MORTIMER WHEELER

JACQUETTA HAWKES

MORTIMER WHEELER
Adventurer in Archaeology

—

WEIDENFELD AND NICOLSON
LONDON

ISBN 0 297 78056 5

Printed in Great Britain by
Fakenham Press Limited, Fakenham, Norfolk

Contents

Illustrations

Rik talking to his Indian students at Harappa, 1946 (*private collection*).

With the Governor-General of Pakistan at the opening of the Pakistan National Museum, April 1950 (*private collection*).

The Archaeological Section of the India Museum, Calcutta, 1948 (*private collection*).

'Animal, Vegetable, Mineral?', 1953 (*Popperfoto*).

Punch cartoon for the 'Buried Treasure' series, 1954 (*Punch*).

Rik visiting an excavation site on the Wye Downs, Kent, 1954 (*Topham*).

In conversation with Elizabeth Allan at the Foyles lunch to celebrate publication of *Still Digging*, 14 January 1955 (*BBC Hulton Picture Library*).

In Egypt (© *Roger Wood*).

Lecturing at Delphi during a Swans Hellenic cruise (*private collection*).

Confronting one of the carved birds from Zimbabwe (*private collection*).

A problem of stratification, India 1959 (*private collection*).

Talking to President Ayub Khan of Pakistan, 13 July 1964 (*Popperfoto*).

Sharing a joke with Barbara Cartland and the Duchess of Bedford, 1965 (*Popperfoto*).

With Magnus Magnusson during the filming of 'Sir Mortimer Wheeler' in 1971 (*BBC*).

A reminiscent drink after filming (*BBC*).

At a reunion of the 42nd Light Anti-Aircraft Regiment (*private collection*).

In 1971 (*BBC*).

LINE DRAWINGS

Acknowledgements

THIS LIFE of my old friend Rik Wheeler has taken a very long time to complete – far longer than I, in my ignorance of biographical writing, could have imagined when I began. The patience of the publishers is certainly a matter for acknowledgement.

Meanwhile I have been discovering the difficulties caused by the fallibility of the human memory, the extreme variation in the extent of the records at different periods and all the other snags familiar to experienced biographers.

Sources of information left by Wheeler himself are substantial though uneven. In 1954 he wrote his biographical work, *Still Digging*, in which he incorporated a selection from the letters, sometimes slightly emended, that he had sent to his friend Cyril Fox while soldiering in North Africa and again when running the antiquities service in India. It also includes the greater part of some sketches and verses describing Second World War experiences which were privately printed in 1944 under the title *Twenty-Four Hours' Leave*. *Still Digging*, though valuable, is episodic in structure and after his early years contains almost nothing about the author's personal life. Some very personal details about his marriage to Mavis de Vere Cole are to be found in the book about her, *Beautiful and Beloved*, by Roderic Owen and her son Tristan.

There are illuminating essays giving Wheeler's feelings and views about archaeology in *Alms for Oblivion*, while his theory and practice as an excavator are set out in *Archaeology from the Earth*. In *The British Academy 1949–68* Wheeler tells much about his own work as a part of the history of the Academy. There is also much to be learnt from his many more specialized archaeological books and excavation reports.

While office files covering most of Wheeler's career from London Museum days onwards contain thousands of letters dictated in characteristic style, unofficial letters are in short supply. There are the few that he wrote in boyhood to Spielmann, the series to his schoolboy friend, Theodore Cribb, written between leaving school and his twentieth year and letters written to his wife Tessa and sister Betty while serving overseas in the First World War. I have drawn upon a few letters written to me. For the rest I have found little of value beyond the two series to Cyril Fox and those, very different in feeling, addressed during his foreign travels to his personal assistant and helpmeet, Molly Myers. Most of these date from the later 1950s and 1960s. Wheeler kept diaries only during his voyage to North Africa in 1942, for the days of the Second Battle of El Alamein and of his raid before entering Tripoli. The first of these is unpublished, the other two originally appeared in *Twenty-Four Hours' Leave*.

I hesitated over introducing the first person to the book since its sporadic appearance in the text might annoy the reader. However, I found in practice that it seemed natural to allow myself to appear when I was in fact involved or when calling on my own knowledge or judgement.

For the most part, however, I have depended on the help of others for information. All whom I approached gave it most readily, supplying written memoirs or submitting themselves to interviews. Several of my informants remained unruffled when I badgered them more than once during the long course of the work.

I should like to begin my acknowledgements of help given with members of Rik Wheeler's family. To his son, Michael Wheeler QC, I am grateful not only for information and hospitality, but perhaps even more for the enthusiasm with which from the first he urged me to undertake the biography. Knowledge that he wanted me to be the author buoyed me up when, in those deadly middle reaches of the writing, I came near to despair. His daughter Carol volunteered an account of her own relationship with her grandfather. I owe much to Rik's sister, Mrs Amy Bailey, my principal informant for the early years; after our meetings she answered many queries by letter and spontaneously furnished further memories of childhood as they returned to her. She also put all family photographs at my disposal. Rik's brother-in-law, the husband of Betty Wheeler, supplied further facts and a family tree.

First of my other informants I would like to thank Molly Myers. Her close association with Wheeler over the last thirty years of his life gave a rare coherence to her knowledge of his working life, of his travels, illnesses and everyday habits. She allowed me to use all his letters to her. Since so many of Wheeler's files were stored in her house she was also called on to help Harriet Geddes, a rarely intelligent and capable research worker whom I was lucky enough to employ to scan this mass of letters and other official documents.

Among very many archaeological friends and colleagues of Wheeler's I perhaps owe most to Glyn and Ruth Daniel. They not only gave me verbal accounts of their numerous important contacts with my subject, but Glyn supplied written notes and comments. Nowell Myres was also extraordinarily generous with his time, writing with his own hand and when he was far from well a very full account of certain Welsh excavations and of his side of the Verulamium dispute. Miss Kitty Richardson was another indispensable informant about the Wheelers' excavations, particularly on their human side, and about the French expeditions – and so, too, was Mr Bill Wedlake, who kindly allowed me to see a memoir he had written on these subjects. Mrs Hencken (Thalassa Cruso) was yet another deep well of knowledge about Rik Wheeler as man and archaeologist – which she shared with me through talk, letters and a memorandum. Professor Stuart Piggott kindly allowed me to read in advance of publication his obituary of Wheeler written for the Royal Society, and to make use of the bibliography. The late Sir Max Mallowan similarly supplied me with his Memorial Address.

Archaeologists whom I should like to thank particularly for interviews or written answers to my questions are Mr Leslie Alcock; Miss Beatrice de Cardi; Dr Molly Cotton; Miss Margot Eates; Professor Christopher Hawkes; Lady Fox; Mr Huntly Gordon; Mrs Rachel Maxwell-Hyslop; Mrs Joanna Harper Kelley; Dr Ralegh Radford; Professor David Stronach and Lady Wheeler.

A number of people helped me over limited aspects of Wheeler's activities: I will thank them approximately according to the order of appearance of their contributions. Mr Roderick Thompson, assisted by colleagues, provided the records for the years at Bradford Grammar School; Mr Randolph and Mr Evelyn Cribb gave information about their father Theodore (Canon Cribb) and kindly allowed me to use the letters to their father and to reproduce two drawings from them. Mrs Forster of University College hunted out College records and Wheeler's contributions to its *Union Magazine*. Mr Peter Farrar of the Hull College of Education gave me the results of thorough research into Wheeler's service in the First World War and was responsible for identifying the correct location of the 'butte de Warlencourt'.

For the London Museum years Mr Martin Holmes provided much personal information and a most useful memorandum; Miss Margot Eates was also immensely helpful here, as was Mr W. Henderson; Miss

Joanna Clark made a fruitful scrutiny of the Museum records. For work in India Mr B. B. Lal supplied a most amusing and interesting memoir, while Mr Robert Raikes told of his work with Wheeler on Indus Valley hydrography.

For the Second World War the late Mr John Ward-Perkins gave an account of his long service with Wheeler from Enfield days through the North African campaign, and Lord Goodman supplied critical recollections of the period when the 42nd Regiment was in England. Mr H. J. Wheeler, a sergeant in the Regiment, came forward with useful details of its actions in Africa and some regimental stories. Mr John Hopkins, the Librarian of the Society of Antiquaries and Mr F. H. Thompson, the Assistant Secretary, helped me to scan the minute books and other records. For the British Academy, Lord Robbins gave a fine presidential view, while Mr Richard Griffiths gave an inside account of Wheeler's dealings with the Treasury on behalf of the Academy.

Finally, for the last phase, Mr R. K. Swan furnished personal impressions of Wheeler as a regular Swan Cruise lecturer and organizer. Mr David Collison brought new light and warmth into the story with his account of the making of the television biography and the friendship that grew from it.

I also owe thanks to the following: Mrs Audrey Bennett; Lord Bledisloe; Mr G. C. Boon of the National Museum of Wales; Mr Dermot Casey; Professor Grahame Clark; Mrs Duncan Christie; Miss Tessa Dunning; Miss Juliet O'Hea; Dr Kenneth Oakley; M. Claude Schaeffer.

Stanwick ▲ Sites of Wheeler's main excavations
Ilkley Places associated with Wheeler's life

Durham •

Stanwick ▲

• *Ilkley*
Baildon Moor •   • York
Bradford •   • Leeds

• Manchester

▲ **Segontium**

Wroxeter

ENGLAND

• Birmingham

• Cambridge

Brecon Gaer

Colchester ▲

Verulamium
▲

• Oxford

Enfield

Caerleon ▲   **Lydney**

Cardiff •

Thames
London

• Bristol

Cadbury Castle ▲   *Cranborne Chase*
•
Southampton

• *Hodhill*

Maiden Castle
▲   **Bindon Hill**
▲

W A L E S

Trent

Severn

Usk

0   20   100 miles
      50   150 km

Prologue

MORTIMER WHEELER WILL rise from these pages as a Hero figure. Of that I feel sure even as I write the very first words of my book. Over the past months I have been talking of him with men and women who knew him in all the conditions of his adventurous yet devoted life. Some spoke of him with unqualified awe and admiration. Some had passionately loved him. But not a few began by insisting on their disapproval or even plain dislike of the man. Almost without exception, however, as recollection followed recollection and the mountain of his achievement was piled up by their words, conjuring up a living presence – or a ghost of the most extraordinary vitality – these censurers ended by conveying admiration as irresistibly as those who had confessed to it from the beginning.

As for my own estimation, and perhaps as a biographer, particularly a woman biographer, I ought to examine it here. I can claim what must be the best foundation for judgement: a very great liking for Rik Wheeler. I first met him when as an archaeological student at Cambridge University I was sent one bitter February to join a field study group at Cranborne Chase in Dorset. He was then already a great man in the small, coherent world of British archaeology which I hoped to enter. I remember exchanging wry glances with him when, on a hilltop in a freezing wind, Christopher Hawkes, whom I was soon to marry, expatiated on the local earthwork with his habitual thoroughness. From that time, though with many intermissions, I enjoyed his company, his talk, his power to brighten the day. Much the same things delighted or amused us. We got on well together. Those unaccountable dictates of the psyche or of the flesh determined that I should never be in love with him, and that, too, I take to be an advantage. On the other hand I count it a disadvantage that I never worked with him, an experience which, by all accounts, could be terrifying as well as immensely profitable.

While I was living in the archaeological world, yet outside his own realm, I more often heard Wheeler attacked than praised. Certain scholars and moralists found much to criticize, and if I thought that their criticism sprang more than they knew from jealousy of his extraordinary success as a man of action in love, war and his profession, I could see that it was sometimes rational enough. Nor did I see perfection in him myself: I tend to have too much detachment rather than too little.

In declaring, then, that I expect to present Mortimer Wheeler as a Hero figure I do not announce an idolatrous biography, but use the word rather in its epic sense. It has been said that he belonged to the heroic age of archaeology, and it must be true that a young, unformed subject such as he found it gave more opportunity for great enterprises and towering reputations. In my opinion, however, it would still today be possible for modern archaeologists in the mould of Layard, Schliemann, Arthur Evans or Woolley to appear among us if the whole spirit of the age were not against it.

Our small children are no longer encouraged to have dreams of lordliness or of great deeds and their educators normally avoid talk of honour, pride or rulership. Science and technology have destroyed the glamorous mask of war and very nearly ended the age-old tradition of heroic combat. The armed forces are no longer generally admired. Even in the learned world science and technology have tended to dehumanize the humanities. All this has gone with the tide of egalitarianism among individuals and among nations, with its condemnation of authority, success and wealth. The century of the common man has taken much both psychologically and materially from the strong and fortunate in favour of the weak and unfortunate. Such an era, dominated, as some would say, by the feminine principle, has its own great virtues. Yet, while it remains doubtful whether the meek are about to inherit the earth, our age could not fail to set the anti-hero on the throne.

I have become more and more convinced that to understand Mortimer Wheeler's personality and life story it must be recognized that from the end of the First World War onwards he lived as an epic hero in an anti-heroic age. It is quite probable that for such a man to live in a yielding society enhanced his powers, giving him the drive of a blade cutting through cream cheese. On the other hand values, ethics and behaviour that would have been accepted or won glory in a more heroic age had to appear outrageous or deficient in compassion and humility to those committed to our present ideals.

I have said 'had to appear' because I believe that in most of us such reactions are superficial. All our ancestry, all our history, have implanted willing deference to the naturally dominant male, the leader born and bred. It remains within us, always potent and ready to resume its sway in time of crisis and war. This suppressed sense of deference seems the most likely explanation of the curious ambivalence in all those who, as I have said, came to bury Wheeler and stayed to praise him. Naturally simple people, people belonging to simple or traditional societies or accepted hierarchies, and all females who allow their instincts to prevail, have no such contradictions to overcome. I shall record the uninhibited devotion given to Wheeler by such individuals, from batmen and museum assistants to women friends and colleagues.

This natural response was perhaps at its best and most spontaneous in India, a land where the epic still lives and veneration is unstinted. It was also the land of Mortimer Wheeler's greatest feats of regeneration, organization and discovery. What he accomplished there in the four years of his mission appears almost superhuman and it is therefore only to be expected that on his return visits, particularly the last at the age of eighty-two, he was received with semi-divine honours. These were paid to him by those who had worked with and known him, from the humblest to those who had taken over his leadership. As though by a little miracle I have at this moment of writing found on my desk a postcard addressed to him from Delhi on 21 December 1957. It is wonderfully expressive, for all its quaintness, of the natural responses I have tried to suggest. It is neatly typed on a card with a picture of Mahatma Gandhi carrying a child in his arms.

Dear Sir Wheeler,

In my buoyant thoughts of approaching CHRISTMAS, I just saw a tall and stately figure this year among the recipients of my reverential regards and warm greetings for the season. Kindly permit me to say, Dear Sir, it was none other than Sir Mortimer Wheeler, the great Archaeologist, who inspired us all with his great lore and smart physique with only a half pant and an open shirt on a wintry evening, while over three score young, on the occasion of our reception to him last month. With warm greetings and sincere prayers that you may be spared for long and peaceful years of active and creative work for the good of mankind.

S. Madhava Rao. Garden Superintendent.

No one can deny that Wheeler was possessed of a daemonic energy. In his Memorial Address, Sir Max Mallowan expressed this as being 'driven onwards by "Seven Devils" which resided within him'. Others have preferred to translate daemon in the sense of genius. This is a word now used on so many levels as to have no constant meaning. If one takes the highest, the possession of extraordinary creative powers of intellect or imagination, Mortimer Wheeler cannot be called a genius. He came to have a vision of human history that enabled him to see each discovery of its traces, however small, in its widest significance. He had the imaginative power to put life into the past and convey this vitality with a mastery of the spoken and the written word few in his field could equal. Yet he was hardly an original thinker or one much concerned with ideas beyond his own work. Nor was he an artist in the most exalted sense, although he had great artistry, sensibility and an appreciation of style, form and finish. Indeed, as will appear, he was criticized by a few who supposed that they spoke in the name of science or scholarship for wishing to turn archaeological reports into works of art.

Wheeler certainly had many of the attributes that would give him the entrée to the world of genius on broader terms. He was a true innovator in archaeology, an inspired teacher, had the dramatic gifts to enable him to spread his own enthusiasm among multitudes. He developed powers of command and creative administration that brought him extra-ordinary successes in energizing feeble institutions and creating new ones. In this way, almost as much as by his more personal achievements, he added to the riches of our western world, helped to shore up the defences of our threatened civilization.

Again, Mortimer Wheeler would have a high ranking for genius among those who see it in an infinite capacity for taking pains. (I am not among them, although I find that this familiar definition was finally shaped by a Miss Hopkins of Cambridge.) Having now scanned the mountains of files that his working life left behind, I am much more aware than before of the extraordinary pains he always took to reach his own standards of excellence. Secretaries from the early days have told that he was a ruthless wielder of a red pencil. Letters often had to be retyped many times but were always sent promptly, and as well laid out as they were crisply worded. Lectures and speeches, even those for the most modest occasions, were written, revised, polished, rewritten. His books, whether popular or specialist, were scrutinized in detail at every stage, carelessness of editors or printers calling down his wrath. How he found time for so much painstaking amid all his active work and travel is in itself a painful question. Work was to him near the Godhead and to it he sacrificed leisure and nocturnal hours. He expected his wives, women and friends, and all who served him, to do the same.

Perhaps the judgement should be that Mortimer Wheeler was a man of talents that were raised to a higher power by his extraordinary and highly concentrated energy. As I reflect again upon that energy, it seems to me that Sir Max's 'Seven Devils' will not do. Surely they would have driven him hither and thither through his lifetime? People have often called him restless, and that he certainly was in the sense of shunning rest. Yet far more than most men he drove himself ahead along a single line of intent as surely as a Roman engineer drove his road through unknown forests, hills and plains from point to point towards its chosen destination.

Towards the end of his life, asked under the glare of television lights whether on looking back he saw his years as fulfilling a plan he had laid down for himself, he replied, avoiding the absolute, that he liked to think so. From the age of nineteen, he said, when he abandoned his ambition to be a painter because he saw he would never be a great one, he was soon set on what was to be a lifelong course to raise the art and science of archaeology to the high place he saw for it, and to spread some appreciation of the subject as widely as possible among the public.

On this same occasion, the making of a 'Chronicle' programme of his life and work, he declared that he did not think much of chance, believing with Gibbon that 'the wind and the waves are on the side of the ablest navigator'. He went so far as to say that he had done everything that he wanted to do, 'for if he had not, he would have done it'. Perhaps such a claim came too easily from an old, eminent man enjoying the afterglow of his glory, but it was not so far from the truth.

There is no doubt that he owed both the fulfilment of his 'archaeological mission' and the success of so many enterprises within it to exceptional powers of forward planning. Here his greatest triumph was achieved in India. It will be told how, in 1944, Brigadier Wheeler, having helped to plan, and having survived, the Salerno landings, found himself in a small private cabin in a ship sailing in slow convoy to India, where he was to take over the post of Director General of Archaeology. He had never been to India, and he had been hastily mugging up its history. Yet on this voyage out he devised the most economical possible strategic plan for the elucidation of India's ancient civilizations. On arrival he had it immediately dispatched to his vast and demoralized staff scattered over the subcontinent, 'to tell them exactly what I was going to do. And every one of those things we did ... we did.' Uttering these words before the 'Chronicle' camera Wheeler struck a fist into an open palm, his face alight with the memory of it all. It was a moment that seemed to sum up his whole professional life.

'Forward planning' is a passable phrase to apply to Wheeler's way of doing things but it has the nasty mechanical sound of modern jargon. That he was able to think ahead so effectively can be ascribed to the living quality of imagination. As I have said, he lacked the artist's creative gift, but imaginative thinking was one of the mainsprings of his being. 'Reasoned imagination'; 'an informed and informing imagination'; 'a controlled imagination' – the phrases occurred again and again, as often as he proclaimed his ideals of what man in general and archaeologists in particular ought to be.

It was this faith in imagination, well-harnessed by knowledge and scepticism, that made him insist that a good archaeologist must always remember that his 'proper aim is to dig up people', not mere things, and that 'archaeology is a science that must be lived, be seasoned with humanity. Dead archaeology is the dryest dust that blows.' With this went his conviction that any young person enlisting as an archaeologist should do so partly for the sake of adventure. In private conversation he would speak with his most brutal scorn of those whose scholarship he felt to be of the dry-as-dust kind, of those who thought more of technology than humanity and (worse still) of those young men whom he suspected of too much concern for safe jobs and pensions.

One can see that his own dedication to imagination and adventure brought about a paradox in his attitude towards archaeology that must emerge in his biography. From the days following his demobilization in 1919, when he saw himself as a 'survivor' with a mission to create a new archaeology, he always insisted on the necessity to make it more scientific. Going back to the forgotten skills of Pitt-Rivers, he set himself to develop the General's techniques, especially the science of stratification, and to apply them in excavations carefully selected to provide knowledge where it was most needed. When at last he achieved his long delayed plans for an Institute of Archaeology he had it proclaimed as essentially 'a laboratory: a laboratory of archaeological science', a place that would bring to the study of civilization 'something of the function which the laboratory has long fulfilled in the study of chemical or physical science', and where the archaeologist would seek 'the collaboration of the geologist, the botanist, the palaeontologist. . . .' Yet during the second half of his life, when so much that he had advocated had come to pass, Mortimer Wheeler began to fight for humanism against the inroads of science and technology. This change of heart is frankly and eloquently set out in his *What Matters in Archaeology*. Here he laments the passing of classical education, insists that any study of history must recognize 'the Nobility of Man' and makes a plea to 'save archaeology from the technicians'. Anyone who knew Wheeler could not have doubted that if barricades had to be erected he would be on the side of the humanities.

All this is very fine – and very fine, on balance, I believe Mortimer Wheeler to have been – but is it not noble-sounding to the point of the impossible – and, worse still, of dullness? What in all this has become of the disapproval I have mentioned, of the antagonisms he provoked in an anti-heroic world? How can I justify my suggestion that he was something of an alien in his time and place?

One could take first of all what appears to be the simplest truth: the fact that Wheeler not only distinguished himself mightily in the actual fighting of two wars, but always admitted to having 'enjoyed' them, found them 'interesting'. By the time of the second (which he fought when well over the permitted age) he was perhaps too inclined to scorn younger men who did not seek active service. These sentiments did not go down well in a society generally more interested in pacifism, least of all among all those highly educated colleagues who, on their own terms rightly, had preferred to exercise their minds well away from battlefields.

From the beginning of the Second World War, when Major Wheeler was commanding his battery at Enfield, he was already being referred to as Flash Alf. I believe that this nickname was in part adopted as a conductor to carry off emotions, running all the way from reluctant admiration to spite, felt by these non-combatants. On the other hand, as will be seen, Wheeler was at that time showing an absurd excess of military zeal, with an insistence on bull and minute points of discipline, that might well be considered inappropriate to the volunteer force of highly competent citizens that he was commanding. This personal militarism, embellished by the most glassy of boots and a moustache that now grew wider and more bristling, certainly contributed to the Flash Alf image. Significantly, however, while the sophisticates who gave him the name did so with amusement or malice, the soldiers of his Regiment who esteemed and even loved him, used Flash Alf affectionately and continued to do so long after the war when he attended regimental reunions.

In the opinion of Lord Goodman, who was one of the intelligent volunteers, his commanding officer of those early days was playing a dramatic role – the role of a conventional soldier, which inevitably in his hands became larger than life. I think this is true. How far it was conscious it is difficult to say. It may have been fostered by some sense of alienation. So far as I know, with the exception of John Ward-Perkins, a member of the London Museum staff whom he himself enrolled, not a single man with whom he had worked during the inter-war years was to don uniform with the intention of fighting.

It would be ridiculous to suggest that a man who was able to turn a thousand very unmilitary civilians into a first-rate regiment, then to distinguish himself so much as a fighting man as to be made a brigadier after El Alamein and sufficiently as a strategist to be appointed to the group planning the Italian landings, was all the time acting a part. Mortimer Wheeler had made himself into as brave a man as any hero; warfare had from the first appealed to his love of adventure and enabled him to develop powers of imaginative planning and control.

Yet the idea of Wheeler playing roles is an important one. If it was well exemplified in his part of army officer, most of all in those early war days of bull and bullying and in the two extraordinary 'acts' of daring-do that he devised, one in each World War, it was also apparent throughout his life and was at the root of much of the disapproval and suspicion levelled against him – by women more than by men. In a period and social milieu with little sense of formal style, his manner of turning on his charm as though with a flick of a switch provoked accusations of insincerity, falsity or even deceit.

That he was often insincere beyond the demand of ordinary good manners is true enough, but often it was no more than role-playing: he was in the part of good guest, admiring male or charming host. When the part was over the charm would be switched off and that, when observed, doubled the offence. Occasionally the performance had an ulterior motive, but I think this was rare. It was certainly not his line of approach for women he wished to bed or men whose service or professional patronage he needed. One source of so much play-acting was, I am sure, a deep-seated psychic insecurity sternly suppressed since childhood.

The habit of self-dramatization was a very real obstacle to easy companionship and communication even among friends and intimates. It helped to form an outer shell of wit, showmanship and swordplay that could be entertaining but very irritating if one wanted the company of the man himself. It was a shell that could be broken in various ways, but not without effort. Carol, one of his two granddaughters, established a good relationship with him by direct attack. There had been a family dinner – which would probably have brought out the worst in Wheeler since it was a matter of principle with him that there was no reason why he should like or seek the company of his relatives. He had been holding forth, and not listening, and the young schoolgirl was 'bored and fed up'. When in the stream of artificial talk he said something offensive to her, she told him with point and heat just what she was feeling. The result? Her grandfather laughed aloud and they 'met' for the first time. Thereafter they enjoyed a long and lively relationship which brought solace to him in his last years.

Another characteristic of the Hero in Mortimer Wheeler that provoked indignation in some breasts was his ruthless power of command. Even in his Memorial Address Sir Max spoke of him as 'a fire-breathing giant . . . relentlessly, inflexibly driven to achieve his aim by a mechanism which enlisted the help of lesser mortals and compelled them to bow in his path'. Another, who knew him well in war and peace, used a different language in saying that Wheeler looked for 'good subaltern material' and then drove the chosen ones to the limits of their endurance.

It will appear how during the twenties and thirties Wheeler, together with his wife Tessa, whose authority came from sweetness, built up a growing band of devoted and trained followers for excavations, museum work and other services and labours. With this band scattered by the war, Wheeler immediately enjoyed the more absolute command of battery – then regiment. So on to India where he was soon slave-driving a huge and generally devoted staff (the others were sacked). It is irresistible to compare Wheeler's role in these settings with the king and his band of warrior Companions in the heroic age of Greece, or the Germanic north. He drove his followers in Atlantic rain, in bitter cold and tropical sun and at all hours of the day and night; he could be brutally critical and terrorize by rages that seem to have been some more, some much less, calculated. At the same time, like royal Companions, they shared in his victories and had full credit for their own, while they received the royal gold in the form of counsel, teachings, testimonials and support for their own ventures. In general those 'lesser mortals . . . compelled to bow in his path' were loyal, and most of them gained immeasurably from having known his command. Of course there were groans, mutterings and occasional faction, but then protest against true authority is always enjoyable. The Wheelers' great excavations at Verulamium and Maiden Castle are said to have been exceptionally happy as well as successful. Devotion was probably at its height in India and mutterings loudest in the early regimental days. But even those enlisted citizens who grumbled most and made the unkindest comments on Flash Alf were, as Lord Goodman recalls, in reality very well pleased to have a commanding officer who was so much talked about and attracted so many stories for or against himself.

In thinking of Mortimer Wheeler as an authoritarian, which he undoubtedly was, and as a tyrant, as he sometimes chose to be, one must remember all those contrary qualities that helped to redeem him even in an anti-heroic age. First and most important in a man of his kind, he had absolutely nothing of the Master Builder in him. He was always glad to see young men and women rise to distinction and did all he could to help them on their way. Then he was never pompous or self-important, for he had a true sense of humour. Indeed, the style he most often affected was one of flippancy. If the circumstances allowed, he favoured those who stood up to him – as the story of granddaughter Carol reveals. This side of his nature must surely be recognized in the name by which he came to be almost universally known. This fire-breathing giant, this bestriding colossus, was known to all and sundry, and usually addressed by all and sundry, by the little name of Rik. How few things that can be said of any human being contain the whole truth and nothing but the truth – and therefore how difficult are the ways of biography!

Such difficulties are not at their least in estimating Rik Wheeler's relationships with women. Women were of immense importance to him and he enjoyed and made use of them in a marvellous variety of ways. It might be said that his often conspicuous promiscuity would be more acceptable now, in the heyday of permissive misrule, than it was at the time. I doubt, however, whether such a statement has much truth in it: his whole style as womanizer and lover was so far removed from present *mores*. The easy confusion of group or communal sex, the notion of unisex, or the theory of sexual equality in its latest form, would all have been abhorrent to him. His own range of sexual relationships was wide and included those of emotional equality and esteem, but always he wanted to relish rather than blur *la différence*.

Once again it would be nearer the truth to say that Rik Wheeler's sexual activities would have been normal and unquestioned for the Hero. His women would have fallen into place as queens, favoured concubines, members of his harem or captives of war. One very great distinction must be admitted as an adaptation to the modern world. With almost all the important women in his life and many lesser ones as well, he enjoyed a strenuous professional working relationship side by side with the amorous one. There was a time and a place for everything.

At the lower, or least important, range of Rik's women was a supply of young girls – including, I have been told, the domestics of at least one country house. Perhaps these encounters do not deserve the name of relationships, since many were little more than one night lays. Rik knew and accepted his lusts, believing (contrary to common belief) that their satisfaction was as necessary to him as the air he breathed, providing the fuel that drove him forward.

Some among these girls, while hardly qualifying as mistresses, roused and enjoyed Rik's affection, passing from mere sexual encounter to an intimacy that involved listening to him, soothing him, doing him small services. They would not be forgotten but be looked on with a lasting fondness and interest. On the other hand, in this endless stream of young girls were a few, perhaps most of them students, who were very much in love with him but knew no reward except in their passion. These he may usually have treated with some delicacy, at least to the extent of not allowing them to know how many others were enjoying what they were denied.

In addition to all the girls who revolved round him like asteroids round the sun, Rik, like most men, must have savoured many brief passages with women met on his innumerable cruises and other travels. Any who were attractive, light-hearted and unlikely to interfere with his work could be enjoyed. He was an extraordinarily swift hunter. I doubt if he ever went with prostitutes: what need could he have for such expenditure or what time to spare? He once told me how, having gone to Paris with one of his few close men friends, to his surprise this companion at once swept him off by taxi to a brothel. Rik took this unexpected opportunity to talk to his girl about her life and opinions. This may be a trite story, but at least it is true and one that he took some pride in telling.

Rik could never be sexually faithful even to the mistresses he loved, yet he felt himself to have been faithful to each in his fashion. There were two or three in the London Museum years, exceptional young women with fine looks, minds in many ways equal to his own, and with the character, vitality and temperament to offer the 'resistance' – flint to his steel – that he needed to kindle his fires. This image is too hard to represent the total relationship, for he also wanted companionship and affection, the enjoyment of talk on any and every subject such as is the greatest resource of true marriage.

With young women of this quality he could provide intimacy as rewarding as any that can make up that total human being, man and woman together, head, heart and loins. The shell fell away, he could be simple and wholly honest about himself and meet in that sharing of emotions which creates a true equality of the sexes. With them he seems to have avoided the rough treatment that he meted out to some of his lesser sexual partners.

It may be that in his forties Rik had lost a little of the easy potency of youth. He certainly liked to generate excitement. He was rash in the richly erotic letters he could entrust to the post, and reckless in making love in places where discovery would have been publicly embarrassing. Any woman highly qualified as a mistress, however, could only delight in these adventures as much as Rik himself did.

One of those whose qualifications were highest has said that some of the happiest times she remembered were with Rik and also some of the unhappiest. Pain must always have been an ingredient in the experience of any woman deeply devoted to him, for he had an utter carelessness of a woman's feelings in his switching of loves and swift pursuits of lesser game. Here, indeed, is one of the truly baffling contradictions in his character, this mixture of a cruel insensitivity with enduring kindness and generosity, for the redeeming fact was that Rik did maintain his affection and friendship with virtually all the women he had loved, keeping in touch with them, advancing their work and fortunes over the years. It was here, surely, that his claim to be faithful in his fashion found meaning. He declared, 'All my mistresses make good marriages. I see to that.' If the first part of this arrogantly joking announcement is true, the second certainly is not. He was in fact naïvely jealous of the men friends of all his women, even of those whom he had never sought to possess. If his mistresses married well it was because he had roused them, taught them, fulfilled them and made them suffer.

One cannot doubt that Rik Wheeler was well aware that his infidelity, far more than his unpredictable temper, caused suffering, yet I do not think that it gave him pleasure. It is true that his sexual handling of some girls was rough, but even here it was not true sadism but a desire (not admirable, certainly) for instant mastery. His behaviour was dictated by something both better and worse than mere carelessness of other people's sufferings. It can be likened to the manner in which he drove all those he commanded in peace and in war to excesses of mental and physical endurance. There was, however, one undeniable difference. While Wheeler himself was always to the fore in these other trials, as lover or philanderer, with the exception of a few humiliations and once being enthralled by a woman who equalled his infidelity, he can have felt little pain beyond that 'ache across the belly'.

The talented mistress who probably knew her lover best, and forgave him most, recognized him to be an 'insatiable Moloch where young women were concerned', yet concluded that he 'managed the tricky task of keeping everybody happy most of the time with impressive skill'. The pity of it was that this feat was not maintained after marriage.

Very much like the father who had been so close to him, Rik Wheeler was a bad husband.

Many have said that he should never have married: I would only say that his character would have escaped its worst blemishes if he had not married a second and third time. I do not suppose that any one of his three wives would have been so poor of spirit as to have wished that they had never known the relationship. The common notion that men who marry more than once tend to choose similar types of woman may often be true, but is the opposite of the truth in Rik Wheeler's case – as will appear in these pages. Tessa, Mavis and Margaret were totally unlike one another and so were their marriages.

There are a number of people, both men and women, who will never absolve Mortimer Wheeler for his philandering, still less for the undoubted pain and misery that he caused both Tessa and Margaret. Yet perhaps such utter condemnations are a part of the negative spirit of the present time. All delights must be forbidden if they are dangerous. One can take the analogy of fireworks – most fittingly, indeed, since they are the film-maker's favourite symbol for sexual activity. As I remember well, to select and let off fireworks was a source of rare excitement, pleasure and even of joy to children. A few were hurt, so now all must be denied their delight.

To understand all is to forgive all. If I apply the partial truth of this piece of wisdom to Rik Wheeler, I seem to perceive, obscurely and confusedly, the light of some general absolution. If he used people, both his 'subalterns' and his women, if he drove them North, East, South and West and at times to dire limits, this was in some way a product of his proclaimed belief in the Nobility of Man, in human dignity. It appears preposterous to associate ignoble behaviour with nobility, and putting others to indignity with dignity itself. Yet I believe this particular man, feeling the need for challenges, for perpetual self-testing and goading, consciously or unconsciously extended his compulsions to others. They, too, must accept and endure. Perhaps there could be a tenuous link with his youthful experience of Passchendaele, which he embraced because in it he had known the worst.

I do not understand all; I may be seeking excuses. Undoubtedly some of Rik's sins were no more than excessive self-indulgence compensating for excessive discipline in his work. Nevertheless, if there is to be forgiveness, it must lie in that direction.

—

CHAPTER I

A Good All-Round Sort of Boy

The truth is that he was born in Glasgow. All that was romantic in his nature made him wish that it might have been Edinburgh. I am sure he never claimed that beautiful city as his birthplace, yet neither did he like to mention Glasgow. The truth is, however, that Mrs Robert Mortimer Wheeler bore her first child in Glasgow where, in that year of 1890, her husband was earning a frugal living from lecturing and writing. The event may have been awaited with more than usual anxiety by Robert, who had been married before and had lost his wife in childbirth.

His second wife, Emily Baynes, had family connections with that ancient and once austere centre of learning, St Andrews. She was the niece and ward of Thomas Spencer Baynes, a Shakespearean scholar at the University. Within a year or two of the birth of their son (such is the perversity of fate) the Wheelers moved to Edinburgh, where their elder daughter, Amy, was born. As she was just two years younger than her brother and grew to be a bright and lively little girl, she was bound to be his childhood companion – and on occasion, it seems, something like his willing slave.

The future Sir Mortimer Wheeler's earliest memories were to come from the sojourn in Edinburgh. The very first – or so he believed – survived from a walk taken with his father among the lonely 'brown hills' of Braid. As was always to happen on these walks, the very small boy had been struggling to keep up with his parent's unaccommodating stride. They sat by the roadside to rest and as a solitary lark rose above them his father sang a lark song and he did his best to echo it. These were the first words to have lodged in his memory.

> 'To wit, to wit to wee
> There's nobody on airth can mak a shoe for me, for me.'
> 'Why so why so, why so why so?'
> 'Because my heels as lang as me toe.'

It would be natural to mock the idea of relating Wheeler to a skylark, yet something in the lonely scene, the solitary, aspiring bird and in the strangely haunting words must have found a response that caused him to remember them all his life. He was never the uncomplicated extrovert that he could appear to be. To take the significance of this first recollection at its simplest, it is in harmony with a deep feeling for birds that emerges in his boyish poetry and correspondence and which never quite left him. In a letter written when he was thirteen years old he confided that 'though most people would despise it, I find pleasant company [here]– herons, moorhens, kingfishers, hawks and snipe. . . .'

Other Edinburgh memories were of a rapture felt when in a *camera obscura* at the Castle he watched in miniature a white-coated Highland regiment drilling outside, and of terror when he was held astride an old cannon and imagined it bursting into flame. Both were experiences that might remain with almost any small boy, but in Wheeler's case are given point by his adult near obsession with soldiering and the fact that he was to go through two wars in the artillery.

When his son was four years old Robert Wheeler took the post of chief leader writer on the *Bradford Observer* (presently to become the *Yorkshire Observer*), which had its head office in Bradford. The family chose to live in Saltaire, within the parish of Shipley, a few miles north-west of Bradford and part of the continuous chain of towns extending up the once beautiful Airedale as far as Keighley. Wheeler was to feel that 'everything that mattered' in his education was to happen during the ten years he lived there.

The first house was cramped and far from distinguished: one of a row of semi-basement houses in Moorhead Lane. For Saltaire itself there was much to be said, however. It was easy to walk up on to the moors, or to the wooded ravine of Shipley Glen with its surrounding parkland. It was also easy for Robert to bicycle the four miles to his Bradford office.

Bradford itself was both prosperous and progressive, its narrow streets, some steep and cobbled, with their solid yet ornate buildings of blackened freestone, full of vigour and Victorian confidence. This confidence found its apotheosis in the busy Wool Exchange, built in the 'Venetian gothic' style, and in the Town Hall, with its parade of English monarchs and the unexpected tower boldly copied from the Palazzo Vecchio in Florence.

The wool trade was booming in those days and Bradford, its world capital, grew with it. The town was to be created a city soon after the Wheelers' arrival. In many ways, though stubbornly Yorkshire in character, it was also cosmopolitan, linked by trade with the ends of the earth. Very many languages were to be heard on the floor of the Exchange. To native and imported wools, alpaca and mohair had been added – and I can vouch that one of its two or three hundred mills was soon to receive a bulky consignment of Chinese pigtails.

Most important for the intelligentsia, among whom the Wheelers were to be numbered, had been the influx of cultivated German Jews, who had enriched the cultural life of Bradford, particularly its music. Their liberal presence may also have encouraged the exceptional progressive energies of the native Bradfordians, who by no means content with maintaining the excellence of their Grammar School and technical institutions, successfully led the way in educational services and municipal undertakings of many kinds. Bradford was also a cradle of the Labour movement: the *Yorkshire Observer* took a keen interest in the Independent Labour Party which Keir Hardie had founded there just before the new leader writer claimed his desk.

Although the intellectual and social climate of the city must have been as bracing as the fresh moorland airs that penetrated its smoky hollow, it was these moors themselves that can be said to have had an even deeper and more lasting effect on the young Wheeler. Beyond Shipley Glen the country rises steeply to the dark, heathery expanses of the moorland between Airedale and Wharfedale, reaching a height of over thirteen hundred feet on the famous Ilkley Moor. Up here walkers can feel a thousand miles away from the industry they have just left behind them, its noise giving way to the wild cries of curlew and the cluck of grouse. They can also feel many thousand years distant in time, for this is an ancient landscape and scattered with the relics of the living and burial places of prehistoric man.

To the west of Shipley and Bingley there lay greener and more wooded country, surviving fragments of the former beauties of Airedale, crossed by streams running down from the moors above Harden. All in all it is no wonder that most Bradfordians in those days before the rule of the motor car were great walkers, thinking nothing of twenty miles in a day – for the more dedicated among them would often cover forty.

For the family settling at Saltaire, then, their surroundings, even if they seemed unaristocratic and provincial after Edinburgh, offered them plenty to enjoy in both town and country life. Robert Wheeler was ideally equipped to see that opportunities were not wasted. Wheeler was to be very much a father's boy and was deeply and lastingly influenced by his unusual parent, particularly during the formative decade at Bradford.

Robert's early days had been full of promise of the conventional sort. His own father was a tea merchant of Bristol, who now lived with his wife and her many cats on that farm in Gloucestershire where he and his family were often to spend their holidays. Robert for a time intended to become a Baptist minister, but experienced some revulsion of feeling and escaped to Edinburgh University, where he became both a successful student and a militant freethinker. He seems to have possessed the unusual combination of intelligence and exceptional good looks with diffidence and lack of personal ambition. For a time he and his first wife moved in a quite distinguished intellectual circle in Edinburgh and he was able to develop his love of the arts while lecturing in English literature. After the tragic death of his young wife, however, he turned towards journalism and after a time was recommended to the *Bradford Observer* by a local editor who was a Bradford man, and so began a professional career which allowed him to pursue and give expression to his own interests. This was to be his way for the rest of his life and, although bringing him no fame and very little money, it must have suited his nature, for, as his son was to feel, he kept within him 'an inexhaustible spring of happiness'.

The very breadth of his interests and this ready happiness may have kept him from worldly success. His greatest enthusiasms were for music and the visual arts as well as for literature. He saw to it that his children were steeped in Shakespeare – and here, presumably, his wife was at one with him. He recalled how Amy taught herself to read at an early age 'by following people about with a volume of Shakespeare's sonnets and insisting upon spelling out every word....' He himself memorized vast quantities of poetry and other literature – a habit which was to stand him in good stead when he went blind and had to pass the last ten years of his life in darkness. He was a true bibliophile and filled his home with books of every kind, some no doubt acquired through his newspaper, others bought second-hand or for their antiquarian interest.

In addition to these more usual cultural interests, Robert Wheeler had a passionate feeling for men of action and their deeds, from great historical and national heroes to humble local people whose lives he liked to explore. While he could not afford much travel for himself, he could imagine scenes of adventure in wild and distant lands. Finally, and even more surprisingly, he was also a countryman, with great practical knowledge of natural history and a fondness for fishing and rough shooting – acquired one must guess during his boyhood in the West Country. All these multifarious enthusiasms he was eager to share with his family and most of all – inevitably – with his fast-growing son.

At this point I have to decide how best to refer to the young Robert Eric Mortimer Wheeler. His parents first called him Boberic, his infant tongue shaped this into Bobedy, which in turn was modified to Bobs. This became his usual name in the family, but his second name was occasionally used and he sometimes signed himself Eric. I have decided to prefer it for the sake of continuity with the nickname of Rik or Rikky, given by his first wife and sustained for the rest of his life.

It was in many ways an attractive family that moved to Saltaire in 1894. Photographs taken a year or so later show Eric as an extraordinarily pretty boy, with a mass of golden curls and large, intensely-gazing eyes, dressed in an appropriately romantic style with buckle shoes, velvet suit and wide ruffles. 'Totsy' (Amy), no less pretty in a gentler way, sits on the floor at his feet. The story is that a bird had flown into the studio and the only way to induce Bobs to keep still for the pose was to put it into his hand – when he controlled both himself and the bird's wild flutterings.

Whether the children owed their good looks entirely to their handsome father cannot be told, since their mother remains a shadowy figure. There is a tradition that she had begun some academic work of her own but that the strain of night study, together with her domestic burdens, proved too much and she had to forsake it, after a partial breakdown. She became a nervous, anxious woman and suffered from poor health. Almost every winter, while living in the cold and smoky north, she developed pneumonia. Nevertheless, she seems to have managed the household well enough, with the help of a young maid. She also had the responsibility of teaching her son and daughter, for they did not go to school until they were seven or eight years old. She gave them regular morning lessons. Robert Wheeler confessed to being 'perhaps unduly sceptical as to the advantages of overmuch teaching in childhood', believing that more was to be learnt at home from adult company and reading.

No doubt this was a sincere conviction, and he certainly gave much time and loving thought to fulfilling it. There was, however, another reason for the unusual delay in sending the children to school (which greatly troubled their mother) – the Wheelers were often hard up. Robert not only lacked ambition but refused to concern himself about money. The family lived thriftily in some ways, including the use of bicycles even when travelling a considerable distance for their holidays. On one of their holidays they took a lonely cottage of the kind that could be rented for a shilling or two a week in those days and there they lived like 'castaways' on such food as they could shoot, trap or gather – rabbits, ducks and mushrooms.

It was, of course, Emily who suffered most from the struggle to make ends meet, and it was probably this that was the first cause of a worsening relationship with her husband. For the sad truth is that in their personal lives their marriage was not a success. Amy, in her eighties, has summed it up with telling simplicity: 'They did not get on well together. He was a wonderful father but a bad husband.'

As is almost bound to happen in a family where the parents are emotionally at war, the children were also to some extent divided, tending to take sides with one parent or the other. With the Wheelers during the Bradford years, Amy, though she felt the stress of the situation, was able to share in some of the benefits bestowed by the 'wonderful father'. Eric not only wholly identified himself with his father, but absorbed the antagonism and as a small boy was often deliberately naughty and hurtful with his mother. He seems long to have remained distant and inconsiderate towards her.

No need to draw on psychological theory to reach the conclusion that this sacrifice of a loving maternal relationship must have lastingly affected the boy's own emotional growth. At the time it may have heightened the natural boyish tendency to despise, or pretend to despise, girls, and later, although it most surely did not prevent him from loving them, may have encouraged the less amiable aspects of his philandering. Those most convinced of the inescapable sway of child-hood experience might argue that, having based himself on his father, he carried the model within him and reproduced it when he himself became the 'bad husband'. Or again that the emotional divisions within the family caused the inner insecurity that his sister always saw in him and to which she attributed his urge to show off: in fact, the genesis of Flash Alf. Yet this is dangerous ground: why should the boy who modelled himself on an exceptionally unambitious parent himself develop exceptional ambition?

That Robert and Emily 'did not get on well together' is a fact, but the importance of its emotional legacy must be left to personal judgement. The ill effects that it had on the Wheelers' family life at this time can easily be exaggerated. Parents and children had many good holidays together, while at home, on fine Saturdays, they would often set off on their bicycles with food for a day's picnicking. Every Christmas they would board the steam tram for Bradford to enjoy the dress rehearsal of the pantomime – for which Robert had free pass tickets. Eric and Amy were so excited by performances they had seen on the stage that, stark naked on their way to bed, they would re-enact them in the semi-basement kitchen. One Christmas a small crowd had gathered on the pavement to watch the pair in this innocent nude show before their parents saw what was happening and brought down the curtain.

The children were high-spirited enough to keep the house lively, and soon began to develop their own interests and games. They also filled house and garden with pets, keeping dogs and cats, guinea pigs, pigeons, an owl and many wild creatures, terrestrial and aquatic. Both were great readers, but whereas Eric loved to paint but was never to have an ear for music, Amy had some musical gift.

The boy sometimes tyrannized over his sister, particularly in making her play soldiers with him. The following note, which must have been written when he had been at school for some years, supports Amy's memory of this, but suggests, in spite of the high condescension, that his tyranny could be benign.

My dear Totsy,

How is your little dolly getting on? How is Granny and Frump? I bought some Boer soldiers, and I am going to have a battle at Ladysmith when you come back.

From Eric

The Wheelers were as hospitable as they could afford to be, and among the more frequent visitors were members of Emily's family. One of them was Thomas Spencer Baynes' widow, a stout lady of strong character, much respected in St Andrews. She was a favourite with Eric, for he welcomed both her company and her generous tips. The children were less appreciative of the visits from Emily's sisters, who they always referred to disparagingly as the Maiden Aunts. Eric cannot have eased his relationship with his mother by subjecting them to a campaign of practical jokes that went so far as snakes in the bath.

A few stories surviving from his early years have some relevance for Eric's later character. As a very small boy he was much attached to a young maid called Alice, probably the first to be employed at Moorhead Lane. His sister remembers how he would beg 'Anice, Anice, scratch my head'. This curious indulgence, beginning in the days of golden curls, is remarkable in having persisted through Wheeler's adult life. Devoted girls at the London Museum had been called to minister to the Director in this way, and I was amused to discover that each of them seemed quite unaware that the privilege had not been hers alone.

When Eric was about five years old he was walking with his father on the Lancashire coast near Silverdale when he disappeared and became totally lost. It was always remembered by the rest of the family as a proof of courage and resourcefulness that somehow, all alone, the small boy made the long journey home.

Perhaps because his father drew him so much into an adult world, Eric thought little of the company of other boys and (like any child of sense and sensibility) detested children's parties. It was always difficult to drag him to them, and once, when he had been obliged to go to a Christmas festivity given by the proprietor of the *Yorkshire Observer*, he became so desperate that he suddenly cried out, 'Damn this party, take me away from it!' Later his father warned him that men had been burned at the stake for saying what they thought.

Then there was the occasion when Amy, having stolen strawberries from a dish, lied to her mother about the misdeed. Amy to Eric: 'Do you think God saw me take those strawberries?' Eric to Amy: 'God sees everything, that's the devil of it!' A riposte which shows that already at the age of seven he possessed clarity of thought and expression.

While such tales and incidents afford glimpses of Wheeler's innate character and also of his family life, what really mattered during the Bradford years must be found in his close and continuing relationship with his father. Robert was to write that his children were 'friends and chums and meat and drink to me'. It was, however, to his obviously gifted son that he gave most of his time and thought and hope. He was to exercise his profound influence equally in the mental world of books, the arts and ideas of hero-worship and in the outdoor world of country lore and skills.

In *Still Digging* Wheeler has himself written a delightful account of their relationship. It cannot be bettered and there is little that can now be added.

That Robert took his son on country walks from an astonishingly early age has already been established by that earliest memory from the hills of Braid. On most afternoons, unless prevented by Pennine rains, they set out together. In Wheeler's memory his father 'Never abated his pace for my little steps . . . I hopped and skipped beside his long striding legs . . . and I learned to walk in an abnormally fast and ungainly fashion.' (It is quite true that all his life he had a most curious gait and it would seem churlish to doubt that this was its origin.)

All manner of things occupied the pair of them on these outings. They might watch birds, collect flowers, look out for rare butterflies. Or they might chance on some delicious adventure, as they did on the day when they met with some gypsies and learnt from them how to recognize strange but edible fungi. Often as they went Robert would quote poetry from the richly varied store of his memory.

Among all their doings on these excursions the most pregnant for the future was, of course, their pursuit of relics of the past, so plentiful in the country over which they ranged. Wheeler was to recall the discovery near Saltaire of a cup-marked stone, never before recorded, and surreptitious digging, under cover of mist, into a barrow on Baildon Moor. This was undoubtedly his first excavation, and perhaps the last to be entirely unsuccessful. Further afield, Ilkley was a centre of interest. There they admired the Anglo-Saxon crosses in the churchyard and filled their pockets with potsherds from the Roman fort, while Ilkley Moor was the best of all hunting-grounds for flint implements.

In a number of the home magazine which, as will appear, Eric edited and largely wrote when he was eleven to twelve years old, his earliest archaeological article has been preserved. It deserves to be given in full:

'OUR ANCESTORS'
A series of chats

Almost every one of us must have wondered at some time or other how Prehistoric man lived; how with a few sharp stones he could have made his home, got his food and defended himself. Well, his weapons, which were his chief things, were very often made out of flint, which was chipped until a sharp edge was got. These were fastened onto a stick or a piece of horn, and with these he defended himself and got his food. Many of these weapons have been found, some still very sharp.

How did they live?

They dug pits and covered them with logs of wood. Imagine to yourself; your father making your home, scraping away for all he was worth, using bad Celtic, fearing that the thunderstorm, which was threateningly sailing over the horizon, would burst before he had made his home. He would think himself lucky indeed if there was a cave near.

(R. E. M. Wheeler.)

Here, already recognizable, one can say with at least some seriousness, is the mind that was always to be steadfast in the belief that, with the help of imagination, archaeology must aim 'to dig up *people*' and not merely dry-as-dust artifacts. It is also worth noting the early imprint on this mind of the old idea that Ancient Britons lived in deep pit-dwellings, for it was one Wheeler was to cling to a little too long when, some thirty years later, it was being disproved.

All in all, there is plenty to justify his declaration, 'Looking back, I can see how in those impressionable years the insidious poisons of archaeology were already entering into my system.' These 'poisons' undoubtedly lingered, but at the time hunting antiquities probably had less appeal than other outdoor sports. Wheeler was to recall how 'From the years when I first toddled alongside my father, I was taught to carry my stick as though it were a gun, with all the formality and respect that so dangerous a toy demanded.' When promoted to handling the real thing, and allowed to shoot pigeons and sparrows or other small birds pilfering the corn, he had to eat all that he killed – for that was the parental law laid down for him. Often in the summer he would make his supper of plump sparrows cooked with dripping in a stoneware jar.

This backwoods approach to sport went with skilful trapping and above all learning how to move silently, observantly, to feel himself 'a wild thing among other wild things. . . .' In these matters he learnt not only from his father but also from Will the poacher, a local character with whom he was able to identify a favourite hero, Cutliffe Hyne's Thompson, a Yorkshireman who followed the same profession.

The boy also became an enthusiastic angler, preferring fly but not above bottom fishing when it was all that was to be had. At home he often fished the Leeds and Liverpool canal or the reservoirs visited on the Saturday outings, but it is unlikely that he did not also try the local becks – for he certainly watched trout lurking in them. On holidays he and his father spent much of their time with rod and line, sometimes having to show the true fisherman's patience – as in the Isle of Man, where they came back day after day with empty creels. On the other hand one of the attractions of the grandparents' Gloucestershire farm was a stream near the house where big trout could be caught. The following extract from the magazine, written when Eric was eleven years old, probably refers to fishing a reservoir, for the scene is

A hot summer day in Yorkshire. A light western breeze blows across the tranquil lake. [where] Little perch, with the red fins and armed bodies . . . lazily paddle themselves out of their beds of weed. . . . The small, greedy fish are cautious and they start by nibbling one end of the worm. Suddenly the float is tugged under. I seize my rod and strike. I land a very small perch. . . . I throw the little fish back into the water in disgust, and put a fresh worm on, a purple one such as fish like. . . . Presently my float gives a bob and then goes under. Ah! This is something like a fish!

This thorough grounding in country matters was to stand Wheeler in good stead. Although he never turned to the conventional, social forms of sport, all through his life, whether in his native land or in wild and distant parts of the globe, he would seize opportunities to take up gun or rod. More than once he was to do so of necessity, to fill the pot. Even more important was the fact that a feeling for nature became a part of the ground of his being. As he himself saw, 'These are the things that matter. . . . They are bred in the young body and the young mind – bred in the boy who learns to carry a stick as a gun and to tread the paths of the wild with comprehension.'

He was soon to respond to the lure of London, and in later life Wheeler was to appear very much an urban man. He had no thought, until the very end, of retirement to a country cottage but preferred a little house in a narrow street near Piccadilly Circus. Yet without the long and intimate relationship with Yorkshire woods and moors that he owed to his father, he would, I am sure, have been a different kind of person.

If Robert Wheeler expected his small son to keep up with his long stride he was no more accommodating over mental exercise – or so it seemed to Wheeler when in retrospect he declared that 'From my earliest years he treated me as an adult mind.' When rain kept them indoors the two would spend afternoons together in the study, with Robert taking down books to read extracts and explore any subject that appealed to him. In those 'earliest years' there was much Eric did not understand, but it did not pass clean over his head. Some of what he heard, whether in talk or reading, lodged within to germinate as the boy himself matured.

Perhaps more influential than literary or general ideas was Robert's romantic passion, already mentioned, for heroic deeds and great adventures. The boy evidently responded with enthusiasm equal to his own and came to develop a particular admiration for outcast men of all kinds, from Thompson the poacher and Dick o' the Fens to Hereward the Wake and Robin Hood. It is good to know that even in heroic literature Eric had discrimination: while in sympathy with Cutliffe Hyne's Thompson, he rejected the doings of his more famous creation, Captain Kettle, as 'mere melodrama'.

Wheeler records of this time, 'When I wanted to enjoy a pleasant melancholy, Don Quixote perennially supplied the need. There sometimes seemed to be a faint touch of my father in him.' It is worth quoting a letter he wrote in response to the gift of a *Don Quixote* from a Mr Spielmann – with whom, as will be seen, the family had struck up an unusual acquaintance:

You could not have sent me anything that I like better. I have already a dumpy little abridged 'Don Quixote' which I bought for threepence at a second hand bookstall. It is a London issue 'Printed by the Booksellers', but my copy has also the imprint of a Halifax bookseller.

It has two little vignettes by an engraver of the name of Stephenson. I am very glad however to have the copy you so kindly sent me, partly because I have been interested in comparing the different translations of which we now have three or four, and still more because it will be a pleasant thing to keep as coming from someone who edits a real Magazine of Art.

This is good writing for a boy of twelve, and the content proves how far the sessions in his father's study had led him in an understanding of books and how they could be used.

The correspondence with Mr Spielmann belongs to what can be distinguished as a second, more expansive phase of the Bradford decade. Just before his ninth birthday Eric had entered Bradford Grammar School, an ancient foundation housed since 1873 in one of the blackened buildings near the centre of the city. It was a matter for parental pride and pleasure that he was put straight into the second form. Before long Amy went to the neighbouring Girls' Grammar School. They travelled in by the steam tram, but never, as Amy recalls, rode together.

It must have been at about this time that the family was able to move from Moorhead Lane to a house nominally in Shipley but closely abutting on Saltaire. Hurst Garth was a big, semi-detached, stone-built villa, standing in its own garden with open fields and some woodland between it and the river. It was large enough to allow the children, for the first time, to have bedrooms of their own. Eric chose one on the top floor with a wonderful view over Baildon Moor – which he often tried to paint.

The larger house was to be much needed, for in the spring of 1902 an event occurred that must have surprised and shaken the family: after an interval of over nine years another baby was born – a girl who was to be known as Betty. Amy was evidently annoyed by this late arrival, for she complained of her howling, heaviness and interference with the family habits. As for Eric, when told the baby was a girl, his only comment was 'What a waste of time!'

It was when Betty was still an infant in arms that her brother and sister launched an enterprise which, with its sequel, has briefly illuminated this period of their lives. In July of 1902 they wrote the first number of a magazine entitled *The Arts of the Day*, and edited by R. E. M. Wheeler. Three of the earliest issues survive, all dating from the summer of 1902, the last including accounts, from a 'special correspondent', of the Coronation procession and illuminations at Bradford.

All the illustrations came from Eric, and most of the articles and poems, although under a variety of pen-names. In addition to *Our Ancestors*, already quoted, the elaborately written coronation pieces and an earnest review of a life of Rembrandt, most items concern holiday doings and natural history. The rule was that everything had to be 'true' in the sense of non-fictional, although an exception was made of Eric's poems, as they were, his sister said, 'as true as most'. It is sad that no later numbers are preserved (when the title seems to have been changed to *The Magazine of Art*), since they contained judgements on their elders 'so true we dare not let the magazine go out of the family' – as Amy was to confess.

Towards the end of the year, entirely on her own initiative, Amy wrote to the editor of *Little Folks*, telling him of their rival publication. She ends, 'The worst of our magazine is that it has not a very big circulation, as it is only read by our Father and Mother, but they think very highly of it. I am dear Editor, your hated rival Amy Wheeler (age 10 and 2 months).'

The professional editor, evidently struck by Amy's spirit and humour, put the children in touch with Mr M. H. Spielmann, then running the *Magazine of Art*. An exchange of magazines, books and letters followed, Mr Spielmann having responded in 'a most kindly and sympathetic spirit'. It appears that he particularly praised Eric's art work. In her first reply to Mr Spielmann Amy wrote,

The 'He' editor was very pleased with what you said about him. He is twelve years old, and twice as tall as I am, and is a nice boy when he likes. But I never thought about being proud of him. I suppose I must try. He says he is going to be an R.A. or a tramp when he grows up. Mother says he may be both.

A little later, in March 1903, Robert Wheeler began a long letter to Mr Spielmann, 'I think it is high time that another middle-aged editor (47 years and 6 months, alas!) should join the ring,' then thanked him profusely for his kindness to 'the youngsters' and confessed that although he had known nothing of the beginning of the correspondence, latterly he had been vastly enjoying it as an 'eavesdropper'. Mr Spielmann's letters, he declared, 'were doubly pleasant to me as an independent voice in approval of the bairns who are friends and chums and meat and drink to me'. He continues,

I should perhaps say that in the production of their little Magazine . . . I have neither part nor lot, and that it comes to me as one of the few things in their lives to which I am an outsider. Once in six weeks or so, for the space of two or three days, there are signs of conspiracy afoot . . . . There are confabulations in corners, retirements to attics and cellars . . . and in due time a new number of the magazine is born. In the main the boy, as the elder, is the brain of the partnership. . . . I was especially interested in your comments on the boy's sketches. For good or ill he has had a small Oil accepted at the Bradford Spring Exhibition this year and his interests run predominantly to Art. At the same time he is a good all-round sort of boy – good enough, I mean, to make the ultimate specialization uncertain. So far, he has had no teaching on the art side; I feed his interest to the utmost of my power with pictures and books, but, for the rest, leave him to find his own way.

After the first, Amy's lively letters to Mr Spielmann have little of significance to say of her brother, except in recording that they were all sick on the way to a holiday in the Isle of Man (she has told me that Betty was sick on her mother's boa, a rather grizzly Edwardian scene). Wheeler, to his intense mortification, was always to suffer from sea- and air-sickness.

Eric's own letters to his fellow-editor are spread over the year 1903, beginning with his acknowledgement of *Don Quixote*. One tells how the local farmer allows him to shoot over the meadows round Hurst Garth, but they are mainly of interest in showing his keen interest in painting. In the spring he wrote, 'I envy you at London just now among all the good pictures. Some day I hope that father will take me down to see all the galleries, then I shall die happy. I am looking forward to the summer and to some out-door sketching when it is a little warmer.'

Another letter shows how substantially Robert was feeding his artistic interests:

It is very good of you to offer to send me more art books, but I don't quite know what to say about them. My father gets me a great many, and it seems greedy to wish for more. I have almost all the different series of picture reproductions that have been published lately, and a number of artists' lives and art histories and gallery catalogues, and we get the 'Magazine of Art' and the 'Studio' and the 'Connoisseur'. The instruction books I have are some little yellow ones published by Rowney and Windsor & Newton many years ago, and Wylie's book on sea painting. We also get the Munich 'Jugend' and sometimes some of the other foreign Magazines. So that every day or two when I wake up in the morning I find a fresh picture book by my bedside.

In the autumn he confesses, 'I have been doing more shooting and fishing than painting this season, and now it takes all my time (and my father's) to do my homework, but I have not lost my art interest – it is still the one thing I most care about, next to "growing out doors", as Whitman puts it.'

The impression left by the three magazines and the Spielmann correspondence is of an active, civilized family pursuing many ideas and interests with lively enjoyment. In all this (under the paternal aegis) Eric naturally played a leading part. An appraisal of the quality of his contributions to *The Arts of the Day*, however, is a little disappointing since it tends to be well below that of the letters. The best writing is in the carefully observed accounts of the countryside and its wild life. Pieces such as those on the Coronation have vigour but are conventional in content. The one approach to comedy, 'In ye Olden Times as Now', is a dramatic dialogue, in mock-mediaeval English, in which Eric is sent on his bicycle to fetch 'a right goodly, plumpe cheeke of ye very best poarke' from the butcher and suffers misadventures.

The poems, alas, show no divine spark and are almost wholly derivative. 'The Folly of Love', for instance, though of some interest since it shows Eric's absorption in the heroic ideal, concerns a warrior 'clad in steel with Falchion good', while 'The Guardian' is a lament over the grave of a beloved where a willow tree is 'Almost embracing my sweet one,/As she lies beneath the ground'. Even nature poems, such as 'The Cuckoo', generally lack the direct observation of the descriptive prose. One poem deserves to be presented because, while exceptional in using such personal responses, it also manifests the influence a classical education was already exerting on the boy:

'IMPROMPTU'

Far from the noise of a city,
Revelling in my solitude,
I walk by the side of a river,
Like Narcissus, wondering at his image!
The brown rats by the water
Make a merry ripple;
Chased by Zephyrus, fleet footed,
Come the joyous, dancing gulls;
The bright plumaged king of fishers
Is there, in all his glorious coat;
Here are reflections, bright and clear,
In the river, from the bank –
And as I walk I marvel not
That Hylas in delighted ecstasy
Went with the nymphs that tempted him.

The watercolour paintings in the magazine are also derivative, mostly showing conventional romantic subjects. Female faces are quite skilfully rendered, but their extreme insipidity makes one suspect the dictates of those little yellow books. Cover designs and their lettering show a sense of design and plainly relate to the posters which Eric was already painting and which he was to turn out with immense enthusiasm all through his school and college years.

If altogether Eric's contributions to his *Arts of the Day* are neither better nor worse than one would expect from a clever boy of his age, they are perhaps exceptional in one characteristic way. They show his command of purposeful energy. When all his other activities are allowed for, the effort needed, with Amy's help, to compose, write out, index and illustrate these magazines is impressive. It seems to have been maintained for at least a year.

The history of the magazine and the Spielmann correspondence that has brought a direct contact with Eric, on either side of his twelfth birthday, can be wound up by a letter he wrote over a quarter of a century later, in 1929, when he was Director of the London Museum. Evidently something had led M. H. Spielmann to write to him and he replied,

Dr R. E. M. Wheeler has an unusual pleasure in acknowledging Mr Spielmann's charming postscript. The identification of Dr Wheeler with the small co-editor of a certain Magazine of Art in Yorkshire is correct, and the recollection of Mr Spielmann's righteous indignation and inspiring encouragement still ranks amongst the most attractive memories of that distant period. Associated with all this is the remembrance of a pilgrimage to Halifax or Huddersfield (or some other place which no Yorkshireman begins with an H) to listen, with admiration akin to reverence, to a lecture by Mr Spielmann either on Watteau or on the Wallace Collection, or both.

Dr Wheeler only hopes that he may be privileged to renew that remote acquaintance, and that, if and when Mr Spielmann is in town, it may be possible for the rival editors to lunch or dine together.

Wheeler was to judge that 'By and large, my school was of no great moment to me, save perhaps that it confirmed in me certain prejudices which I had developed in contact with my father.' The prejudice he had most in mind was against organized ball games of every kind, for which he had then, and always maintained, 'a deep-seated and barely tolerant contempt'. It is mainly of interest as proving the schoolboy's strong individuality and tenacity of purpose that throughout his five years at Bradford Grammar School he played no games at all save one cricket match, when he was conscripted for his form as eleventh man. It was also, however, of importance since it left him relatively free to spend the afternoons with his father – himself at liberty since he was 'a working journalist whose dinner was his breakfast'.

This total avoidance of the playing fields was achieved without any loss of standing among the other boys. Indeed, when he was thirteen and in the classical fifth form, one of the football teams made him an honorary member, appointing him to 'draw their posters and programmes' for them and nominating him as their RA. This assignment he may be said to have combined with his classical studies, for the first poster he devised for them showed 'a *full Bacchus* trying to kick a goal'.

To have brought off this coup, Eric must already have won respect among his fellows: there was no fear of his being considered a milksop, his gifts as an artist were probably over-estimated, and he may have begun to show that ability to dominate 'lesser mortals' that was to grow with time. There was no doubt, either, about his intellectual ability, and that counted for much in the Grammar School of those days.

The master most able to recognize and foster this ability was J. E. Barton, a Newdigate Prizeman who combined teaching Latin with a far-reaching intelligence and the gift of stimulating schoolboys to make full use of their own. He had a further bond with Eric in that he already possessed a love and knowledge of the visual arts that he was to develop when he became a widely influential headmaster at Wakefield and Bristol.

When Eric first went to school Barton's star pupil and the leading light of the group of bright boys he had drawn to himself was Humbert Wolfe. Wheeler was to remember his delight and sense of liberation into the realities of a greater world when the whole school was given a holiday in honour of this Olympian's Oxford scholarship. By the time he himself had moved far enough up the school he felt that he had 'in a measure' taken Wolfe's place in the Barton circle.

He was not to occupy it for very long, since in 1905, when Eric had just (precociously) reached the sixth form, his father agreed to take over the London office of his newspaper. On hearing the news, Barton sought an interview with Robert Wheeler to protest against a removal that would deny his son the near-certainty of a scholarship. 'You are not taking him away from Bradford, you are taking him away from Oxford,' he declared, and for him Oxford was the goal that any sane man of intelligence must choose. Eric stood stoutly behind his father's decision. Had he not written at twelve years old that if he could reach London he would 'die happy'? He stayed on for the autumn term and his fifteenth birthday, taking his Oxford and Cambridge certificate with a first class in arithmetic, history and Greek. This was to be the end of his school-days. In the Christmas week of 1905 the whole family moved to Carlton Lodge, West Dulwich. Soon Robert Wheeler was to say, in his last known letter to Mr Spielmann, 'My wife does not yet take quite kindly to the change ... but the children and I are happy.'

There is no question that in later life, when he mingled with an elite still largely drawn from Oxbridge, Wheeler would have liked to be an Oxford man: an honorary degree from the university was to give him intense pleasure. This was not to say that he regretted the decision for London. It is quite possible that had he gone to Oxford and been a great success there he might have been led into the accepted paths within the groves of academe and so failed to cut the new trail better suited to his nature and his talents. It is possible, but by no means certain since in most ways Wheeler understood himself well enough and would probably have turned from conventional scholarship as firmly as he turned from the playing fields of Bradford Grammar School.

Robert Wheeler seems to have found Carlton Lodge, in South Croydon Road, for himself. He wrote of the place that it was 'propped up into a sort of habitability'. Presumably the house was cheap as it was dangerously dilapidated, but it suited the family quite well, having plenty of room for the five of them and, like Hurst Garth, standing in its own garden.

By now it may have been Robert's lack of faith in classroom teaching rather than lack of money that determined him not to send his fifteen-year-old son back to school. Instead he gave him some five shillings a week for travel, lunches and all the other expenses needed to pursue his 'further education' in that heaven of his past longings: London. If it seems an eccentric course to have adopted, it was probably a safe one, for the boy was not only well ahead of his years in book work but full of driving interests that would never allow him to be idle. As Amy recalled, the Wheelers had long ago recognized that he was 'meant for success'. Moreover he was pledged to combine his London ventures with working at home to prepare for his early matriculation.

Eric himself certainly plunged into his new, free way of life with an exalted sense of adventure. Most mornings he took the train up from Dulwich to Blackfriars Station, from where he set out, map in hand, to walk to whatever gallery, museum, building or thoroughfare he most wanted to explore. His leading passion was still for the visual arts, and his favourite haunts therefore the Victoria and Albert Museum and the National Gallery. Some days he might stay near home and enjoy the choice little gallery in Dulwich Village or do some painting in the park. Indeed, the many hours he spent with the masters of watercolour at South Kensington and with Turner in Trafalgar Square were not intended solely for appreciation but as an advance towards a future career. His desire to become a painter had not weakened. Although Eric spent most of his time in such earnest cultural pursuits, he could not fail to open himself to all the riches of Edwardian London that could be enjoyed with a purse so thin that to spend more than four pence on lunch rocked the financial week. He observed, often with a sardonic eye, a variety of spectacles, from the Lord Mayor's Show to bloody bouts in an East End boxing saloon. He wrote to his school friend, Theodore Cribb, 'I'm enjoying myself here "no end".... What with shows, unlimited picture exhibitions, and celebrities, my spare time is fully, if not well, occupied.'

Although in retrospect Wheeler himself felt that the Bradford time had been all-important for him, these two years between school and university, when he was a student of all London, must almost have balanced it on the scales of experience. If in the West Riding he had learnt what it was 'to be a wild thing among other wild things', now he must have discovered what it was to be a civilized youth alone in a great civilized capital. For he was nearly always by himself in these explorations. Surprisingly, there was nothing precocious in his sexual development: during these fifteenth and sixteenth years he was quite untroubled by it. Although what he did and experienced must have been valuable (he never lost the pleasure that comes from reading the buildings of a city street like a pictorial history), it was the absolute command of himself and his days that was most significant. Alone, but not lonely, mind and senses fresh and acute, responsible for planning the expenditure of every day and every penny, this time must have increased his natural resourcefulness and perfected that armour of self-containment in which he was to move through his crowded and amorous life.

It was a necessity of this age of adolescence that Eric should grow peacefully away from his father. Occasionally they were together in London, attending an exhibition or a concert – for Robert, who was a lobby correspondent and now walked the street in morning coat and top hat, was expected to keep his readers in touch with the artistic life of the capital. Afterwards they might retreat to the Fleet Street office, where Eric was initiated into journalistic discipline, writing strictly compressed paragraphs for the 'London Letter'. Nor did he fail to keep his promise to work for his London Matric. Early mornings and evenings at Carlton Lodge saw him toiling at his books.

Why it had been arranged with the London University authorities for Eric to break the rules by sitting the examination before his sixteenth birthday is not recorded – nor was fate to allow him this distinction. Already groggy when he presented himself for the first day's papers (Wheeler was never to consider illness a sufficient reason for inaction), he collapsed on the way out and had to be nursed through a dangerous fever.

This was in the summer of 1906; early in the new year he duly matriculated, although, as he told Cribb, it was 'shocking of me not to have got a first but I have been most awfully lazy, or rather London has been most awfully interesting, so that I didn't deserve one'.

Eric began his letters to Charles Theodore Cribb when he moved to London, while his school friend remained in Yorkshire. They throw patches of light on his later teens no less welcome than the illumination of his earlier boyhood by the magazines and the Spielmann correspondence. They almost certainly owe their preservation not to their written contents but to the art work lavished on their covers and occasionally on the inner pages as well. The postal sorters must have been astonished at having to distinguish addresses that formed an integral part of elaborate paintings covering the entire faces of the envelopes.

Cribb was much devoted to nature study, and it may have been this that first drew the boys together at school. During Eric's last year at Bradford they had been collaborating in the production of a school magazine, a hand-produced affair probably started by Eric himself as a sequel to a number of short-lived form magazines he had run in the past. He now wrote, typed and illustrated the school magazine, while rather oddly attributing it to Cribb under his nickname of Byron. Theodore Cribb was in fact the Business Manager, an office which involved circulating the single copy of each issue among masters and boys at the charge of one penny per day.

The early letters (the first dates from April 1906) manifest an eagerness on Eric's part to keep in touch with his Bradford past, since he had volunteered to serve as Art Editor of their paper under any General Editor Cribb chose to appoint. Although, inevitably, this scheme came to nothing, he continued to write to his dear Theodore for no less than five years, right up to the time when he was preparing to take his BA at University College.

The letters are full of youthful facetiousness, sometimes rising to wit, and scattered with private jokes and teasing. Keeping to his school name of Remy throughout, he began by inscribing himself 'Your affectionate chum', then 'thine', 'thine eternally', or 'Your humble and admiring friend'. Yet despite their jokiness, these are letters speaking from a strong attachment which Eric cherished and was determined to

One of Eric's illustrated
envelopes to Cribb

maintain. He often urged his friend to visit him, did small commissions for him in London – and invariably wrote on natural history topics when his own interest in them must have been fast receding. His old admiration for his 'chum' must have been hard to sustain as he himself prospered in the Metropolis while Theodore floundered and at last was glad to land a job as a bank clerk in Skipton. He never faltered, handling the relationship with perceptive sensitivity, omitting or making little of his successes and always insisting that his friend would make his name as a naturalist. When he heard the details of Cribb's job he reminded him that Bernard Shaw had started as a clerk on an even smaller salary and wrote, 'It will be by natural history that you will make your mark, but in the meantime – £35 a year! While you are *earning* that, my college course (with no particular object) costs my poor unfortunate parents at least as much, and I don't know when I will earn a penny.' While at this time Eric felt it necessary to encourage his friend in the face of what seemed dismal prospects, Theodore was to have a belated but quite successful career, not in natural history, but in the church, becoming an honorary canon of Birmingham.

As a testimony of friendship these letters can hardly be faulted. Nor should the odd originality of the decorated covers be ignored. Nearly all are illustrative of matters within: they are skilful, sometimes really funny, and must have cost considerable time and trouble. As a whole, however, the letters are much constrained, bound, perhaps, by the limitations of the friendship itself. For the writings of an intelligent youth advancing into manhood, they contain astonishingly few general ideas, feelings or comments on the outside world. They may be said to be cribbed, cabined and confined.

The very last, dated March 1910 and written after a long interval, bears one of the best drawings – of Eric cheering as he waves a letter announcing Theodore's promised arrival in London. They are to meet the next week and do some 'excursionizing' together. What happened is lost in oblivion. Did they perhaps come together only to discover that they no longer really knew or liked one another? However it happened, it can, I believe, be recognized as the end of a uniquely innocent, selfless and faithful relationship upon Wheeler's part. Probably it had long been kept alive only in his imagination.

While Eric's habits, and those of his father also, were greatly changed by the move to London, something of the old family ways continued much as before. They still went for holidays together. The first summer, for example, took them to the seaside at Herne Bay, whence they visited Canterbury, and Eric's enthusiastic interest in the cathedral

C.T. CRIBB, Esq.,
THE VICARAGE,
SHIPLEY,
YORKSHIRE.

The envelope showing Eric's father
'seized with a mania for boating'

probably established his enduring enjoyment of Gothic architecture. The next year they spent four weeks at St Leonards 'in a country full of interesting castles', and went on to stay in an artist's house at Walberswick, where Eric tried his hand at riding, rowing, swimming and sailing.

The strongest links with the past were, however, established by Robert Wheeler in his evident determination not to be altogether cut off from nature and the outdoor life. His early explorations from Carlton Lodge discovered an island in the Thames near Weybridge and he took the family for a few days' camping there. This was the beginning of what was to become an important part of their shared activities. The following summer Eric informed Cribb that his father had been 'suddenly siezed [his spelling was still not quite as reliable as he thought] with a mania for boating'. He had in fact bought a sailing dinghy from Gamages and converted it into a 'water caravan' with a tented roof. At first their attempts at sailing her from the island base exposed them to public ridicule, but by autumn Robert and Eric, alone together once more, took the boat up from Weybridge to above Henley, covering some dozen miles a day 'through ripping scenery. . . . It was awfully jolly, though very cramped.'

Thereafter, as Amy remembers, the family went camping at Weybridge as often as three times a year; they rented a pitch on the island and added to their amenities until they had three tents and a cook-hut as well as the dinghy. These holidays were cheap, healthy and enjoyable. Eric particularly enjoyed fly-fishing from the dinghy, inducing his sister to get up early to row for him. Even then he did not restrain his brotherly impatience, but would call out, 'More to the right . . . to the *right*, I said. . . .' She guarded her sisterly patience and there was shared delight in that small boat on the early morning Thames. Sometimes Eric hunted rare snails for Theodore – and to the end never ceased to urge him to visit their camp: 'It is just the sort of thing you would revel in – aquatic monsters in quantity.' His friend never came.

Their waterside holidays brought a boon to the Wheelers of an altogether unexpected kind. If at the time of the removal from Bradford Emily did not 'take quite kindly to the change', the warmer, cleaner air of the south, together with these camping days, restored her to good health. Through the rest of her long life, and she lived to be eighty-four, she suffered only one more attack of pneumonia.

Emily Wheeler may have been the one member of the household who could at least in part welcome another removal. It is a safe guess that she did not greatly appreciate having to look after a house 'propped up into a kind of habitability', however much her husband and children valued its advantages. In the spring of 1908 Eric wrote to Theodore,

Please note change of address. We were too much for Carlton Lodge – it was becoming quite cracked, so we determined to leave it while we had the chance. We are in a typical semi-detached villa which is, however, most fortunately on the only hill in the district, so that from my window I can see over miles of chimney tops to the two most famous gasworks in England – those of Battersea and Westminster. . . .

The new address was 14 Rollescourt Avenue, Herne Hill, in south-east London.

After his matriculation Eric had plunged directly into reading hard for another examination: the Intermediate Arts, which he was to take the following summer. Wheeler himself came to feel that his drive for examination successes, accompanied as it was by physical excitement, had had a compulsion other than the academic. At this time the little dragon of sexual energy, with such a puissant life ahead of it, was beginning to claw its way out of the egg. Under its still unrecognized power, 'examinations took upon themselves less the character of an ordeal and increasingly that of an orgiastic ritual.... I ascribe the classical scholarship which I acquired at this period to subliminal sex rather than to superior sense.' He was probably right, but I think one can add to sex his desire, as an isolated youth, to test himself against others, and perhaps also the mounting force of that passion for work that was to dominate his life.

Classical Studies

WHEELER WAS CERTAINLY wrong when he claimed in *Still Digging* that it was the scholarship which he won through subliminal sex that enabled him to go to University College, for the Cribb letters reveal that it came to him only through the Intermediate Arts examination, taken when he had been there for several months. Writing to his friend in the spring of 1907, he said he was preparing to go 'to some college in October', and at the end of that month declared that university term had come upon him so unexpectedly that he was obliged 'so to speak to pack up my things and catch the next train'. It may well have been that the choice of University College among the possibilities offered by London University was a chancy one, but it cannot be believed that his approach to his academic purposes was so casual. Because he wanted to spare Theodore's feelings he always made light of his university activities. His own true feelings are better judged by his statement that the college in Gower Street, with its massive pediment and rotunda, was to be his 'real home' for the next five years. Real perhaps, but not actual, since he continued to live with his family and had to make wearisome daily train journeys from West Dulwich and later from Herne Hill.

University College in those days was a place of moderate size and considerable distinction. The Provost, Gregory Foster, was an administrator rather than a man of learning and ambitious in promoting the growth and influence of his college. Looking back, Wheeler was inclined to blame him for a policy that was to transform it from being 'a college in the truly academic sense', where everyone knew everyone else, into 'a hypertrophied monstrosity as little like a college as a plesiosaurus is like a man'. These harsh words anticipate Max Mallowan's similar if more mildly expressed judgement on the metamorphosis of Wheeler's own foundation, the future University of London Institute of Archaeology.

When Wheeler joined the college soon after his seventeenth birthday it possessed faculty professors with high reputations in both the arts and the sciences. Among those who taught him, A. E. Housman was by far the most distinguished. He had published *A Shropshire Lad* ten years before, and now professed Latin in what his pupil described as 'the take-it-or-leave-it principle' – in scholarly austerity, remote from his students. For Greek, Wheeler had Professor Plat, and also sat under Ernest Gardner, who, though he occupied the Yates Chair of Archaeology, in fact taught the history of art – and of Greek art in particular. Nevertheless, it was Gardner more than anyone else who encouraged Wheeler as a post-graduate to embrace the more earthbound forms of archaeology. He also supported him in the earliest steps of his career.

Among Wheeler's fellow-students he seems most of all to have rejoiced in the friendship of Paul Nash, one of the young men of high promise who was to survive the hideous slaughter of young men of promise that was only half-a-dozen years ahead, yet would have been totally unimaginable to them all. Others were William Strang, to become Permanent Secretary of the Foreign Office, and Andrade, the physicist.

Stafford Cripps was at University College during these years, but as a graduate considerably senior to the rest. Wheeler saw something of him, since Cripps was President of the College Union when he himself became editor of the *Union Magazine*. He was immensely impressed by the older man's personality, the manner in which he dominated a room simply by entering it. On the other hand, in his opinion, Cripps was taking no very active part in the intellectual or political life of the place: 'He remained a remote and brooding genius.'

Editor of the *Union Magazine*? There is something touching in Wheeler's adherence to old ways. From the launching of *The Arts of the Day* at eleven years old to the time he graduated there can have been very few years when he was not editing a magazine of some kind. The same is true of his poster-painting, cartoons and caricatures. He was probably executing these during most of his time at college. Writing to Cribb in December 1908, he told how he had been put on a Bazaar Committee and had painted 'a huge and monstrous poster which cost me many sleepless nights. Now, as they judge art by inches, they measured it and pronounced it successful.' At the end of the following year, when the college held a mock election, he was 'called upon to do a series of cartoons' and soon afterwards he wrote of 'a few feeble attempts at poster drawings or caricatures, done against time, mostly'. Among surviving posters the largest, probably the 'huge and

The caricature of A. E. Housman

monstrous' one, is excellently designed and executed, while of his caricatures that of A. E. Housman has been applauded. Other examples of this kind of handiwork are the coloured drawings on the Cribb envelopes. They include an effective caricature of Edward VII on horseback. 'It is meant to represent a well-known monarch who can no longer be classed among the light-weights and who was with me at the trooping of the Colours yesterday – a gorgeous affair. Upon my soul, I never in my life saw such a tun of man as our Most Gracious Majesty.' Another shows a diminutive working man with big boots gazing up at an immensely tall and grotesque Lord half-extinguished by his coronet. Wheeler had no sympathy with what he called the 'Down-with-the-lords-give-the-working-man-a-chance business', yet he drew the cartoons for those who had. It was a relationship very much like the one he had forged at school with the football enthusiasts.

Wheeler derided his efforts as poster artist and cartoonist, and probably quite genuinely thought little of them. Yet they were involved with his deeply rooted ambition to become a painter. In the letter of 1908 describing the success of his Bazaar poster, he wrote that some of his friends 'got the notion into their heads that I was a budding President of the Royal Academy, a Raphael in disguise, an infant prodigy, mainly, I think, on account of my long and curly locks. . . .' Yet, despite the mockery, he goes on to tell Cribb, 'next term I think of working in the Slade School of Fine Art where my drivelling scribbles will, I am afraid, be estimated at their real worth'.

The plan was put into effect. Through fixed determination Wheeler won permission to enrol at the Slade, the prestigious art school attached to University College. The place had a personal attraction for him since Henry Tonks was on the faculty as assistant to the Slade Professor – whom he was later to succeed. He had become a hero of Wheeler's, partly because he had sacrificed a promising career in medicine for art's sake, and partly because he felt that his scientific training gave him a clear-headed approach to art-teaching. So, in the spring term of 1909, the eighteen-year-old classical student, then about half-way through his honours degree course, began to direct his footsteps away from the lecture rooms dedicated to Hellenic and Roman studies towards the studios and life classes of the Slade.

It was a foolish business; it meant cutting much of my classics, and, in particular, it involved the constant cutting of Housman, for the very good reason that Housman cared least about his individual students. Yet in the long view my glimpses of the Slade were probably a good thing. This was just after the great phase of Augustus John, Orpen and Albert Rothenstein, and the

Slade was still in the first flush of the world's art schools. Sickert, McEvoy, W. W. Russell were hovering round it.... It was a promised land into which I wanted above all things to enter.

In addition to his pleasure in the general ambience and the hope that he was on his way to fulfilling his treasured ambition, he had the satisfaction of being taught drawing by none other than Tonks. Yet one cold winter's morning, as he left the studios, presumably at the end of a year's attendance, he experienced a sudden realization, produced by what failures cannot be known, that he lacked the talent to be more than 'a conventionally accomplished picture maker'. He took an immediate decision and walked away from his 'promised land'. He never returned to the Slade.

The decision must have caused anguish to a young man who had cherished dreams of becoming a great painter since early boyhood. It was the right one to take. With one exception, his surviving work shows nothing more than competence. The one exception is an oil portrait of Amy which has real painterly quality. It remains as a memorial to years of hopeful striving bravely ended.

His training in drawing, his study of lettering and layout for his posters and cartoons, were to be a little useful in his archaeological career. Yet the roots of his vain ambition went deep and could not be destroyed. In reminiscent mood he was to write,

Every spare moment of my busy boyhood was used up in the production of an endless succession of water-colours, oil colours, pastels, in a fruitless endeavour to express and evacuate some complex or other that inflamed my mental inside. To me every thought, however abstract, assumed (and assumes) a shape and colour.... Later when in my university days I dabbled in Greek philosophy, even the eidos took upon itself a nebulous form, rather like a Hobbiah.... This pictorial reflex, though I never succeeded in projecting it, has served me, on the whole, in good stead: it has helped me to objectify most things that have happened to me, and has so enabled me to spend my life, happily enough, encloistered in a picture gallery.

In spite of all the cutting of classes and lectures necessitated by his excursions to the Slade, Wheeler's undergraduate course went smoothly. After winning the small scholarship during his first summer at college, he began to find further ways of saving his 'unfortunate parents' from all expense. Towards the end of the following year (1909) he wrote to Cribb, 'I have actually been indulging in really hard work; the old classics of course, for the B.A. which I take (D.V.) next October. Moreover I gather a few necessary crowns by inflicting unfortunate youths with the rudiments of the Latin tongue. They think, poor victims, that they will attain the heights of matriculation, the Cambridge Senior etc. I pray they may!' One of these victims was 'a scented Egyptian'. He also earned a few guineas by writing.

The really hard work made a distraction from the disappointment of the break from the Slade which happened at about this time. It was not enough, however, to make up for lost hours and Wheeler got only a second in his BA examinations. He was to press on, working in his spare time, to take his MA in 1912, at the end of those five years when University College was his 'real home'.

For the rest his undergraduate life was much like any other young man's at that period. He was involved in various rags and peccadillos, and was caught often enough for the resulting fines to be a serious tax on his finances. His sexual drive was now advancing from the sublimated orgy of exam-taking to more natural pursuits. Most of his encounters were presumably with women students, but none was of much significance until he fell in love with Tessa Verney.

At the opposite extreme of undergraduate affairs, he came to serve on many committees. As he told Theodore Cribb,

Go to a college for committees! If they want half a crown for a new letter-box they form a committee to collect it. If they want to decide the date of some dinner or other they form a committee and hold half a dozen meetings. They have captured me and condemned me not indeed to the galleys but to the committees, which is almost as bad. . . .

Such was Wheeler's initiation into committee work, that part of the British way of life that was to claim so much of his time when he was in full career. His account of it suggests that he had not yet lost the sense of isolation induced by the years wrapped up in his father's company and as a lone hand in London. He participated in university doings but as something of an outsider.

It was in much the same spirit that, as has been said, he served the politicos of the college in their mock election. This was at the time when Parliament had been dissolved after the Lloyd George budget was defeated in the Lords, and the student body was largely on the side of 'the working man'. Wheeler was never to manifest much interest in politics, but his temperament, values and ambitions made him a natural conservative. Already in his school debating society he had opposed a motion 'That this House cordially approves of a socialistic system of Government'. Among all the letters to Cribb there is only one which, without political bias, has to be judged objectionable in tone and feeling. In poor rhyming verse it makes fun of the suffragettes' demonstration in Parliament Square. He was then only sixteen, but later he commented scornfully on the 'Medicals of the College' who have been 'making asses of themselves à la suffragette'. He also liked to mock cockney accents, but this was a universal indulgence of the period.

Of the ephemera fossilized in letters to his friend a few have the interest of the unexpected. Wheeler attended the 1908 Olympic Games at the White City and confessed that they aroused his 'wild enthusiasm and patriotism'. Yet when Ernest Shackleton visited the college, fresh from his early Antarctic exploits, Wheeler's sense of the heroic was not aroused. 'He stirred the hearts of two or three schoolboys (not including myself) and a few susceptible young females. His little old ship was rather more inspiring ... stinking of oil and grease and arctic explorers.' In 1909 there was a recruitment drive for the Territorial Force created the year before in response to the German threat. The following summer Wheeler wrote, 'Have you been swindled into joining the Terriers yet? I don't know whether the craze has penetrated so far into the wilderness, but here we are just overrun with 'em.' He went on to say that Gellert, a form-mate of Bradford days, was one of those now in camp 'playing at soldiers'. There was to be a total change of heart before August 1914.

The very last sentences that 'Remy' was to dispatch to Theodore reveal an unexpected enthusiasm for the drama. Having sacrificed his high hopes of the Slade, he was seeking relief from the 'humdrummery of student life through an occasional excursion to some really good theatre'. He begged his friend to overcome what seems to have been a puritan's disapproval of a supposedly sinful institution. 'I wish I could convince you that some of the very highest and *purest* art is to be found on the stage. There are, of course, *some* exceptions, as there are inevitably in everything (even the Church). . . . Preaching again! But I feel strongly on this point, and only wish that you would give the theatre a chance.' It is not altogether surprising that soon after this solemn exhortation was penned his friendship with Cribb and his last personal involvement with Yorkshire came to an end.

Working for a university degree gives all those young men and women who undertake it at all seriously a simple and energizing sense of purpose. They are like knights enclosed in armour, intent only on success in the lists. Those are most fortunate who are further armed with a more or less clear idea of what direction they would wish to take when the prize is won. Otherwise when the charge is over and the armour removed the young graduate is apt to feel naked and aimless. Wheeler was among these less fortunate. His one fixed desire – to be an artist – had been denied him and, as he told Cribb, he had started to read classics at University College 'with no particular object'. Now, in 1910, he was a Bachelor of Arts, but one for whom nothing was certain except the looming problems of adult life. He was as hard up as ever, perhaps increasingly concerned with his sexual life, had no job in prospect and, much worse, no conviction as to what kind of job he wanted.

It is true that, like many of those suffering from post-examination blues, he was soon to seek a cure by entering the lists again (for his MA). In those unenlightened days, however, this could not be done free of charge. He was to be saved by none other than the Provost, who must have recognized in Wheeler a poor young man of ability. After the BA was added to his name, Gregory Foster sent for him and offered him the post of private secretary to himself at a salary of £100 a year. Soon afterwards his status and earnings were advanced when he was made publications secretary, a position for which his chain of editorships must have helped to qualify him. He was thankful for this unsolicited support, although he had no intention of settling down within the obscure security of the college system.

During the four years between the Provost's intervention and his enlistment in Kitchener's army, Wheeler took two steps of immense importance for his personal life and his public career. He courted, then married, Tessa Verney and became committed to archaeology. Yet because so little is known of how these steps came to be taken or of their environment this span of years gives an impression of emptiness. It most certainly was not an hiatus in his affairs and yet it has the appearance of one.

In term-time most of his day must have been occupied by secretarial duties and working for his second degree – for in London a graduate has to work for an MA, unlike the superior procedure at Oxford and Cambridge, where he need only first wait and then pay. At home he was probably still sharing in the family camping and other holidays – since he was certainly doing so, and with youthful enthusiasm, to the very end of his correspondence with Cribb.

When Wheeler first met and loved Tessa Verney she was reading history at University College. Very small and slight, with dark-brown wavy hair, she was blessed with long lashes that made her eyes seem enormous. She was lively, very intelligent and with a charm incarnate in an enchanting smile. She could not fail to be popular – indeed, throughout her life almost everyone loved her in one way or another. When

Wheeler appeared on the scene she was being courted by a young Mowlem, heir to the family of building contractors, and was inclined to look on him with favour. That the penniless Wheeler seems to have had no difficulty in winning her away from a well-placed rival with such comfortable prospects is evidence that he was beginning to develop that attack and ascendancy over lesser mortals of which hitherto there had been only a few hints.

Tessa Verney was the happiest proof that a difficult and disturbed early childhood need not produce a difficult and disturbed personality. Her own mother was, or at least is known to have become, an admirable character, but with a dash of some quality, probably simple reckless-ness, that brought great troubles on her head. It is thought that her maiden name was Annie Kilburn and that she belonged to the prosper-ous Kilburn family of Bishop Auckland in Durham. Her history remains hazy, but she certainly launched her injudicious career at an early age when she made a hasty, very probably runaway, marriage. Her husband was a Mr Mather, and to him she bore a son, John – fated to become something of a wanderer and to spend much of his later life in South America.

It may have been with Mr Mather that Annie first went to South Africa, and that he deserted her there – unless he left her only through death. She was to tell her grandson Michael that she had been in Johannesburg in the nineties when there was hardly a two-storey build-ing in the township. Tessa had in fact been born in Johannesburg in 1893. Her father, John Verney, was a doctor, but remains an even less substantial figure than his predecessor. Certainly Annie had to fend for herself, and also, it can hardly be doubted, for her little girl, in cruelly difficult circumstances. The experience left her with an incurable loath-ing of black men.

When Annie returned to England she was able at last to secure a relatively happy and peaceful existence, living with a chemist called Theophilus Morgan Davis. She did not marry him, very probably because it was not known whether Mather, or Verney if he had been her husband, was still alive. However, she came to be recognized as Mrs Morgan Davis, and, inexplicably, sometimes adopted the Christian name of Agnez.

Tessa was devoted to her adoptive father, whom she called her guardian, and owed much to him both personally and for providing her with a settled family home. Probably it was he who, recognizing her abilities, enabled her to develop her interest in history at University College.

Wheeler must first have been attracted to Tessa at about the time when his thoughts were turning towards archaeology for his future career. If he had once welcomed Professor Gardner's not very imaginative handling of Greek art as a partial assuagement for his aesthetic longings, he was later to record that 'It was his teaching that drove me ultimately and not unwillingly into professional archaeology of other kinds.' Whether those pockets full of Roman sherds from Ilkley and all the other archaeological ventures of his boyhood influenced his choice, who can tell? The choice was made, and his own life work and Tessa's were determined.

The decision was not, however, to mean an immediate divorce from his classical studies, since then and for a long time afterwards his archaeological interests were to be concentrated on the western frontiers of Rome.

In that pre-war decade, knowledge of Roman Britain was being advanced both by scholarly, armchair studies and in the field. Two of the most significant excavations were at the Roman town of Viroconium near Shrewsbury ('Uricon', a link here with Housman) and at Corbridge near Hadrian's Wall. The English archaeologists, and particularly J. P. Bushe-Fox, who dug at both places, were coming to realize how valuable pottery could be for dating purposes. This had been recognized for the high-quality imported table wares such as the familiar red 'Samian', with its identifiable potters' marks, but now it was appreciated that everyday domestic pots and pans could also be dated with reasonable accuracy. The lead in this work was coming from the industrious, methodical and well-endowed German specialists. As Wheeler was to write in his earliest considerable archaeological treatise, that on Rhenish pottery,

Modern Excavation is rightly learning more and more to piece together the history of Roman Britain from its potsherds. In this connection, the relative scarcity of classified remains from British sites has given the immense mass of carefully marshalled material in the Rhenish museums an unrivalled importance for purposes of comparative study.

Wheeler was in touch with the Roman archaeologists and himself joined the Wroxeter excavation as a student during the 1913 season. He had a clear enough vision of the problems to discern a most promising opportunity for research in such comparative studies. He was, then, already feeling the attractions of pioneering in a neglected subject, especially since it combined activity in the open air with the historical studies he understood. There was, however, a small element of chance in his final commitment. Looking back upon this moment from old age he was perhaps heightening, but not falsifying, its chanciness when he said: '. . . by a process of sliding this way and that, I landed up in archaeology. It was in 1913, for the first time as far as I know in the history of academics, somebody founded a studentship in archaeology, and my professor at University College, Ernest Gardner, suggested that I might just as well apply for it.'

This studentship had, in fact, just been established by London University, together with the Society of Antiquaries, to honour the memory of Sir Augustus Woolaston Franks, late of the British Museum. Although the honouring did not stretch beyond £50 per annum for two years, Wheeler took the professorial advice and duly appeared with several other applicants before the selection committee. By that time he had his MA, had routed young Mowlem and become publicly engaged to marry Tessa.

Among other eminent selectors were Ernest Gardner himself and Sir Arthur Evans – famous for his discovery of Minoan civilization, announced a dozen years before, but who had also made a striking contribution to the understanding of Celtic Britain. Wheeler evidently satisfied the committee with his plan for research into Romano-Rhenish pottery and was immediately accepted for the Franks award.

He had been given what he wanted, he could look forward to his visit to the Rhineland, but now that he was committed he was suddenly dismayed by the worldly difficulties confronting him. He left the room, wondering how he was to survive on less than half his present modest income. He had burnt his University College boat.

As I walked away slowly and thoughtfully down the long corridor, I became aware of light footsteps hurrying after me. I turned and found myself looking upon the small, slight form of Arthur Evans, a little breathless with his running. 'That £50,' he said in his quiet voice, 'it isn't much. I should like to double it for you.' And he was away again almost before I could thank him.

Sir Arthur could well afford £100, but probably few other rich men would have done as much or acted with such discreet promptness.

Wheeler himself acted very promptly in setting out on this, the very first of his truly innumerable archaeological journeys. It was also the first time he had been abroad. It must have been an exhilarating experience to find himself alone in a foreign land, free to do anything he could afford and with a clear plan of work to give purpose to his days without unduly fettering him. The romantic beauty of the Rhineland was in harmony with his tastes and the architecture a revelation to one who had been able to respond even to the castle in the neighbourhood of St Leonards-on-Sea. Whether he had money for Rhenish wine or inclination for Rhenish maidens cannot be told.

In each museum he made full-size drawings of the jugs, jars, urns and other pots with which he was concerned – a task that must have given him pleasure, particularly when he was dealing with vessels rich in classical ornament or charged with the strange, comical faces of a more primitive tradition. When, later, these drawings were perfected and reduced, they made the most elegant, accurate and stylishly laid out of any archaeological illustrations being executed at that time. Unfortunately neither thesis nor drawings were ever to be published.

Soon after Wheeler had returned to London with full notebooks and portfolios, vacancies were advertised for 'junior investigators' with the English Royal Commission on Historical Monuments. Six young men were to be tried out in competition for three permanent appointments. The Commissions (for England, Scotland and Wales) had been set up some five years before to record and publish – but not conserve or excavate – every 'building, earthwork and stone construction' older than 1714. In that dawn it was not yet apparent that this was a task that could last for many generations.

The work was not well suited to Wheeler's qualifications, for in practice it principally involved the study and drawing of historical buildings, domestic and ecclesiastical. However, professional jobs in archaeology were very few and Wheeler decided to apply for a vacancy. As he was strongly backed by Professor Gardner, the Franks studentship cannot have been considered an obstacle.

Wheeler was obviously a strong candidate for the Commission staff – indeed, in many ways far too strong for so lowly a post as that of a junior investigator. Nevertheless, it had to be recognized that he lacked skills essential for the survey of buildings, and he was appointed on probation with the understanding that he would acquire them. He promptly arranged to work at night in the Architecture School of University College and there 'pursued with industry the elements of building construction and architectural drawing'. He was to find this training valuable far beyond its immediate purpose, in particular as giving a final touch of professionalism to his long experience as an amateur draughtsman.

The English Commission was then working on the County of Essex, and when he joined it in the autumn of 1913 his immediate assignment was to the parish church of Stebbing. If he was still somewhat at a loss when confronted with its heraldry, rood screen and other and deeper mysteries of Gothic architecture, his senior colleague led him to drown his anxieties in potations of whisky and milk. There would be few men of twenty-three today who had not tasted Scotch, but such was the case with Mortimer Wheeler on that memorable day.

After this initiation he worked for the three probationary months and was duly given one of the vacancies. Nor was he to be kept too long to struggle with our mediaeval heritage. As had probably been intended all along by Gardner and other elders, in the early summer of 1914 the Commission appointed him to make a survey of the Roman remains in Essex, a charge which, in theory at least, was more appropriate to his long years of classical education. In practice he was to have little time to do more than assemble some odds and ends of material. There survives a small leather-bound notebook in which he compressed all the information he had gathered about the buildings, roads, cemeteries and other remains of the principal Roman foundation of the county, and one-time capital city of Roman Britain: Camulodunum, or Colchester. Rough and cramped though they are, his notes are most painstakingly done and include all the references he could find to the chance discoveries made during past centuries. It was no doubt this familiarity with Roman Colchester that encouraged him, when briefly stationed in the town during the war, to employ men from his battery to make surreptitious investigations of the famous Balkerne Gate.

In the little Colchester notebook Wheeler wrote in a vigorous, masculine hand very close to that of his fully formed style and in marked contrast with the poor, sloping handwriting of all his letters to Theodore Cribb. This change can be seen as representing the strengthening and development of his adult personality that was taking place as he left his student days behind him. It was a process soon to be completed by the years of authority, stress and frightfulness brought by the First World War.

The greatest of the new responsibilities that he assumed during that summer of 1914 was his marriage to Tessa. So far as his family was concerned, Wheeler had tended to be secretive about his relationship with her, although this was his first serious love affair. Perhaps he was already adopting the attitude, for which he has been understandably much criticized, that led him to insist that there was no reason why anyone should feel especially close to his family and relations. Tessa was never to share it, but was always to do her best to keep in touch with both her husband's kin and her own. It was she who insisted, probably after their engagement, on arranging to meet members of the Wheeler family at University College.

The marriage itself was celebrated in an obscurity that now seems conspicuous. It can be assumed that the Morgan Davis's were there to support Tessa and give her away to her irresistible lover. It is a likely guess that her mother, after her own matrimonial recklessness and disasters, may have attended this excessively quiet wedding with some regret for the greater security and grandeur that she would have anticipated for Tessa had the bridegroom been John Mowlem. Robert Wheeler was present, but Emily heard nothing of her son's marriage until it was over. This was the unkindest cut of all, and one that caused her much grief and hurt.

There was, however, to be very little time for private happiness or unhappiness before the war came, with such terrible suddenness in its final stage, to shatter everyday life and the plans of the young. Wheeler was among those who, fired with patriotic and heroic ideals, hastened to volunteer, since the war would soon be over, and he was eager to be fighting the enemy. It was to be three years before he was sent overseas, straight into the very worst horrors of the Western Front.

For his first seven months he was to remain in London as an instructor in the University of London Officer Training Corps. It was early in this period, in January 1915, that his son Michael was born. In the light of what was to come, it is probable that, outwardly at least, Wheeler made as little of his fatherhood as he had of his wedding day. He lived now for guns, horses and the command of men.

CHAPTER 3

—

Then A Soldier . . .

DURING THE EARLY summer months of 1914 Rik Wheeler's main professional preoccupation was with his new responsibility for the survey of the Roman remains of Essex. In the conduct of his work for the Commission he learnt much from one of his seniors, the worldly-wise and able Alfred Clapham, later to be a close friend. In his domestic life, the emotion of his new role as a married man was heightened by Tessa's pregnancy. They appear to have been living together in the Wheeler family house in Rollescourt Avenue, Herne Hill.

At that time the British public at large had little thought of being involved in a European land war: it is true that there had been anxieties about the growing might of the German navy, but the main concern was with the Home Rule Bill and the problem of Ulster, with its threat of civil war. All through July this was seen as the darkest cloud hanging over the country, while the violence done by and to the suffragettes was the other centre of political battle. Most people had taken very little heed of that unfortunate assassination at Sarajevo, and it therefore came as a thunderclap from an unexpected quarter when on 28 July Sir Edward Grey, the Foreign Secretary, made a grave announcement concerning the Austrian ultimatum to Serbia. Even then there was no immediate expectation of Britain's involvement; that did not come until the ensuing Bank Holiday weekend, when hundreds of thousands of excited citizens remained in London to hear the news of mobilizations and invasions across the Channel. By the Sunday night vast crowds, knowing that France had been attacked, swayed outside Buckingham Palace, singing their national anthem and the 'Marseillaise'. The Bank Holiday was prolonged for three days and by that time war had been declared. On 5 August the popular and well-trusted Lord Kitchener was appointed Minister of War and within a few days had made his appeal for a hundred thousand recruits to be enlisted 'for four years or the duration of the war'.

Wheeler must have made an early decision to volunteer, for a fixed plan to begin the ordering of his survey by excavating an early Roman site in central Essex during August was abandoned without hesitation. Now that there was no question of 'playing at war' his scorn for the 'terriers', expressed five years before, had probably long since vanished in the face of realities. The inference is that he immediately joined the University of London's Officer Training Corps, for he was with them when on 9 November 1914, he was commissioned 2nd Lieutenant, with the position of Instructor. His appointments over the next three years are enough to show that he proved to be an excellent one, a fact unsurprising in retrospect since he was to be a brilliant teacher and trainer in practical skills when peace returned.

That Rik Wheeler took so readily and successfully to army life and later to action and command in the field is, however, more surprising, since his previous ways, tastes and abilities would seem to point against it. His dislike of team games, his lack of interest in badges or positions of authority at school and college, his love of solitary country pursuits, his youth-long ardent desire to be a painter, and even his recent devotion to historical research, do not suggest a soldierly nature. He had shown independence and strength of character, and his taste for editing and his immediate plan to straighten the tangles of Roman Essex indicate a fondness for good order. Yet the overall impression is of a loner, a young man who wanted to follow his own interests and who had manifested no power of command or desire for it.

It is true that his eager response to his father's romantic admiration for heroic men of action would have heightened the dream of performing great deeds on the battlefield that was shared by most of the young men who rushed to answer Kitchener's appeal. That, however, has little to do with success in putting a stream of raw and sometimes rough young men through the elements of gunnery.

He remained with the University College Corps until the following May, and it was during this time that Michael was born. He was then posted to the Royal Field Artillery (Territorial Force) and shortly afterwards, just before his twenty-fifth birthday, he gained his captaincy. For more than two years he was to remain a battery commander, first of field guns and later of howitzers. Both these commands were with training brigades permanently stationed at home. Thus it was his evident success in training and commanding men even younger than himself that prevented Captain Wheeler from being sent overseas and so vastly increased his chances of survival.

He was stationed at various localities in England and Scotland, and usually Tessa seems to have been able to follow, enabling him to taste something of family life. A snapshot album shows him holding and later playing with his small son on a beach, in gardens, a farmyard and other pleasant country places. Sometimes he clasps Michael in front of him on the saddle of a solid, highly groomed charger. In these little photographs Tessa may be looking on, with her quick, irresistibly charming smile.

One studio photograph shows Wheeler when he was stationed at the Redford Barracks in Midlothian. He is booted and spurred and he is leaning lightly on his cane, yet the stance is aesthetic rather than military, relaxed as his unstiffened cap; his face, despite the small moustache, is soft, while his expression, as he gazes into an imagined distance, still has some of the wide-eyed intensity of his small boyhood.

Through all the time that Rik Wheeler served in the training brigades, making no more adventurous excursions than from one dreary set of barracks to another, he was striving to be sent overseas. When the break came, in 1917, it was sudden and events moved with great speed. Since July the horrors of trench warfare had reached their most frightful pitch in the long-drawn-out Battle of Passchendaele, originally launched in the vain hope of reaching the Belgian coast. By the autumn the Second British Army under Plumer was fighting on the Ypres salient, one of the objectives being to make the salient more secure by winning the higher ground in which Passchendaele itself lay. The Germans were holding this country with pill-boxes and counter-attacks, and were making effective use of mustard gas. The British had gained some ground with constant pounding by their artillery, but the ceaseless slaughter of young men was putting a fearful strain on home reserves.

It was not, however, until October, in the last phase of the battle, that Wheeler was posted to the 76th Army Brigade RFA. This Brigade had been in France and Belgium for a long time, and in July, at the beginning of the Passchendaele offensive, had been moved to Novara Farm, near Brielen in Belgium. In October it had suffered heavy losses and Wheeler found himself rushed across and within a day or two of his embarcation spending a night in the wagon lines just behind the front.

This was almost certainly the night of 20 October and the plight of the Brigade had become far worse while Wheeler was in transit, for that day, as its War Diary records, the Colonel, several junior officers and the Brigade staff had been gassed at their HQ. The next morning Wheeler was sent up to the guns across ground recently surrendered by the Germans. He was immediately put in command of A Battery, taking the place of a Major who had been among those gassed. That same day the newly promoted Brigade commander and yet another Battery commander were gassed and a subaltern and several men killed or wounded.

It seems that no real breakdown followed this loss of so many officers, for the Brigade took up its place for the big attack soon to be launched. They formed the Left Group of artillery covering the advancing infantry. A Battery was positioned on a mud-blocked stream in such a way that the guns recoiled into water – as described in Wheeler's letter below. It was from here that the acting Major, as he now was (his appointment was to be officially dated to 21 October) fired his first creeping barrage – one that had to be maintained over a period of no less than three hours. He was to keep the barrage map as a memento, and this it remains, yellow and tattered, a touching relic of Wheeler's week of action in the Battle of Passchendaele.

An account of this grim week, which he always maintained was to solace him in all future trials because in it he had 'known the worst', is given in a letter he wrote to Tessa on 29 October, when the 76th Brigade had been withdrawn across the French frontier to Nieurlet, near St Omer. It is shorter than the version written for *Still Digging*, but has the advantage of being more personal and being penned immediately after the experience itself:

> Rest Billet
> France
> 29.10.17 (Monday)

The scene has changed, and I am writing this in a little French (or, rather, semi-Flemish) farmhouse, 20 miles from the firing line & as you see, on the French side of the Border. The Brigade has come out of the line for a few days rest, after being in the line for many months, so that my first baptism of fire only lasted a week. And ye gods! what a week! To cut a long story short, I reported to the Brigade on the Sunday following my embarkation, spent the night at the wagon line about 3 miles back from the front line, & the following morning went up to the guns over ground which not so long ago was Boche. Shells were of course coming over, but fortunately for the moment things were relatively quiet. I was at once posted to command A/76/RFA. Their major had been gassed the previous day. He is still in France, but if & when he goes down to the base I shall get my majority. (You see, he is at present still nominally on the Brigade). One of my subalterns, a boy of 19, had just got the D.S.O. (almost a record for age) & another has the M.C. Several of my men have decorations, & I have just recommended another.

I cannot attempt to describe the conditions under which we were fighting. Anything I could write about them would seem exaggeration but would in reality be miles below the truth. The whole battlefield for miles is a congested mess of sodden, rain-filled shell-holes, which are being added to every moment. The mud is not so much mud as fathomless sticky morass. The shell-holes, where they do not actually merge into one another, are divided only by a few inches of this glutinous mud. There is no cover & it is of course impossible to dig. If it were not for the cement pill boxes left by the Boche, not a thing could live many hours. The guns are all in the open, & – most phantastic of all – many of them are in full view of the Boche. I must not say much about my own Battery's position, but, to give you some idea of it, our gun was in water up to its breech, &, when it recoiled, the breech splashed under water. The gunners work thigh deep in water. Their spirit is perfectly wonderful. They are red-eyed, & hardly any of them (or their officers) can speak above a whisper – gas & cold has got them by the throat – but they stick it marvellously. They are out to win.

My own little headquarters, where I and my telephonists lived, was in a little German pill box consisting of 2 compartments, each about 6 ft. × 4 & about 5 ft. high (or less). The map shows it to be on the site of a farm, but the farm has disappeared. The strength of this little pill box enables me to write this letter. During the six days I was up there the pill box received five direct hits from 5.9s when I was inside. The place rocked like a ship at sea, but stood firm. As an example of the spirit of the men (many of whom are Irishmen), the cook was one day making dinner behind the parapet in front of the pill box door, when a 5.9 hit the parapet & filled the rice with mud. Instantaneously was heard the plaintive voice of the cook – 'Gawd! It's gone & spoilt the blinking puddin'!'

My week at the guns was a very crowded one. On the day I reached the gun line an attack had just taken place & I had to go forward & reconnoitre a forward position in view of a possible move. This forward position consisted merely of some waterlogged shell-holes on the skyline in full view of the Boche. A party of men under the captain of the Battery had gone to try & dig on the position the day before, but 5 of the men were killed & 7 wounded. The captain marvellously escaped unhurt. However, orders were that the position would probably be occupied, so I took a party of men up at dawn next day & we built a sort of track into the position. Fritz very kindly spared us, but it was not the sort of job I should care to do in my spare time.

Next day was more or less uneventful, except that we were pretty heavily shelled. An unfortunate driver, taking up ammunition, had both his horses killed & his leg blown off at our door. We tied him up & got volunteers (one of whom I have recommended) to carry him through the shell fire to the dressing station. He died as he got there. We then had the rather exciting job of pulling the dead horses clear of the road to let the traffic by. A very exciting five minutes. The one advantage of the mud is that it to some extent smothers many of the bursting shells – otherwise casualties wd. be more than doubled.

During the next 2 days we fired regularly by way of preparation for the new attack on the third. The morning before the attack I went forward to the front of the ridge to do some observing. I must confess to getting the wind up, but got through the job all right. On the night before the attack, I went over a mile of battlefield to our Brigade H.Q. to synchronize watches. The battlefield at night is a wonderful sight – flares & rockets going up above the front, blazing ammunition dumps lighted by shell fire, occasional searchlights, the continual flashes of the guns, the whistling of the shells, & the throbbing of the bombing planes overhead. Bombs I really don't like. Everywhere are falling bombs on both sides of the line. And last night, a few miles from this rest billet the archies were going strong.

On the morning of the attack we fired the barrage for several hours, the gunners working splendidly under tremendous difficulties.

However, enough said at present. Here we are, still up to our eyes in mud – our horses in a plowed field – nominally resting. The one redeeming feature is the absence of shell fire.

So the recruit has had a varied week & has grown shell-weary under conditions which will very possibly be better when he next goes into action. It is a wonderful experience, which I would not have missed for worlds.

It is a remarkable fact that in a postscript to this letter conjuring up a week of extreme danger and frightfulness, Rik Wheeler asked his wife to send him a rubber bath, one of the kind without a stand and which he thought could be bought at Andersons.

So long as he remained overseas Rik seems to have written often, and when the war allowed, regularly, to Tessa. She herself wrote frequently and whenever possible sent sweets, chocolates and other 'luxuries' that were always enthusiastically welcomed. Rik had early assured her that there was no need to send food since they were not starving nor living off bully beef but 'fed like kings'. To prove his point he gave a typical menu of a five-course dinner supported by beer, port and coffee. His requests for articles to be sent out to him were sometimes exacting, as when he demanded that his field boots should not only be registered but well packed, and again when a pair of light-coloured pinky-yellow riding breeches were to be bought and altered since in the standard Army and Navy cut '(a) The knees do not fit quite tightly enough in front; (b) They are not quite full enough in the end.' These sartorial details were illustrated by sketches.

Wheeler also received letters from his parents – although, surprisingly, his father appears to have been a poor correspondent – from his sister Betty (still referred to as Baby), from John Mather and other members of the family, even including Aunt Annie, one of the despised Maiden Aunts of Bradford days. He begged for more photographs of Tessa and Michael and again and again insisted on his eagerness for mail. 'Letters from home just make all the difference.... They are

waited for hungrily and their arrival always puts new heart into things.'
In short in the matter of correspondence Major Wheeler felt and
behaved exactly like the most ordinary of serving soldiers, whole-
heartedly accepting the importance of family relationships.

The 76th Brigade was to remain at the Nieurlet rest billet for three
weeks, during which time Passchendaele and its ridge were captured
and the battle deemed to be over. He assured Tessa, 'All is well with the
world.' Only the weather remained awful.

Soon he was to escape even that. On 12 November his Brigade
received word that it was to be transferred to Italy, information that
Wheeler conveyed home in words designed to pass the censor: 'Instructions just come. As the National Poet saith, "Better far off than near, be
ne'er the near." But not immediately.'

Those who believed in Guardian Angels on the side of the Allies
might well have assigned a private one to Mortimer Wheeler. To have
been kept safely at home for three years and then sent out when
Passchendaele was nearly over, but in time to be given as a lifelong
possession that one week in which 'to know the worst' was amazing
good fortune – crowned and secured by the dispatch to Italy.

During the wait represented by 'Not immediately' Wheeler seized a
chance to taste again one of the pleasures of his boyhood. Somehow he
heard of 'a proper old poacher type – a real French version of a Dick of
the Fens', said to be adept in duck-shooting. Long before the crack of a
November dawn Rik groped his way to the old man's cottage and they
set off together in an ancient boat with four decoy ducks and a drake
stowed on its bottom. The ducks squawked and the guns flashed and
rumbled far away as they paddled through willow-hung dykes. At last
they reached a mere, anchored their decoys and manned a hide on an
islet. There in the icy dark they waited, the old man from time to time
holding out the drake to encourage amorous quacking. As Rik was to
tell Tessa,

I watched with a sort of double-barrelled 5.9 in my hands. Happily I had no
occasion to fire this piece of ordnance. We sat there through the grisly dawn –
the poacher and the major – and the quacking of our decoys, though answered
at a distance, brought no prey within range.

And so we sat for a couple of hours, with no companion save an occasional
snipe which flashed past, and the crows which were just beginning to move to
their feeding grounds. . . . I proposed breakfast. Our procession back took us
past 'D' Battery as they were watering their horses, very much to their
amazement. 'Autre jour, possiblement' the old man said as we parted.
'Possiblement' I replied.

So ended an escapade that brought home no bacon, but was sweet as a private escape from the war and an exercise in nostalgia. Rik was never to lose his love for such vagaries, even when youth had been left far behind.

The transfer of the 76th Brigade to Italy was, of course, occasioned by the calamitous defeat of Caporetto. For months the Italians had been thrusting against the Austrian defences in the Alps, when on 24 October, during Wheeler's week of Passchendaele, Ludendorff launched the victorious Austro-German attack. The Italians lost a quarter of a million men and thousands of guns captured in the battle and were driven back to the River Piave. No less than five British and six French divisions were sent to reinforce them and in late November an assault on the Piave was driven back.

The gunners of the 76th Brigade did not reach the new line in time for this engagement, since they entrained only on 20 November and it was two weeks before they came within the sound of the firing line. Meanwhile Wheeler had in many ways enjoyed the slow erratic journey through the French and Italian Rivieras. This was his first view of the Mediterranean and he responded with new delight to the flat brown roofs, the scattered villas and 'the cold clear sunlight, blue sea, red cliffs and dark green pines and olives'. Moreover, he was able to record that 'Our progress through the Riviera was in the nature of a triumph. . . . The people turned out and cheered and threw flowers and oranges at us. Italy was more sober, but here and there displayed legends such as "GOOD HEALTH AT OUR ALLIES" or "WELCOM TO OURS BRAVE ENGLISH".'

After six days of this the Brigade detrained and began its trek eastward, across the north Italian plain, billeting each night in small towns and villages – where the commander saw to it that his Battery secured the best billets, including one night 'a great big chateau' that other troops had not dared to enter. By early December they could hear the guns, but were not moved up to the front, becoming instead a flying column or mobile reserve. This involved further continuous trekking and billeting, moving some dozen kilometres a day 'from Campanile to Campanile', usually keeping close to the Alpine foothills, 'within easy earshot of the war'. One of the tasks of this mobile relief was to hunt out Italian deserters. In general conditions were so easy that diversions were organized: a Battery paper-chase and a rugger match. This was always to be remembered as Rik's one and only appearance on a football field. 'It was a fearful rag. The Italians enjoyed it immensely – shouted and laughed and thought us quite mad. In fact our parade discipline, our continual "cleaning up" and our wild games are a complete mystery to them all.'

Just before Christmas the flying column was lucky enough to be called to a halt for a while in the small village of Silvelle, where Wheeler and his Captain were billeted in the house of the priest, a very convivial old fellow with an ancient gramophone and a taste for chartreuse. On Christmas Day they ate two dinners, one in the Sergeants' Mess and one, complete with goose and plum pudding, in their own. The last drink of the day was a toast to the King of Italy – in chartreuse.

The next morning, strengthened rather than weakened by what had gone before, Major Wheeler made a strenuous expedition recorded in one of the last of his surviving Italian letters:

I went up to see the war and reconnoitre battery positions on the tops of the mountains. Motored out to the foot of the mountains and then climbed up the endless mule tracks. Steeper than the roof of a house, and of course as rough as they make them. If we go into action there we shall have to get guns up these paths – a bit of a problem. Scenery wonderful. Went up to a village well above the snow line and drank to a battery in action. . . . The civilians still live at the top of these mountains, amongst the soldiers. A very peaceful war – saw only two Bosche shells burst all day! When one thinks of that and of Passchendaele one laughs and is happy. How on earth the Italians were ever driven back across these mountains beats me and all of us. We looked down on the plains of Italy . . . with the silver river winding for miles into the mist amongst white towns and villages. As we came down at the end of the day the setting sun just for a moment set the top of the mountain aflame with scarlet light. The next moment it was gone and we tumbled down the almost vertical path in cold grey dusk.

A hard day's work, but not a bad war. The men are all very pleased with their Christmas.

It was while he was still pleasantly billeted in the priest's house that Wheeler and a brother officer took the 'Twelve Hours Leave' in Venice described with an excess of artifice in *Still Digging*. The nub of the story was that the two young men, bored and frozen as they were propelled through falling sleet round melancholy canals, resolved to seek adventure. The outcome was that they twice found themselves at the window of the same unwanted prostitute. A sad little tale, punctuated by a stray bomb let fall by a passing aeroplane.

Rik's last letter from Italy was written in the New Year. He was in the highest spirits, announcing it as 'one of the brightest days in my existence'. For six weeks his life in the mobile reserve had deprived him of all mail, but now a fine batch had arrived. Moreover, the officers and men of his Battery had just fared very well in a distribution of medals. He thanked Tessa 'for carrying out his behests', and so presumably the pinky-yellow breeches had reached him, duly adjusted. Their shade had been chosen as protective colouring in the Italian landscape, but they were not to serve him for long in this capacity. Vast and terrible powers would soon determine that Rik Wheeler would have once more to don the old greenish breeches of the Western Front. A few days later, however, on 13 January, still happily unaware of what was in store, he lectured to an audience of officers on 'Artillery in Open Warfare'. This very ordinary occasion is made extraordinary by the fact that it is the only one on which the name of Major Wheeler, an outstanding officer soon to be decorated and Mentioned in Dispatches, appears in the official War Diaries of the 76th Brigade.

During February 1918 it began to be known that the Germans were preparing a big offensive on the Western Front. With troops released by the Russian collapse, and spurred on by the promised arrival of the Americans, Ludendorff had to try to divide and crush the French and British armies while there was time. Clemenceau having insisted that they should extend their line southward to the Oise, the British forces were dangerously stretched and short of reserves. In the north round Arras the Third Army, under General Byng, was relatively well-manned, but south of him to the Oise General Gough's Fifth Army was vulnerable.

On 21 March, in a thick early morning mist, the Germans struck with three times as many divisions as the combined British armies. Gough's forces were driven back and pierced, and, though never quite routed, were so hard pressed that on the evening of the second day Gough had to order a retreat to the Somme. Meanwhile Byng was able to hold his main lines and the attack on Arras failed. The situation, however, was extremely grave, with the Germans nearing Amiens.

The Italians had been clamouring to keep their Franco-British reinforcements, but such demands could no longer be countenanced. It was on 24 March that the 76th Brigade RFA received its orders to entrain for France at Castelfranco. So it was that just four months after being dispatched from France to Italy, Wheeler found himself steaming back from Italy to France. This time the journey took only five days, ending at Vieux Rouen. His luck was holding, for the Brigade had been assigned to the 2nd Division of Byng's Third Army, and by the time he reached the line on 12 April this part of the northern front had been made stable. He was now back to a point some fifty miles south of his action at Passchendaele.

Later Wheeler was to refer to the ensuing period before counter-attack was possible as 'months of stagnation', but at first he was cheerful enough. Indeed, owing to his temperament and his relative good fortune, he was less affected than most by the mood of grim but weary determination that had by now settled on most hearts both in the armies and at home. After his first week at the front he was to describe, 'as an example of the spirit that prevails', how he watched a daring foray into the German lines and commented, 'No, there's nothing beaten about the British Army.'

Characteristically, Wheeler's immediate concern was to secure all possible good order:

Yours truly is in bed in the brand new little bedroom which he has had builded for himself today. A hole in the side of a ditch, six German steel railway sleepers overhead, surmounted by a large iron gate and a layer of sandbags. Tomorrow large chunks of plundered concrete will crown the edifice, which will then be covered with grass and dandelions. Inside it is bon. It contains mine and Wilcox beds, and the floor is tiled with tiles from the ruined village and covered with a square foot of carpet. Ammunition boxes let into the wall hold shaving kit and one of your parcels of sweets. Two pictures you sent me adorn the walls. . . .

He was equally active in more purely military enterprise:

Another unintended tribute to my camouflage, which I have been further improving. A Signal Officer . . . came up and asked where the guns were. He had them marked on his map but he couldn't find them. It was pointed out that they were only 30 yards from him.

Am digging vasty dugouts. I expect by the time they are finished we shall be moved.

Not, of course, that Rik Wheeler was entirely unaffected by the changed mood of the time. It runs through what is surely the most sensitive piece of writing he confided to Tessa, a piece, moreover, which illustrates that 'pictorial reflex' that enabled him to spend his life 'happily enough, cloistered in a picture gallery':

Wet underfoot, but a warm spring day, and the larks singing – silly asses, when they might be singing ten miles further back. However, 'spose they're as wise as we darned silly mortals who fling bits of iron and infernal stinks amongst the dandelions. Two hundred yards away is a little garden that was just being re-dug among the shellholes of an old battlefield. When we came, the little hand-barrow was still standing beside it with its last load of earth, but it now carries ammunition when the days are misty or the nights dark. Little fruit trees have just been planted and they still flutter their labels, of which I enclose one – sent from England to the villagers who had come back and were starting afresh. . . . The War, as run, seems a silly business, but the very fact that everybody is fed up makes them all the keener to go through anything to finish it.

If the Third Army remained almost stationary during the perilous months of the spring and summer, there was still plenty of fighting to be done and the artillery was active. As Wheeler put it, 'We don't work in the afternoon, save for occasional firing, but confine our efforts to morning, evening and night.' From their side the Germans maintained a regular nightly bombardment.

Meanwhile Ludendorff had thrown vast forces into France and Belgium, and with the free use of mustard gas and bold new artillery tactics they had many successes. All through April the danger of breakthrough was very great. However, with the unified command under Foch, the Allies were never quite broken and with their increasing use of tanks and the arrival of the Americans in significant numbers the tide turned in their favour. In July the Germans suffered set-backs and on 8 August the Fourth British Army won a victory so telling that Ludendorff knew his offensive had failed. The Fourth continued the pressure until 21 August, and on that same day the main British counter-offensive passed to the Third Army.

Wheeler described how 'a new current of energy and expectation suddenly burst upon the waiting army' when they knew that at last they were to attack. On the rainy night of 19 August, along with the rest of the 76th Brigade, Wheeler's A Battery took up a position on a ridge near the village of Adnifer, remaining there through the following day. The Third Army's opening attack on the twenty-first was to have the limited objective of advancing eastwards on a nine-mile front to the embankment of the Arras–Albert railway. Initially this would involve crossing some six hundred yards of no-man's-land to seize the well-fortified German lines on the opposite side of the valley. The plan was for the 2nd Division to lead the advance at 4.55 am, and for the artillery to move forward eighty minutes later, with the 76th Brigade in the van. Moreover, a section of A Battery was to push ahead in close support of the infantry.

There was a heavy ground mist that night through which the moon shone dimly. This was the same good fortune that had favoured the Germans exactly five months before when they had launched their offensive. Nature's screen hid the tremendous activity as infantry, cavalry, light tanks and artillery made preparations for zero hour. On the ridge the gunners were able to set their fuses by torchlight without fear of betraying their position. All was done by midnight, and those who could slept for a while under the blanket of mist. It was during this tense night of waiting that Rik wrote a farewell letter to his wife.

By dawn the mist was thickening into a fog so dense that Wheeler had to make his way to all his gun positions to assure himself that they were ready for action.

Thanks to the fog, the surprise was complete. The gunners on their ridge had their count-downs to that curious zero of five minutes to five. Then a tremendous barrage was thrown across the valley onto the German lines, bringing the enemy their first news of the onslaught. Everywhere thousands of men, scores of commands, knew their precisely appointed tasks and moved to execute them; yet for the most part they were invisible to one another, hardly able to see more than forty yards. A strange, ghostly battle.

At the moment appointed for A Battery to move the command had no notion what was happening to the attacking infantry: at his Colonel's behest Wheeler sent out a mounted patrol to get information, but when that, too, seemed to be swallowed up by the fog, the Colonel gave word for the Battery to advance to find, if it could, its appointed position in no-man's-land. There was difficulty in bringing up the limbers and horse teams since the track had been smashed by German fire; it was accomplished, however, and A Battery set off at a trot down the road to the ruined village of Ayette, hitherto on the front. Wheeler's Battery thus became the first in that sector of the offensive to make the crossing of the British lines. Soon after, the first signs of the fighting were encountered when passing a dressing-station where wounded, mostly Germans, were being brought in. Already prisoners were serving as stretcher-bearers.

The conditions in no-man's-land were frightful, the ground being honeycombed with shell-holes, the fog thicker than ever and the whole area swept by the German guns. Somehow the teams stumbled along what was left of the Ablainzeville road until they passed the German trip wire and Wheeler settled his guns in what he rightly estimated to be approximately their intended position.

The great need was for news of the battle and observations for the guidance of the guns, and Wheeler rode forward with his signallers in an attempt to obtain them. They soon had to dismount to grope their way through wire and shell-holes; the road they had to follow in the fog drew concentrated fire. They were thankful indeed to come upon the recently abandoned German front-line trench: 'Now, blown to pieces by shell-fire, flattened by tanks, choked with scattered equipment and mangled bodies.' Sheltering there were a few infantrymen munching a breakfast of bread and bully beef, with a dead British soldier close beside them.

Wheeler and his signallers struggled on to the Courcelles ridge under a continuous curtain-fire. Sights such as are to be expected in the rear of a battle line came strangely to them through the fog: an advancing troop of cavalry, a slaughtered artillery team of horses and their riders, riderless horses, stretcher parties with British and German wounded, a batch of German prisoners – whom he found excessively obsequious. One sight in particular he was to remember: a horse that sank backwards into a concealed shell-hole until only the terrified beast's head could be seen above ground. It was dispatched by an officer, but 'For many days afterwards the horse's head, odoriferous and shrunken, haunted the unholy spot and put the fear of all the horse devils into the passing steed.'

While the fog persisted no observations were possible from the ridge and its commander returned to A Battery, where he found his gunners had performed prodigies of digging to make cover for themselves and the guns. They had been lucky, but at about this time a shell hit one of the Battery's teams as it brought ammunition. One can picture the death of men, but the frightful carnage resulting from the blowing to pieces of a team of six horses is hard for the outsider to imagine.

At about one o'clock the fog began to lift and soon the sun was shining and the hum of aeroplanes was added to the noises of battle. Now August heat took the place of fog, and as there was no water for miles around the already exhausted horses were consumed by thirst. Wheeler went forward again with his signallers. The infantry had passed Courcelles hours before and now, supported by dismounted cavalry, was held up not far from the railway. Wheeler, followed by his signallers unrolling their heavy cables, advanced from the observation post on the Courcelles ridge, the intention being to establish a telephone link with the Battery. If the shelling was lighter, there was now a deadly machine-gun fire from the Germans by the railway embankment. For Wheeler it was a change very much for the worse. 'A shell is tangible . . . but the rustling of machine-gun bullets is that of the evil spirits of the night. They are round and about one, almost between the fingers of one's hands. . . .'

The contrast with the morning was complete: from his new observation post on a ridge top, Wheeler commanded a view of the entire battle front, from the thin line of British outposts below him to where the

German machine-guns were putting up unapproachable fire from the fortified embankment, and, beyond it, to where columns of reinforc‐ments were being rushed forward. The frustration was painful. The confusion in the later stages of the advance caused by the fog had allowed the enemy to reform, and now, worst of all for Major Wheeler, his laboriously laid telephone line had been broken and he could not send word to the gunners of all the tempting targets there before his eyes. A Corporal was sent back with orders to get the cable restored at all costs. It remained dead for another agonizing half-hour. The 'cost' had been the Corporal's life: he was to be found shot through the head by a machine-gun bullet.

Meanwhile a line of whippet tanks in open formation scheduled to attack at this hour came over the ridge crest but attracted the fire of several German batteries. One was immediately smashed – a 'living tomb' as Wheeler was to write. It was his first experience of one of the horrors of mechanized war with which he was to become familiar. The whippets turned back, followed by a single gun from the forward section of A Battery, which, as it chanced, had made its dangerous way onto the ridge in the hope of supporting their charge.

The battle was over for the day. In spite of the final frustrating check, the British forces had done well. They had in fact taken the first step in the great advance that was to carry them onward to the Belgian frontier and the armistice. The next few days were to be in many ways decisive. Moreover, it was at this time that Rik Wheeler staged a deed of personal heroism that won him his Military Cross and was never to be forgotten by those who knew him. It might have been called reckless had it not been perfectly successful.

The next day saw a pause for consolidation before the great attack of the Third and Fourth Armies in conjunction, long planned for 23 August. Early on the twenty-third, Byng launched his onslaught, the 76th Brigade taking its part in the opening barrage. During the morning the British succeeded against stiff resistance in crossing the railway and advanced eastward to capture Gomiecourt, while the 76th were moved forward to fresh positions, though still on the west side of the embankment, near Achiet le Grand.

We come now to Rik Wheeler's famous exploit of capturing two German guns, which he describes so well in *Still Digging* under the heading of 'The Butte de Warlencourt'. According to him it was executed on this day, 23 August, for he says it was two days after the initial attack in the fog. This must be an error, for not only is it almost inconceivable that the Colonel would have given permission for such a dangerous escapade on the day of the main advance, when the Brigade had been in action for some ten hours, but Wheeler himself recorded that he was tempted to the deed on 'a busy but slightly tedious day', when 'things had settled down' and his Battery was only engaged in some sporadic shelling. This agrees perfectly with the entry for 24 August in the Brigade's War Diary: the laconic statement, 'Harassing fire, work on positions, reconnaissance'.

There can be no reasonable doubt that this was the date of the Butte de Warlencourt episode. There is little interest in the extension of time by twenty-four hours; it is more remarkable that Wheeler must also have mistaken the place. The mound which, bristling with German machine-guns, seemed to tower above the two field guns was not the Butte de Warlencourt, which in fact stood four miles to the south. Wheeler's own account of his positions during that week, the more detailed description of the advance in *Deeds of A Battery*, and the official Brigade War Diary all combine to make it quite impossible for Wheeler to have operated well to the south of Bapaume. His feat must in fact have been executed at another, nameless, mound of the same proportions as the Butte, standing just to the west of Sapignies, a village to be captured the very next day – 25 August.

It is unlike Wheeler to make a topographical slip of this kind: he has left us a hint as to how it may have happened. He introduces his story in *Still Digging* by recalling a moment many years later when his friend, O. G. S. Crawford, was pointing out a mound visible on an air photograph of the Bapaume region. Wheeler intervened, declaring that he knew the mound too well, it had once appeared to him 'almost as high as Everest'. It seems that he must have heard the name of the Butte de Warlencourt for the first time on that occasion and understandably assumed it to be the 'awesome castle-mound' of his memory. He tells us that he never revisited the place.

The day, then, is 24 August and the setting between the ruined villages of Achiet and Sapignies. Back at his old observation place on the ridge, but with the Battery now stationed not far behind him, Wheeler spotted two German field guns on the slope beyond the British outposts, with their dead teams (presumably a dozen horses) lying around them. The castle mound, some fifty feet high, rose beyond and above them on the skyline. He saw that the guns could be seized from under the noses of their owners and he saw himself doing it. By way of justifying such a deed he argued that not only would it prevent the Germans from reclaiming their property, but that the field pieces could be used to fling back captured German gas shells.

In the afternoon he put his case to the Brigade Colonel, who turned it down flat. Only a damned fool would challenge the deadly threat from the mound, with its machine-guns nests. Then, unaccountably, the Brigade Colonel had second thoughts. He rang his A Battery commander and gave his consent to the foray, providing a smoke screen were laid over the mound.

Wheeler's call for volunteers to man two six-horse teams was promptly answered by a sergeant and five drivers: the sixth driver, 'a known shirker', hesitated, but came in, perhaps hardly as a volunteer. So they set out through a bright summer evening, Major Wheeler on his charger leading the procession of the two teams and their limbers, with the Sergeant bringing up the rear. They went down the ridge and crossed the railway, startling the British outposts as they trotted past them into no-man's-land. Wheeler admitted to having already known a 'slightly strained feeling about the ribs and a growing sense of the silliness of the whole affair'. Now the danger was sharply increased for, something having gone wrong in the rear, the smoke shells that had been blinding the mound suddenly ceased.

Luckily, however, the smoke had hardly dispersed before they reached dead ground below the hill and could approach their goal unobserved. Wheeler and three others dismounted to hitch the German guns onto the British limbers. They did not fit. The limbers would have to be taken together with the guns. The four struggled to extricate them 'from beneath the unimaginably heavy carcasses of the horses'. The return procession, now longer and more encumbered, was saved from total exposure only by the clouds of dust raised by its own wheels. A shell landed close beside it, causing no casualties, but adding smoke and confusion to the dust. When Wheeler rode back to inspect he found that the rear gun had come unhitched and had been left a fearful hundred yards behind. He could not tolerate partial success. Sending the Sergeant on with the leading team, he circled back with the other to rehook the errant German weapon. It proved a difficult job for so few hands, 'but another shell landing nearby served as a timely stimulus'. Dusk was falling when they rejoined the Battery without further serious misadventure. During the night the gunners saw to it that the captured guns duly returned many of their gas shells to the enemy.

In his account of this action, which would surely have taxed the goodwill of any Guardian Angel, Rik Wheeler made a confession that is revealing of the inner conflicts of his nature. It so happened that one of the drivers of the team he led back for the missing gun was the scallywag whom I had put in at the last minute, and I observed him as the team turned in the dust. His blue moonlike face had lost all expression, his mouth and eyes were wide open like those of a corpse, his legs were clattering at the sides of his saddle and only the balance of long habit kept him in place. I recall a sudden and unforgivable urge to put a bullet through his head. (Poor fellow)

Soon after their safe return, when Rik was thanking his men for all they had done, he received a call from the command to recommend two names for decorations. He selected the Sergeant but then 'Chose a driver (quite irregularly) by lot, and wondered ... whether the scallywag would draw the winner. In fact, he did not – but he might have done.'

After due process the Sergeant was awarded the DCM and the lucky driver the MM. Major Wheeler got his MC, with the following citation:

Lt. (A/Major) R. E. M. Wheeler, R.F.A., T.F. attd. A/76th Bde. R.F.A. For conspicuous gallantry and initiative. While making a reconnaissance he saw two enemy field guns limbered up without horses within 300 yards of the outpost line. He returned for two six-horse teams, and under heavy fire, in full view of the enemy, successfully brought back both guns to his battery position and turned them on the enemy. He did fine work.

If this deed, this heroic prank, has proved memorable, it has not been generally appreciated that it was a brief personal interlude in many days of dangerous and slogging battle. In the early hours of the very next morning the Battery was taking part in the opening barrage of another general attack that was immediately successful, the infantry capturing Béhagnies and Sapignies, an area including the notorious mound. Presently A Battery was advanced some five miles to the Sapignies ridge, where it was met by its commanding officer, who, as usual, had been reconnoitering in advance. No sooner had he put it into action than it was strafed by a squadron of low-flying aircraft as well as by field guns. In the afternoon, when Wheeler was once more forward directing ranges, the Germans launched a barrage of high-explosive and gas shells so ferocious that the crews of A Battery took cover. He returned to find three guns active; a gallant subaltern, suspecting a counter-attack, had left cover to fire a gun single-handed, an action which had inspired a few others to follow him. One gun had been knocked out. Wheeler promptly redeployed his available men, he himself manning No. 6 gun. Soon all five were firing at high speed, and although the Sergeant was hit by a splinter he remained in action until at last the German barrage died down.

This was perhaps no more than a particularly grim moment in the everyday life of an artillery officer during an advance. If one looks back over the previous twenty-four hours it is easier to see how, on his return to civilian life, Rik's idea of the possibilities of human endurance, of what could be meant by a day's work, was to appear somewhat excessive to more ordinary mortals.

By this last week in August the general British, French and American offensive was rolling forward. Even those at home, rationed, short of food and fearful of over-optimism, began to realize that the news was now of almost continuous advances, of the capture of prisoners and arms. In this Byng's army played its effective part.

There were, of course, small checks and setbacks, for the German morale had not cracked. In these the 76th Brigade suffered its share. One night before the end of August it had to make a withdrawal from the intensity of the shelling and gas bombardment, while on 18 September, by which time the advance reached the banks of the Canal-du-Nord, there was another ferocious artillery duel as the Germans counter-attacked. All the crews had been forced to take cover, when Wheeler and his officers ran forward and manned A Battery until, at the sound of their firing, the gunners left shelter to join them. Presently other batteries followed their example, in this way, as it proved, breaking up the attack of the German infantry. It seems that it must have been due to Wheeler's usual exacting zeal that his guns had been sunk in deep pits and so remained secure, whereas the neighbouring battery had all its guns smashed and sixteen men killed.

Until this time the German retreat had been slow and strongly contested, and it remained Ludendorff's intention to stand for the winter on the Hindenburg Line, where he was already massing reserves. Haig, however, thought otherwise and his conviction that his forces could break through determined Foch to strike for victory within the year. A general offensive was launched during the last days of September. On his sector of the Third Army front Wheeler's Battery was involved in a fierce, swaying battle round Fremicourt and Marcoing that lasted through the days and nights from 27 to 30 September. This combat of movement demanded tremendous endurance, though casualties, except among the horses, were slight.

It was during these same days that the Hindenburg Line was broken on a wide front, Dominion troops playing an outstanding part. With disasters also in other theatres of war, Ludendorff lost his nerve and put out feelers for an armistice. Soon, however, he attempted a rally, and fighting on the Western Front was by no means over. All through

October and into November the 76th Brigade remained in action, firing creeping barrages as Byng's army advanced, swinging now in a more northerly direction across the Nord department towards the vital junction of Maubeuge.

That the German resistance was still determined is apparent in one of Rik's few surviving letters to Tessa. The eleventh of October was

A day of rest (and rain) after a somewhat strenuous period. We are at the moment resting in what was three days ago a none too pleasant battery position but which is now already a 'back area'. Beside me is the tiniest of tabby kittens, which I carried back the day before yesterday from a village which had two hours previously been in the hands of the Boche. His name is Wamby, and his taste in food is peculiar. When I brought him back to the 2 foot excavation which we called our Mess I offered him a good old breakfast of milk and ham and eggs, but he turned up his little nose and meeowed piteously. Then, inspired, he rushed at my shaving water and gulped down the lot!

This letter ends with a request showing that, characteristically, Rik was preparing for his teams to do him credit in time of victory: 'Do you remember the shop near King's College, Strand, where I bought the bit? If you do, would you order from there for me six metal horses' tail combs and six pairs of scissors suitable for trimming horses' legs. Many thanks.'

On 9 November, when the Brigade was on the outskirts of Maubeuge, the War Diary recorded, 'It was impossible to advance over the River Sambre as all the bridges were blown up.' For 11 November the entry reads, 'At about 9.30 a.m. the news is received that hostilities will cease at 11.00 hours.' So Rik Wheeler learnt that he was to be a survivor. It was a responsibility to the dead that he was to take with deep seriousness.

A week later the Brigade set off on the long drive across Belgium. After being held up a few days at Heyd, on 13 December Rik scribbled a little note from Germany to say, 'Today we crossed the frontier in pouring rain. Drenched and very busy.' Before Christmas they reached Poulheim, near Cologne, where they were to be stationed for several months. Christmas Day itself offered the occasion for uninhibited celebration. Rik Wheeler sent home a comical hour-by-hour programme of his day, which had involved, before his own Battery dinner, riding round to drink healths with the Colonel, all the other batteries, the Sergeants' and the Men's Messes. The quantity and variety of the drinks, ending with 1875 brandy and champagne, was staggering – and, indeed, all concerned went to bed very tight indeed. It must have recalled the similar rites of the last Christmas Day in Italy, but gloriously expanded by peace and victory. The letter ends,

However, on Boxing Day *every* officer turned out for bare-back exercise, and I took the battery at a gallop across country. Very good for the liver.

By the way, you will see in the 'Times' of Dec. 24th that yours truly is mentioned in Sir Douglas Haig's dispatch of Nov. 8th (along with thousands of others). Still, 'Mentioned in Dispatches' is, I suppose, worth being.

Many months were to pass before Major Wheeler was demobilized. The Brigade was at Poulheim until late in March, but he was to remain in Germany until full summer. We learn only from a stray remark in his commentary to the 'Chronicle' biography that he saved himself from tedium during this long delay by writing up and expanding his Franks studentship research on Romano-Rhenish pottery. It seems he had already determined to use it as a doctoral thesis. He said 'At the end of the war . . . .I was put in charge of a district in Germany which included a number of museums and was near the big museums of Cologne and Bonn. I continued my work . . . on my studentship there. . . . When I came out of the army I had my thesis in my pocket.'

His last letter was written from Bliesheim and dated 26 July. There is a hint in it that Tessa may have been looking for somewhere for them to live, but he was evidently not expecting to be discharged at once since he asks for a German dictionary to be sent out and says, 'Today, I have started to send away my horses. The beginning of the end, though the process will be a long one.' If, then, he was right when he stated in *Still Digging* that he was demobilized (or 'disembodied') in July, there must have been some very sudden dispensation from the powers above at the War Office. It looks as though he could hardly have been home before August.

When Wheeler wrote from Bliesheim Tessa had just received the farewell letter he had addressed to her nearly a year before.

If I remember the letter you mention rightly, it was never intended to reach you under the present happy circumstances and should have been long ago destroyed. It was written in the village of St Amand, South of Arras, just before we went into action, and my servant carried it until the Armistice. However.

Since this letter was in fact treasured by Tessa and then by Michael Wheeler, it seems justifiable to take that 'However' as a posthumous permission to reproduce the opening passages here. They are less intensely personal than what follows in a most moving message of farewell, but are still valuable for their illumination of Wheeler's inner nature. His words show how fully realized was his expectation of death, how deep his love for Tessa. These were emotions almost wholly concealed in the ordinary letters he addressed to her. Furthermore, this message, pencilled on two flimsy sheets during that misty night on the ridge, is witness of the truth, known only to a fast-diminishing few, that behind all his masks, often in stark contradiction to his actions, Rik Wheeler could harbour strong and tender feelings:

I am writing this on the eve of going into action. We are taking up position on the crest of a hill and we and Fritz will shake hands across a valley. You will receive this only if he shakes hands too hard.

I need not say that life is very sweet to you and me, Tess – so sweet that I dare not think too much of it lest I should cling to it rather than to duty. I lie awake at night and dream of you, and when I sleep you are my dreams. So much happiness sometimes makes one fear that it cannot last.

CHAPTER 4

Wales: A Pattern Is Set

RIK WHEELER WAS to write of his five war years as an 'interlude', and within his rising archaeological career that is what they were. Yet they were just as obviously a part of the continuous development of his character, shaping and hardening it and bringing out qualities that might have remained latent. In this way his soldiering years did affect his career as an archaeologist: they assured its high success.

By far the most telling of the latent qualities to be elicited and hard-wrought by the experiences of the second half of his twenties was the power of command and with it a belief in the need for authority. So long a time of unbroken responsibility for men and horses, for all their weapons and gear, all their training and transporting, would have been enough even away from battlefields for him to discover that he possessed that power, and, one can be sure, that he enjoyed its exercise. But to that initial discovery there was added the tests of endurance and courage of which we have now gained some inkling. There had been many grim occasions when Wheeler had seen how the advance planning of positions, the leading, or sometimes driving, of his men to excep-tional labours, could make all the difference between life and death. One can understand how he came for the rest of his life to believe in the rightness of command and of exacting the utmost from himself and those under him.

With these developments in his character and outlook, there also surfaced the tendency to despise and discard the 'shirker' or incompe-tent that was acceptable in war but could be culpable in normal life. Even then, as will appear from time to time, harshness or intolerance might be mitigated by that twinge for the 'poor fellow', a little contemp-tuous, perhaps, but enough to produce real and sometimes secret kindnesses.

The husband who returned to Tessa and four-year-old Michael was,

then, a markedly different and more formidable man than the one she
had known during the first year of their marriage. Yet they had kept in
close touch through their constant letter-writing, and it can be seen as a
lucky chance that the letter that revealed his feelings as none other did
should have come to her just before his return. There is every reason to
think that their reunion was an ardent and happy one.

Professionally, however, Rik Wheeler could not rejoice in his condition. Immediately there was nothing for it but to resume his humble
post with the Royal Commission on Historical Monuments. If there
were financial difficulties in adjusting family expenses from the relative
opulence of the £800 a year he had been earning in the army to the
pittance provided by the Commission, it was far more difficult to make
the psychological adjustment from years of command, movement and
intense experience to the humdrum, unchallenging existence of a
Junior Investigator. Wheeler no longer possessed the humility for such
a position and did not intend to settle into it for a long run.

For the present Rik, Tessa and Michael occupied a flat in 16 Taviton
Street, near Gordon Square. It was small, on the top floor and without a
lift, but conveniently near the Commission's office at No. 23. Here Rik
released the last ambitious expression of his urge to paint: he decorated
the flat with murals of battle scenes. As Michael remembers them, they
gave pride of place not to guns but to aeroplanes. These premises, with
all Taviton Street, were later demolished to make way for the empire-
building of London University.

The Royal Commission was still busy with Essex, and during the war
had begun to prepare the reports that were to be published in four
geographically divided volumes during the early twenties. In all of them
except the first Wheeler is thanked for work on the Roman monuments
and for 'revising' accounts of them. Taking up his job once more, he
was still very much concerned with the Roman period both on the
Commission's behalf and on his own. In particular he saw much to be
done at Colchester, which was full of remains of the Roman imperial
past both above and below the ground.

The museum was housed in the Norman castle, and here Wheeler
had deposited the plan of the Balkerne Gate, the massive eastern
gateway through which the London Road entered the Roman city. The
diggings that he had directed there in 1917 while waiting to be sent
overseas were unconventional, even comical, but undeniably effective.
A considerable chunk of the gate was upstanding but a public house
covered a large part of it. Rik Wheeler determined to clear out and
develop burrowings below the pub made by a local antiquary, and for

this purpose each evening led his groom 'of melancholy but co-operative nature', his batman, a gunner of unmilitary temperament who had been a student at the Slade and sundry volunteers from his Battery who were ready for a lark and a drink. By the light of a candle, lying prone or supine in the tunnels and scrabbling the earth into sandbags, they contrived to clear and to map much of the complicated walling of the gate. Meanwhile they were entertained by the lively and profane talk of the citizens standing at the bar overhead – citizens who would soon make them welcome when they went up to wash the dust of ages from their throats.

Now, on his return to Colchester, Wheeler worked up the plan and wrote an article on his interpretation of the design and history of the Balkerne Gate, publishing them in the Essex Archaeological Society's *Transactions* for 1920. It was, as he said, his 'first contribution to the literature of learning'. Another such first-of-many can be recorded for this same year when a photograph of Dr Wheeler excavating Roman pots on a site near Colchester Castle appeared in the press.

At much the same time the castle itself provided the scene for a manifestation of his habitually quick co-ordination of eye and idea. A local savant offered to take him down to inspect the 'dungeons' below the great Norman keep. There he was confronted, in the dim light, by two long, vaulted tunnels largely constructed of a kind of shuttered concrete. Almost at once Rik turned to his companion 'and I looked him in the eye. . . . I must have looked like an owl, and I said, "Dungeons, dungeons be damned."' He had seen at once that the vaults were not mediaeval nor related to the plan of the keep above. It did not take long to establish the truth that this vaulting, packed with earth, had supported the podium of the huge Temple of Claudius which that conquering emperor founded for his own official worship and which was soon to be destroyed by Queen Boudicca. This discovery, which already bears the stamp of Wheeler's dramatic flair, he was to publish the next year (1921) in an esteemed national periodical, the *Journal of Roman Studies*, where he had already placed a more general paper on Roman Colchester.

So, at his usual headlong speed, Wheeler laid the foundations of his reputation as a Roman archaeologist. Meanwhile he had also to take part in the general work of the Commission. As he commented, 'Listing seventeenth-century cottages for the Commission was great fun, but it led nowhere either professionally or financially.' The one immediate step he could take for the advancement of his civilian career was the successful submission of the thesis he had completed in Germany for his

University of London D.Lit. Henceforth, until he was knighted, he was always to be publicly known as Dr Wheeler.

The other move he attempted was to extract a living wage from the Commission. With this very reasonable ambition, he tackled its Secretary, George Duckworth, 'a smooth Edwardian placeman with a fair knowledge of wine but none whatever of archaeology'. Duckworth's tactical response was of a kind once familiar to young authors seeking more money from substantial publishers: he took Wheeler to the Garrick, gave him an excellent lunch during which nothing was said on the all-important subject, then, on the way back to the office, told him that more pay was out of the question. Duckworth rounded off this refusal (can it be believed?) by enquiring whether Wheeler was aware that there had been a war.

The Secretary had badly misjudged his young guest's temper, or the soothing effect upon it of the Garrick's fine Sauternes. According to Wheeler it was no more than an hour after their abrupt parting that he noticed an advertisement for a post in Cardiff that combined that of Keeper of Archaeology in the National Museum of Wales with a newly created lectureship in the subject at the University College of South Wales and Monmouthshire. He applied for it at once, saw Cardiff for the first time when he went for an interview, took an over-hasty dislike to the city – and was appointed to the job.

Wheeler's application for the Cardiff appointment had been backed not only by his old benefactor from University College days, Sir Gregory Foster, but also by the Secretary whose official tight-fistedness had been so largely responsible for his making it. Whether George Duckworth regretted the loss of its ablest Investigator or, on the contrary, felt that the Commission would be happier without the threat of such a caged lion, cannot be told. A curiously worded paragraph in the second volume of the Essex report suggests, but perhaps unintentionally, a certain indignation over Rik's departure so soon after reclaiming the post that the Commission had kept for him. It reads, 'We have to deplore the loss, through promotion, illness or death of (among others) Robert Eric Mortimer Wheeler, who has accepted a post as Keeper in the National Museum of Wales and Lecturer in the University of South Wales.' The only aspect of the loss that Rik himself deplored was quitting London, that powerful centre of his ambitions, for a provincial capital.

Yet in reality the strange background to the new appointment was to provide just the right conditions for Rik to establish his reputation through exceptional personal achievements. As part of the grandiose civic centre built in Cardiff's Cathays Park, a plan had been agreed in 1905 to make this the setting for a state-aided national museum for Wales. The Corporation agreed to give the site and the entire collections of the old municipal art gallery and museum, hitherto poorly accommodated in a part of the public library. A charter had been granted two years later, but the actual building had progressed so slowly that it had been caught by the war and now consisted of a handsome stone façade with nothing behind it but a silent wilderness of concrete and scaffolding. Further construction had been halted, for money was short and Cardiff had been hit by a post-war slump. Meanwhile the collections remained in their old quarters. Although in 1912 the archaeology department had been added to the miscellany of fossils, natural history bygones and 'reproductions of metal and ivory work illustrating various periods of art and civilization', conditions were all against its development. By the time Rik Wheeler arrived in Cardiff it seemed that nothing could shift the weight of inertia and debt to set the concrete-mixers turning once more and provide the façade with a museum. Whether anyone concerned had more than the faintest surmise that the new Keeper was the man to generate the necessary energy appears unlikely.

If on the museum side of the appointment there was a burdensome inheritance from the past, full of snarls and obstructions that had to be shifted before its promise could be released, on the academic side all was free and open, a virgin field on which the first Lecturer in Archaeology could plan and build as he saw fit. The creation of the university post was the outcome of the growing interest in the subject and the recognition (by a few) of its academic possibilities, that were evident before the war and were now reviving.

Wales had not been too remote to be reached by this archaeological tide. H. J. Fleure, Professor of Geography and Anthropology at Aberystwyth, and John Ward, Wheeler's predecessor as Keeper, had carried out some reasonably competent excavations and field studies, while the learned journal, *Archaeologia Cambrensis*, founded as early as 1846, and the Cambrian Archaeological Association which had grown out of it, did much to advance antiquarianism towards a more scientific archaeology. There were also a number of local societies and museums throughout the Principality that might be small and impoverished but could well be stimulated and led in the new direction. In addition the Royal Commission on Ancient and Historical Monuments (Wales) was making good progress with its surveys.

The Wales of 1920, then, was far from an archaeological desert. What it lacked was any unity of purpose or understanding. In addition to the much relished antagonism between north and south, local loyalties and divisions were fortified by its mountain walls. As his short spells of work in Essex showed, Wheeler was already a man who sought coherent strategy, order and wide views.

Once he knew he was to be a survivor, and a survivor unshaken in his dedication to archaeology, Wheeler had been brooding on the needs of his infant science and how he could best serve them. He saw that while there were excavations going on in many parts of the country, some badly done, some much better, they were hopelessly haphazard and lacking in strategic purpose. He was a humanist, seeing archaeology as a new instrument for the reconstruction and writing of history, but he was clear that it would remain a very poor instrument unless excavators greatly improved their methods and, moreover, worked to a strategic plan – what he called 'controlled discovery' – with historical objectives clearly in view. In his own specialist field of Roman Britain, for example, he was convinced that Professor Haverfield's fine distillation, the *Romanization of Roman Britain*, had carried the subject as far as it would go without fresh evidence. That could only be won from the earth, and by following the new methods he believed he had within his grasp.

At some time, perhaps while he was still at University College, more probably through the Royal Commission, Rik Wheeler had come across the four large tomes, in royal blue and gold, which General Pitt-Rivers had published privately between 1887 and 1898. These volumes, *Excavations in Cranborne Chase*, contained the meticulous and prodigally illustrated records of the many sites, prehistoric and Romano-British, that the General had dug on his own vast estates in Dorset. While still a professional soldier he had developed an over-riding interest in archaeology, and now this inheritance, coming to him unexpectedly and late in life, gave him possession of both monuments and the wealth needed to dig and publish them as well as he knew how. A powerful and independent mind, together with his sense of order and command and the skill in surveying acquired in the army, enabled him to reach standards unique in his time.

Wheeler had been quick to recognize this, and what astonished him, and is still astonishing, was the fact that the man and his works had been almost totally neglected during the two decades since his death. 'Nobody paid the slightest attention to the old man. One of his assistants had even proceeded to dig up a lake-village much as Schliemann had dug up Troy or St John Hope Silchester: like potatoes. Not only had the clock not gone on, but it had been set back.'

Wheeler conceded that there had been a few exceptions to the generally poor technical standards of pre-war excavation in Britain, but they had been isolated and personal, not related to any accepted body of theory and practice. Then he and his young contemporaries digging at Wroxeter in 1913 had been feeling their way towards better methods. Of the five undergraduates who had shared in these ideas, he alone had survived the carnage of the war. The thought of this at once intensified his sense of isolation and his conviction that as a survivor he had been entrusted with a mission on behalf of the dead. Certain that Pitt-Rivers had already shown the way, he determined that his immediate 'path lay backwards, to the forgotten standards of Cranborne Chase, before advancing to new methods and skills'.

The leading precepts that Wheeler learnt from the great pioneer are plain enough, and although it is true that he was able to advance beyond them, they were to be fundamental to his work throughout his whole career as an excavator. First, and this came readily to him after his years as a commanding officer, was the precept that the director of a dig must train a disciplined team of assistants and that no spade or trowel should be wielded except under the eye of an expert supervisor.

The second but greatest of the laws was that the purpose of excavation could only be successfully served by the most careful observation and recording of the stratification of deposits and buried structures so that their relative ages could be established and their nature understood. Wheeler wrote, 'In practice, Pitt-Rivers's method was to record every object in such a manner that it could be replaced accurately in its findspot on the recorded plan and section. That is the essence of three dimensional recording, and three dimensional recording is the essence of modern excavation.' The 'Wheeler Method' in excavation that was to dominate the inter-war years depended upon the perfecting of the uses of stratification. We shall find that he developed very definite ideas about the pictorial aspect of recording, particularly the drawing of sections, that reflected his mind and temperament and were therefore to provoke some opposition in those differently constituted.

The third rule relates to the second, but was clearly differentiated by the General himself. He wrote in the introduction to his first volume,

excavators, as a rule, record only those things which appear to them important at the time, but fresh problems in Archaeology and Anthropology are constantly arising, and it can hardly fail to have escaped the notice of anthropologists that, on turning back to old accounts in search of evidence, the points which would have been most valuable have been passed over from being thought uninteresting at the time. Every detail should, therefore, be recorded in the manner most conducive to facility of reference, and it ought at all times to be the chief object of an excavator to reduce his own personal equation to a minimum.

Rik followed this precept in general, but perhaps did not quite accept that minimizing of 'his own personal equation'.

Finally General Pitt-Rivers insisted that excavation reports must be not only fully and accurately but also promptly published. This behest Wheeler took very much to heart and obeyed in all his excavations large and small – with one exception. Indeed, he has, with some reason, been criticized for preparing his Reports at too great a speed. Yet surely he was justified in his utter condemnation, on one occasion cruelly expressed, of those who let the years go by without publication while dust and forgetfulness mount over their discoveries, and perhaps at last death has its victory. This for him was the greatest of sins, more dire even than lifting antiquities like potatoes. Nor has it grown less with the progress of archaeology. Indeed, the vast increase in the number of excavations, particularly of urgent 'rescue' digs, together with the need to digest a welter of detailed reports on everything from beetles to spectroscopical and thermo-luminescent analyses, have meant that many a professional has failed to meet the General's last precept and digs on in the shadow of a back-log of unpublished work.

When Rik removed himself and his family to Cardiff in August 1920 he had in fact determined, in a largely pragmatic fashion, the nature of his professional life. He had wrapped the mantle (or was it a military cloak?) of Pitt-Rivers about him, and although his aims remained essentially historical, he was clear that they were to be attained through more systematic and more technically proficient digging and the study of antiquities already in museums. What was most original in this approach was that he was giving to the archaeological method its own primacy as a source of history and an academic subject, a concept that was widely disapproved of among the more scholarly, literary or philosophical historians of our old universities.

Wheeler knew that from his base in the National Museum and University College he would be able to put what were essentially practical ideas into practice, while at the same time fulfilling his duties as Keeper and Lecturer. Although he saw that it would have to wait for changes at the top, he also had the ambition to be the hero who would slay the Giant Sloth and get the museum built, opened and fully functioning.

On the purely archaeological side of his mission he was eager to excavate and while developing his technical skills to establish an overall understanding of the Romans in Wales. Because of the limits of his own knowledge and experience he planned to concentrate on Roman sites – and on military Roman sites, since in what had remained essentially an occupied country they held the key to the more general history. He also realized, however, that it was up to him to get a total grasp of Welsh archaeology, not neglecting a prehistory stretching back to the cave dwellings of Palaeolithic Man. Such must be the scope of a National Museum and of the lectures and courses of study through which he hoped to 'secure for archaeology a recognized place in the curriculum of the Welsh University'. It did not take a genius to see how plans for his own excavations could be married to his academic aims: his students were to be enrolled to take part in them, the best trained up as a skilled staff, later to be fit to carry on the work of exploration on their own account.

Perhaps the most remarkable, because the most unexpected, feature of Rik Wheeler's strategic plan for Welsh archaeology was that which he himself described as political. He understood the highly localized interests of the Welsh and the fact that most of them felt no loyalty towards the distant and un-Welsh city of Cardiff.

Wales, save when united in opposition to England, was an aggregate of parish pumps rather than a nation. The thirteen counties could not for a moment be expected of their own volition to focus on Cardiff; the last thing that the mountains were prepared to do was to come to Mahomet. It was for Mahomet to go to the mountains. And if for Mahomet we substitute a young and rather determined Englishman, that is what happened. My senior colleagues were sometimes disturbed by my frequent absences in the hills, but I knew that my policy was right. . . . I took the museum into the highways and byways of Wales.

By tireless travelling, by offering help to the 'poor little museums up and down the country', by lecturing to local societies and other small humble audiences, and when possible through his excavations, he was able to make the Cardiff Museum truly national and to create a federation of museums centred upon it that was to stand the test of time. It was a largely selfless enterprise and one that does not match the picture of Rik Wheeler as one ever in pursuit of publicity and aggrandisement.

Although Wheeler may have displeased his elders by being too often away among the mountains, he did not neglect his keepership. John Ward had not only held the post for a very long time, he had ended his tenure with a very long illness. His successor's earliest recorded undertaking was to sort out the specimens which had accumulated while the department was without a head – a frustrating task since there was virtually no exhibition space. Before long there was so much to be done that Rik and Tessa kept camp-beds in the office of the old museum, to enable them to sleep there after late night work.

By 1921 the 'rather determined young Englishman' and his family had settled in lodgings in Cathedral Road, where they lived until Wheeler gained the directorship of the museum. While he had taken on far too much work to be able to spare the time for Michael that Robert Wheeler had devoted to him, and would never have found it in his nature to say that the boy was his 'food and drink', he did so far emulate his own father as to begin Michael's initiation into riding, fishing and shooting. While family excursions and holidays such as he and Amy had enjoyed in their Bradford lives could not be repeated, Rik from the first assumed that his family would share in the outdoor life of his archaeological digs. Through all his boyhood and youth Michael recalls only two family holidays, one at a seaside resort near Calais (which he believes his father hated) and the second a Mediterranean tour that was a rough prototype of later Hellenic cruises. Otherwise holidays for him meant his part in the toils and pleasures of digging. As for Tessa, her inclinations and talents alike soon led to her becoming her husband's partner in the direction of all their excavations.

Wheeler himself was impatient to launch that part of his Cardiff schemes that depended on excavation. He longed to justify his belief that he could follow and then improve upon Pitt-Rivers's methods, and his only experience so far, his digging in Essex, had been very small beer indeed. He did not have to wait too long before an ideal site presented itself. Some tentative exploration had begun at the Roman fort of Segontium, a fine site overlooking Caernarvon, and now, in 1921, with what promptings one cannot tell, he was invited to take charge. 'The chance was gladly seized simultaneously to deal with the historical problems of a site which was pivotal in the Roman occupation of Wales and to evolve the necessary techniques for doing so.'

Wheeler began this, his first major excavation, in July and worked on for six weeks, sacrificing his leave to do it – a practice that was to become habitual with him. He repeated it immediately in a second season (1922) at Segontium which was to prove rewarding. The principal buildings of the fort were cleared, while finds included such pleasing items as brooches, hundreds of coins, a statuette and an altar inscribed to Minerva.

Altogether the Wheelers must have been satisfied with their first joint venture in 'archaeology from the earth'. They were feeling their way with growing confidence, he particularly in the uses of stratification, she in the handling and recording of artifacts. Presumably, too, responsibility for the commissariat and for looking after the needs of the few students employed on this dig already fell upon Tessa.

Since in the retrospect of *Still Digging* Wheeler discusses the two topics, stratification and the association of students with his excavations, in connection with Segontium it seems right to follow his lead, with the understanding that what is said in large measure applies also to future excavations, even though they saw great advances in technical complexity and refinement and in the number and expertise of student trainees.

Wheeler had not failed to put into practice Pitt-Rivers's precept for prompt publication, having written full seasonal reports for *Archaeologia Cambrensis*, to be followed by his earliest excavation report in book form, *Segontium and the Roman Occupation of Wales*. These were illustrated by his own hand, notably by the sectional drawings that in his later works were famous for their elegance and clarity – and widely imitated. In his autobiography Wheeler wrote,

I reproduce as a sample a key-section drawn in 1922 through the strong room ... of the fort. The section displays a certain crudity but, with the privilege of advancing age, I can say that it has all the right stuff in it: the clear interleaving of the original structure with dated coins, the cascade of vegetable mould which streamed down the steps when the building was deserted ... the infilling of masonry debris when the garrison returned years afterwards and cleared and rebuilt the structure, and the successive floorings (with their significant contents) with which the cellar was ultimately filled and sealed. The whole bones of the matter are there and ... it is fair to boast that, *at the time*, our sections were unapproached anywhere for expressiveness and integrity.

In this method of recording the stratification revealed by carefully cut sections used by Rik and his school the strata were firmly outlined, filled with symbolic representations of the various types of soil, stones and the like, numbered, named and interpreted. In the field he insisted that each stratum as it came to light should be similarly numbered and named. As he wrote in *Archaeology from the Earth* (1954), 'I like to see my sections plastered from head to foot with orderly arrays of labels.'

In short the Wheeler method produced a highly schematic rendering of actuality which was also a definitive interpretation of its meaning. It has already been suggested that there were a few archaeologists who were critical of this method and, moreover, that the division closely

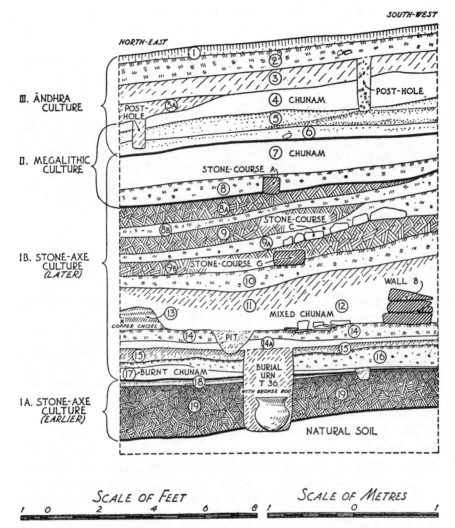

SOUTH-WEST

NORTH-EAST

Ⅲ. ĀNDHRA CULTURE

POST-HOLE

POST-HOLE

④ CHUNAM

Ⅱ. MEGALITHIC CULTURE

⑦ CHUNAM

STONE-COURSE A

STONE-COURSE C

IB. STONE-AXE CULTURE (LATER)

STONE-COURSE G

WALL 8

MIXED CHUNAM

COPPER CHISEL

PIT

BURNT CHUNAM

BURIAL URN T 36 WITH BRONZE ROD

IA. STONE-AXE CULTURE (EARLIER)

NATURAL SOIL

SCALE OF FEET

SCALE OF METRES

An example of Wheeler's method of recording stratification: a section from Brahmagiri, Mysore State, India, showing three cultural phases with overlaps

responded to the temperaments of those concerned. Rik's sections, equally with his writing style, were clear-cut, positive, authoritative. The sections of the opposing school, which Rik called the pictorial or impressionistic, attempted a more or less natural representation of actuality and were therefore lacking in definition or confident interpretations by the delineator. Those who favoured it tended to be

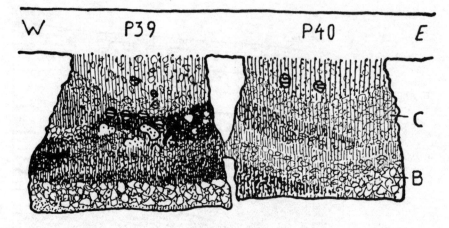

Bersu's 'pictorial' method of section-drawing

tentative thinkers, reluctant to commit themselves until some ideal moment when all evidence could be weighed, and meanwhile keeping their historical view flexible – or hazy like their sections. There is, of course, some wisdom in their cautious approach: Rik Wheeler did on occasion go too far in imposing his mental will upon the evidence and in being unwilling to change his conclusions. On the other hand it is true that even if it proves erroneous, clear and decisive statement will produce correspondingly clear contradiction, whereas otherwise all may remain nebulous.

Wheeler himself was characteristically sharp in his disapproval of the pictorial method, stating his case in *Archaeology from the Earth*. As his exemplar he chose the work of the German archaeologist Gerhard Bersu (who made important excavations in England), since Bersu followed it with artistry, whereas in the hands of 'mere delineators' he judged it inevitable that 'chaos will prevail'. Having reluctantly admitted that Pitt-Rivers 'occasionally, though not normally' used the pictorial style in his sections, he continues,

The strata are not outlined but are . . . differentiated from one another by what may be called a sort of chromatic shading. The result is an *impression* of the section, more akin to a photograph than to a diagram. . . . The impressionistic technique cannot be defended on the grounds that it is less conventional; in its own fashion it is no less conventional than the linear technique, only, it is a different convention. And it has this crowning disadvantage: it lends itself to nebulousness, to a blurring of detail and a lack of precision in diagnosis. . . . Any medium or convention which is likely to encourage woolly thinking is to be deprecated: and, save at its rare best, the impressionistic technique is woolly.

Roman military sites in rocky Wales did not offer many opportunities for complex or crucial uses of stratification: nothing to compare with the challenging importance of the vast ramparts and ditches of the prehistoric hill-forts of England, or the city mounds of India, that were to confront Wheeler in later years. Nevertheless, as the emphasis he put on the little section at Segontium shows, he had already consciously established his principles and all that was to follow was their elaboration, magnification and refinement.

Looking back, Wheeler saw himself at Segontium standing on the threshold of his career as a great excavator; he also recognized this early dig as the beginning of another aspect of his commitment: the teaching and inspiration of the young. He wrote of it in *Still Digging* with a sentiment and lofty earnestness unusual with him and enough to provoke incredulity in a sceptical generation – though they were genuine enough. Rik did care very much about his training up of young people to follow in his footsteps. If there is any falsity, it is one of omission. He gives no hint that he tended to show favour only to those he himself had picked out, or how hard he drove, and variously used, his young men and women. Nor is there any hint that when one blood transfusion from an old pupil was a sharp criticism he did not receive it well.

At Segontium on a small scale we began, too, that association with students which was to enter into our normal practice. I remember being deeply conscious at this time of our loneliness in the field of archaeological excavation and of the responsibility which the hazards of the age had thrust upon our shoulders. It became a mission – one which I have never since forsaken – to gather the younger generation about me in all my field work, to inculcate it with a controlled enthusiasm, and to give it in the formative stage a sense of direction, or at least of the *need* for direction. In return these young people have served as a recurrent blood transfusion into my own work. Whether in England or Wales, in France or the East, they have been encouraged to work with me in their tens and hundreds, and my debt to them is beyond acknowledgement.

Among that first little band of chosen students at Segontium two were destined for distinction: Victor Nash-Williams, one of Rik's original students at Cardiff, who in due course became Keeper of Archaeology in the National Museum and did much for Welsh archaeology, and Ian Richmond, then an Oxford undergraduate, a brilliant man who was to be a leading light in Romano-British studies, although essentially a scholar rather than an earth archaeologist. Rik was always to admire

Ian's superior intellect and literary quality, although their long relationship was to be unhappily marred at last, as will appear, when Rik somewhat savagely broke the code and spoke ill of the dead.

After two seasons of digging, quite long ones for those days, the work at Segontium was judged to be completed and a new site was to be chosen that would further both the political and archaeological strategies. This clearly pointed to a comparable fort in South Wales. The Romans had held down Wales by a network of roads linking garrisoned forts, and if in the north Segontium was a 'pivotal point' in this system, the same could be said of the Gaer near Brecon in the south. This is a fort in a beautiful and sequestered spot in the Usk valley, lorded over by Brecon Beacons and once garrisoned by the *ala Vettonum*, a cavalry regiment originating in Spain. Wheeler confesses that in addition to its undoubted strategic advantages he was attracted to the Brecon Gaer by his knowledge that the Usk swarmed with salmon and trout.

So for the two summer seasons of 1924–5, during which they lodged at a farmhouse, Rik and Tessa Wheeler conducted a modest but very successful dig in idyllic surroundings. The peace of the valley and the enfolding mountains, freedom from the publicity and resulting crowds of visitors that were to follow with the more ambitious projects of the future, together with innocent yet congenial company and the pleasure afforded Rik by the 'fishful Usk', seem to envelop the excavations at the Gaer in an atmosphere all their own. If it would be going too far to see them 'apparelled in celestial light', they do show something of the 'glory and the freshness of a dream' – and one never to recur.

The congenial company was largely provided by two young Wykehamists from New College, Nowell Myres and Christopher Hawkes. It is a proof of the high reputation the Wheelers had already established that a formidable lady, Miss M. V. Taylor, who presided over the Haverfield Library at Oxford, decided to dispatch these two star scholars to learn from them the rudiments of excavation and the archaeology of Roman Britain. I can witness that my former husband was to look back on the weeks at the Gaer as an extraordinarily happy and rewarding time, while Nowell Myres has given me some account of it:

The work at the Brecon Gaer was on quite a modest scale and was not conducted in a blaze of publicity. Rik himself treated the excavation as the agreeable background to a fishing holiday. He would begin the day by directing Christopher and myself, and the handful of unemployed Welsh navvies who comprised the labour force, what we were to find, and would then disappear, suitably equipped, in the direction of the river. In the evening he would return, not always overburdened with trophies of the chase, listen to what we told him of the day's work on the dig, and explain to us what he thought it meant. Meanwhile Tessa coped with all the organizational and administrative chores which a dig entails, including the provision of enormous picnic meals. Apart from their son Michael . . . and occasional visitors, there was no one else there at all.

As a picture of the whole two seasons' digging at the Gaer, this memory has to be taken as somewhat heightening the truth. The Director did sometimes regard it as more than a background for fishing, just as the party of four gifted people was sometimes diluted by more ordinary students. Yet Rik himself conceded that 'On the whole, it was the happiest and least anxious of all my enterprises.' Perhaps the dream-like atmosphere that envelops this episode in recollection owes something to the fact that Nowell Myres became deeply attached to Tessa in a true sympathy of spirits. Nowell recalls of this 'profound admiration' for a woman still young yet ten years older than himself that 'Tessa herself seemed to welcome it, for she needed at that moment in her life an understanding friendship with someone, however innocent, on whose devotion and discretion she could place absolute trust.' It was now five years since Rik had returned from the war, and Tessa was discovering the difficulties of marriage to an extraordinary man with the domestic and emotional flaws of most exceptional human beings. She was entirely devoted to him and was beginning to overwork herself in response to his demands and for the sake of his career. Whether or not he was already guilty of minor infidelities, there is no doubt she was already suffering from the tyranny his passion for work imposed on their life together. In the valley of the Usk both threats were far away, Rik was securely there at his charming best, while the presence of an adoring young man of Nowell Myres's quality brought true solace to her remembered troubles.

Congenial company of a very different kind was provided by a visit to the Gaer from that great but eccentric couple, the Flinders Petries. He was at that time seventy years old and newly knighted. Rik had probably come across him at University College, London, where he professed Egyptology. He was always to feel admiring affection for the old man, accepting his unconventional methods and honouring his genius. On this occasion while Rik angled Petrie went off to plan stone circles with the help of a bamboo and a visiting card. One day he and his wife Hilda had to be rescued from a hedge where they were besieged by an infuriated bull.

.   .   .

Wheeler had taken a big step upwards in his career just before the start of the Brecon Gaer excavations. Indeed, having such laurels to rest upon must have encouraged him to relax for a few weeks and enjoy his fishing. Since his appointment in 1908, the first Director of the National Museum of Wales, W. E. Hoyle, had presided over the birth and subsequent arrested development of the institution. In the Museum Handbook it is still recorded of him that he was an expert on squids, octopuses and cuttlefish and had bequeathed a large collection of these creatures 'preserved in alcohol'. In 1924 ill health obliged him to retire.

In his handsomely printed application for the directorship submitted in June of that year, Wheeler set out his proposed policies with an authority and confidence that would have been considered presumptuous in an ordinary young Keeper seeking promotion. Nor was he afraid to offer thinly veiled criticism of the existing regime. He began, not unreasonably, by saying that he would give precedence to raising funds to make habitable the museum he hoped to direct. He then stated the conviction, on which he had been working, that 'It is essential that even in the remotest parts of the Principality the existence of the National Museum should be known and its influence felt. The present position in this respect leaves much to be desired.' He went on to develop the related theme that as local museums inevitably had a sense of rivalry with the National Museum they should be pacified by measures of aid such as his 'affiliation scheme'. More unexpectedly, he concluded, 'I would emphasize my conviction that museums have an important part to play in the educational system of the country.' It must have been partly due to this belief, not then very widely held, that the Welsh Museum School Service was soon to set an example to the rest of Britain.

Passing on to his personal qualifications, he suggested that while archaeology gave him a sympathetic understanding of the sciences, 'My own training in boyhood and youth was primarily that of an art student, and it was through the study of ancient and mediaeval art that I first approached archaeology.'

The breadth of Wheeler's interests were further stressed by the three eminent and carefully selected writers of testimonials, two, Professor Fleure and Robert Bosanquet, with Welsh associations, and the third the highly influential Charles Peers, then Director of the Society of Antiquaries and Chief Inspector of Ancient Monuments. The adjectival riches of testimonials may always be suspect, but those supplied by these men were out of the ordinary. They recognized Dr R. E. M.

Wheeler as possessing energy and efficiency, vision and personal power; steadiness; a rapid, accurate and indefatigable ability in his work; the qualities of leadership – enthusiasm, self-reliance and promptitude. . . . Since there seems to be a lingering tradition in the museum that, while Tessa was universally beloved, her husband was unpopular, it is worth noting that Peers credited him with 'a most attractive personality' and Bosanquet with 'tact, kindness and unselfish readiness to give credit to others'.

Rik had been genuinely surprised when, with no museum experience, he won the departmental appointment, but now there can have been little doubt in anyone's mind, including his own, that he would be given the Directorship. His achievements during the four intervening years had been remarkable. He had more than a score of substantial learned articles to his credit, including a few on prehistoric subjects, he was on the councils and committees of half-a-dozen national societies, including the Board of Celtic Studies, and had been elected a Fellow of the Society of Antiquaries in 1922. These things all in addition to his excavations and administrative and missionary work for the National Museum, his considerable successes as a university and public lecturer.

Among the publications listed in his application for the Directorship Wheeler had been able to include '*Prehistoric and Roman Wales*. (About to be published by the Oxford University Press)'. The following year (1925) it duly appeared, the first book that he had written for the general reader. Ultimately based on some public lectures, it had been 'scribbled hastily in railway carriages and country inns' during his travels among the hills. Indeed, it was largely as an instrument of his unifying strategy that he had designed this 'comprehensive survey of ancient Wales in relation to the prehistory and early history of the adjacent lands'.

Books of the kind are now so commonplace that it is hard to realize what a pioneer effort this one was in its day. Starting with 'Cave Man', more than three-quarters of a lucid, well-ordered volume was devoted to prehistory, with no special favours allowed to the Roman period. The author was certainly justified when he wrote, 'Looking back on it and on the utter negation from which it emerged as a germ of future achievement, I am less dissatisfied with it than a single-minded and unfettered archaeologist has any right to be.'

So, at the age of thirty-three, Rik Wheeler rose to join the company of the professional Top People, and would never again have to make formal application for a job. Henceforth they would be offered to him. He had also seen to it that he would have a first-rate lieutenant, for he had persuaded Cyril Fox to leave Cambridge to take his vacated place as

Keeper of Archaeology. Cyril, a most vital man with energy and enthusiasm equal to Rik's own, had been developing original ideas and methods in relating early human settlement to its geographical setting. He was to become one of Rik's few close friends, perhaps the only one with whom he was able to drop all masks and be absolutely natural and at ease. Cyril was also the biographer's friend in that he alone among men preserved many of Rik's letters.

On becoming Director, Wheeler immediately set about redeeming his pledge to get the museum completed. In 1922, 'in order that at least a portion of the Museum building might be opened to the public', the City Council had borrowed enough money to furbish a small section. Overcome by extreme caution, they had, however, failed to launch an appeal, so that two years later not only had inertia set in once more but there was a large and expensive overdraft.

Wheeler's opening move was a private sortie into Whitehall to induce the Treasury to increase its grant. This was the first of his persuasive visits to the holders of the money-bags which in the future were to do so much for science and learning. The secret of success was then, as later, to arrive with a precise objective clearly stated and evaluated and to present it with the evident determination and ability to carry it out.

Next the home ground had to be prepared by battling with, and finally ousting, the ineffectual alderman who held the key position of museum treasurer, and his replacement by Sir William Reardon Smith (Bart), a wealthy shipowner who had already contributed handsomely to the building funds. Between Director and self-made baronet there sprang up a warm personal relationship quite independent of the give-and-take of money. Rik felt an immediate liking for the man who had first gone to sea as a cabin boy in a brig and had sailed the seven seas before becoming owner of a shipping line. The fact that he loved to hear him tell of his adventures is proof, if one were needed, that the new Director had not lost the taste for heroic tales instilled in him by his father. It may be that, even without this friendship, his realization that the museum was leaving the doldrums under inspiring command would have led Sir William almost to double his earlier gift. It is certain that after his appointment as treasurer, in November of 1925, he went to Wheeler's office and wrote a cheque for £21,367 4s 9d – the amount of the overdraft.

With the bank account out of the red and the Treasury grant substantially increased, building could be restarted and the appeal launched at last. Gradually further galleries were opened until within two years (in 1927) King George V and Queen Mary came down in their sober dignity to declare the National Museum of Wales open. By that date, however, the Wheelers had left Cardiff.

The directorship had brought with it a number of personal advantages. One of them was in the shape of an agreeable, capable and ever-willing secretary. Captain Archibald Lee might have been designed to meet Wheeler's needs – except that he was something of a character in his own right. He was equal to all his new master's exacting demands, and all possible burdens were put upon him. 'Leave it to Archie' became a regular formula in the National Museum during Rik's hectic years and remained so for long afterwards.

The domestic advantages of a higher salary were very considerable. The Wheelers were able to leave their Cathedral Road lodgings and move into a new house they had built for themselves. It was in a suburban setting among other houses, but it had a pleasant garden – a new experience for Michael. Above all it was the first real home of her own that Tessa had known, after ten years of married life. She rejoiced, and happily did not know that all her work and pleasure in it were soon to be sacrificed and that she would be condemned once more to cramped and unlovely rented flats.

Nor, until the beginning of 1926, had Rik himself any foreknowledge that he would soon be tearing up these very tender family roots. On top of his high-pressure administration in the museum (for not quite everything could be left to Archie) he was working on two big schemes, one for more ambitious excavations and one for academic archaeology. As events of this 'year of decision' were to develop, they were to come into embarrassing conflict – but that again could not be foreseen.

Having written *The Roman Fort near Brecon* as a counterpart for South Wales to what the Segontium monograph had been for the North, Wheeler determined that the next strategic advance must be 'the examination of the great legionary fortress from which the Gaer and its fellows had depended, as it were the prehensile fingers of a strong hand'. This was Caerleon, the Roman Isca on the Usk estuary, where it had commanded the southern approaches to highland Wales. Isca had an obvious appeal for Rik Wheeler: it was large (fifty acres) and offered the opportunity, always dear to him, of adding to recorded history by archaeological exploration.

Outside the walls of the fortress lay a well-preserved oval amphitheatre, built by the Second Legion for use both as a weapon-training ground and a stage for games and entertainments. It was known to local folklore as King Arthur's Round Table. Cogitating where best to start the digging of so huge a site, Wheeler decided upon the amphitheatre, since it was well-known, free of later buildings and 'likely to attract the considerable funds required for a long-term programme of work'. This magnetic quality, he saw at once, would owe much to the fortuitous connection with King Arthur.

Wheeler has been accused of shameless exploitation of this romantic name as a money-spinner. The accusation is true, but Wheeler's action was hardly more shameless than the use made of largely irrelevant biblical associations by excavators in the Near East, particularly (a few years later) by Leonard Woolley of Noah's Flood at Ur. At that time, when the tax-payer was spared, the sentimental and uncritical had to be induced to subscribe.

Hopefully, though without any precise expectations, Wheeler announced his project to the press. The bait was immediately snapped up: the *Daily Mail* sent their man to Cardiff and within a few minutes, round about midnight as it happened, an agreement was made that the paper would provide £1000 for exclusive rights and daily reports on the uncovering of King Arthur's Round Table. It proved to be no more than a first instalment.

Nowell Myres, who was very much involved with both excavations, contrasted the Gaer, 'the last excavation conducted by the Wheelers on ... an old-fashioned family basis', with Caerleon, 'the first in which Rik's genius for publicity set a new fashion in the conduct of British excavations'. If the contrast is perhaps somewhat heightened, this undoubtedly was a turning-point, and since Rik Wheeler's 'genius for publicity' was one of the things about him that was most to provoke his later critics, raising the scholars' hackles alarmingly and causing them to growl or snap, this is the moment when the subject should be examined.

In seeking the roots of this quality (if quality it was), some, including Nowell Myres, have discovered them in his family background: in his father's profession and his own early if slender experience of writing for the papers. I do not think that this is apposite. Robert Wheeler's journalism had from the first been in art criticism and leader-writing, hardly involving him in ordinary daily reporting or building up news stories. Of course his son was familiar with newspaper offices and had some knowledge of the ways and needs of journalists. Also it is true that Rik's English style was slightly influenced by his father's (essentially Victorian) journalistic writing and his lessons in speed and compression were valuable to him when at the height of his fame he was bombarded with requests for special articles. But all this has little to do with what is implied in a genius for publicity.

I am sure that Wheeler began to use the press with predominantly pure motives. He had from the beginning believed that if archaeology was to grow and to contribute to civilized values it had as much need of popular interest as of academic recognition. Pitt-Rivers himself had regretted the lack of archaeological publicity in his day, declaring, 'If ever a time should come when our illustrated newspapers take to recording interesting and sensible things, a new era will have arrived in the usefulness of these journals.' Not very much later G. M. Trevelyan wrote, 'If historians neglect to educate the public, if they fail to interest it intelligently in the past, then all their historical learning is valueless except in so far as it educates themselves.'

Wheeler more than once quoted and sincerely believed in these ideals. Related to them, more practical but almost equally blameless in itself, was a second motive: to raise money. In the twenties and thirties, when there were almost no public funds available for excavation, this motive was a real and urgent one. It is true that in addition to grants from the Society of Antiquaries and other learned societies the Wheelers' excavations were largely financed by appeals circulated to concerned individuals, but the contributions wrung from the visiting public through collecting boxes and the sale of literature, cards and insignificant antiquities such as potsherds and bones was important. At Maiden Castle, for example, where the publicity was highly organized, they met nearly one-quarter of the total expenditure. The first, totally unexpected, success in securing the sponsorship of the Caerleon excavation by a newspaper was not repeated, but subsequently the press coverage that Wheeler did so much to attract brought the crowds to his digs – with money in their pockets. It can hardly be doubted either that the interest and occasional excitement built up by what the critics regarded as ballyhoo stimulated a generous response to the private appeals.

Wheeler, then, always sincerely believed in the duty to spread an understanding of archaeology among the people and the desirability of taking a little of their cash in fair exchange. In *Archaeology from the Earth* he includes a section on how to handle publicity and its results as a normal part of an excavator's methodology. Now that tax-payers' money was being made available, he felt more than ever that the public 'must be cultivated and rewarded'. In the light of experience he added that for students to guide parties round the complexities of a dig was 'an admirable training in clear thinking and simple exposition'. He regarded all 'vulgarization' as a test of cogency and as an antidote to jargon and obfuscation.

As for Rik's personal role in all this, it was inevitably ambiguous. There are few human beings who are honestly indifferent to publicity if it comes their way, however much their reactions may differ. Of these, backing into the limelight is the most objectionable. In the fifties, when television brought Rik tremendous public acclaim on his own account, we shall find that he did not attempt to conceal his enjoyment of it. But in these earlier days the position was difficult. He wanted to popularize archaeology and attract a large public to his digs, yet could not fail to know that the response of the press depended very considerably upon himself. I have known a number of individuals who were accused of publicity-seeking and in most cases have judged that they did not seek it but attracted it. Anyone (and they are rare) who has a powerful personality, energy, independent ideas and a forceful way of expressing them will attract hungry journalists or other newsmen. Rik Wheeler, plainly, was just such an individual and inevitably he responded, so that some, though at this stage not very much, of the publicity stuck to himself.

The disapproval felt by a few for this personal aspect of the 'genius for publicity' was perhaps largely a matter of taste, but more often than they realized it involved suppressed envy. Much more important were the serious criticisms of scholars who believed that catering for press and public on excavations had ill effects on the work itself. One criticism was that large numbers of visitors, many of whom were no more than curious sightseers, took too much time and energy and produced a hectic atmosphere, while the sale of bits and pieces was undesirable in itself and might encourage pilfering and treasure-seeking. There was some truth in this, but the compensating advantages were very great.

The most serious criticism, in which, as it happened, Wheeler's earliest pupil-assistants, Nowell Myres and Christopher Hawkes, led the way, was that because Wheeler thought it necessary always to have clear and simple stories for journalists and the public he tended to leap to conclusions too soon and then either to cling to them too long or produce a series of different stories, leading to incredulity.

Members of the Wheelers' regular team of excavators deny this, claiming that his interpretations remained flexible and that he did no more than follow the evidence as it emerged. Undoubtedly Rik did make mistakes, as every pioneer must, but also, more culpably, was inclined in his reports to give an excessive appearance of finality. I do not think, however, that this had anything to do with publicity stories but everything to do with temperament and style. Just as at Sapignies Rik could not bear to return without the second gun, without his plan being completed, so he was determined that his major Reports should not only be well-arranged, lucidly written and finely illustrated, but that they should show a completeness of form, a clarity of historical diagnosis. We are in fact back with the issue of the sectional drawings: he set out problems with honesty, but liked to draw a firm outline round his conclusions. Let it be agreed, then, that Wheeler was sometimes too sure of being right, too ready to accept his own authority, but the idea that pleasing journalists and the visiting populace affected his thinking deserves to be forgotten.

To return to 1926 and to the plans for the excavation of Caerleon, I have said that these were to come into conflict with a second ambitious scheme that Wheeler was developing at this time – one for the aggrandizement of archaeology as an academic subject. Wheeler records his thoughts in *Still Digging*:

In the latter days of my directorship at Cardiff, my mind had been turning increasingly to the need for systematic training in a discipline which was now emerging from the chrysalis stage and was incidentally now in the public eye. Students were increasing in numbers; archaeological posts were slowly beginning to multiply. Something had to be done about it, and, looking round in my war-depleted generation, I could see no one but myself to do it – such was the poverty of the land. During the early months of 1926 I drew up a detailed scheme for a university Institute of Archaeology such as nowhere existed in this country.

Wheeler seems always to have been quite clear that such an institute would have to be in London, a conviction justifiable in itself and serving his long-felt and deep-seated desire to establish his own base in London. To be among the lower ranks of the Top People and settled on a provincial eminence was not what he wanted either for himself or for the advancement of archaeology. He was to describe how, after Reardon Smith had come to the rescue and he was sure of success in the completion of the National Museum, he was invaded by a sense of anti-climax and a desire to escape:

The future was assured: a great deal too firmly assured for the liking of a young man with remoter and more presumptuous horizons. If my boots were not to grow too large in Cardiff to enable me to jump out of them, I must jump now. I leapt therefore into the first pair of shoes which presented themselves to me, back to London.

The shoes he was offered were the London Museum, then established in Lancaster House. Events inside his head and outside it must have moved very fast, for while Reardon Smith presented his cheque in November of 1925, only two months later Rik had told Lord Kenyon,

President of the National Museum of Wales, that he was an applicant for the post at the London Museum likely to be made vacant by the retirement of the then Keeper, Mr Harmon Oates. The letter from Charles Peers that Wheeler records as having arrived 'one morning in 1926', inviting him to the Keepership, must either have been written in the first week or so of January or was not the initial invitation but a confirmation after Wheeler's appointment had been secured. In the next chapter the story will be told of a struggle over the succession that was waged at quite an exalted level during the early months of the year. What is certain is that when Rik was drawing up his schemes for Caerleon and an institute he already knew that he was very likely soon to be moving to London. Indeed, the formulation of the plans for an Institute of Archaeology must have been prompted by that knowledge and his dream of putting them speedily into effect.

Wheeler accepted the Keepership in the early spring, and although his official appointment was not to begin until July of 1926, it was quite evident that he could not direct the Caerleon excavations scheduled for the summer and autumn. The intervention of the *Daily Mail* made the whole matter more irrevocable and urgent. Tessa could take on advance preparations for the dig, and later for its direction, but hardly for the supervision of the first crucial season at Caerleon. The Wheelers looked round to find a qualified substitute, at short notice and in a scene where few such existed. As Nowell Myres has modestly written, 'It must have been Tessa who, when all else failed, cast me for this very unsuitable role.' It was certainly she who persuaded him to accept it. Her argument that to have been in charge of an important Romano-British excavation would add greatly to his qualifications counted for much less with him than his desire to come to her rescue in time of trouble.

So with Rik still doing some master-minding in the background, and Tessa rushing down when she could spare time from moving her household to London and coming to terms with her new life there, Nowell, then aged twenty-three and between his Finals and an Oxford Fellowship, took successful charge of King Arthur's Round Table. Willy-nilly, to redeem Rik's pledge, every evening he had to supply the *Daily Mail* with a newsworthy bulletin on the day's discoveries.

When in October Nowell was obliged to quit Caerleon, Tessa assumed the direction. But then it was obvious that the excavations were going to last very much longer than had been anticipated, and it caused him great distress to leave her with such a heavy burden. He knew she was overstrained and far from well, for on more than one of her summer visits she had suffered alarming black-outs. This is the first indication that Tessa was not sufficiently robust to bear the ceaseless pressure of work that marriage to Rik entailed and which she accepted so willingly.

As it turned out, she had to toil away on the amphitheatre for another eight months, enduring hard winter conditions and with only occasional weekends in London. She did not leave until the history of the building had been established and it was ready to be put into the hands of the Office of Works.

Rik himself chronicled Tessa's return to the almost equally uncomfortable conditions of their London life. For nearly a year now he had been hurling himself into all the activities of the new job. 'When she had eventually completed the long and difficult task of fulfilling our commitments at Caerleon – a task to which she devoted skill and diplomacy of a high order – Tessa joined me and trebled the efficacy of the attack.' There was to be no rest.

Apart from the crisis over the Caerleon excavations, the Wheelers' departure from Wales was not altogether happy or propitious. On the personal side there was the very great sadness Tessa felt at leaving her house and garden almost before she had begun to enjoy them. Professionally it was not difficult to criticize Rik for quitting the National Museum so soon after he had assumed the Directorship. He justified it by the claim that he had set the place moving towards an assured future, and that in Cyril Fox he had secured an ideal successor. In these circumstances he felt 'an inward assurance of right judgement' and that he 'could depart with a clear conscience'. Welsh opinion differed. As Lady Fox recalls, the move provoked unconcealed ill-feeling in Wales among a few who thought that Wheeler had used the National Museum of Wales as no more than a stepping-stone in his career. In a way they were quite right. Rik himself was frank enough about his ambitions and his awareness that the Principality, for all its mountains, could not offer him those 'presumptuous horizons'. Both criticism and departure were inevitable.

Looking back, the six years that Rik Wheeler spent in Wales can be seen to have done more than lay the solid foundation for his future. They had yielded the first considerable excavations and Reports; the first popular book; the first success in civil administration; the first exploitation of publicity; the first step into the professional elite. All were important, but what is most striking is the extent to which the Welsh achievements set a pattern which was to be repeated again and again during Rik's lifetime, on a larger scale. At the centre one can place a cultural institution in a thoroughly bad way, providing a stiff challenge; grouped round it, opportunities for archaeological research, academic foundations for the training and employment of students, and the establishment of expert teams. The closest similarity was between the little Principality and the sub-continent of India, but much the same elements can be seen in the London Museum pattern and at the British Academy. India was, of course, to be by far the greatest challenge, but the London Museum was to involve the biggest gamble and the longest, grittiest effort.

CHAPTER 5

The London Museum

BEFORE RIK WHEELER arrived in a whirlwind of progress the London Museum had been like no other. It was the sole national museum, duly funded by the Treasury, that was local in its scope. Moreover, the Treasury grant was so small that in staffing and finance it was no better than a poor relation to some provincial establishments. Looked at from another side, however, it revealed a face of exceptional grandeur. It had no merely nominal royal patronage but the personal interest and attachment of the royal family. Outwardly, too, it was palatially housed.

It had been founded largely through the enterprise of the second Lord Esher who, recognizing that London should have a museum of its own, recommended it as a memorial to Edward VII. The memorial idea was not pursued, but King George and Queen Mary sustained their interest in the project, supplying Coronation robes and many other royal mementoes. They took Princess Mary and Prince George with them to the inauguration ceremony in the spring of 1912.

The museum's first home was in Kensington Palace, but just two years later it was moved to Lancaster House, a setting no less royal since, as it faces Stable Yard, it is very much a part of the St James's scene. Originally built for the Duke of York as Stafford House, the present handsome but rather heavy pile was completed in early Victorian times and contains a splendid hall and double staircase designed for grand receptions. It was Lord Leverhulme who acquired the mansion, now to be called Lancaster House, and presented it to the nation. In the twenties the museum was sharing the premises, very uneasily, with the Government Hospitality authorities.

Here, as with the National Museum of Wales, development had been checked by the war; although Rik was being too harsh when he described the place as 'derelict' and 'a junk shop', it was certainly a survival from an amateurish past, a storehouse of purposeless and ill-assorted collections. The first Keeper, Guy Laking, a friend of the royal family and a dashingly imaginative if somewhat erratic character, had been succeeded by a man of a very different type, though equally ill-qualified: a Mr Harmon Oates, referred to by Rik as 'a dull and pompous commercial traveller'. Also on the staff was G. F. Lawrence, as Inspector of Excavations, a post largely concerned with rescue work on the sites of new buildings. This was a responsibility which must have confronted Lawrence with ethical problems, since he was himself a well-known collector of antiquities, employing workmen to keep watch for him on building sites. Both men were due to retire early in 1926.

Lord Esher had kept a strong personal influence at Lancaster House: some were later to refer to it as having been his toy. He was chairman of the governing Board, where his principal co-trustees were the weighty Establishment figures, Lord Burnham and Lord Lascelles – a trio of Viscounts. Lord Esher had supplied money for such acquisitions as were not private gifts, and his son, Colonel Maurice Brett, was an Assistant Keeper and guide-lecturer.

With the retirements in prospect, Esher was eager for his son to succeed Harmon Oates and in the November of 1925 he wrote to Maurice (whom he always addressed as Molly and in terms of deep affection) concerning the best tactics to secure the keepership. It was a government appointment and the crucial question was whether to get the Trustees' consent to the plan at once and spring the recommendation on the Treasury, or to delay while lobbying in high places for support. Esher himself was 'for trying to get the succession considered *now*. The atmosphere seems favourable.' In fact he evidently delayed, for at a meeting of the Board on 13 January the appointment was discussed. 'It was unanimously decided [by the three Viscounts] that Lord Esher should see the Prime Minister and ascertain whether, in the event of the Assistant Keeper's name being proposed by the Trustees as Mr Oates' successor, it would receive favourable consideration.' This he did within a day or two and received the reply that he should 'set in motion the usual official notification'.

Esher may by now have known that a dangerous counter-move to his plans for his son was afoot, for he seems to have decided that he must make his strike at once. On 18 January he wrote to Oates, instructing him to get in touch with Burnham and Lascelles to seek their consent either for another immediate meeting or for their agreement that a memorandum which the Keeper had prepared recommending Maurice Brett as his successor should be forwarded to the Treasury *as their own*.

There seems to have been no change of intention among the Trustees, for Burnham replied to the Keeper that he considered a meeting unnecessary – indeed, that he would not attend one – and that the recommendation of Brett for Keeper should go to the Lords of the Treasury without delay.

The opposition, the supporters of Wheeler for Keeper, was moving with equal speed and more power. It would be excessive to call it a conspiracy, but it does appear to have conducted its campaign through private and personal contacts that probably centred on the Society of Antiquaries, possibly under the leadership of the Director, Charles Peers. It was on 20 January that Lord Kenyon, as President of the National Museum of Wales, wrote to Lord Burnham, 'Dr Wheeler tells me that he is an applicant for the Directorship of the London Museum,' and went on to say that, as he had been much impressed by the exceptional energy and ability Wheeler had shown in Wales, he felt he must support his claim 'to such an interesting post'. Two days later this was followed by a personal letter to Lord Burnham from Walter Godfrey, a leading Fellow of the Society of Antiquaries who on this occasion chose to use the Society's writing paper. It is this letter alone that gives some idea of what had been happening behind the scenes.

. . . my excuse for writing to you is the anxiety felt by London antiquaries in a decision which I believe the Trustees of the London Museum are about to make. It is common knowledge that . . . no reliable expert has been available to watch the excavations which proceed daily in the City in the various building reconstructions. In nearly all these cases the whole strata recording Roman and Mediaeval London are destroyed, and the absence of detailed observation is a calamity.

It has been hoped in many quarters that on the retirement of Mr Harmon Oates of the London Museum the services of an archaeologist of proved reputation might be obtained. . . . There is one candidate who stands out as pre-eminently fitted for this work, and that is Dr R. E. Mortimer Wheeler, MC, D.Lit., FSA. . . . He has proved himself a brilliant exponent of just those things which touch most on the antiquities of London. If he could be prevailed upon to exchange Cardiff for London, it would be an event of very great archaeological moment. . . .

I am sure that all prominent antiquaries will endorse my view, and feel that the London Museum has a great opportunity for performing a vital service towards the elucidation of the history of London.

This emphasis on the need for an experienced archaeologist to supervise building excavation sites was evidently the line being followed, quite rightly, by the pro-Wheeler party. It was mentioned by Lord Kenyon, and again a little later in a letter, obviously inspired by the campaigners, from the council of the London Society. It is noteworthy that all these missives were addressed not to the Chairman of Trustees but to Lord Burnham, presumably because it was felt to be too embarrassing to address Lord Esher rather than for any suspected weakening on Burnham's part. He was evidently still firmly behind Esher when the first two letters were being composed.

It would be interesting to know what active part, if any, Rik Wheeler himself was playing in this struggle within the Establishment. What is sure is that his backers and his candidature were to prove irresistible. Burnham plainly had to give way over his strongly expressed opposition to another meeting, for one was held on 3 February. It must have been a curious affair, with the three noblemen closeted together; Oates and Brett were excluded since the agenda concerned them. Lord Burnham, as he was bound to do, presented the letters from Godfrey and Kenyon 'recommending the name of Dr Mortimer Wheeler for the Keepership of the Museum'. They then proceeded to consider a draft document for the Treasury, recommending the name of Maurice Brett for the Keepership of the museum, thus completing their business.

Evidently the Trustees were genuinely uncertain as to what the outcome would be, for some three weeks later Lord Esher wrote to his son, 'I wonder when we shall hear about Mortimer W.? You have been *very* good all through this affair. So unfussy and reconciled to any eventuality. Which ever way it goes you will benefit.' At another meeting early in March the subject seems to have been left alone, save for a vote of thanks to Harmon Oates for 'his invaluable services'. When, on 14 March, Viscounts Esher and Burnham met yet again all had been decided. Maurice Brett was in attendance still as Assistant Keeper, while 'The newly appointed Keeper, Dr R. E. M. Wheeler, was also present.' A letter from the Treasury appointing him had just been received and was read at the meeting. Probably feeling that he could not decently leave Cardiff at once, Wheeler had asked to defer taking up the post until 1 July. This was agreed, and meanwhile the ever-patient Maurice was to run the museum and G. F. Lawrence's tenure as Inspector of Excavations was extended until the autumn – when, with an archaeologist as Keeper, the post was to lapse.

Lord Esher's reactions to his defeat were ambivalent but not without some magnanimity. A strong tradition lingered in the museum that he had been very angry, and he undoubtedly ceased to fund purchases, leaving Wheeler virtually without money for acquisitions. On the other hand in the letters that he showered on Maurice Brett after Wheeler had assumed office he commented, 'He will keep everything buzzing, which I like' and 'Damn Mortimer. And yet I feel as if he was a wholesome tonic.' Within a month he reports, 'A nice letter from Dr Wheeler which I am answering.' When he chose to be tactful Rik could be a master of the art. The two were to work together in reasonable harmony.

The decision to leave Cardiff for London meant a tremendous fall in living standards for Rik and Tessa. His commencing salary was £600 a year, and this was not raised to £900 until 1930 – by which time Tessa was earning a little as part-time lecturer. They had originally hoped to ease the stringency by lodging in Lancaster House, but this plan was frustrated by the interests of Government Hospitality, and they moved instead into a semi-basement in 2 Cardinal Mansions, Carlisle Place, near Victoria Station. Once again, as in his childhood, Rik was living below ground in rooms open to the peering glances of passers-by.

It was for these quarters that Tessa had to part with her Cardiff house and garden, and where the Wheeler family was to stay for over six years. In Michael's memory the flat was of a fair size but gloomy, while Tommy, a girl secretary who will appear again, found it dark, unhomely and unused. She had the impression that Rik, and presumably Tessa also, never much wanted to return there. The unattractiveness of their home encouraged the practice of spending half the night at the museum, together with a small but growing number of assistants and students. The main purpose was for work, but they also inspired a warm sociable atmosphere that became more homelike than that of the unloved premises in Cardinal Mansions.

Michael was now attending the Dragon School at Oxford. In sending him to this prestigious and loftily intellectual preparatory school, Rik was setting him on the highly privileged educational progress, denied to himself, that would lead his son by way of public school to Oxford. During those parts of the school holidays when they were not away excavating, the three of them would often eat out at Stone's Chop House, but on the return journey would leave the bus one stop early to save fares.

This family aspect of the Wheelers' life must not be forgotten when considering the gloomier accounts of their first London home. Indeed, when much later Rik's philandering and love affairs, combined with his equally insatiable work-drive, were making Tessa wretched, she told a young confidante that they had been very happy together when poor, living in a basement flat and 'giving friends bread and cheese – when there was any cheese'. Now, when they were better off and successful, happiness had flown.

The drive of ambition for archaeology and for himself that had made Wheeler so ready to accept the London Museum, in spite of the material sacrifice and risk involved, was a most powerful one. He not only gave up the security of the Welsh directorship, in which he could have remained (as his friend Cyril Fox was to do), with the certainty of a knighthood and opportunities for peaceful research, but also at about this time he turned down the offer of a dignified seat in the purely academic world: a newly established professorship at Edinburgh University. Although he was always attracted by a challenge such as that presented by the condition of the London Museum itself, the leading motive force behind the drive was to fulfil his dream of founding an Institute of Archaeology. He arrived, as he said, with the blueprint for it in his pocket, and with high hopes that it might soon come into being.

Fulfilment was to prove much harder and slower than Wheeler had anticipated. In fact, almost exactly a decade was to pass between his arrival at Lancaster House and the opening of the Institute. For more ordinary mortals ten years might not have seemed too long for so great a project, but it was an unconscionable time for Rik Wheeler. He dashed into all the immediate jobs that confronted him as Keeper, but behind every important initiative lay the blueprint.

These initiatives largely conformed with the pattern established in Wales, being directed towards the reform and vitalizing of the museum, together with its responsibilities for the rescue of London's antiquities, towards the recognition of archaeology as an academic subject by the University of London, towards the training of students and the formation of a team of experts and, finally, towards excavations that would increase knowledge, advance techniques and bring glory to British archaeology. All these actively interrelated goals were to be pursued for their own sake, but also as tributary to the grand purpose of the foundation of the Institute.

The most urgent and open task confronting Wheeler when he took up office was, of course, to tackle the museum itself: there he was, in charge of the great, neglected house, with its assorted contents, extending from valuable jewels, royal robes and fine costumes to the oddest bric à brac and quaint peep-shows. After he had been there for just a week Maurice Brett wrote to his father, 'Here things are quiet. Dr W. is rearranging the cases, collecting all the scattered examples of different things and putting them together. He is also busy on the general guide.' These charmingly simple words refer to the beginning of a process that

Wheeler himself described more vigorously: 'The London Museum had to be cleaned, expurgated, and catalogued; in general, turned from a junk shop into a tolerably rational institution.'

As though he were being warned that the outside world cannot be completely excluded even from the best laid plans, before he had been installed two months he had to cope with a much publicized theft. On 31 August the *Daily Chronicle*, among other papers, proclaimed, 'Daring Theft From London Museum. Show Case Rifled. For the first time in the history of the London Museum, a robbery occurred yesterday. Oliver Cromwell's watch was stolen in broad daylight.' The loss of the Protector's timepiece, an egg-shaped mechanism, the dial engraved with 'a view of Worcester cathedral and two rabbits browsing', attracted considerable attention. The new Keeper sent a firm but forgiving memorandum to the Sergeant in charge of the retired policemen who, in insufficient numbers, guarded the collections, emphasizing the need for the keenest vigilance, especially in such small rooms as the 'Duchess's Boudoir', where the watch had lain. Before long the waves in the teacup had subsided.

The task of rationalizing the exhibits and vastly improving the style of display was one that stretched far into the future after that first week. It was soon to be integrated with the mounting of special exhibitions, and with educational work, including the setting-up of children's rooms and so forth. It was a minor proof of the imagination and humour that saved Rik from many of the failings that might have gone with his character that in his 'expurgating' he spared the large working model of the Great Fire of London, which, with its crimson exuberance of flame and smoke, was to delight us all for years to come. On the other hand he was probably equally right to suppress the array of stuffed seagulls with which the first Keeper had enlivened the remains of a Roman boat from the banks of the Thames.

As part of the same first wave of museum reform Wheeler swept away a strangely amateurish system of listing accessions in favour of one based on running annual numbers, and at the same time introduced a fully descriptive register of the collections. Both these innovations have stood the test of time and are maintained in the new Museum of London.

The general guide which, as Maurice Brett witnessed, Wheeler began to write during his first days at Lancaster House was on sale by the end of the year as *A Short Guide to the Collections*. It was the first quick step towards a vigorous policy for museum publications. Lord Esher wrote of it, 'I am very pleased with the "Guide". Thank goodness we have your motive power behind our old machine.' Already by August Wheeler was sending out circular letters and otherwise collecting material for the first period guide, *London and the Vikings*, which, like its successors dealing with Roman and Saxon times, contained original research and new ideas as well as serving the popular interest. By 1930, which was to be a crucial year of advance for the museum, Wheeler was able to say that he had four guides out and two in the press. Almost all the work on them was done after dinner in Lancaster House – for, as Rik said, he seldom went home before midnight.

Another weighty matter that demanded the Keeper's attention during these early days was the proper supervision of building sites for the record and rescue of Roman and mediaeval remains – what Lord Kenyon called 'London underground'. It was his qualifications for this work that had been most strongly urged by Wheeler's supporters for the keepership, and the shocking losses that were being suffered every year had built up the pressure for action, particularly among Fellows of the Society of Antiquaries. Wheeler himself had recently been elected to the Council of that august body and was therefore more than ever in touch with its leading figures. The problem was to some extent linked with the needs of his old masters, the Royal Commission on Historical Monuments, which, as it happened, was just beginning a survey of Roman London. (Rik must have been gratified to learn that it was to follow the lines he had laid down at Colchester.)

A meeting of all interested parties had been called at the Society of Antiquaries within a fortnight of the new Keeper's arrival at Lancaster House. He had already sent his views to Reginald Smith, the British Museum representative, and it is astonishing to find Wheeler saying afterwards that he had been given no chance to present them to the meeting. It was generally understood that, with its absurdly small staff and the impossibility of inducing the Treasury to allow any substantial increase, it was out of the question for the London Museum to be responsible for the rescue work. Instead, all hope for the essential financial backing was centred on the City of London Corporation. In Wheeler's original, optimistic plan he envisaged the Corporation pro- viding the services of both an architect and a qualified archaeologist for the regular supervision of all sites. The conference at the Antiquaries, though indecisive, also favoured a solution that would depend on the generosity of the City in providing an Inspector of Excavations. Wheeler, however, with his usual quick grasp of situations, had sensed from the first that the Corporation would claim that they had such an official in their own museum, whereas it was evident that the Guildhall had totally failed to keep a watch even over the City area, and had no trained archaeologist available.

Nor, most certainly, did Rik Wheeler want to see any such advantage being given to the Guildhall. He wrote to that great and truly noble figure, Lord Crawford, who, with all his other involvements with art and culture, was then President of the Society of Antiquaries, expressing his misgivings and urging that there must at the very least be an expert committee empowered to superintend any individual appointed by the City Corporation. Otherwise, he wrote, 'I venture to express my conviction that it would be an unhappy ending to a well-intentioned effort on the part of the Society of Antiquaries.' Later, the City Librarian, responsible for the Guildhall Museum, submitted a report on actions taken or intended which involved the appointment of an unpaid and virtually unqualified inspector. Wheeler, judging this document to be specious and useless, wrote again to Lord Crawford to suggest that it was intended to throw dust in the eyes of the Library Committee, to 'give the Guildhall authorities a running start' and in effect to frustrate all plans for serious reform.

Later again, he was hopeful of persuading the Lord Mayor or the City Companies either to put pressure on the Corporation or themselves to fund a qualified inspector. Addressing a friend, he declared,

... the annual salary required for an adequate Inspector of Excavations need not exceed £350, and if the City Corporation of London, which is already streets behind other cities in the country in the care of its antiquities, cannot produce this small sum I feel sure the City Companies would show the way. I know of no other city in Great Britain which leaves its museum to fend for itself under the supervision of a solitary clerk. . . . And when in addition to this we remember that *every day* in several parts of the city historical evidence is being dug up and irreparably destroyed without record or observation, one can scarcely believe the obtuseness of the City Corporation which is so blind to its own obvious responsibilities!

There is no doubt that Rik Wheeler found the Guildhall Museum an irritating thorn in the flesh. It could be seen as a rival, for while it was, strictly speaking, a local museum concerned only with the City of London, whereas his own museum was national and covered the whole of Greater London, it had enviable wealth and influence behind it. He openly admitted that he wanted the two to be merged – and one need not ask which museum would swallow the other. Certainly he was an interested party, but no less certainly he was justified in his belief that the Corporation, with its museum a poor adjunct of the Library, could not, or would not, provide the proper archaeological care for London underground. Even after the war, when Roman Londinium was being explored before the rebuilding, the City Corporation was to be censured for its niggardly and short-sighted policies.

As for the outcome of the grand initiative of 1926, after a period of contention and stop-gap improvising the Society of Antiquaries itself assumed responsibility for the employment of a Director of Excavations, to be based at Lancaster House. The provision was still inadequate, since funds were short and the Director was paid according to work done – a system known at the museum as 'ten bob a hole'.

If the urgent matter of rescuing London's buried antiquities was not to be satisfactorily dealt with until after the war, the blame can be laid on the miserably poor establishment of the London Museum that persisted through the first four years of Wheeler's regime and was only slightly improved thereafter. Considering the size and grandeur of Lancaster House and the range of the museum's responsibilities, it appears grotesque that the Treasury grant was under £5000 and that the Keeper had at his command, on the administrative level, two part-time Assistants who were also lecturers, with a total salary bill (including his own) of £1300. There was also, of course, a small clerical and technical staff, porters and an odd-job boy. The Keeper had to exert himself to secure trifling improvements from the Office of Works, such as a decent sales counter in place of 'a small and very unsuitable table'. Sometimes, it is true, he wrung some amusement from these ploys, as when he sought to have passages better lit

... not only in the interests of the Museum public, but also in those of the Oriental and other Potentates whom our hospitable Government entertains here from time to time. The spectacle of an Indian Rajah, covered in diamonds, standing beneath the dim light of a remote electric fitting, which might appropriately grace a workshop or lavatory, is a romantic one but scarcely worthy of an Empire upon which the Sun never Sets. . . .

Nor were the Government Hospitality people themselves very helpful, turning down Wheeler's request to use their dining-room as a rest place for visitors equipped with a few seats and 'appropriately depressing periodicals such as the Burlington Magazine, the Connoisseur etc. . . .'

During 1927, when the Royal Commission on Museums and Galleries was starting work, Wheeler and Lord Esher made an effort 'to put the staff of the Museum on a working basis' and won a few minor posts from the Lords of the Treasury, usefully enhanced a little later when Tessa was awarded her part-time lectureship. On the other hand Wheeler's hopeful suggestion that a saving could be made by combining the Keepership of the National Portrait Gallery with his own fell on deaf ears.

More substantial progress in staffing was delayed until 1930, when the Royal Commission published its report. This recommended that if the London Museum was to play its part as a model local museum and educational centre its establishment must be increased, while a purchase grant should be made by the Exchequer, 'if not to meet the major needs of the Museum, at least to enable it to take advantage of occasional opportunities'.

The Commission made no precise recommendations under these heads – all was to be settled between the Trustees and the Treasury. Wheeler immediately began to marshal his forces, and a committee was set up to prepare a case for the Treasury.

Within a few months a deputation to Whitehall had been arranged, including among the eminent Trustees Ernest Makower, a wealthy silk merchant and connoisseur. The Wheelers had succeeded in so far captivating Makower and his wife that they became the museum's greatest benefactors, contributing from first to last some £20,000.

The fateful day was fixed for 14 October, when the Museum representatives were to be received by Sir Russell Scott. Wheeler had briefed them well with facts revealing the striking progress already made – in numbers of visitors, publications, the making of acquisitions. He laid much emphasis on educational advances, from lectures to school-children and their teachers to the encouragement of higher studies and research. There was also the good news that as a family memorial to Lord Esher, who had died that year, an Esher Research Studentship had been endowed and was soon to be announced.

Led by Lascelles, who had succeeded Esher as Chairman of Trustees, the strong museum troop was duly received at the Treasury and was successful in securing the still modest requests for an improved establishment and an acquisitions grant. It seems, however, that, to prove they were not soft the Treasury authorities raised the Keeper's salary to £900 rather than to the £1000 which had at one time been suggested.

The year 1930, then, was a turning-point in Wheeler's reign at the London Museum. The leanest years were over, the Treasury had given its stamp of approval and might be expected to continue to allow small financial favours. The increase in staff led directly to another change of atmosphere, although of a very different kind. The new Assistant Keeper, appointed in the following spring under the new dispensation, was a girl of such remarkable appearance, attributes and abilities that her presence was felt in every nerve of the museum's establishment.

This was Thalassa Cruso (her mother's maiden name was Robinson) who had been at the London School of Economics, had some archaeological experience and a strong personal interest in the history of costume. These were the qualifications the Keeper gave to the Trustees. She had many others. She was extraordinarily attractive to look at, with a brilliant complexion, bright blue eyes and that rare feature, an irresistible nose – finely cut and straight but relenting towards a retroussé tip. It was a nose that could quiver or snort. Her figure was very slender for those days, with a boyish carriage and stride. These happy endowments were made more telling by an immense, almost comical, intensity and spiritedness. She was quick-tempered and could be brutally outspoken, making many a young man quail. She had a rapid, clear intelligence and enough forcefulness to prove a successful Director of Excavations. It need hardly be added that she was less popular with women than with men, some of them judging her to be hard and ruthless.

Thalassa Cruso's arrival quickened the pace of the museum and the pulses of its inmates, male and female. It so happened that her appointment coincided with the award to Gerald Dunning of the first Esher Studentship – for research on mediaeval pottery. He was in every way her opposite: convivial yet slow, heavy-seeming, patient, faithful. He had already been about the museum and was the special object of Tessa's benevolence, since he had been all but starving himself to save enough to marry on. It is a proof that Rik, in spite of his intolerances, could appreciate a variety of men that he established an enduring and affectionate relationship with the Dunnings – whose daughter was to be called Tessa.

Quite apart from additions to the regular museum staff, the population of Lancaster House was on the increase. This same year of 1930, as will be told, saw the initiation of the Wheelers' era of major excavations. Since leaving Wales they had not ceased to dig, but now they were to lead undertakings on a scale far greater than anything attempted before. As in all excavations, the greater part of the work had to be done not in the field but indoors, and the doors that opened were those of Lancaster House. Material from the digs was inevitably brought there, followed by members of the excavation teams to sort, study and prepare it for publication. Back rooms and top rooms were kept busy.

There were, of course, many continuing museum activities of a more orthodox kind. Perhaps the most important from the point of view of making the place known to a wider public was the staging of special exhibitions. One of the first to attract popular attention, and which will serve as a sample for all the rest, was entitled 'Parliament and Premier-

ABOVE: Eric's parents, Emily and Robert Wheeler, *c.* 1890.

Eric with his sister Amy. He is holding a live bird in his hand.

Emily and Robert Wheeler in the family camp at Weybridge.

Eric in his late 'teens.

Examples of Rik's early posters and cartoons drawn at school and at University College.

Wheeler standing in an 'aesthetic rather than military' stance when he was stationed at the Redford Barracks, Midlothian, 1915.

Tessa, at about the time of her marriage.

Dame Margaret Lloyd George visiting the excavations at Segontium, 1922. Rik is on the left and Tessa in the background.

Tessa.

Maiden Castle, Dorset: an aerial view of the Iron Age hill-fort with excavations in progress. The small trenches follow the line of the 'Long-barrow'.

Wheeler's grid method of excavation, first developed here at the Eastern entrance of Maiden Castle.

Routine excavation in the Roman city of Verulamium.

The opening of the Institute of Archaeology, 1937, by the Earl of Athlone, Chancellor of the University of London. Left to right: the Academic Registrar, Wheeler, the Chancellor, the Vice-Chancellor and Lord Harlech (then Colonial Secretary). Kathleen Kenyon is on the right in the foreground.

Huelgoat, Brittany, 1938: Dr Claude Schaeffer visits Wheeler's excavations on behalf of the French government. Left to right: Schaeffer, Wheeler, Ralegh Radford, Kitty Richardson and Sean O'Riordain.

Rik and Mavis de Vere Cole after their wedding, 16 March 1939. Augustus John turns away.

ship'. The idea for such a display seems to have been Rik's own, and he rightly claimed that 'no similar exhibition has ever been held before'.

The aristocratic, distinguished and wealthy Trustees and other friends of the museum were invaluable in assembling a show of this kind. They gave or lent exhibits and borrowed them in high places. Lord Lascelles provided relics of Canning, Lord Burnham of the Disraelis, together with the famous dagger which Burke threw down upon the floor of the House. Lord Esher presented the Duke of Wellington's coat, trousers and boots, while Lord Wellesley added 'the umbrella used by the Duke of 1832'. Mrs Lloyd George produced the pen her husband had used to sign the Treaty of Versailles.

The vein of mockery ever-present in Rik Wheeler's mind led him to enjoy such relics with their popular appeal and slight absurdity. On this occasion he particularly responded to the then Prime Minister's pipe. Stanley Baldwin's drooping briar was as much a part of his image as Churchill's cigar was to be of his, so it is only a little surprising to find Maurice Brett writing to his father, 'Baldwin's pipe arrived today'. Rik, who for this and all other exhibitions, took great pains to organize appropriate publicity, recognized the possibilities inherent in this prime-ministerial symbol and approached an official of London Transport with a request to display it on 'small posters on the carriage windows'.

This tactic was only partially successful since the reply was that stickers for car windows could not be contemplated in addition to the poster designed by Rex Whistler already in the press. The official, however, so far relented as to add that he would be interested to see the illustration of the pipe, 'in case we may decide to print a double royal bill. . . .'

The affair of Baldwin's pipe serves as a reminder of a principle always observed by Wheeler in his handling of public relations. He was steadfastly against the employment of professionals, as much in the London Museum as on excavations. He extended this from PROs to guide-lecturers, having an especial horror of the parrot chatter of those who knew not what they told. Only those who fully understood what they were talking about should be allowed to interpret it for the public.

'Parliament and the Premiership' was only one of many special exhibitions that helped to make Lancaster House a lively place, the kind of museum that all kinds of people with all kinds of interests expected to visit from time to time. They involved the Keeper and his staff (including Tessa) in a great deal of work, but were well justified.

Perhaps Wheeler was never at heart a dedicated museum man or one with that passion for collections that leads to great success in attracting acquisitions. Yet he did not neglect this aspect of his responsibilities, one which was made more onerous by the fact that in addition to pursuing desirable acquisitions he often had to extract money from various sources to pay for them. The museum files are full of letters written in this cause about objects ranging from the Great Seal, and the cap, gloves and stomacher worn by Charles I at his execution, to the toothpick of the royal martyr.

The proud owner of the toothpick insisted on concealing his identity. One can be sure that the Keeper would have composed his letter of approach to this gentleman with his characteristic grin: a lifting of the upper lip and drawing in of the lower, a raising of the eyebrows and tipping back of the head.

My Trustees are anxious to bring together, by gift or loan, a representative collection of relics relating to Charles I and to exhibit them in the Entrance Hall of the Museum. They wonder whether, under the circumstances, you would be kind enough to consider the possibility of lending the famous toothpick for this purpose and so enabling them to add materially to the interest and variety of the proposed exhibition. I need hardly say that the collection will be under guard night and day, and that absolute security can therefore be guaranteed.

This letter is discreetly veiled, but it is on the record that Tessa acted as an effective censor when she heard some particularly angry or scathing letter being dictated to an individual whom they could not afford to antagonize.

Lancaster House enjoyed one peculiarity in its acquisitions programme. The royal family continued to make gifts, and Queen Mary in particular took a careful personal interest in the collections. The Keeper would receive notes written in her sloping hand, 'I am sending you 1. dark blue velvet cloak trimmed with ermine worn by Victoria Princess Royal at her christening in 1840 or 1841' and the like. She paid occasional informal visits.

One of the most generous donors, both of objects and of money for purchases, was, of course, Ernest Makower. The most valuable of his gifts was what Wheeler described as 'the very gorgeous saddle-trappings used by the first Duke of Marlborough during his ceremonial visit to St. Paul's after the Battle of Blenheim'. These, together with a loan from Lord Spencer of even more gorgeous Marlborough silver, were made the centre of a special exhibition. Mr and Mrs Makower were also as eager as Dr and Mrs Wheeler to 'get the Museum better known to the public'. With this end in view they gave silver cups to be awarded for essays submitted by boys and girls of London County Council schools and presented with a suitable flourish. This scheme was successfully launched in 1928, and was followed the very next year by another, far more ambitious, that was to prove a lasting triumph, not only attracting a new public to the museum but genuinely enriching London life. The Makower concerts of classical music held during the summer months right through the thirties were on the highest level of excellence. After each concert the conductors and soloists left their signatures in a book, and to turn its pages today is to be dazzled by a galaxy of famous names. Among conductors were Sir Henry Wood, Sir Thomas Beecham and Malcolm Sargent; among pianists Schnabel, Myra Hess, Cyril Smith and Clifford Curzon. Leon Goossens produced his inimitable sounds; Arthur Bliss played a most active part and so did Robert Mayer; the LSO, LPO and other orchestral groups performed, as did the Griller Quartet.

The initiative and most of the money came from the Makowers – although the Keeper won permission from the Treasury to make a sixpenny entrance charge. Wheeler, who acted as Secretary, may not have got great joy from the music, but he did from the company and the glitter of these occasions, so fittingly staged in the great entrance hall. He remembered the concerts warmly enough to leave an account and defence of them in *Still Digging* – where he had little else to say about his London Museum days:

These concerts were a great success. The audience consisted of an astonishing medley of critics, music students, tradesmen, guardsmen with their girls, passers-by and pilgrims of all sorts. They stood or sat about on the stairs or balconies or vacant patches of floor, without any special provision; indeed the slight discomfort contributed to the sense of informality and adventure. No stage separated listener from performer, and the resultant sense of intimacy gave an unusual quality to the scene. 'But what has music to do with a museum?' asked the caviller. 'A museum, my dear sir, is a home of the muses. Why should we turn Euterpe into the storm?'

As the next chapter will make plain, the Wheelers' deepest concern during these Lancaster House years of the twenties and thirties was still for the advancement of British archaeology. Rik had in no way retreated from his ambitions or his sense of mission as a leader in that advance. Tessa supported him whole-heartedly here as in all things. Thus excavation and ceaseless preparations for an academic institute dominated their lives, and for such work the London Museum could be no more than a useful base. Yet Rik has now been shown as an active Keeper, probably putting as much energy and imagination into the job as most curators with no wider preoccupations.

It is possible to catch personal glimpses of Wheeler in this role – in which hard work and emotional involvements were so often intertwined. They come from the cherished memories of his staff, from the humblest to those lieutenants who were themselves to become distinguished. There is no doubt that, with Rik as the towering Father Figure, Tessa the caring and comforting Mother (often in school holidays with Michael at her side), the staff became part of an enlarged family life lived behind the scenes of the splendid display rooms known to the public.

Rik's own office was a well-proportioned and dignified room on the ground floor, with windows looking out over the garden. Leading off it was a narrow apartment occupied by the long succession of his secretaries, conveniently provided with a little staircase leading to the first floor. Tessa had two small rooms (now occupied by Gentlemen's Lavatories). Gerald Dunning and Cottrill, his successor as Inspector of Excavations, had appropriately modest quarters near the kitchens.

An important feature of the domestic regime of the museum was a communal lunch, at which all the salaried staff, the researchers who were found working space in the museum and friendly visitors ate their packed meals together. The Wheelers' sandwiches were daily fetched for them, by a willing underling, from Capella's, an Italian restaurant just across the way. These gatherings kept everyone in touch with one another's doings and ideas. Later in the day tea would be brewed in the governmental kitchen.

Two such remarkable heads of house as Rik and Tessa were of course closely observed by those 'below stairs' and became the subject of innumerable jokes and stories. Rik's loves and sexual activities were well understood and newcomers were warned that they must always knock and wait before entering the Keeper's sanctum. He was, however, venerated to an extent that would today appear incredible if it were not vouched for by more than one survivor, particularly by Arthur Trotman, who joined the museum as a lad soon after Rik was installed. He recalls how, when the Keeper was expected (and Wheeler was often away from the museum), porters would slip into their best brown coats and everyone smartened up and took precautions against trouble – down to seeing that no dust was anywhere visible. Trotman declares that almost all of them held their chief in deep respect and many were in awe of him. Trotman himself well understood how that could be, for when, as a new boy, he drove a drawing-pin into some precious object he received a tremendous dressing-down from the Keeper and went in misery. A day or two afterwards, however, Wheeler went up to him, said, 'How are you, boy?' and grinned at him. The world was restored.

Walter Henderson, a sterling character who had entered the museum in 1915 after losing a hand in the war and acted as Wheeler's first secretary, was one of those who most reverenced him. He recalls how on one occasion the Keeper seized an offending secretary by the neck and threw her out, yet he insists that Wheeler was normally very kind to 'all wage-earners under him'. Even the ejected secretary returned after three weeks of recuperation. When Henderson could no longer cope with the secretarial work he was replaced by a woman sixty years old and uncomely at that. Wheeler, much annoyed, saw to it that succeeding appointees to the exacting post of secretary were, as far as possible, young and pretty.

At a time, then, when paternalism was not frowned upon Rik Wheeler exercised it with a blend of sternness, understanding and occasional ferocity that proved wholly acceptable. Not even in the army was his authority surer or more absolute. Tessa, meanwhile, soothing all with her native sweetness and taking the weakest under her wing, was quite simply beloved by all these humbler servants of the museum. She was known to them, it seems without a breath of derision, as 'the Angel'.

The attitudes and duties of Rik's personal secretaries were, of course, infinitely varied. 'Tommy' (Mrs Audrey Bennett), appointed during the 1930 reforms, declares that she must have been the stupidest secretary Rik ever had. She was one of those who had no difficulty in admitting that she adored him and was blissfully happy through most of her three years in his service. She records that he could be cross over such trivial things as the filling of his pen, but in general was patient, and never threw so much as a telephone directory at her.

In her case he could even forgive some inefficiency. She has never forgotten one occasion when a telephone call came through from the Ealing Archaeological Society to ask whether their lecturer was on his way, since an audience of five hundred was awaiting him. Wheeler was in fact at the Society of Antiquaries, and Tommy realized with horror that she had completely overlooked his engagement. In misery and dread she went to Burlington House and hung about until he came out. She told him what had happened. Instead of the expected rage, he put a hand on her shoulder and said, 'Poor old Tommy.' Once, when Tommy had chosen the wrong moment to do something particularly stupid, Rik barked at her, 'You are sacked – and you can leave today.' At lunch time she made for the park by the narrow walk along the side of Lancaster House. She had just entered it when she saw a tall figure with a familiar walk turn in from the park end. She could not retreat, but found it both fearful and embarrassing to have to walk and walk towards Rik between the confining rails. As they passed one another he said, without looking at her, 'Be at your desk at 2 pm.'

When they worked late at the museum Tommy did her stint of hair-ruffling. She records that she stood behind him for the purpose and no word might be spoken.

Some years later, in 1936, a young woman of a very different kind became Rik's secretary. This was Beatrice de Cardi, who had been so far inspired by a course of his University College lectures as to offer herself for the job and so begin a distinguished career in archaeology and a life-long friendship with her old chief. As a girl of critical or even sardonic judgement, simple adoration was not for her. Yet in a practical way she served him as devotedly as the rest, often staying on for his late-night working sessions, darning and cooking for him the while and ready to undertake the hair-ruffling routine, sometimes by the hour.

When, as we shall see, Rik's infatuation with Mavis de Vere Cole was dominating his sex life, Beatrice was sometimes sent out on shopping missions to find presents that might be pleasing to this most *exigeante* mistress. Sitting in her narrow office, she often heard stormy sessions with girl friends and others raging on the other side of the door. Though seldom provoking them herself, she was witness that Rik's occasional outbursts of rage 'could be quite shattering'. Beatrice was also one of those who discovered that he could be very jealous if any of his women had men friends, even when his own sexual interests were not involved. Yet predominantly she found him kind and affectionate and in her later career he was always ready with advice and practical help.

In her judgement of Wheeler in the office of Keeper, Beatrice de Cardi is one of the few who is prepared to be critical. She feels that while he had extraordinary powers for setting up and inspiring new or moribund institutions, he could be faulted in his everyday, detailed administration. It may well be that in the later thirties, when Tessa had gone and the affairs of the Institute were pressing, he became more careless and relied too much on unsupervised delegation of duties. Even this, however, is not the opinion of Martin Holmes, who joined the museum in 1932 as Rik's only male secretary. Holmes's impressions deserve quotation:

His outstanding characteristic . . . was his capacity for keeping his immense energy under control. Even his occasional explosions were rapidly calculated and as rapidly brought to an end when they had performed their function of letting off steam and it was time to get back to serious work. This was what made it possible for him to pursue so many interests and keep in intelligent touch with all of them. His correspondence was enormous. He would frequently dictate some fifteen or twenty letters a day on a wide variety of subjects, not to mention the long articles or memoranda which he would write out by hand – Heaven only knows when he found the time to do it. . . .

Having described the 'combination of inspiration, imagination and hard, unflagging energy' that he and Tessa put into their plans for an institute, Martin Holmes continues,

Very much the same principles governed his administration of the Museum itself. The collection was never allowed to become, or to seem, stagnant; new acquisitions as they came in were put on exhibition in the entrance hall and in due course moved on to be exhibited in their appropriate rooms. Special exhibitions were held at intervals. . . . All this meant a great deal of work for everybody, and for him most of all, but it was readily accepted and zealously performed. He paid his juniors the compliment of delegating appropriate sections of the work to them, and seeing in due course they got the credit for it, but at the same time his roving and knowledgeable eye was always alert to notice any error. . . . Even when one might think him to be safely occupied with the birth-pangs of the Institute, or with his excavations at Verulamium or Maiden Castle, he might suddenly be found striding round the galleries, glancing this way and that at the material exhibited and ready to round on one with a sudden question about something that one might not have thought he had ever heard of. And, in all the years I served him, I never knew him to lay the blame for anything upon the shoulders of a subordinate. . . .

Here is high praise indeed, perhaps too noble-sounding to be acceptable as the truth. Yet, even allowing for some administrative backsliding, I believe Holmes's tribute to have been true enough in its positive claims. What inclines one to drop one's eyes from so exalted a portrait is the knowledge of the very much less admirable doings that Rik Wheeler found time for among all his achievements as the presiding genius of Lancaster House. One real truth must be that with a subject of many contradictions there can be many portraits, none of them false yet none of them absolute.

——

CHAPTER 6

A Dream Fulfilled:
The Institute of Archaeology

ALL THROUGH THE pre-war years in London, when Rik Wheeler was, according to accepted wisdom, in the prime of life, his professional work had three main drives: the building up of the London Museum; the creation of 'a full dress academic institution' for archaeology; excavation for the advancement of knowledge and of its scientific techniques. All three were inextricably mingled, yet have to be partially distinguished.

'Pending the establishment of the Institute of Archaeology of my dreams, the shadow of a research institute was already coming into being at Lancaster House.' This admission, made in *Still Digging*, reveals in which of the three his heart was most engaged. His salary came from his Keepership and we have seen that he earned it more than adequately. It is probable that, with the summing-up of time, his excavating and excavations will be judged to be of the most lasting value. Yet this dream, which he had brought with him from Wales already written down, was his dearest ambition, his leading light. As a dream, held to with equal tenacity for about the same length of years (a decade or more), it can be likened to his youthful vision of becoming a great painter. The difference lay in its fulfilment in substance – not, indeed, with all the glory of a dream, but remarkable enough.

The Wheelers arrived in London confident that, with their well-thought-out plans and their determination, the pavements would turn to gold. It is a small sign of their proselytizing ardour that within the month of their arrival in the capital Rik had used the quest for an inspector of London excavations to get a few paragraphs in the *Daily Mail*, emphasizing the urgent need for more trained archaeologists. 'Supposing this new post is created, where is the man to be found to fill it? There are not sufficient archaeologists in the country to fill the vacant posts. . . .'

Wheeler himself wrote, 'The first task in 1926 was clear enough: to prepare the ground by infiltration.' This they did tirelessly over the preparatory years, undeterred, if disappointed, that the course was to prove such heavy going. Meanwhile they did not neglect what might be called the opposite face of infiltration: that of attracting people and institutions into Lancaster House.

The London Society, which had supported Wheeler's appointment, was at once eager to be more closely associated with Lancaster House, and some two years later, 'By the courtesy of the Trustees of the London Museum', moved their headquarters there, paying rent for rooms on the top floor that helped to supply the salary of a part-time lecturer – none other than Tessa Wheeler. Also involved in this move was the London Survey, a private group then very active.

Of rather greater significance in this development of the museum as a centre of learning was the attachment of the Royal Archaeological Institute, a once distinguished society which had fallen into decline. Rik saw it as another worthy object for his powers of reviving the moribund. The Institute held a meeting at Canterbury in 1929, when plans for this transfusion of energy were made. Rik wrote to a friend in Wales,

We have just returned from Canterbury where the Archaeological Institute has been holding a timid orgy ... the rumours which you hear are true. The celerity with which the old Institute is overtaking itself, however, should not be ascribed to me alone. We have made a complete clean up and really are going ahead now.

As Honorary Editor he promised the rapid appearance of belated volumes of the *Journal* and went on, 'Meantime we need new members, in order that the Institute may become a real power in the land, and I hereby appoint you Chief Recruiting Agent for South Wales. Remember that all who join now will get the arrears of volumes without extra charge.'

The laggard volumes duly appeared and Wheeler soon followed his usual plan of delegating much of the work by persuading Christopher Hawkes to serve as Secretary, with Thalassa Cruso as his assistant. Christopher remembers that, on being summoned to Lancaster House to discuss the job, Thalassa (recently appointed) was produced as a lure to encourage him to accept it.

The three of them were effective in making the Royal Archaeological Institute, if not 'a power in the land', at least a thriving and lively society. Thalassa served it well, but not as a contributor to what had become an excellent journal. Rik had told her to write an article on Neolithic pottery, but when it was found that Stuart Piggott was already working on one it was agreed they should collaborate. It proved that Thalassa, who was not deeply interested in Neolithic pottery, had only collected a few photographs and written THE BEAKER LAND-MARK on a scrap of paper. Rik ordered Stuart to assume total authorship – thus happily securing what was to be a classic contribution to prehistory.

Having raised the society from its sick bed, Wheeler brought it under his roof. He must have fixed up with Christopher Hawkes that a formal application should be made between them, for he wrote, 'My dear Secretary, My Trustees have considered your Council's petition for the use of Lancaster House as the registered address for the Royal Archaeological Institute...'. The Trustees graciously granted the petition.

This progress in associating more and less learned bodies with Lancaster House was not without value in making it 'the shadow of a research institute', but was of far less significance than the infiltration of the seats of power and influence in the world outside. In one such seat the Wheelers were already well-placed: the Society of Antiquaries of London. That venerable institution, with its dignified premises on the west side of Burlington House, could be turned to very good account both through its corporate undertakings and through the support of individuals or groups of Fellows. Though not wealthy, it was far better endowed than any other society in the field and also offered the best channels for publication, in the *Antiquaries Journal* and *Archaeologia*, a massive, heavily illustrated tome, appearing irregularly and with a strong aroma of a richer, more gentlemanly past. On the other hand the Research Committee issued special Reports, and it was in this form that the Wheelers' principal excavations were all to be published.

Meetings held in the lecture room, with its rare pictures, Corinthian pilasters and uncomfortable mahogany benches, could be grand occasions. No Fellow was better equipped to command them than Rik: his somewhat histrionic lectures on his excavations were to pack the room to the point of suffocation.

Rik and Tessa had no difficulty in penetrating the Society of Antiquaries. Indeed, as we have seen, Rik's appointment to the London Museum had been largely brought about by leading Fellows and he was already on the Council when he came to London. He was soon on the

Research Committee, while Tessa was to follow him onto both bodies in due course. When, in the crucial year of 1930, Rik was to attain the Executive, the control of the Society was well suited to him, for the recently elected officers, the Secretary, Director and President, were now for the first time all professionals and all in sympathy with his aims. The Secretary, Alfred Clapham, still with the Royal Commission on Historical Monuments, though not an archaeologist, was Rik's mentor and old friend; the Director, Reginald Smith of the British Museum, although he looked as if he never saw the light of day, was a much respected, if old-fashioned, prehistorian, while Charles Peers, the President (soon to be knighted), widely influential, with a finger in every well-crusted pie, had been Rik's active champion since Cardiff days.

Not that everyone at Burlington House welcomed this new man who had thrust among them, powered by a dangerous mixture of ability, ambition and missionary zeal. The Antiquaries was becoming more sharply divided between the old antiquarian Fellows, with interests well represented by *Archaeologia*, many of them gentlemanly amateurs and devoted to mediaeval studies, including heraldry, and the rising party of the archaeologists, who had mud on their boots, potsherds in their pockets and 'science' on their lips. These 'dirt archaeologists' might also in fact be scholars and gentlemen, but they roused the hostility of the more die-hard antiquaries.

The Wheelers had themselves already done much, perhaps more than anyone else, to strengthen the progressive party in British archaeology, but ideas and aims such as theirs were spreading, sometimes directly through their influence, sometimes independently. There was the Chair at Edinburgh, now filled by the formidable prehistorian Gordon Childe, and a degree course in Archaeology and Anthropology at Cambridge; Christopher Hawkes was soon to conduct excavations from his base at the British Museum; Nowell Myres and others were spreading the infection even in Oxford. In most of the centres of learning traditional historians and classicists, who believed that the human past could only properly be discovered through written documents and works of art, were opposed, disdainfully or virulently, to those who believed that the discoveries of the spade were no less credible. It was primarily against British and European archaeology, and most of all against prehistory, that this antagonism was aroused. Oriental excavators largely escaped it. They were recognized as true humanists, inheritors of Layard and Rawlinson, with no dangerous thoughts of a scientific approach to humankind.

Inevitably, with this division strongly felt within the Society of Antiquaries, Wheeler, as the most powerful personality associated with the diggers, appeared in a mephistophelean light to the die-hards (sometimes known collectively as the 'Heralds'). In truth Rik was always happiest when the spade could be used to correct or extend written history, and, moreover, he appreciated, if with a grin, the curious survivals beloved by the Antiquaries: the President's cocked hat on the table at meetings, and the ancient formalities of election that involved the possibility of 'blackballing' and formal admissions solemnized with a silver mace. He positively relished such games as the election of Fellows to or their exclusion from the elite club of the Cocked Hats, but here his influence was likely to be used in directions displeasing to the Heralds' party.

In practice the faction was recognized and overall peace maintained by an agreed balance in appointments and policies, and it was not until the famous disputed presidential election of 1949 that something like war was to be declared – with Wheeler as one of the protagonists.

While their entrenchment within the Society of Antiquaries was valuable to the Wheelers, ensuring widely disseminated support for their cause, the greatest efforts for an Institute of Archaeology had to be put into more positive campaigning.

The idea was first declared to the public in 1927, when Rik lectured to the Royal Society of Arts on 'History by Excavation'. He had already proselytized Reginald Smith, who, as a prehistorian, was open to persuasion, although he himself had no understanding of scientific excavation, preferring to conduct his studies from his museum desk. Smith was to prove a useful ally at this meeting, for, speaking after the lecture, he told the audience 'that Dr Wheeler had a scheme in mind for founding in London a sort of school or institute for training young archaeologists, especially in fieldwork', adding that it remained to be seen whether the lecturer was as good at money-raising as at excavating, but that 'he wished Dr Wheeler all success in any attempt to make archaeology into a national movement'. Wheeler himself then leapt up to declare that in a nutshell the problem was £70,000, the sum required for the creation and endowment of an efficient school of British archaeology.

This was only one among many lectures given by the Wheelers as honest propaganda for British archaeology in general or the Institute in particular. Tessa did not spare herself in going out to talk to local societies and the like, lectures now forgotten but effective at the time in spreading the word far and wide. Rik also lectured, wrote letters, dropped words into important ears and never missed an opportunity to put his case to archaeological gatherings.

All this helped to prepare the ground, but it was obvious that success depended not only on hard cash but also on securing a place in the academic world of the capital. London University had not as yet been touched by the dawn light of scientific archaeology; only classical archaeology, mainly art history, and Egyptology were established, and modestly at that.

As an alumnus of University College who had been awarded a Fellowship, Wheeler saw a possible opening there, and presumably explored it. In 1928 the college assigned a new lectureship to him, but it was a tenuous affair, unpaid and unrenowned. It was useful, however, in providing him with a few university students, and he arranged to give his lectures at Lancaster House. He followed this up early the next spring by staging an ambitious exhibition, 'Recent Work in British Archaeology', at University College itself. He had secured Lord Crawford as chairman of the organizing committee, wrote personally to the art editors of national newspapers and arranged a press day, with special photographic facilities.

His reward was a full and favourable press coverage, to which he himself contributed an eloquent article in the *Western Mail*. In it he contrasted the attention paid to discoveries made in Egypt and the Orient with that given in 'our own poor, neglected country'. There was no need, he insisted, to look abroad for archaeological interest when so much exciting work was being done in the British Isles. A version of this exhibition was later shown in the London Museum – in time to impress an important international congress then gathered in the city.

This whole enterprise, with its characteristic combination of flair and thoroughness, was certainly gratifying to University College and proved how much public enthusiasm could be aroused for British archaeology. It was a move towards Rik's avowed intention that 'the University of London, through University College, had to be led gently into the garden and up the right path'.

Wheeler seemed to attach disproportionate importance to another move in this policy: the endowment at the London Museum of the Esher Research Studentship, which, as has been said, was announced in the year of advances, 1930. The family, wishing to commemorate their father's long devotion to the museum, had provided funds for two-year grants for research into some chosen subject in the history or archaeology of London. Wheeler wrote of this event at the time as part of 'the increasing effort of the Museum to encourage higher education and research' and continued, 'The institution of this studentship marks a completely new line in Museum activities in this country. . . .' Rather much, perhaps, but then it was intended to impress the Treasury. Moreover, the students did in fact do some valuable work, particularly Dunning's innovative study of mediaeval pottery, which was to prove of the utmost importance for the archaeology of the period.

Of far greater significance for leading University College up the right path was the raising of Wheeler's lectureship onto a proper footing, and the establishment of a post-graduate diploma. He had always sincerely believed that archaeology should be taught as a post-graduate subject when students had a wide enough understanding of history to appreciate the true purposes of excavation as an approach to the human past. It was a part of his essential humanism.

The diploma course started in quite a small way, with a handful of students and a haphazard teaching programme. There was a much-liked geologist, Professor King, who took them on expeditions, and Wheeler persuaded a young graduate, Kenneth Oakley, to give a lecture on the Old Stone Age. (Here I cannot resist an aside, to prove that Rik could be a good adviser to the young. At the end of his school-days Kenneth went to him to ask how he could enter archaeology. He at once recommended the boy, who was not an historian, to read geology and approach archaeology from that direction. Kenneth obeyed and became a distinguished expert in human palaeontology and palaeolithic archaeology, to the advantage of science and himself.)

At the centre of the diploma course were the lectures Wheeler delivered twice weekly at Lancaster House. They covered all time, from the earliest Stone Age to the Roman. Most of his listeners were prepared to forgive any sketchiness in their matter for breadth of vision and inspiring enthusiasm. Some lectures were delivered while the excavations at Verulamium were in progress, and Stuart Piggott, who was one of the first to enroll, recalls the characteristically dramatic manner in which Rik handled this situation. He cherishes a 'recollection of the class assembled, and on the hour hearing the screech of the brakes as the grey Lancia shot into the gravel sweep of Lancaster House and the excavator leapt up the steps to appear in time to lecture on the Lower Palaeolithic, or perhaps the Belgae'.

Severe critics maintain that the university authorities were inclined to disapprove of the Diploma in Archaeology for its inadequacies and because it was rumoured that anyone who attended Wheeler's two lectures per week would be passed. This was not strictly true, since at least one early student, whose intellect was not her strongest suit, was twice failed. Perhaps some of the results were based on personal judgement, but were none the worse for that. Certainly a large proportion of those enrolled were sufficiently inspired to advance to successful careers. Moreover, I can bear witness that the weaknesses of the London course were closely paralleled in the new Tripos at Cambridge. Pioneers cannot expect perfection.

For Wheeler himself the important thing about his lectureship and the diploma was 'that prehistory was now, for the first time, on the books of the university. I took a breath and prepared for the final assault.' He had penetrated the academic hide of London and now had to turn to that second essential: the provision of hard cash.

The years of infiltration had won the Wheelers many supporters, of which the triumvirate ruling the Antiquaries was undoubtedly the most important. Yet the first golden ingot heavy enough to tip the scales for the Institute of Archaeology came from an unexpected quarter. That it came at all is to the personal credit of Rik himself, revealing a capacity many would deny him: that of an attachment for a man very different from himself through a disinterested recognition of his quality and greatness.

This was the eccentric genius, Sir Flinders Petrie, last seen measuring up stone circles with a visiting card while staying with Rik and Tessa at the Brecon Gaer. During the earlier days of the Institute campaign Wheeler heard that, as Professor of Egyptology, Petrie was incubating magnificent ideas for the accommodation of archaeology in the new university buildings in Bloomsbury then being planned. He sought him out, and the old man (he was born in 1854) generously agreed on full collaboration; an oddly contrasting pair, they had happy times together seeking to harmonize their dreams for the future. Nothing immediately came of these confabulations, perhaps because Sir Flinders's ideas were grandiose to the verge of fantasy. In 1932, however, there was to be a sudden advance. The Petries were now intending to retire to Palestine and it became an immediate practical necessity to find a suitable and important home for his large archaeological collections. These were mostly from excavations in Palestine and were stored, with some disorder, in a vast array of packing-cases.

Some generous spirit, hearing of his embarrassment, offered Petrie £10,000. He, with at least equal generosity, assigned it to Wheeler, stipulating only that space and uses should be found for his Palestine material when an institute was created. Although the gift was only one-seventh of the sum that he and Tessa had judged to be the minimum needed for an endowment, Rik determined that it was enough to launch his attack.

Luckily the principal of London University at that time, Sir Edwin Deller, was in sympathy with the project, and with his support the University of London consented, after much negotiating, that it should go forward. Wheeler turned to his other most doughty champion, Sir Charles Peers, and prevailed on him to be chairman of a committee to appeal for public support. Rik assigned himself the secretaryship, and Tessa took upon her small but enduring shoulders the burdensome office of Appeals Secretary. A manifesto was addressed to *The Times*; Peers summoned a conference of all interested societies to discuss plans for the Institute.

So now, after six years when progress seemed deadly slow, the Wheelers found their goal within sight and they braced themselves for the final effort. Tessa put all her exceptional powers of persuasion into money-raising. She did all she could to charm it out of individuals; she tackled the City Companies, a territory as strange to her as archaeology was essentially incomprehensible to its denizens.

She did wonders. Money came in, although, looking back, it must be admitted in modest amounts. Only one Mary Woodgate Wharrie gave handsomely: in those days archaeology had not the kind of recognition and repute to attract wealth such as that which Samuel Courtauld had recently provided for an Institute of Art, enabling it to open in a very grand style in that same year of 1932.

When, two years later, the London University Institute of Archaeology came officially into being it existed only on paper, with no premises and no full-time staff. However, a strong Management Committee had been set up, again under the chairmanship of Sir Charles Peers.

The first students to be formally enrolled were Rachel Clay and Barbara Parker, two intelligent girls who were to have useful careers in archaeology. In their strangely immaterial academic settings, these pioneer students presently forsook British archaeology and turned instead to the East. This shift, in Rachel's case, was due in part to the positive attraction of discoveries in Western Asia, but also to the extreme disapproval she felt for Rik Wheeler's personal life, as it was to be observed in the mid-thirties. Whatever its motivation, this turning to the light of the Orient was to prove of value to the future of the Institute, as the students' demand for tuition in an unestablished subject was to lead to its provision. In all their academic difficulties it was Tessa who proved invariably helpful in finding them classes and tutors.

This preference for oriental studies can also be seen as part of a change that was affecting the growth of the infant Institute as a whole. No one knows just what outlines were drawn in the original 'blueprint', but it seems certain that Wheeler's first intention concerned British archaeology alone. Then fate, in the not inappropriate person of Sir Flinders Petrie, had intervened. The Wheelers, as beggars, could not be choosers, and for Rik there was no dangerous compromise in welcoming Asia within his province. His one avowed intent was for a post-graduate school to train professional archaeologists in the skills and objectives of purposeful excavation and fieldwork of all kinds. There was no reason at all, as he himself was to prove so brilliantly, why such professionalism should not be employed as advantageously in the East as at home.

Meanwhile the most urgent need was to find a lodging for an institute which for the present had no roof of its own. Tessa took on the greater share of that most depressing of pursuits – the search for decent accommodation with little money to pay for it. How often did she set out hopefully on some wearisome journey, only to find a place too large or too small or squalid beyond hope of redemption? As Rik wrote, 'We scoured London for the impossible – a large building at next to no rent.' Then at last they achieved the impossible: they found St John's Lodge in the green heart of Regent's Park.

It was a piece of amazing, if well-earned, good fortune that the Wheelers should have come upon this house, derelict since it had served as a wartime hospital, standing beside the little inner ring road that was part of Nash's grand design for the Royal Park. The oldest part of the Lodge, in the 'Grecian style', was one of the villas included in this scheme, but it had been greatly enlarged in early Victorian times by Sir Charles Barry, in what Rik called 'Barry Italian'. He always found genuine enjoyment in architectural manners and so welcomed having so stylish and historic a home for the Institute, shabby though it was. Moreover, it contained two libraries with ready book-shelves and a ballroom more than big enough to house the contents of the Petrie packing-cases. Perhaps the greatest good fortune of all, St John's Lodge, being Crown property, came under the jurisdiction of the First Commissioner of Works, who at that time was Mr Ormsby-Gore (later the fourth Baron Harlech), who had all the sympathy that went with a very real interest in archaeology.

Even with the First Commissioner's support there were inevitable delays in securing the tenancy. In July of 1935 Wheeler wrote to Sir George Hill of the British Museum (briefly substituting for Peers as chairman of the Management Committee), 'My wife has stirred up Crown Lands, with the result that the lease of St. John's Lodge is, I am told, being "speeded up", a very relative term!' At last, however, negotiations were completed and the lease was secured at a peppercorn rent. 'Crown Lands', no doubt, were glad to find tenants who would take on the responsibility for repairing and maintaining their shamefully neglected property.

While the restoration of the Lodge began and Tessa continued her fund-raising and other labours for the Institute, Rik had the delicate task of enrolling a staff before accommodation or adequate salaries were available for them. He himself had accepted the post of Honorary Director, and some other specialists were to serve temporarily for little or no pay. In that same letter to Sir George Hill Rik was preparing the way for what was to prove an important appointment. Referring to the secretaryship of the Management Committee, he wrote, 'I propose to suggest Kathleen Kenyon for the job. She is a level-headed person, with useful experience both in this country and in Palestine.'

Kathleen was a daughter of Sir Frederic Kenyon, the eminent biblical scholar, later to succeed Sir George as Director of the British Museum and to precede Wheeler as Secretary of the British Academy. She herself had been one of the Wheelers' early trainees in digging and was by now a leading member of the excavating team. At this time nearing thirty years old, she was an immensely able and formidable product of St Paul's and Somerville – she had in very truth been a hockey captain. Lacking in grace in her appearance and writing of English, she became a good administrator and a great excavator by sheer weight of character. She could command her work-force, whether of British labourers or felaheen, with complete authority. Her appointment to the Management Committee, duly secured by Rik, was to mean her secretaryship of the Institute itself, a job she was to hold for over a decade, including a spell when she was Acting Director during Rik's absence at the war and in India.

In the post-war years Max Mallowan, recalling the days when he occupied a chair at the Institute, said of Kathleen Kenyon, 'Woe betide those who opposed her, or were not of the same mind. I was often asked how we got on together at the University and I always replied, "Perfectly, because I always gave way."' It is therefore not surprising that after their long association in excavation and high archaeological affairs, Rik's relationship with Kathleen became stormy and suspicious.

The year 1936 opened with the highest promise for Rik and Tessa. After so much hard work, so many delays and frustrations, their dream was near fulfilment. Their institute was in being, and a worthy home was being prepared for it; the Maiden Castle excavations were going very well indeed and arousing widespread interest in British prehistory. Wheeler himself – it is now hard to believe – had never been even so far east as the Levant: his beloved foundation was going to be much involved with Asian studies and there was every good reason for him to acquaint himself at least with the nearer shores of the Orient. In the early spring he had raised sufficient funds to enable him to arrange what he called 'a solitary pilgrimage to the Levant'. It must be admitted that there were personal reasons, as well as the shortage of money, that counted with him in his decision to set out alone.

In *Still Digging* there is a lively account of the voyage on a French liner from Marseilles to Port Said. Rik was travelling First Class, but soon wearied of the company and 'fled to the lower classes'. In the Second he encountered an oil technician who, on hearing he was an archaeologist, exclaimed, 'Coo —— *that's* an OUT-OF-THE-WAY JOB'. Penetrating still lower, Rik found in the Fourth a merry, racially motley crew who were dancing to a drum and banjo. 'There alone in the whole vast ship, it seemed, were real, living people, uninhibited by Oxford Greats and unemasculated by Cairene lubricity.' Then, to his astonishment, he recognized among them a handsome, well-born young archaeologist, Peter Murray-Thriepland, who proved to be going out to dig under Sir Leonard Woolley. At the sight of this young man, whom he knew slightly and was to encounter again in his personal life, 'In my ridiculous boiled shirt I suddenly felt heartily ashamed of myself. Of course, that was the way to travel, sitting at night in the swinging shadows above the churning propellers amongst these happy polychrome outcasts. . . .' He admits, however, that he eventually went up to his stateroom and took a bath.

In Egypt Wheeler visited the W. B. Emerys on their Nile houseboat and was taken by them to see their soundly conducted excavations among Old Kingdom tombs at Sakkara. Travelling up through Sinai to his principal destinations in Palestine, the Lebanon and Syria, 'alive with excavators of many nations', he immediately, as he had antici-pated, found much to criticize or condemn. At several excavations, perhaps most notably that of the Americans at Megiddo, there was an abundance of equipment and work on a large scale but 'such technical standards as had not been tolerated in Great Britain for a quarter of a century'. There was no real mastery of stratification, and in general methods of discovery and recording were lamentable.

Depression was lifted for a while by a visit to the great historic site of

Ugarit, on the Syrian coast, where the digging was being directed by the brilliant Alsatian, Claude Schaeffer, in the company of his charming and domesticated wife, Odile. Rik was soon to encounter Claude in his official capacity during his expeditions to northern France, and often after that on Unesco conferences and the like. On this occasion Odile served up a plump chicken, a rarity in that part of the world, stolen for her by a grateful murderer, one of the convicts who provided the labour at Ugarit.

Rik also found comfort in the company, for some part of his time in Palestine, of a remarkable young woman, the then reigning sovereign of his love life, a fact that it seems should be recorded for the effect it must have had in his reactions to the impending tragedy.

Of the end of this, his first introduction to the continent that was to mean so much to his career, Wheeler wrote, 'I left the Near East sick at heart, ferociously determined to make my new Institute in London first and foremost an effective medium for the enlargement of technical understanding. Without that, archaeology of the sort which I had witnessed was in large measure destruction.' So, with this ferocious determination, he set out for home. He had been away six weeks, with no fixed address and no contact with the world outside his uncharted travels. He had come by sea and determined to return over land: at Aleppo he boarded the Transcontinental Express for Boulogne. In Paris his coach was shunted through those dark and mysterious byways of the *chemin de fer* then so familiar to European travellers. When they brought him to the Gare du Nord he secured a copy of *The Times*. Turning the pages for his first news of the home country, he came upon the obituary column, and the heading TESSA VERNEY WHEELER. She had died three days before, on 15 April, after an operation. In his letter of appreciation to *The Times* Sir Frederic Kenyon had written with unconscious truth that 'her husband was away, *largely* in pursuit of his archaeological studies' (italics added).

Rik Wheeler was to describe this terrible event in his life out of context in his autobiography, placing it at the end of his account of the First World War. This he did in order to set it beside his week at Passchendaele: in the battle he had experienced the worst in physical suffering; now, almost twenty years later, he was to feel the worst in mental pain and misery. As he sat there in the railway carriage his first instinct, his first bodily reaction, was for anaesthesia. 'I pressed the bell-button and ordered a double brandy. My unfocussed eyes turned from the unreality of the printed page; at the same time a kindly numbness entered into my mind and threw it also out of focus, a condition in which it was happily to remain during the following days. . . .'

In London a friend of Rik and Tessa, Molly Cotton, had been meeting every boat train with the intention of breaking the news to Rik, should he arrive in ignorance of it. She gave herself this task because from a chance encounter in Jerusalem she alone knew his whereabouts and also that his travels had not been altogether solitary. Molly was perhaps the most fully mature human being in the Wheelers' archaeological circle, and for this good reason had been able to understand both of them and accept the dark element in their relationship.

Molly Cotton was waiting at Victoria Station when Rik arrived, and although the particular service she had intended was not necessary, he was thankful for her support then and for a long time to come. She it was who drove husband and son to the Golders Green Crematorium. Her presence was doubly welcome, for Michael, who all his life had been so close to his mother, could hardly endure her loss, and, although he did his best to control it, felt bitterness against his father. In his misery, he could hardly fail to blame Rik for the tremendous burden of work Tessa had accepted, however willingly, and for the unfaithfulness (some part of which he knew) which had caused her so much unhappiness.

When Rik had said goodbye to his wife six weeks before she was as well as usual and he believed he had her blessing. She knew of his current love affair, but whether she had any inkling of his pursuit of it on this journey can never be known. He recorded of their final parting, 'I remember turning back as I went down the stairs of our little Park Street flat, and can still hear the words which followed me in her quiet voice: "Goodbye – and remember, you are very precious."'

No doubt there are many to whom, knowing the circumstances, Rik's account of Tessa's death, presented in *Still Digging*, will appear as sickening humbug. Yet those of us who were his friends, or who had some understanding of his complexities, cannot wholly accept this judgement.

Rik had truly loved his wife and was still very fond. He recognized how much he owed her and was proud of her achievements; he took pleasure in their public image as 'the Wheelers'. Moreover, her death was quite genuinely a dreadful blow to him and one which he never forgot. The far from admirable truth seems to be that he knew she would not desert him, and had come to accept her as the rock on which much of his life was founded. That being so, he was prepared to trample on her feelings, trusting to her endurance and forgetting that rocks can be removed.

The last phase of their twenty-two years together had brought Tessa much misery: there are many witnesses to that. She had undoubtedly found satisfaction in her success as an excavator and in her growing reputation as an archaeologist in her own right. She must have found it, too, in the building up of the Institute, in which she played so substantial a part. But Rik was at his most libidinous during the thirties (his forties) and he took no pains to conceal the fact. Whether they were working at Lancaster House or in the field, his amours could be conspicuous and Tessa had to witness all the evidence: scenes of jealousy when one mistress was being supplanted by the next; girls turning crimson at the sight of her husband, and in one case jealous hostility towards herself. The tension between them must often have been great: once, at Maiden Castle, when Rik came up unexpectedly from behind and put his hands on her shoulders Tessa fainted.

Those of us in the archaeological world who were not in their immediate circle could not fail to know something of these affairs, but it was usual to say 'Isn't Tessa wonderful?' and to believe that she handled them easily, accepting them as an inevitable part of life with Rik. This was not so. Several times in the museum she was caught in tears and on one occasion, with rare over-dramatization, she took Rik's revolver to Mr Henderson, begging him to keep it out of her way. When a girl diploma student found Tessa in such floods of tears in her office that she could not, as she had before, pretend that they were due to hay fever, she confessed their cause, but insisted that all allowances must be made for her husband. He had genius, she was the plodder. This girl, who came to know Tessa well and to receive her confidences, felt sure that she believed she had lost Rik and lived in dread that he would abandon her. Michael, too, knew that his mother was fearful that one mistress or the next would carry him off.

Almost all those who moved in the Wheelers' orbit were devoted to Tessa. Nearly all of them felt intense sympathy with her and some have never ceased to condemn Rik for the utter carelessness and insensitivity of his treatment of her.

There is one close observer of those years who finds it possible to take a much harsher view of Tessa, what might be called a psychological hard line. As the critic, though prejudiced, was certainly giving an honest opinion, it is right to set it out here:

It seemed to me Tessa used his insulting behaviour – which was to be found in his actions but never in the way he spoke to or of her – to launch a cult round herself as a brave little woman battling with superb courage against all odds, a cult which continues to this day. She undoubtedly was made very unhappy, but I thought she could have checked him had she chosen to do so. His ambitions were such that he would not have risked a divorce. . . . The fact that she never used the power she possessed over him is one of the reasons why I feel she 'fed' him.

Such an interpretation of the relationship will be almost universally condemned and denied – and I think rightly. Some women will fight by any means to keep a man: Tessa was not one of them; the mere thought of a threat of divorce to hold the man she adored would have gone wholly against her nature. The idea that she actually encouraged her husband to find girls, that she 'fed' him, seems to me preposterous. It is a psychological possibility, true enough, but a woman playing such a part could not have inspired the admiring affection felt for Tessa by men and women of every kind. She could not have possessed the expression, the smile, that Tessa never lost.

If this brutal judgement does relate, at a distance, to an acceptable truth, it is this. Very many women like to be dominated by their men, and such women, naturally, were always drawn to Rik Wheeler. Some among them may go further and develop some degree of emotional masochism. It is possible that Tessa was one of these. Yet, after all, it must be remembered that she is known to have looked back to the happy time, the time before Rik's behaviour became so nearly intolerable, with profound regret.

There are those sentimentalists who believe that Tessa Wheeler died of what is summed up in the phrase 'a broken heart'. That view, too, is hardly to be believed. Although her small body must have had some toughness to endure the overwork, the absence of holidays that had become habitual, Tessa was not altogether strong. She had suffered black-outs as early as the Caerleon days; towards the end of her life she developed an internal ulcer, and this, together with the stress which presumably caused it, had aged her face and perhaps reduced her stamina.

Tessa had resolved to have a small operation performed on her foot while Rik was in the Levant. That he did not know of this is vouched for by their archaeological colleague, Ralegh Radford, who chanced to meet her in the street after Rik had left. She told him about the operation, and also that she had said nothing of it to Rik. It was hardly a serious enough matter to call for a cover-up lie. She was normally well and cheerful.

For the work on her toe, Tessa entered a nursing home, but while there she developed severe pains, diagnosed as appendicitis, and was removed to the National Temperance Hospital, off the Tottenham Court Road. When she was opened up her appendix proved to be in a perfectly healthy state. On 14 April, after four or five days, when she appeared to be making a good recovery, she was visited by Molly Cotton, just back from Palestine. Molly found her in good spirits, looking forward to a visit that evening from Michael and talking of how soon she could go home. Michael, who was now up at Christ Church, Oxford, had been performing in an OUDS production of *Richard II* and his mother had heard it broadcast.

That evening Michael turned up as arranged, bringing an Oxford friend with him, and they were quite merry together. At 2 am Michael was woken up at the Park Street flat by the telephone bell. It was a summons to go at once to the hospital, and when he asked for news the voice only repeated that he was to go at once. So certain did he feel of disaster that, on encountering a doctor at the Temperance Hospital, he asked at once, 'Is she dead?' The reply, which to Michael's ear was uttered in sickeningly jolly tones, was 'Oh yes, she died a couple of hours ago.' Tessa had suffered a pulmonary embolism which had proved fatal.

The next morning the same young woman who had found Tessa weeping and had gained her confidence came to the hospital with flowers. A nurse who had attended Tessa broke the news to her and went on to declare that her patient 'need not have died', that 'she had no will to live'. This was merely a nurse's impression, and is inconsistent with Tessa's cheerful optimism of the day before. It needs to be recorded, however, for echoes of such words may have contributed to the idea of death from a broken heart.

Sober evidence suggests that there is no need to look beyond normal medical explanations for the tragedy. It may be that Tessa did not have the best possible medical attention – a wrong diagnosis leading to an unnecessary operation – and probably neither hospital nor surgeon were of the top flight. Certainly, too, she was tired and had the added strain of preparing for the final run-up to the opening of the Institute. On the other hand she was looking forward eagerly to that consummation of her work.

The general opinion at the time was that Rik was very much to blame for his carelessness of his wife's health, for allowing her to drive herself so much too hard in conditions for which he himself was responsible. That judgement, strongly shared by Michael, who had been an observer at close quarters and for so long, was a fair one. Rik's behaviour and the unhappiness it caused may have contributed to the general stress, but it most certainly did not affect her will to live.

Tessa had gone, but the strenuous life and all the enterprises in which she had been involved went forward much as before. For the vacation, Rik and Michael continued to live uneasily together at Park Street. On the night of Rik's return, indeed, the young man felt that he could not face a meal there alone with his father and they dined at the Athenaeum. Michael, who was to forget much of his own inner resentments, remembers this dinner as the first occasion when he tried to come closer to his elusive parent. He believed his support was needed since Rik not only felt the blow of Tessa's death very deeply, but would have to face a rising wave of censure among those who had loved her. This effort, however sincere it may have been, was not to be lastingly rewarded.

Wheeler was determined that the Maiden Castle excavations must be completed, declaring that they should be carried out as a memorial to Tessa herself. On these terms he persuaded Molly Cotton to take her place as Deputy Director in the field.

Up to this time Rik's loves and dalliances had caused very little trouble during his digs and were not even universally known. During this sad season of 1936, however, very strong antagonism was generated, particularly among the women members of the team, not only for what had happened but when it became obvious that the Director had no intention of changing his ways. Rik Wheeler was not a man to allow any sense of guilt to affect his conduct. He had not hesitated to have love affairs that caused Tessa unhappiness: he would see no sense in denying himself when she could not suffer. So there, on the nobly carved hilltop in the beautiful and peaceful Dorset countryside, the atmosphere was highly charged.

That winter Rik suffered another loss in the death of his father at the age of eighty. For years he had seen very little of him, but the ending of a relationship that had been so close must have affected him. Robert had remained at Herne Hill with Emily although their feelings had grown no fonder.

During the war Robert had been able to fulfil something of his heroic ideal. By the use of an 'experimenter' he had actually succeeded in tapping German radio and regularly used the information for his paper – probably the first journalist to do so. He also made a practice of leaving his midnight desk to go on patrol among the docks in all weathers. The strain of this voluntary night duty may have caused the blindness that struck him in his mid-sixties. For years after this he had continued to write leaders and reviews. He also kept up the family camping at

Weybridge, darkness failing to end his pleasure in it. He had finally given up work only after he had had a stroke some eight years before his death.

During this most difficult time the younger daughter, Betty, often went to relieve her mother, although her marriage to William Usher had taken her to Beaconsfield. It was Usher's opinion that his brother-in-law should have done more to help his parents. It must also be said that the recognition *The Times* obituary gave to Robert as one of the best informed parliamentary correspondents and a fine critic of the arts makes Rik's pronouncement that his father was 'a failure' in his career appear unduly harsh.

Rik and his sisters attended the funeral in what must by then have been a rare family reunion. Betty was to become a successful physical training mistress, a rowing enthusiast and a leading Girl Guide. In spite of his general antipathy to such doings, Rik was much closer to her than to any other member of his family, spending several Christmases at Beaconsfield. He grieved at her early death. She was to be the only member of the Wheeler family not to reach an eightieth year.

When the season had closed and the aftermath of indoor work was in train Wheeler's main preoccupation was with the opening of St John's Lodge. The date had been fixed for 29 April 1937, almost exactly a year after Tessa's death. There was much to be done in assembling further teaching collections, in procuring cabinets to take the place of packing-cases and at least a modicum of scientific apparatus. There was to be provision for archaeological photography, for conservation and repair, for soil analysis and so forth. Money was still desperately short, but fortunately a handsome gift from Sir Robert Mond provided for much of this equipment.

Some students from the days of the 'paper' Institute were still about and others arrived, while a skeleton staff was somehow held together by Rik's enthusiasm for the future. Appointments were made in Near Eastern and in Biblical Archaeology; the Honorary Director himself, together with Kathleen Kenyon, 'plodded on', as he put it, with Pre-historic and Roman Britain.

For the opening day a distinguished company of college principals, professors, museum directors, a cleric in the person of the Dean of St Paul's, and benefactors represented by Sir Robert Mond and Ernest Makower, assembled in St John's Lodge. The exterior of that charming mansion was now in good order, though it was always to remain a little shabby and makeshift within. The platform had been furnished with handsome gilded chairs and two palms of the more drooping variety.

Onto it mounted the Earl of Athlone, splendid in the gold facings of the Chancellor of London University, the Vice-Chancellor, Sir Charles Peers, Mr Ormsby-Gore, the Academic Registrar and Dr Mortimer Wheeler. A silver mace, much larger than the one displayed by the Antiquaries, lay on a table before them.

The principal speakers were to be Peers, Athlone and Ormsby-Gore, who had recently been promoted from First Commissioner to Colonial Secretary and who was to succeed his father as Lord Harlech in the following year. They had been fully briefed and almost every word that fell from their lips that day had immediately or previously been put into their heads by the Honorary Director.

Sir Charles, having welcomed the Chancellor, gave a brief history of the establishment of the Institute and then defined its objectives. 'It was necessary that the student should find three things – materials for study, instruction in the treatment of antiquities, and training in archaeological method, in research and in the recording of research. That was the irreducible minimum.' This minimum, however, could be extended to an involvement with 'all phases of the story of Nature and of man'.

Peers ended with a view of the future, insisting that 'they looked forward to much greater things, and particularly to finding their permanent quarters in the great new buildings of the University in Bloomsbury. . . .' Athlone took up this theme of the temporary nature of the present arrangements, declaring that 'although he was formally opening the Institute, he was in reality only laying its foundation stone'. The Lodge was adequate for the present and he thanked the authorities of the Crown Lands and the former First Commissioner for their sympathetic help in acquiring it. Even more than Peers, the Chancellor, who had persistent difficulty in pronouncing 'archaeology', then emphasized the scientific direction of the Institute, which was to

provide a laboratory which would fulfil in the study of civilization something of the function which the laboratory has long fulfilled in the study of chemical and physical science. . . . As the study of civilization became more intensive, more detailed and more accurate increasing need arose for the collaboration of the geologist, the botanist, the palaeontologist, and other workers devoted to the study of the physical universe.

The special importance which he went on to attach to the Palestinian collections and British excavations in that country reveal how wholeheartedly Wheeler had now accepted oriental studies within the Institute's programme. This conversion, together with his disapproval of the standard of digging in the Levant, which had shocked him a year before, may also be seen in Ormsby-Gore's words when he rose to thank the Chancellor. Having referred to 'the vacant and derelict eyesore in Regent's Park' about which he had been beset with Parliamentary Questions while First Commissioner, he declared that it could have served no better purpose than to train competent archaeologists to work not only in Britain but 'in those countries where we had imperial responsibilities'. Wheeler spoke only a few of his own words himself, devoting them largely to the idea that the future of archaeology lay with the universities. There was, of course, a desperate need to induce London University, whose Chancellor and Vice-Chancellor were sitting beside him, to follow mere recognition of his Institute with a substantial endowment.

After declaring the Institute open the Earl of Athlone unveiled a memorial to Tessa Verney Wheeler. It was a black marble tablet, inscribed in elegant Roman lettering, set in the library wall. It evoked a palpable living presence to all of us there assembled.

In the purposes and ideals that Rik Wheeler had caused to be uttered on that opening day there is already a hint of a divergence of thought that was to lead at last to his disenchantment with some of the results of archaeological science and technology. The laboratory is not at all a good analogy for the type of institute he had initiated. In a sense the science of chemistry is contained in its laboratory. Wheeler rightly saw that the knowledge, skills and techniques of the natural sciences would and should be increasingly employed by archaeologists but always for him they were tools to be used for the extension and illumination of history. As he declared when looking back from 1954,

... our institute ... was founded primarily as a workshop in which the relevant sciences could be interrelated and assembled in a humanistic environment and to the better understanding of humanity. It represented the culmination of my efforts, begun almost *in vacuo* after the First World War, to convert archaeology into a discipline worthy of that name in all senses.

No one in 1937, or even in 1954, could have foreseen how in the sixties and seventies a new generation of archaeological scientists were to become so wholly committed to ingenious techniques, computerized statistics and attempts to apply scientific laws to the human past as often to be obliged to ignore all the higher faculties of their species. Certainly Rik could not, for he had nothing of the natural scientist in him, either by nature or nurture. He was a being mentally compounded of the arts and humanities, for whom man was 'Noble' or he was nothing.

In 1954 he could well be satisfied with what he and Tessa had created, for in many ways it was during the post-war decade that St John's Lodge came closest to providing a 'humanistic environment', where creative historical teaching and research could be pursued. In a few years the wish that the Institute should be rehoused in Bloomsbury was to be granted. We shall find it moving to a glassy new building in Gordon Square.

To understand Rik's vision of his institute, it has to be appreciated that he always saw it as closely linked with excavation. The scientific aids to be developed there were for the most part intended to make the higher purposes of selective excavation more effective. This relationship hardly had to be formulated, since all through the embryonic years at Lancaster House the Wheelers were in fact using such staff and equipment as they had to conduct excavations that were a great advance in British, and indeed world, archaeology. There on the platform, in his dark suit and academic gown, with well-groomed hair, Rik looked urbane and distinguished. He might almost have been mistaken for the Master of a college. Soon he would be back in his old digging clothes, lord of the trenches and earthworks. That was where he was at his best and where he most liked to be.

CHAPTER 7

Digging Up People

OF THE THIRTEEN years between Wheeler's return from Cardiff to London and the outbreak of war, there was not one when he was not supervising an excavation, and for the greater part of the time he was actively directing excavations on a scale never before attempted in this country. At Segontium and the Brecon Gaer he had been to some extent learning the craft. Now, although he continued to improve his methods in digging, recording and publication, he was already a master, and, moreover, had command of first-rate assistants whom he and Tessa had trained.

Kathleen Kenyon, who knew Rik so well as a director in the field, wrote after his death, 'Excavation method was only one of Rik's contributions, perhaps not even the greatest, but I put it first since it was the basis of all else he did. . . . Admittedly, nowadays, many minutiae are added, but I doubt if anyone goes to the heart of interpreting a site as he did.' This judgement is universally accepted, and probably most archaeologists would also agree that the two principal excavations of the thirties, those published in the splendid volumes, *Verulamium* and *Maiden Castle*, saw Rik, with Tessa at his shoulder, attain his apotheosis as an excavator. It is true, as has been mentioned, that the Reports were to be criticized by a rising generation as too stylish, positive and finished, but in them, and in the brilliantly directed work which they recorded, Wheeler surely approached his own ideal. The totality of his achievement in India was to be even more important, more extraordinary in its extent, and less open to criticism. The two English excavations remain his most fitting monuments because they were the most perfect on his own terms.

During the early years at Lancaster House Rik was too busy building up the London Museum and establishing his own power base in London to consider such ambitious undertakings. Also he and Tessa, despite their hurried exit from Wales, were still involved with the Principality. Even after her return from Caerleon in the summer of 1927, much remained to be done at the amphitheatre and they both had to pay frequent visits, as well as preparing for its publication in *Archaeologia*. In spite of its embarrassing start, this dig ended very happily. The history of the building from the time it was first constructed by soldiers of the Second Legion from the nearby fortress was firmly established and the whole place cleared and restored. It was now easy to imagine the arena, with the legionaries drilling there, or when wild beast and other shows were staged and the banks of wooden seats were alive with spectators. As a crowning gesture of generosity, the *Daily Mail* presented the monument to the nation.

Early in 1928 Wheeler was able to announce that the excavation of the amphitheatre was finished – although work on the legionary fortress was to continue for years under the direction of his faithful disciple, Nash-Williams. Plans were now already afoot for the Wheelers to shift to a site not very far from Caerleon (near enough for them to keep an eye on the restoration work), yet one which could be called English. This was in Lydney Park, on the southern edge of the ancient Forest of Dean, in that part of Gloucestershire that lies west of the wide Severn estuary and is by nature a part of the Welsh foothills. The setting was almost as agreeable as that of the Brecon Gaer, for the site itself is on one of many wooded spurs running down to the river: as Rik wrote, it 'commands a vista of luxuriant forest and spacious estuary which can scarcely be matched for beauty even in a county of pleasant parklands.... The spur is flanked by deep glens ... and the whole deer-park, whereof it is now a feature, had been enriched by many generations of the Bathurst family with a great variety of timber....'

It was an enlightened move by the head of the Bathurst family, the then Lord Bledisloe, that led to the re-excavation of the well-known remains of antiquity on his estate. Early in the nineteenth century his great-grandfather had laid bare a temple and other Roman buildings on the spur, one part of which stood just high enough to win the name of Dwarf's Chapel. For that age the digging had been thoroughly done and, even more surprising, well-recorded. After various vicissitudes, a version of this record had been published just half a century before Lord Bledisloe appealed to the Society of Antiquaries to arrange for the rescue of the ruins, by then neglected and overgrown.

Charles Peers, glad enough to use the services of the star performer whom he had recently helped back to London, was one of those who invited Rik to accept the commission. To tackle a site already stripped by gentlemen of the romantic age of antiquarianism usually has few attractions, yet Rik welcomed it as 'a pleasant task'. He probably liked the country and the prospects of fishing, but he was also tempted by the challenge to prove that, with expert digging, the place could still be made to reveal its history.

He said of Lydney Park that chance enabled him to 'assume the study of a site upon which I had already set my eye', while at the same time confessing that this dig was, in a sense, 'an interruption in the ordered programme of fieldwork I had mapped out'. Although there was truth in this, the Lydney excavation can be seen in itself as just right for an intermediate stage between the Wheelers' Welsh campaign and their two great undertakings in lowland England. If, geographically, the place was a perfect half-way house in this advance, so, too, was its archaeological content. In Wales they had been concerned with the neat, well-regimented installations of the Roman military; now they were introduced not only to the far more varied and untidy remains of civilian life of the Roman age, but also to the pre-Roman natives and the survival of these humble Celtic folk under Roman rule.

In the *Report on the Excavation of the Prehistoric, Roman and Post-Roman Site in Lydney Park, Gloucestershire*, published jointly by Rik and Tessa in 1932, their first to be issued by the Research Committee of the Society of Antiquaries, Rik initiated what was to be his regular practice of opening the record with a brief summary. There can be no better way of presenting the historical findings of those two summer seasons of 1928–9 than by reproducing it here.

A 'promontary fort', or small embanked hill-town, five acres in extent, was established at Lydney in or shortly before the first century BC and was subsequently, during the second and third centuries AD, occupied by a Romano-British population, engaged to some extent in iron-mining. An intact iron-mine, not later than the third century AD, has been partially explored. Soon after AD 364–7 a temple, dedicated to the otherwise unknown deity of Nodens, was built within the earthwork, and with the temple, which was of unusual plan, were associated guesthouse, baths and other structures, indicating that the cult was an important centre of pilgrimage. About the end of the fourth century, the buildings were surrounded by a precinct wall; but, later, they fell into decay, and the final phases of occupation, co-inciding probably with the fifth and sixth centuries, is represented by a reinforcement of the prehistoric earthwork. Amongst the 'finds', the prehistoric pottery and brooches, the Roman bronze figurine of a dog, the hoard of small sub-Roman coins, and the post-Roman brooch are noteworthy.

This masterpiece of compression shows how well Wheeler succeeded in extracting the evidence needed for so complete a reconstruction, even from a previously cleared site. This was possible because, as he said, the Bathurst diggers had dug down to the floors of the Roman buildings and then stopped. This brought them plenty of coins and pleasing objects for the curio cabinets of the great house, or to give away to friends and relations, but for archaeologists reliable dating evidence is to be looked for below floors rather than above them. With the abundance of coins and dateable pottery on the site, Rik had no difficulty in setting up the sound chronological framework that was always his prime objective.

The Report as a whole is of interest as being the prototype for the Wheelers' later, more important and grandiose publications. The volume is logically ordered on what became a standard scheme, well laid out and lettered and illustrated with Rik's own elegant plans, sections and drawings of mosaics and small finds. In all this his own designs were enhanced by the high standards of the Oxford University Press.

In his record of an excavation that had something personal and light-hearted about it, Rik allowed himself to indulge his fondness for figure-drawing. In a little reconstruction of the Nodens establishment in Roman times, he not only peopled it with busy inhabitants, but enlivened the foreground with the portrayal of a young deer quietly looking down on the scene.

The Lydney dig must in fact have proved quite a pleasant task. The work was not too strenuous, there was no great mass of earth to be shifted, and, although the prehistoric earthworks were duly sampled, no huge and complicated sections had to be cut. Moreover, the history being revealed was consistently interesting. It was surprising to find a pagan religious centre thriving through the last half-century of Roman rule, and for the site to remain inhabited, though with some return to barbarism, after that rule was ended. The discovery of an iron-mine (with the pick marks of the miners well preserved), unique in being securely dated to the Roman period, was a totally unexpected bonus.

Then again Rik could enjoy himself making the historical comparisons always dear to him. Perhaps the most interesting was the inference that the pilgrims flocked to seek the help of Nodens mainly as a god of healing. Many figurines of dogs, presumably votive offerings, had been found at Lydney, and the commodious bath-house was evidently a public building. 'Now in the classical religions, the dog is most widely associated with cults of healing. At Epidaurus, dogs sacred to Asklepios were kept in the temple, and are recorded to have been instrumental in healing by licking the affected parts.' Furthermore, 'At Epidaurus,

Wheeler's reconstruction of the Nodens establishment

also, baths were added to the temple-settlement of Asklepios in Roman times, and bathing was frequently prescribed by the god ... as a curative measure.' From this Wheeler inferred, though cautiously, that his obscure Celtic deity shared some of the attributes of the divine physician of the Greeks. Cult objects suggest that Nodens also had powers over the sun and the sea: as Rik wrote, 'Fishermen from the Severn must have toiled up the narrow, rocky path to this shrine.'

One incident occurred during the second season at Lydney that is of uncanny interest since it seems to raise Rik's famous archaeological intuition to the level of magical divination. One day during the lunch break he was sitting on a wall of the bath-house beside one of the more dilapidated mosaics at a point where a hole in the *tesserae* had, in ancient times, been patched with rough cement. 'Beside it lay a pick, and the conjunction of idleness and opportunity was too much for me. I drove the point of the pick into the cement patch. ... As the lump of cement came away, the dark soil beneath it was of a sudden freckled with minute green specks.' The specks proved to be 1,646 tiny coins, *minimi* so small that they filled only half a teacup. They represented some kind of inflation in the sub-Roman economy of the fifth century.

It was characteristic that, Rik having found the hoard in this extra-ordinary way, Tessa, with Michael's help, laboured over the classification and wrote the account of the coins in the Report. Rik commented, 'When a newspaper a few days after the discovery hailed it as "King Arthur's Small Change", the shot was nearer the mark than it had the right to be. The Lydney Hoard, veritable symbol of the Dark Ages, would alone have justified our two seasons work on that lovely spot.'

The company and conditions at Lydney were also agreeable. The Bledisloes were hospitable and much interested in the digging, but were anxious that the tranquillity of their park should not be disturbed by too many visitors. Their wishes were, of course, respected – and easily, since there was no necessity to raise funds. Of the few assistants, one was the young Kenneth Oakley to whom Rik had given sage advice, and another an Australian, Dermot Casey, who was to join the Wheelers' regular team for later excavations and who aided Wheeler at a time of need in India. There seem to have been no women students as yet to cause Tessa anxiety. (The third Viscount Bledisloe told me of a family tradition that none of the housemaids was safe from Rik. I got the impression, however, that this was hardly a matter of fact but rather a sign that the Bathursts were aware of his reputation.)

Among distinguished and useful visitors were Davies Pryce, a wise elder with a vast knowledge of Samian pottery, who became Rik's friend and counsellor, and the brilliant R. G. Collingwood, who was as much a Roman archaeologist as an Oxford philosopher. He was to provide a special report on the inscriptions from the site. An appendix of impenetrable learning on the name Nodens was contributed by a little-known young professor, one J. R. R. Tolkien.

The Lydney excavations wound up satisfactorily and in a sudden burst of publicity. The press was summoned to hear Lord Bledisloe announce his gift of the site to the nation. He was not to be outdone by the *Daily Mail*. The news received sufficient coverage, and on 21 September 1929 *The Times* published a photograph of Dr and Mrs Wheeler accompanying Lord and Lady Bledisloe on a visit to what was left of their ruins.

By the time of these closing scenes at Lydney Park the first stirrings of the Wheelers' next, and far greater, enterprise had already begun far away in the home counties. It was in 1929 that the Corporation of St Albans acquired a stretch of pleasant Hertfordshire countryside to the west of the town, with the laudable purpose of shaping it into a public park, and playing-fields. Their purchase, which lay just across the little River Ver, included the southern part of Roman Verulamium. This historic town, built astride Watling Street and adjoining a ford, was well known to everybody, since some two miles of the embanked city walls were still standing, in places up to twelve feet in height, and enclosing nearly two hundred acres. If they have a sadly worm-eaten appearance, it is because the good Roman bricks were systematically plundered and reused by the builders of the Norman abbey, leaving only flint rubble and brick footings and binding courses behind.

Early the next year the city fathers resolved to seek the counsel of the Society of Antiquaries on the possibility of exploring the Roman site before it was laid out for the enjoyment of their electors. Rik Wheeler was always to declare that he had long before determined that Verulamium was by far the best choice for the much-needed excavation of a Romano-British city – that it was, in fact, a part of his 'ordered programme of fieldwork'. Since the Corporation's prompt application to the Antiquaries seems an unexpected move in the conditions of 1930, it is possible that his thinking had in some way been conveyed to the Councillors. However this may be, the approach was made, the Society was sympathetic, and in the beginning of February a meeting was held at St Albans. It was to seal an agreement that excavations should be carried out and that Wheeler would direct them.

Alfred Clapham, as secretary of the society, Dermot Casey and I attended upon the Mayor and Corporation at a hospitable luncheon which was served to us in the charming Regency town hall overlooking the busy market place. It so happens that I have had a long experience of mayors, and am amongst their most fervent admirers. They represent the heart of England, these proud, courteous, friendly, sensible folk, who rise from their railway-ticket offices and their shops to attend in state to the affairs of their fellow citizens. And the mayor on this occasion was no exception. He was Mr. Ironmonger, the butcher; folk used to come from miles round to buy his honest sausages, and surely an honest sausage is the hallmark of a worthy butcher. We sat at his table, drank an unadventurous Graves, and then rose in turn and made our little speeches.

Whatever thoughts and feelings may pass through the mind on reading these words of Rik's, the essential fact remains that the mayor would in truth get on well with him: he and his successors and their colleagues gave friendly backing to the Director and his work through four seasons.

Led by *The Times*, the press made much of this meeting with the St Albans Council and the decision to excavate. Once action had been agreed upon, a Verulamium Excavation Committee was set up under the chairmanship of the ubiquitous Sir Charles Peers. It was an august body, well able to win respect and subscriptions for the ambitious undertaking. The Marquess of Salisbury consented to be its President; the Earl of Verulam and Mr Ironmonger were Vice-Presidents; Davies Pryce joined the Wheelers to make a triumvirate of Directors of Excavations, while other old friends and colleagues – Casey, Clapham, Collingwood – were among the members. Further worthies of St Albans were also enrolled, so that the London and Hertfordshire interests were well balanced.

The necessity to raise funds is brought out by the fact that the Society of Antiquaries, under whose aegis the digging was to be done, was able to contribute only £200, to be divided between Verulamium and a second major excavation which by chance was to begin in the same year. This was at Camulodunum – Roman and pre-Roman Colchester, and under the direction of Wheeler's former pupil, Christopher Hawkes. Verulamium and Camulodunum had had close historical ties and were directly linked by a Roman road, yet there was curiously little communication between the two excavation teams, despite the fact that Rik and Christopher were still on quite friendly terms.

It was, of course, through the four long seasons of fieldwork in and around Verulamium that the Wheelers recruited the band of assistants, of whom many were soon trained to take considerable responsibility as supervisors. Among those who already had enough experience to take charge of sections were Dermot Casey, who had been at Lydney, and Kathleen Kenyon; Paul Baillie Reynolds, from the Ancient Monuments Department of the Office of Works (where he was later Chief Inspector) was another. Among Rik's list of his 'willing team' there were, not unexpectedly, no less than eight young women, several of whom were blessed with both good looks and ability.

Their names reveal how far the Wheelers were able to carry out their aim for a fruitful combination of their museum and academic teaching with practical training in the field. In addition to Kathleen, whose share in establishing the Institute of Archaeology was to be so great, there were Thalassa Cruso from the London Museum staff, and Rachel Clay and Nancy de Crespigny, who were among Rik's university students. A new recruit, also to be a student, was Leslie Scott, a composed and beautiful blonde whom we shall encounter working with Rik right up to the outbreak of war.

There were many good reasons behind Rik's preference for Verulamium to represent a civilian city in his programme of selective excavation. First and simplest, it was only twenty miles from Hyde Park Corner, yet was set in open country, having escaped the fate of so many Roman towns of being sealed below the streets of later successors. The defences, it is true, were extensively planted with trees, but this was a minor hindrance. Its closeness to London allowed Rik to race up for his lectures and other commitments and also made it accessible to the large numbers of visitors he hoped to attract.

Even more appealing than these practical advantages was the history of the place, so exactly suited to his tastes, in its mingling of archaeological with written evidence, of protohistoric with Roman Britain. From references by classical writers, including Julius Caesar, and from the distribution of inscribed British coins, it was virtually certain that this part of Hertfordshire lay within the territory of the Belgic tribe of the Catuvellauni, and that one of their kings, Tasciovanus, ruled and had his mint at Verulamium. It had also been inferred that his far more famous predecessor, Cassivellaunus, gallant leader of the resistance to Caesar, also ruled from Verulamium, and made his last stand here in 54 BC before his capital, a place 'admirably fortified by nature and art', was stormed by Caesar and he was forced to sue for peace.

So when Rik and Tessa, having made their preparations with all speed, assembled their forces and equipment at St Albans in the summer of 1930, they were in high hopes not only of exposing one of the chief cities of Britannia, but also of discovering the *oppidum* of Tasciovanus and perhaps of Cassivellaunus as well.

It had been generally assumed that the Roman town was built over the native capital, and some even thought that the stout bank behind the Roman walls might be its ancient rampart. The first step in Rik's tactical plan was therefore to test these assumptions. Deep pits were sunk within the southern part of the walled area, while at the same time sections were cut through the defences themselves. No traces of any pre-Roman settlement were found, and the embankment, like the wall, was shown to be no earlier than the second century AD. For Rik, these soundings sufficiently proved that the British *oppidum* had not stood here by the banks of the Ver and must be sought elsewhere.

Its pursuit was to last over further seasons, and even then, so far as King Cassivellaunus was concerned, to have no absolutely certain conclusion. Rik wrote, 'To me the whole episode was of surpassing interest as the first occasion upon which I had to plan my work in terms, not of a site, but of a landscape. Our work in fact extended over five miles of countryside. . . .'

Most excavators, it is safe to say, would have abandoned the quest for the Belgic princes and found quite enough to occupy them in discovering the character and history of a large Roman town. But for Rik the prospect of the hunt, of exercising his tactical sense and intuition, his imaginative understanding of people and their likely actions, was irresistible. When, in later seasons, he had to supervise digging 'over five miles of countryside' there was even good reason to revive his wartime love of horses and riding (shared in their time by the Belgic aristocracy) and approach outlying sites at the gallop. This extension of his responsibilities as Director of Excavations was made possible by the wise agreement between them that Tessa should take charge of their principal and most arduous task, the selective excavation of Roman Verulamium.

When Wheeler came to write his book on archaeological method, *Archaeology from the Earth* (1954), he selected his Verulamium campaign as an example of what he meant by advance tactical planning: 'The conscious and careful sequence . . . present continuously from the outset in the mind of the director.' Although he stated that the problem confronting him there was the unravelling of the history of a Roman and pre-Roman city, it is noticeable that, in fact, his account of that unravelling in six successive stages made only the barest mention of the Roman excavations.

This search in half-a-dozen stages for the Belgae in general and Tasciovanus and Cassivellaunus in particular still provides a good example of the success of Rik's forward planning, even though some errors have since come to light. Stage one consisted of the tests already described, which established the fact that any Belgic *oppidum* had to be sought outside the Roman walls. The next step carried the search only just outside them, to an angular bank and ditch projecting from their west side and extending up the slope towards the plateau forming the western rim of the valley. This earthwork, known as the Fosse, appeared to be earlier than the walls, and excavation (a tedious job supervised by Kathleen Kenyon) proved it to be so. On the other hand it was evidently post-conquest, and Rik judged it 'safe to infer' that it had been raised soon after 61 AD, when Boudicca's sack of Verulamium would have roused the authorities to protect their citizens. (Here, as we shall see, he proved to be wrong.)

Where the Fosse reached up the hillside sherds of native pottery were found in and under it, suggesting that a Belgic settlement might be near at hand. Some years before, Rik's old friend O. G. S. Crawford had reported on a tangle of earthworks on the plateau. Stage three, then, was to investigate these banks and ditches, an archaeologist's nightmare since they were of all sorts and sizes and in Prae Wood horribly overgrown with trees. Dermot Casey was given the unenviable responsibility of disentangling and surveying them, an operation fully launched in 1931. There was, indeed, a Belgic stronghold on the plateau, which imported pottery, especially the glossy Arretine ware from Italy, proved to date from after about 15 BC, the earliest foundation having probably been made by Tasciovanus himself.

Rik, however, was not to be satisfied. He had come to Verulamium with the intention of taking the story back to Cassivellaunus and Julius Caesar: therefore it had to be done, though it carried him further into the landscape and away from his base. Stages four and five involved the surveying and dating of two linear earthworks running to the north and north-east of Verulamium. The first to be tested, the Devil's Dyke, proved to have been dug at about the time of Tasciovanus or a little later, to make a frontier across a strip of relatively open country.

The Devil's Dyke, then, was pre-Roman but no earlier than the Prae Wood stronghold. Having gone so far, it now seemed evident to Rik that this dyke was to be related to another earthwork on much the same line, but on the far side of the Ver, where it headed north-east towards the River Lea. This Beech Bottom Dyke, however, was very much more formidable: with its embanked ditch a hundred feet across and thirty deep it was, indeed, the largest work of its kind in Britain.

It was during the 1932 season that Rik's attention was riveted on Beech Bottom, but no excavation was contemplated of this huge and far removed boundary ditch.

Precisely at this moment fate smiled upon us. A rumour reached us one evening that workmen digging a sewer through a filled up section of Beech Bottom had found a shovel full of silver coins. The workmen were 'foreigners' to the district, it was the end of the day and no time was to be lost. We spread ourselves quickly through the innumerable public-houses of the vicinity and, with an immense expenditure of pints and patience, recovered 'in confidence' forty of the coins 'on loan'. They were photographed and recorded, and were sufficient to show that the dispersed hoard had been deposited early in the second century AD. . . .

When the exact find spot had been established it was seen to be well up in the silt of the ditch, which could only have accumulated to this height after long exposure. Since the earthwork was certainly not of Roman type, it must be pre-Roman. The day after the silver *denarii* had assured him of this fact Rik studied Beech Bottom from the point of view of its purpose. He saw it as designed to bar 'an open tract of country between two river valleys and two fords' – for there was a ford across the Lea here below the north-east end of the dyke corresponding with that across the Ver near the other end, at Verulamium itself. It was already known that Belgic rulers often delimited land surrounding their tribal capitals by running dykes of this nature – a fact even then being further clarified by the excavations at Camulodunum.

Following in imagination the line of Beech Bottom, though the further part of it had been obliterated, Wheeler was struck with greater force than before by the significance of its near approach to yet another massive earthwork crowning raised ground above the ford across the Lea near the small town of Wheathampstead. This was no linear work, but huge ditches with flanking banks, partially enclosing an area of over ninety acres, a stronghold obviously well qualified to be a Belgic *oppidum*.

Here, then, was the target for stage six. Wheeler secured the permission of Lord Brocket, the landowner, to make small test cuts near the ramparts in the hope of finding evidence for their age. He had staked much on this proving to be older than Belgic Verulamium, and watched the digging with concealed anxiety. As the potsherds began to be taken out in quantity from behind the defences he experienced mounting confidence and in the end a minor triumph. This pottery from the Wheathampstead *oppidum* was quite free of the imported wares from Gaul and Italy that were reaching Britain by the time of Tasciovanus. It was all native, and of varieties that could be dated to the middle of the first century BC – that is, to the period of Cassivellaunus.

Rik was able to declare that from the testimony of the sherds 'and the formidable character of the defences, there is no known rival to Wheathampstead as the site of Caesar's last, hard-won victory over his redoubtable opponent in 54 BC'. He was also able to record, in *Archaeology from the Earth*, that this judgement had escaped serious questioning and was able to conclude the account of his tactical advance, 'Thus in six progressive stages, developing gradually and logically from known to unknown, the vista of a formative phase of protohistoric Britain began to unroll itself.'

Although Rik was probably at his happiest when walking, riding or driving his long and low grey Lancia to the more distant Belgic sites, he necessarily spent a great part of his time with Tessa excavating Verulamium inside-the-walls. Here by far the greater part of the work was concentrated, for an area of some eleven acres was extensively dug and there was in addition the excavation of the defences, particularly of the wall towers, which had been lost to view, and the massive gates, the foundations of which were now discovered for the first time.

Since the war it has been usual for students and volunteers to do most of the physical labour on archaeological excavations – though sometimes assisted by mechanical diggers. In the interwar years pick and shovel work was done by labourers, and in this Verulamium was no exception. Unlike some other directors, Rik, with his natural authority and war experience, had no trouble in managing them. In addition to supervisors, there were soon plenty of students, drawn from various universities, and other volunteers, to do the more delicate work with trowels and brushes. As publicity brought more visitors there it is safe to say that Verulamium was the first archaeological site in Britain where the spectacle of numbers of human forms crouched in holes and cuttings became known to the public. Later, of course, it was to become a familiar sight, sometimes strangely resembling a Resurrection scene.

Soon the everyday life of a big excavation was established, with the toilers going off early to their appointed sections and gathering together for a communal lunch – out of doors whenever possible. At the centre of the activity, and a ready shelter when needed, was the excavation hut with its trestles and shelves, surveying equipment, drawing boards and reference books, its storage of all kinds for finds ranging from bones and coarse pottery to coins and brooches. Every item had to be exactly recorded and correctly labelled, for good order was even more firmly imposed here than in Lancaster House.

With Rik's authority and tactical direction in the background, Tessa commanded all ranks of her forces with apparent ease. As Sir Frederic Kenyon was to write of her,

No one who saw her at work in the field, among a troop of assistants, many of them untrained though enthusiastic beginners, could fail to be filled with admiration, alike of her skill as a director and interpreter of the results of excavation, of the patience and good temper with which she dealt with assistants and visitors. . . .

Qualities of patience and good temper were severely tested, since during those four seasons at Verulamium Rik's more serious love affairs involved three of their assistants and in the periods of transition emotions could run high. Yet they triumphed, for all are agreed that this was throughout a more than usually happy dig.

Archaeologically, the first season in the Roman town went well, work being mainly concentrated on the history of Watling Street, on adjoining houses and other buildings and on uncovering the foundations of the great 'London Gate' which had spanned it. From the point of view of public interest the luckiest discovery of the year was an exceptionally fine mosaic pavement of a design based on the scallop shell. A photograph of this, taken when partially exposed and with Rik crouched over it in the attitude of a Moslem at prayer, was often reproduced. It appeared at last as 'Portrait of the Author, 1930' in the front of *Still Digging*. It does at least show a fine head of hair, worn rather long for that time.

Tessa was to take charge of the mosaics. In 1932, when there were several to be lifted, Italians were brought in to carry out this highly specialized task. These experts cost money, however, and having watched them at work on the first, Tessa intervened and to everyone's astonished admiration succeeded in lifting all the rest of the pavements with skill equal to the Italians'. She also undertook the illustration of many of them in colour, working so meticulously that every tessera was in place.

In August of the opening season, when the shell mosaic was on show and there was enough going on to please visitors, the press was made welcome and responded warmly. The Wheelers' old ally, the *Daily Mail*, concentrated on Tessa – whose work at Caerleon had meant much to them. 'A woman with dark wavy hair and smiling brown eyes, dressed in a business-like brown jumper and skirt and brown Wellington boots, is directing ... an important work of excavation.' (This journalistic flight was to be used five years later in obituaries carried by local papers throughout the country.) One reporter was delighted to be asked into her tent and fed on fried bacon.

A little later the *Daily Express* seized upon the idea of a family excavation. Michael, who was now at Rugby, had as usual spent his summer holidays digging, his mother now welcoming his help more than ever before. Under a large headline, WHEELER FAMILY DISCOVERIES, the *Express* gave most space to Michael, telling their readers that he had been an archaeologist since the age of five and now to their reporter appeared to know everything there was to know. Michael's emotions were divided between pride in his first conspicuous appearance in a newspaper and anxiety over possible repercussions at Rugby.

The Roman excavations went ahead at a fairly even pace through the following seasons. For the second, when some forces had been diverted to the Belgic stronghold in Prae Wood, Thalassa Cruso, having joined the museum that spring, began her training as an excavator in earnest and soon became an able assistant. In that same year another recruit was enrolled in a curious way, a proof of the value of 'free entry' of amateurs into archaeology. Huntly Gordon, a son of the manse and of the Gordon clan, had been a professional soldier until after the First World War, and therefore, like Rik, had some skill in surveying. Also like Rik, he was fascinated by great soldiers, and, having read an article on Verulamium in *The Times*, was so excited by the thought of Julius Caesar in Britain that he made his solitary way to Prae Wood, finding the earthworks for himself. He set to and made as good a survey as one man could, then ventured to send the results to the author of the article.

Rik was sufficiently impressed to arrange a meeting, and although they walked the mile of fields up to Prae Wood without speaking, they got on well, discovered they had fought within a few miles of one another on the Western Front – and struck up a working friendship that lasted forty years. Immediately poor Huntly was appointed to assist Dermot Casey in making an accurate survey of the medley of earthworks in and around Prae Wood.

The further exploration of the city was concentrated in the southern area belonging to the Corporation and was largely concerned with uncovering a part of the street plan and the large town houses of the prosperous citizens, with their mosaics and bath suites. Added interest came with the identification of two triumphal arches associated with Watling Street, the first to be found in Britain, and a unique temple of an approximately triangular plan.

The important central area round the forum lay within St Michael's churchyard and the vicarage garden and no work was attempted there during the main excavations. This was true also of the northern quarter of the city, within Lord Verulam's estate, except that during the fourth season the long-forgotten position of the theatre was rediscovered.

Rik Wheeler determined that 1933 should be his last season at Verulamium. He had come as near as possible to locating the Cassivellaunian capital, and felt that together he and Tessa had fulfilled the two objectives of 'the recovery of the historical framework of Belgic and Roman Verulamium' and enough material for 'an attempted reconstruction of the social and economic evolution of a major civic unit . . . during four and a half critical centuries'. He knew there was still very much more to be done and perhaps it was partly to placate his conscience that he arranged for Kathleen Kenyon and his architect, A. W. G. Lowther, to return for another season. Their outstanding achievement was the excavation and planning of the theatre, another building unique of its kind in Britain, and one which has proved a lasting attraction to visitors. There the future excavator of Jericho and Jerusalem had her first experience of commanding a large work force on an important excavation.

One reason Wheeler could give for quitting Verulamium after 'four long seasons' was that a scheme to build a great arterial road on some undetermined course in the Ver valley made it impossible for him to plan ahead. This was a real problem, but one that he might have overcome if, as we shall see, he had not been suffering from an inner revulsion and restlessness and thoughts of an even grander, more challenging enterprise.

Meanwhile he and Tessa had to prepare for the joint publication of their work, again as a Report of the Society of Antiquaries Research Committee. Annual Reports had regularly appeared and every winter Rik had lectured to packed audiences at Burlington House, but much remained to be done: selection of material, writing, perfecting maps, plans, sections and other illustrations according to a most ambitious design. All was in excellent order, for over the years the Wheelers had developed a sound system of site recording. Rik always gave Tessa credit for the large part she played in this advance. In work on the finds, – and particularly on the pottery, of such importance for determining chronology – Rik preferred not to handle the material himself. Instead he would appoint members of his staff to work on it, then summon them to show it to him piece by piece while he made his own notes – and his own deductions.

Hard labour on the Verulamium material had to be done while keeping up with all the fresh obligations generated by their current excavations. Although unhappily it did not appear until later in 1936, the Report was virtually complete before Tessa's death. It was published under their joint authorship with the title of *Verulamium: A Belgic and Two Roman Cities*. It was to provoke the most bitter and long-lasting feud to rend British archaeology between the two World Wars.

The explosion did not occur at once: the slow fuse was burning through the age it takes for reviews to appear in specialist journals. Crawford, who had founded the magazine *Antiquity* during the twenties and edited it in his own idiosyncratic fashion, had sent *Verulamium* to Nowell Myres for a notice. It would not be just to say that Nowell was prejudiced in making his archaeological assessment, but he had inevitably harboured intense feelings against Rik for his treatment of Tessa. Infidelity apart, he felt that for years she had been 'working herself to death in selfless devotion to the promotion of Rik's professional advancement'. Now she was dead and there was no reason not to criticize the Report as harshly as he judged it to deserve.

The notorious review opens with high praise for the perfection of the writing and of 'plans and photographs whose technical skill and artistic excellence are beyond all praise'. It also emphasizes the importance of the excavations and hails *Verulamium* 'as a monument to a partnership which has steadily developed the techniques of large scale excavation of Roman sites'; nor does it neglect the significance of the dig as a training school for the students who flocked to learn from the Wheelers. Then the criticisms begin. The Prae Wood earthworks were not substantial enough to be Tasciovanus' capital; essentially the early Roman city (the Fosse) had not been excavated at all and might have been the centre of the Belgic *oppidum*; much dating evidence was shaky and Rik had been guilty of advancing its interpretation from the possible to the certain; there was too much compression throughout and quite inadequate illustrations of the pottery. Nowell justifies this onslaught by saying that he fears that otherwise the inner weaknesses of so splendid a volume would be overlooked in a chorus of applause.

The explosive force was considerable: waves of excited talk swept through the little archaeological world of those days. A few years before Nowell had had a more amicable brush with Wheeler over his Roman London guide, but no one else had ever ventured to criticize the master in print, and the fact that the attack was severe, came from a young man and concerned an important excavation made it the more heinous. The stir would certainly have died away, however, had Rik not immediately sent Crawford a somewhat intemperate and petulant reply.

As a general defence against the accusation of insufficient evidence obtained he suggested that news of the arterial road, which could have led to excavations costing £5000, had 'failed to penetrate the enviable seclusion of Tom Quad' and asked whether Mr Myres wanted a Report divided into Part I, 'What We Did', and Part II, 'What We Didn't'. He insisted that if Annual Reports and other articles were included quite enough pottery had been illustrated and that, anyway, its classification was far less urgent and vital than the establishment of the historical chronology. He counter-attacked by saying that Nowell had misinterpreted the Prae Wood earthworks, and as for his own excavation at Aldborough, which he had mentioned, everyone knew how inconclusive and inadequate it had been. Rik ended with a slightly contemptuous reference to Bertie Wooster and the necessity of knowing the 'terrain'.

This riposte was unwise, certainly, and unworthy, but I think myself that Nowell was inclined to magnify the frightfulness. However, what really infuriated him was the fact that Crawford did not show it to him in advance and that 'This thoroughly unethical conduct was made worse by his subsequent refusal to publish the admittedly rather tart reply which I felt bound to send him.' Nowell gave me an extract from this Reproof Valiant to Rik's Reply Churlish:

He who discharges a peashooter at Olympian Jove would be very foolish to expect anything less damaging than a thunderbolt in return, and Dr. Wheeler has duly replied with the regulation missile to the review which I do not regret writing on his Verulamium Report.

Nowell must have enjoyed the exercise of his own scholarly wit, but when it was suppressed his indignation was so great that he told the tale of this unethical conduct to all his archaeological friends and long-lasting faction ensued. Eminent persons, and Rik himself, tried to calm him down, but he 'was not prepared to be browbeaten in the matter in which I was so obviously right'. The upshot was that Nowell informed Rik and Crawford that he would never again review for *Antiquity* so long as Crawford was editor. He kept to this with astonishing tenacity: many years later Crawford invited him to review a particularly appropriate book, only to be reminded of the Verulamium affair. As he himself said, 'It is not only elephants who never forget.' To which might be added it takes a good Christian gentleman never to forgive.

This 'unseemly rumpus', as Nowell Myres now refers to it, seems to have stirred such depths of personal feeling that both men lost their undoubted sense of humour. If there had been any laughter in the affair it must be said that Nowell has had the last and longest laugh. Excavations at Verulamium in the mid-fifties proved his criticism to be largely justified, certainly the general one that Rik, in his desire to present his Report with shape, clarity and conclusiveness, had given what should have been tentative judgements the appearance of finality. Although Prae Wood remains as the heart of Tasciovanus's capital, some traces of its extension were found below the northern part of the Roman town, he misdated the walls and failed to find some early Roman features. The simplest and most conspicuous mistake concerned the Fosse; this was not, as Nowell surmised, Belgic, but, on the contrary, dated to the second century AD. Thus the earlier of the Wheelers' *Two Roman Cities* has to be eliminated.

The story ends happily, for although Nowell Myres refused to forgive the sins of *Antiquity*, he did forgive Rik. They were barely to encounter one another again until Rik returned from India, but later, as Secretary to the British Academy, Rik was able to provide financial help and backing for Nowell's Anglo-Saxon research and friendly relations were restored. That this might have happened much sooner is implicit in what Michael was to write to Nowell after his father's death. It has the ring of truth: 'Rik was the first to admit – to me at any rate – that you were right. He admired rather than resented your unfashionable presumption in standing up to him.'

When Rik Wheeler determined to move his main forces away from Verulamium he had been excavating Roman sites almost every year since his demobilization.

For the moment I suffered from a satiety of Roman things. The mechanical, predictable quality of Roman craftsmanship, the advertised *humanitas* of Roman civilization, which lay always so near to brutality and corruption, fatigued and disgusted me.... Now, in 1934, there was an opportunity to break away from the pretentious Roman machine and to transfer our large and experienced following to other aspects of that pre-Roman Iron Age which had already enlivened Verulamium. Once again the new objective was one which I had secretly meditated for several years before the moment came for action.

That objective was Maiden Castle. Archaeologists expressed no surprise, for it was held to be obvious that no other site was large enough, or challenging enough, to satisfy Mortimer Wheeler at this vaulting stage of his career.

As he said, nothing was precisely known of this gigantic Dorset hill-fort, capital of the British tribe of the Durotriges, except that traces of a Roman building had been found inside its ramparts. On the other hand by the mid-thirties knowledge of the British Iron Age had been mounting fast. Not only had there been much digging at sites of the period, including hill-forts, but a theoretical cultural and historical classification had been devised to give order to the welter of material brought to light.

This was very largely the work of Christopher Hawkes. The year after that first idyllic season at the Brecon Gaer, he and Nowell Myres had excavated the fort on St Catherine's Hill, so familiar to them from their school days at Winchester. From the discoveries there, and wider research, Christopher had in 1931 published a paper in *Antiquity*, defining a threefold division of the pre-Roman centuries of Celtic Britain, of which the last was to be associated with the invasions of those Belgae whom he and Rik were then pursuing at Camulodunum and Verulamium. He was soon to publish a fuller study of the Belgae with

Gerald Dunning of the London Museum, a collaboration indicative of the very limited number of professional archaeologists working at that time.

This scheme won general acceptance, and although minor modifications were already being suggested, Christopher Hawkes's classification was bound to form the basis for the Wheelers' interpretation of his findings at Maiden Castle.

The nature and ambience of this 'monstrous artifact', as Rik called the earthwork, were in complete contrast with those encountered at soft and almost suburban Verulamium. Enclosing a long saddle-backed hill to the south-west of Dorchester, the county town of that most beautiful and utterly rural county of Dorset, Maiden Castle was in the heart of the chalk country, with its noble, bare contours, few inhabitants and strangely remote atmosphere. Thomas Hardy could see the vast form from his Dorchester house, Max Gate, and must often have visited it. He wrote an evocative description of the place which Rik did not fail to quote in his Report.

At one's every step it rises higher against the south sky, with an obtrusive personality that compels the senses to regard it and consider. The eyes may bend in another direction, but never without the consciousness of its heavy, high-shouldered presence at its point of vantage.

Although here among the chalk hills there is no feeling of it, the sea is in fact not far away, and is easily reached at the little resort of Weymouth, some five miles to the south.

From the first Rik had determined that the work should be done on a scale proportionate to that of the earthwork itself. About a hundred assistants, students and volunteers took part every season – probably the largest force of the kind ever to be employed on a British dig before or since. The Society of Antiquaries shared their responsibility for the excavations with the Dorset Field Club, and the local interest was further represented by Lieutenant-Colonel Drew, Curator of the Dorset County Museum, who joined the Wheelers as a third Director. Collaboration was certain to be smooth since the Colonel, who had a DSO as well as a Fellowship of the Antiquaries, was an extraordinarily sweet and gentle man. A true story was told of him that when a fire was kindled on the site he suddenly bent down beside it, put his hand among the flames and brought out an ant to save it from the pains of cremation.

Most of the trained assistants transferred from Verulamium, although Kathleen Kenyon had been left to serve there, while Thalassa was soon to launch an excavation of her own (under Rik's surveyance) and, in 1935, with characteristic aplomb, was to marry a rich, good-looking and agreeable American, who was also a professional archaeologist. In spite of all these qualifications, Rik, of course, did not approve of Hugh Hencken.

If these two were absent, two other women members of the team came very much to the fore at Maiden Castle. One was Molly Cotton, who, as we have seen, took over Tessa's role as Deputy Director, and the other Kitty Richardson, a compárative newcomer, but one of such competence and good sense that she became Molly's chief assistant. In the following years Kitty was to go with Rik on the dashing expeditions to France that were to prove such a remarkable combination of archaeological with amorous adventure.

Michael Wheeler, even after going up to Oxford, still devoted much of his Long Vacation to excavation. Here his father gave him the truly fearful task of joining with Huntly Gordon to make a contour survey of the 'monstrous artifact'. When it is remembered that the fort is over twelve hundred yards long, and has three or four lines of colossal ramparts so steep in places that it is an effort to stand upright on them, it will appear that the family of titans would have been more appropriate surveyors than two slight human beings.

New recruits who were to be of the utmost value to Rik Wheeler during very many years were W. C. Wedlake and M. B. Cookson. Bill Wedlake was a West Country man who from the beginning was engaged as a foreman at Maiden Castle, but who soon became very much more than this, being entrusted by Rik with all manner of responsible jobs and becoming a field archaeologist in his own right. Cookie, as he was soon to be universally called, was an employee of a London firm of photographers, and in this capacity had been briefly employed at Verulamium. He was soon summoned to Dorset when the local photographer proved far too slow to serve Rik's purposes, and was found to be not only ingenious and skilful in his craft, but also extraordinarily lovable, and was engaged as a permanent member of the staff. In time he became head of the photographic section at the London Institute and served Rik far and wide until his untimely death.

Rik's relationship with Bill and Cookie showed him in many ways at his best. These two men, so different from one another in character and background, were alike in being among those who were able unaffectedly to admire him as great man and leader, respecting his fine qualities and accepting, even overlooking, his faults. If Rik first drew them to himself because he saw how useful they would be, he also took them as trusted companions, sharing his own love of hard work and adventure. Cookie he was to establish in a good job, while in later years he took pains to help Bill with his archaeological endeavours.

The way of life forming the background to the daily toil up on the hill at Maiden Castle was bound to differ from that at Verulamium as sharply as did its local setting. There could be no frequent dashing up to London for Rik or anyone else. The excavators were very largely isolated, forming a community of their own. Huntly Gordon stayed with the Wheelers at the Antelope Hotel, a privilege that allowed him to witness Rik briefing Tessa on the plans for the day as they breakfasted together. Others among the more senior members of staff lodged elsewhere in Dorchester, while some of the young women lived in considerable discomfort in a girls' school near the site.

A large number of the volunteers, however, preferred the camping life, pitching their tents in the shelter of the southern ramparts, adjoining the large army hut that served as the headquarters. Before long Bill Wedlake was given permission to set up his bed in the hut, and so was on the spot to succour the campers whenever their canvas gave way before south-westerly gales.

In the isolation that brought all the diggers together, social rituals were soon established. The most regular took place on Friday nights, when the company went to one of the three Dorchester pubs equipped with alleys and the staff played the workmen at skittles. After one of these matches Bill Wedlake drove Tessa round about the town on the back of his motor bicycle, while on another occasion the local pressmen, challenged at skittles, presented Rik with a silver cigarette-case in gratitude for his having enabled them to give their readers 'archaeology without tears'. Friday nights were good for esprit de corps and enabled the Directors to become acquainted with their changing band of followers.

At weekends Rik might find time to drive down to Weymouth with a few chosen companions, where they would fish for mackerel and bring home their catch for supper. Sometimes, too, they let off steam at a Weymouth fun-fair. One Gwen Anderson, who, with her Rolls-Royce, was also to provide transport in France, organized cocktail parties at her hotel and bathing tea parties at Bridport.

The many campers up on the hill could not share in all of these doings, but they soon developed a lively social life of their own. A leading figure was Gilbert Carruthers, who organized their meals – which sometimes included rabbits pursued and caught at night by the light of headlights. On Saturday nights they would have supper and drinks in Dorchester, as many as ten at a time piling into the 'dig car', an ancient Morris two-seater with dicky. On fine nights after supper it was the custom to perambulate the ramparts singing camp songs, while on wet ones Carruthers would provide drinks to cheer them before they retired to their damp and flapping tents. Once during each season the campers entertained the Directors and all the non-campers to dinner, drinks and singing in the hut.

Rik encouraged such doings since to some extent they satisfied his ideal of adventure in archaeology and certainly attracted more volunteers. He saw to it, of course, that they did not interfere with strict discipline and punctuality on the dig. Most responded well and were both keen and capable – indeed, for some it proved an introduction to an archaeological career. The few who proved incompetent or idle were condemned, unknown to themselves, to serve on a site secretly named the 'chicken run', where they scraped and brushed harmlessly and in vain.

Publicity was well organized and successful. Each year *The Times* assigned one of the then much-coveted turn-over articles to Rik for a summary of past achievements and future prospects at Maiden Castle. Well-attended press days were carefully staged every week, and as a result during the later summer months a stream of news items appeared in national and local newspapers throughout the country. Sometimes reporters might let themselves go on human interest, as when the *Evening News* informed its readers that 'Sun-burned girls from British Universities are working in trenches on a hill-top near Dorchester with men students from three continents'. There was a popular photograph of Tessa, still in her brown suit and Wellingtons, together with Colonel Drew, making one of those spurious 'examinations' of a gold coin, while a British working man in cloth cap looks on.

As Rik himself recorded, 'Our more conventional archaeological friends sometimes raised their eyebrows and sniffed a little plaintively at "all this publicity of Wheeler's!"' Yet he was satisfied that here as never before they succeeded in spreading factual information so that 'the public for the first time became conscious of the Early Iron Age and the meaning of prehistory'.

For the first two seasons the Wheelers themselves conducted the weekly meetings with the press, and reporters blessed Tessa for her simple clarity in exposition. After her death the briefings were handed over to Margot Eates – who was also made responsible for shepherding and initiating the intakes of raw students. Margot became a part-time lecturer at the London Museum, and will be encountered again when in later years she played a useful part in looking after the interests of both museum and institute.

During the last season public relations gave rise to an incident ironical in the light of future events. Rik was invited by the youthful television authority of the time to broadcast on Maiden Castle. He had no opinion of the new device and, deciding not to waste his time on it, he appointed Margot Eates to go in his stead. She duly presented herself at Alexandra Palace and became the first tele-archaeologist.

In addition to the general public, Maiden Castle attracted archaeologists and a few notables. Not long before his death T. E. Lawrence paid a visit, as did the poet John Drinkwater. During the last season Augustus John came over from his house, Fryern Court, at Fordingbridge. With hindsight this can be seen as the most significant visitation, for John had brought with him a favourite mistress, Mavis de Vere Cole, the sister-in-law of Neville Chamberlain. Rik was to write,

I was wandering about at the east end of Maiden Castle when I saw a curious entourage on its way towards me. It consisted of Augustus John and his party, in the odd clothes they always wore. Mavis was skipping in front on long legs; very distinctive that skipping walk of hers – I was greatly taken with her, straight away.

Here, far from the great world, was the first stirring of the one spectacular folly of Rik Wheeler's life: he had set eyes on the beautiful blonde creature who was to outplay him in the sexual game.

The life and ambience of a great excavation is a creation in itself, and one not without effect on the work in hand. Rik, whose vision and determination had drawn all these people together, and who both enjoyed and dominated the little society he had created, yet concentrated his energy on solving the historical riddles set by the earthworks in all their obvious complexity. Although by now modifications were being suggested to Christopher Hawkes's classification of the British Iron Age into three main phases, any facts Wheeler could establish for the Wessex hill-forts would have to be related to it.

Bill Wedlake has described his impressions of the July day in 1934 when Rik and Tessa first appeared at Maiden Castle to launch their formidable undertaking:

The Wheelers and the London contingent did not arrive on the scene for the first few days. But I well remember Dr Wheeler's arrival at the site. My first impression was of his long striding legs with equally long arms. These were emphasized by a bright yellow, high-necked pullover and an American style wide-brimmed hat. But despite his immediate command of the situation, I detected an underlying nervousness and an anxious desire to be kind to us rural folk. We were first given a 'pep' talk during which he explained, in no uncertain terms, his aims and expectations.

I soon noticed that Mrs Wheeler and the staff which he had brought with him from London were trained almost like commandos to carry out the 'Keeper's' instructions....

Bill, however, was soon rejoicing to discover that he could work with these invaders, that there was none of the 'county' atmosphere he had met on local digs, that status depended on effort and competence. 'In fact I soon learned I had made new friends and it was a pleasure to work with them.'

The aims set out in that pep talk were first to establish the structural development of the fortifications, then to relate this with the cultural history of the various builders, and finally to expose enough of the interior to learn something of how and where the inhabitants lived. As always, Wheeler's intention was to secure the maximum of information with a minimum of labour. Kitty Richardson recalls being greatly struck by the tactical sense that made such economy possible: he virtually never dug in the wrong place. She observed how, when some new move had to be made, Rik would 'disappear for a time to sit among the ramparts deliberating – then emerge and issue orders for the work to be done'.

In fact, it did not require great perspicacity to decide where the first cut should be made to elucidate the structural history. Of the two knolls of the saddle-back enclosed by the ramparts it could be seen from the air that the eastern one had most probably once been enclosed by a single bank and ditch, for the western side of the embankment, where it had crossed the hilltop, was still faintly visible. A trench across it would surely prove that here was the first Maiden Castle, a simple little fort of a kind already familiar for the early Iron Age.

Wedlake and Colonel Drew laid out this first incision, and almost at once Wheeler found himself confronted by one of those unexpected discoveries that are at once the joy and the hazard of archaeological exploration. The first Iron Age settlement was there all right, but hidden below it were the remains of another far more ancient. Some three thousand years before the Celtic tribesmen raised their bank, Neolithic farmers had already enclosed the knoll and lived on it long enough to leave hearths and plentiful litter behind them.

When news of this discovery spread along the archaeological

grapevine one view was that Rik was furious over a distraction from his plan of work that must drag him into a remote prehistoric past where he was a stranger. When later another rather less ancient Neolithic monument came to light and appeared to be an extraordinarily lengthy burial mound the attitude shifted and it was said to be characteristic of Rik to find the longest long barrow in Britain.

Whatever his feelings, and they were probably mixed, he turned to and quickly mastered the essentials of the period, including the rich variety of its ceramic forms. Kitty Richardson, who was in charge of the long mound during the final season (when a weirdly butchered burial was judged to be 'clearly a primary feature of the mound'), found Rik fully committed to his Stone Age responsibilities.

Very properly, however, these remained a side-line; the main energies of the Directors, their trained staff, the thirty or so labourers and the much larger force of volunteers was concentrated on the Iron Age and its problems. The work was divided into a number of sites, each under a more or less experienced supervisor. Wheeler almost invariably chose women for supervisors: they were good at keeping workmen and volunteers happy, and (as Wedlake observed) 'he was able to maintain an absolute and unquestioned loyalty from them'. In supervising the supervisors, Rik and Tessa developed an appropriate collaboration. He would visit each site several times a day to make a rigorous inspection of the work, including the complexities of find-books, layer cards and the like. If any considerable fault was found he would grill the supervisor mercilessly, leaving her shaken or even in tears and with orders to set things right before his next visit. If this proved too difficult, Tessa was alerted and she would hasten to the site, comfort the supervisor and call in assistance to solve the problem. So much did this become a routine that Rik might ask if Tessa had been called and delay his next visit until her rescue mission was completed.

Much of the volunteer force was employed not on the more skilled and important investigation of the ramparts and entrances but in uncovering the remains of dwellings inside the fortress. During all the centuries of occupation the inhabitants had dug deep, ovoid pits into the chalk to serve first for storage and then as rubbish tips. The ground was riddled with them, and their excavation was usually undertaken by pairs of volunteers, who, when they had disappeared below ground-level, would fill buckets with waste to be pulled up by workmen. If it was judged that too much canoodling was going on in any of these snug retreats Tessa would find some more exposed place of work for the young man.

One volunteer was a 'little Dorset lady', who arrived each day by bicycle with food and tools in a governess bag. She laboured most conscientiously in a deep pit and was rewarded at last by finding the skeleton of a pig at the bottom. When the time came for Cookie to photograph it she was told to give it a final brush up, but in her excitement fell off the ladder and onto the pig. Rik, who was looking on, exclaimed, 'By God, the beast has been there for two thousand years and now you have destroyed the damned thing!'

The inexperienced and their mishaps or misdeeds were not tolerated in the exacting work on the fortifications. Here all Wheeler's skill in the placing and interpretation of sections through ramparts, entries, road-ways and ditches was needed to determine the various stages and methods of their construction. Some problems could be solved with his usual economy by cuts at points crucial for the stratification, but as the seasons went by the involved constructional history of the eastern entrance led onto its complete excavation – where the results were to prove dramatic as well as historically illuminating.

The manner in which the actual work was done was also of excep-tional interest, for it was here that Rik first devised a technique that became an important part of the perfected 'Wheeler Method'. During the first season he had tackled the northern part of the elaborate outworks defending the inner gates by the old trench-cutting tech-nique. He found it awkward to do and unsatisfactory in its results. In its place he developed what he called the system of accumulative squares – or sometimes the grid system. This meant sinking a square with sides of at least ten feet, then extending it in any direction by further squares, leaving between them balks of uncut soil wide enough to take a man and wheelbarrow for the removal of dug soil. Each square, of course, provided four sections clearly seen and easily photographed. It proved an ideal method wherever a considerable area had to be coherently explored.

The story that Wheeler was able to compose from his findings was that the original Iron Age fort was built on the eastern knoll in about 300 BC – latish in Christopher Hawkes's first period – while the single rampart was extended to enclose both knolls before the end of the same phase. The Celtic tribesmen, cultivators and cattle-breeders lived in their simple and even squalid huts within this unambitious earthwork for a century or more, when they were rudely awakened and their fort taken over by invaders coming, Wheeler believed, from southern Brit-tany. It was these newcomers who first made Maiden Castle a great stronghold, adding outlines of ramparts and raising the innermost one

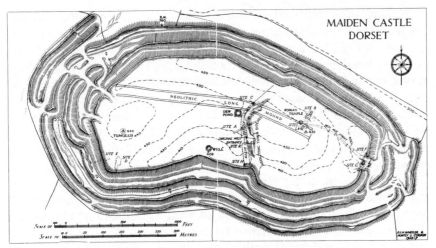

Maiden Castle, Dorset

to a formidable height. The explanation for this depth of defence works, found also in many lesser hill-forts in south-west England, was there for all to see: ammunition dumps in the form of sling-stones (mainly beach pebbles), one containing well over twenty thousand of these missiles. This unique discovery was irrefutable proof that multiple ramparts went with the introduction of sling warfare by the invading chieftains and their fighting men.

Wheeler argued strongly for these people belonging to the warlike Venetic tribes of Brittany, seeking refuge in Britain after their defeat and harsh punishment by Julius Caesar in the year 56 BC. Their general culture could be duly identified with the second phase of the Hawkes scheme. He saw their first strengthening of the defences, great though it was, as somewhat piecemeal adaptations of the old earthworks. After some two generations there was a further, far more purposeful and coherent remodelling of the fortifications, bringing them to their present size and due not to outside influence but chiefly to ambition. The idea aroused Rik's imagination and his sense of military history and its great men.

This phase represents the work of a master-mind, wielding unquestioned authority and controlling vast resources of labour. The whole plan is now knit together into a single unit, with a single personality. The ditches and ramparts ... are remodelled on the same prodigious scale as the mainline of defence; the awkward and hesitant adaptations of the entrances are boldly swept aside, and original and coherent plans are brought into being.... The old lines show through the new only as Holinshed shows through Shakespeare.

Having thus deliberately roused the prejudices of those archaeologists who considered him too literary, Rik went on to quote Thomas
Hardy's admirable description of the entrances: 'The ramparts are
found to overlap each other like loosely clasped fingers, between which
a zigzag path may be followed – a cunning construction that puzzles the
uninformed eye.' It was in the total excavation of the eastern entrance,
even more than in other cuttings, that Wheeler found evidence for the
last episode in the history of Maiden Castle, before it fell to the Romans.
He was once again confronted by the presence of those Belgic rulers
whom he had first encountered at Verulamium. He judged that it was in
about AD 25 that minor Belgic princes and their followers seized the
great fortress of the Durotriges, having probably been driven westwards by the ambitious expansion of King Cunobelin of Colchester.
They found the defences shaped by that 'master-mind' in a dilapidated
state and the settlement within equally neglected; the whole community, it seemed, had fallen into inertia and stagnation. The new
rulers repaired the fortifications according to their own ideas, tidied up
the houses, metalled the interior roadways and introduced their slugg-
ish subjects to some more advanced ideas – the use of coinage and of the
potter's wheel, the drinking of imported Roman wine.

With the Belgae Wheeler was once more approaching his favourite
territory, the frontier between prehistory and history. It was to be
crossed with the coming of the legions and a clash between Celt
and Roman that inspired some of his most eloquent imaginative
writing.

As late as the August of 1936, in an interview for the *Observer*, Rik
announced that the work at Maiden Castle was so nearly finished that
digging would cease 'within the next few weeks'. However, both the
eastern entrance and the neolithic 'long barrow' proved so interesting,
and so evidently had more to reveal, that in spite of his usual impatience, and his eagerness to follow up a reconnaissance conducted for
him the year before in northern France, Rik saw that a fourth season
was essential. It was to prove a fortunate as well as an archaeologically
correct decision.

Just a year after the *Observer* interview, reports began to appear in the
press of skeletons being found within the entrance works. As the days
went by, the numbers reported increased until at last it was realized
that Dr Wheeler and his now desperately busy team of diggers had hit
upon the place where the British dead had been buried after their
seemingly impregnable stronghold had fallen to a savage Roman
attack.

When Claudius sent his army across the Channel in AD 43 the Second Legion, advancing across southern England, was commanded by Vespasian, the future emperor, and is known to have reduced 'two very formidable tribes and twenty *oppida....*' This statement certainly referred to the conquest of the Wessex hill-forts in general and very probably to the Durotriges and their capital. Against a background supplied by the Roman historians, Wheeler was able to mount the physical evidence revealed day by day during that August of 1937, and reconstruct a story that was dramatic yet essentially irrefutable.

Having described how Vespasian evidently decided to launch his main assault against the eastern entrance, Rik let himself go in writing his Report:

What happened there is plain to read, the regiment of artillery, which normally accompanied a legion on campaign, was ordered into action, and put down a barrage of iron-shod ballista-arrows over the eastern part of the site. Following this barrage the infantry advanced up the slope, cutting its way from rampart to rampart, tower to tower. In the innermost bay of the entrance, close outside the actual gates, a number of huts had recently been built; these were now set alight, and under the rising clouds of smoke the gates were stormed and the position carried. But resistance had been obstinate and the fury of the attackers was roused. For a space, confusion and massacre dominated the scene. Men and women, young and old, were savagely cut down, before the legionaries were called to heel and the work of systematic destruction begun....

That night, when the fires of the legionaries shone out (we may imagine) in orderly lines across the valley, the survivors crept forth from their broken stronghold, and, in the darkness, buried their dead as nearly as might be outside their tumbled gates, in that place where the ashes of their burned huts lay warm and thick upon the ground. The task was carried out hastily and anxiously and without order, but, even so, from few graves were omitted those tributes of food and drink which were the proper and traditional perquisites of the dead. At daylight on the morrow, the legion moved westward to fresh conquest, doubtless taking with it the usual levy of hostages from the vanquished.

Having thus described the action, with the deployment both of his love of military history and his journalistic skills, Rik went on to present the evidence for it in some detail. He dwelt particularly on the grisly and touching facts revealed by the burials themselves. He related how the graves had been roughly cut through the ash of the burnt huts,

and into them had been thrown, in all manner of attitudes – crouched, extended, on the back, on the side, on the face, even sitting up – thirty eight skeletons of men and women.... In ten cases extensive cuts were present on the skull, some on the top, some on the front, some on the back. In another case, one of the arrow-heads was found actually embedded in a vertebra, having entered the body from the front below the heart. The victim had been finished off with a cut on the head. Yet another skull had been pierced by an implement of square section, probably a ballista-bolt. The last two and some of the sword cuts were doubtless battle wounds; but one skull, which had received no less than nine savage cuts, suggests the fury of massacre rather than the tumult of battle – a man does not stay to kill his enemy eight or nine times in the mêlée; and the neck of another skeleton had been dislocated, probably by hanging.

To write of skeletons rather than bodies being thrown into their graves is an uncharacteristic lapse on Rik's part. He then went on to show how the corpses must have been buried by fellow-Britons, since they were accompanied by food bowls and a mug, while two of them had joints of lamb between their hands. Many of them still wore such ornaments as armlets and finger- and toe-rings, and one warrior had been allowed to take his battle-axe and knife.

The whole war cemetery as it lay exposed before us was eloquent of mingled piety and distraction; of weariness, of dread, of darkness, but yet now of complete forgetfulness. Surely no poor relic in the soil of Britain was ever more eloquent of high tragedy, more worthy of brooding comment from the presiding spirit of Hardy's own *Dynasts*.

The discovery of the war cemetery made a splendid, Wheelerian ending for the Maiden Castle excavations. The public always loves a skeleton, and here were skeletons in tragic profusion, displaying the marks of battle and making actual one of the best-known events in British history: the Roman conquest. It was summed up poignantly in that Roman arrow embedded in the British spine. Here was 'digging up people' at its simplest and most vivid. No wonder that press reports multiplied and the crowds came.

Since the Institute had by now been for some months settled in its own premises, Rik decided to have the mass of finds divided between St John's Lodge and Lancaster House. He missed Tessa's help in this laborious part of every excavator's responsibilities, but his assistants served him well. Molly Cotton worked with him on the Celtic and Roman brooches, while Kitty Richardson was in charge of the daunting bulk of the pottery. She had to have it very much under her hand and to be always alert, for at any moment Rik might suddenly send for some particular group of sherds from an obscure corner of the dig, expecting to have them brought to him on the instant. Of the other categories of finds, from coins to querns and molluscs to bones, which as usual demanded specialists' reports, the human skeletal remains were perhaps the most exceptional. Just ninety-nine individuals were represented and added a very large percentage to the closely dated remains of the pre-Roman Britons from Maiden Castle. They were small, the men about 5 ft 5 in. and the women about 5 ft (Tessa Wheeler's stature), and if there was little evidence of their lives being nasty or brutish they were certainly short, for it was unusual for either men or women to live much beyond forty.

Preliminary work for the final Report could go forward after the close of excavations, but completion was delayed by Rik's forays into northern France in search of the homelands of his sling-using invaders and then by the outbreak of war. The typescript seems to have been finished by 1941, but the volume did not appear until 1943, by which time the author had been through the Battle of El Alamein, had been promoted to Brigadier and was so completely a soldier that Maiden Castle appeared as a distant dream.

The Report, simply entitled *Maiden Castle, Dorset*, was published under R. E. M. Wheeler's sole name, but was dedicated to the memory of Tessa. Rik began his dedicatory inscription, written in August 1941, by wishing that the book were a worthier memorial to her work, admitting to inadequacies and hoping that a time would come 'for the completion of the task'. He ended with a bleak paragraph:

The manuscript has been prepared for printing amidst the watches of the War.... The wreckage of the present has in these days been more instant to my mind than the wreckage of the past, and *inter arma* I have no heart for studentship. The following pages are less a report than the salvage of the report that should have been written.

By the time he was writing *Still Digging* Wheeler found himself able to judge his monograph less harshly. No one could quarrel with his summary of the very substantial contribution it had made to knowledge or with his modest claim that the sectional drawings were an improvement on his 'earlier efforts'. All except foes would accept his conclusion: 'I think I may justly say that it has a certain basic and enduring value.'

In general time has dealt with *Maiden Castle* and the great excavation it represents rather more kindly than with *Verulamium*. War inevitably delayed serious appraisals, but in 1945 (when he succeeded Rik as Keeper of the London Museum) W. F. Grimes wrote a critical review.

He it was who felt that in his Reports Wheeler aimed more for literary than scientific values, and also that his principle of selective digging led to a neglect of the social and economic aspect of a community that could only be won by extensive excavation of settlements.

In this Grimes was swimming with the prevalent archaeological current of the day. The doctrine of the total exploration of sites to discover just how, where and on what societies had lived was being developed during the later thirties, with the Cambridge school in the lead. It reached a high point in the immediate pre-war years, when the German archaeologist, Gerhard Bersu, was invited over to conduct a demonstration dig at a small hilltop settlement near Salisbury. His exposure of what proved to be a single farmstead was illuminating and did much to justify the new approach, despite its unavoidable expenditure of time and money.

Bersu had been taken by Christopher Hawkes to inspect the Maiden Castle excavations and he made some criticisms of what he saw. It could hardly have been otherwise. Christopher himself had the temerity to deliver a lecture in Rik's own Institute, soon after its opening, in which he, too, preached the dangers of selective excavations, as practised at both Verulamium and Maiden Castle. From that time onwards many of the now established younger generation of Hawkes and Myres used this issue as a platform from which they could sling stones in Rik's direction – in private or occasionally in public.

It is a pity that always and everywhere the new generation comes up fighting and seeks to pull down the achievements of its predecessor, rather than quietly absorbing them – as in practice it must. Of course the pursuit of economic and social interpretations would not have been possible without the historical framework and the advanced methods of excavation for which the Wheelers were so largely responsible. Nor had Rik Wheeler himself been wholly neglectful of social objectives – they were very much in his mind as long ago as when he determined that a Roman city should be excavated. As for Maiden Castle itself, the exploration of the 'town' within the ramparts had been his third aim, only abandoned when he found that four centuries of occupation had left the traces of houses such a bewildering palimpsest as to defy historical reconstruction. It should be remembered, too, that the interior of the fortress was ten times the area of Woodbury – where Bersu was able to uncover only one-third of the area in two seasons of digging.

As for more particular ways in which Wheeler's interpretation of his findings has been eroded by new discoveries and ever-changing opinions, his first two aims, to elucidate the structural history of the fortifications and to relate it to the cultural history of the inhabitants, have not been seriously questioned. Inevitably his views on how the facts relate to the general history of the British Iron Age has been considerably modified after more than forty years of intensive research on the subject, just as Christopher Hawkes's original classification has been modified. It has been shown that the sling-users must have been present well before 56 BC and therefore were not Veneti driven out by Caesar. It now appears, too, that the arrival of the Belgic rulers was earlier than Wheeler thought.

One very definite error, and one that had already provoked Gerhard Bersu's disapproval during his inspection, concerned the numerous ovoid pits sunk deep into the chalk among the huts. Rik had been writing of pit-dwellers as a small boy and was reluctant quite to abandon the idea now, when it had become generally discredited. Although in *Maiden Castle* he conceded that most were storage pits later used to dump rubbish, he stubbornly maintained that some had been used as sheltered rooms, and that in one the occupants had crouched round a fire, eating mutton and throwing the bones over their shoulders. So strongly had this picture taken possession of his imagination that he ignored both informed opinion and the probability that his mutton-eaters would have been both roasted and suffocated.

It is in the interpretation of the Neolithic remains, where Rik adopted the opinions of the learned specialists of the day, that the changes have been greatest. The dating of the original settlement has been pushed back another thousand years or so by the findings of Carbon 14 analysis, while the butchered burial is now thought to be Anglo-Saxon in date. Rik was prepared to take such switches in expert doctrine cheerfully. I recall one occasion when I showed signs of distress at having written something in ignorance of the latest opinion on the subject. 'Yes,' he said. 'It is the latest, but not necessarily any more correct.'

The years between the last triumphant season at Maiden Castle and the outbreak of war were at least as strenuous as any that had gone before, while all through the last year after 'Munich' Rik was inwardly distracted by his realization that war was inevitable and by his determination to take part in it.

In the background the infant Institute at St John's Lodge demanded attention and the London Museum (which had staged its own jubilee exhibition in 1937) could never be entirely neglected. Then Rik had determined that some supplementary digs were needed in connection with both Verulamium and Maiden Castle. Although he delegated the field direction of these to his reliable women assistants, he frequently dashed down to inspect and advise on the progress of the work. One was at Poundbury, a small fort near Dorchester, the historical relation of which with its gigantic neighbour he wished to establish, another a building in Verulamium itself which had been left unexplored. Both were put in the charge of Kitty Richardson, with the expert services of Wedlake and Cookson, and although, like Thalassa Cruso and others before her, she found Rik's inspections most alarming occasions, she also appreciated the responsibility she carried, for it enabled her, relatively inexperienced as she still was, to build up her self-confidence. A third excavation in which Rik was much concerned was directed by Molly Cotton at Silchester. This was an attempt to discover a Belgic predecessor of the Roman town (to be compared with that at Verulamium) and although it was unsuccessful, proving the suspected earthwork to be Roman, it was none the less strenuous. Kitty Richardson has a vivid recollection of a preliminary meeting held at Silchester to discuss plans:

For some reason I went down, driven alarmingly by Rik in that awfully draughty Lancia, at horrific speed, because we were late in starting, we were due to lunch with the others, and he loathed unpunctuality. My map-reading was rotten and I missed a turning in the medley of lanes, but he did not blow his top off and we got there in time.

Kitty was, indeed, one of those young women with whom Rik never blew his top. She confesses that 'he did terrify me out of my wits at times, but when I made some curious error would mildly remark, "I sometimes wonder how your mind works."'

These subsidiary digs and their aftermath of paperwork took up some of Rik's own time, while the preparatory work on the Maiden Castle report had to be fitted in during the winter months. The main effort of this period of attenuating peace went, however, into the surveys and excavations in France.

It had been part of Rik's forward planning to send Leslie Scott with her car to France as early as the second season at Maiden Castle. Not only was the nature of the country on either side of the Channel very similar, but there was reason to think that during the relevant period, from the fourth century BC to the first century AD, there were also close cultural relationships – as was a confirmed historical fact by Caesar's time. Leslie drove her lovely and intelligent self through much of Brittany and Normandy, looking out for many-ramparted forts and scanning local museum collections. As anticipated, the report she brought back confirmed the likely cultural connections and also that the evidence to prove them would have to be sought by the British since the French had little to show.

At that time French prehistory was in the doldrums. The great achievements that had been made in Palaeolithic studies, and the particularly glorious discovery of cave art, had led to complacency and a neglect of all later periods and of advances in scientific excavation. Most local museums were in a deplorable state and although the Musée Nationale at St Germain-en-Laye had notable collections, its direction was unenterprising to the point of apathy.

This state of affairs can be seen as most fortunate for Wheeler, since it meant that he could hurl himself into an archaeological field almost identical with that of Britain in the twenties. In France his methods of rapid selective excavation to establish historical outlines was again perfectly appropriate. He was able to lead the British foray with untrammelled zest: many colleagues judged that it was the most brilliantly executed action of his career.

It was plain that Leslie's reconnaissance had to be followed up with a fuller preparatory excursion before serious excavations could begin. Accordingly during the winter of 1936–7 Rik constituted a three-man survey party, consisting of Leslie and himself, together with Ralegh Radford, who already had some acquaintance with Breton sites. Radford, well known in archaeological circles for speaking at meetings in a high sing-song voice, with eyes closed and swaying to and fro on the balls of his feet, was a scholarly archaeologist and historian who had been Director of the British School at Rome.

The first necessity was to win official permission for a British invasion to excavate French monuments. Like many nearly comatose institutions, Gallic archaeology was highly centralized under the Ministère des Beaux Arts, and the correct way to gain its favour was through the St Germain Museum and its Curator, Raymond Lantier.

It was therefore arranged that Radford should come from Rome to join Rik and Leslie in Paris, when he could introduce Rik to his old acquaintance, Lantier, an art historian with a gammy leg and no interest in fieldwork. The meeting could hardly have been more satisfactory, for the easy-going curator gave them carte-blanche to excavate any two sites which they cared to select – providing only that they got the landlord's permission and obeyed the insurance regulations. The two greatly contrasting Englishmen were then passed on to Claude Schaeffer, with whom Rik had stayed in Syria earlier that year. He showed them such relevant collections as there were, and, as one who had actually done some digging in France, advised them on more detailed planning. Subsequently Schaeffer made the sole official, or semi-official, visit to one of the excavations (Camp d'Artus), while Rik was to dedicate his final Report jointly to Claude and Odile.

That same day the little survey party set off for Rouen, where Leslie's car was waiting, visited a well-known Neolithic camp in the dusk and drove on to their base at Caen.

The three of them set out on one of the more curious of archaeological expeditions. Armed with Leslie Scott's findings and such information as could be gleaned from the old French antiquaries, they swept across western Normandy and Brittany, determined to discover all hill-forts that might further their search for the homelands of the Dorset slingsmen – and select two for excavation. The great impediment was that they dare not be seen trespassing on the lands of small farmers and peasants whose goodwill they might need later on. Instead they held long café-table sessions with the countrymen concerned, worming out information over the wine. It was not easy, for most earthworks of whatever kind had no other local name than the *chatellier*, while at the same time it was likely that mediaeval and later remains were better known to the peasantry than prehistoric ones.

However, they did well enough and Rik certainly enjoyed himself. Ralegh Radford, the better linguist, claims to have been the more successful at picking up clues. Yet, as the odd man out, he was at a disadvantage, and Rik was prepared to treat him unscrupulously. On one occasion, which he remembers with bitterness, he was left to conduct the café enquiries while Rik and Leslie went to buy a picnic lunch. An hour went by and on their return Ralegh learnt that they had spent much of it wandering round a Romanesque church in which he was particularly interested. Rik announced that it was late and they must move on at once. Poor Radford was not to see that church for another forty years.

After crossing much of the Normandy peninsula, filling notebooks as they went, they reached yet another *chatellier*, but one that already had an appeal for Rik, the Petit Celland in the south of the Manche. He knew it to be exceptionally large for the region and with multiple ramparts, and inspection confirmed that it was probably unfinished – suggesting the emergency of Caesar's wars of conquest.

Inspection also proved the place to be quite horribly overgrown with scrub and the most pernicious brambles, but Rik was no more daunted by such threats than he would be by the midday sun in India. Ralegh, with his delicate sensibilities, was appalled at the prospect of pain, but reflecting that he would not himself experience it, readily gave way to Rik's favourable arguments when the pros and cons were discussed at their hotel that night. So one site for excavation was chosen.

They drove westward, perhaps rather scamping the inspection of northern Brittany since Rik had already felt the lure of another, even larger fort known from the antiquarian record, that of the Camp d'Artus near Huelgoat in Finistère. Probably Rik's mind was all but made up before he saw the place. He wrote that 'in the Camp d'Artus we found an *oppidum* after our own heart. . . . We had no hesitation on the spot in selecting it as our starting point.' The difficulty presented here was not brambles but the well-grown State Forest that covered the area. The trees would be an inconvenience, but the need to insure the whole forest against fire threatened to be a more serious problem.

The survey party went on to inspect some small promontory forts along the coast. Presently Ralegh Radford had to return to Rome, leaving Rik and Leslie to drive eastward. Fate was unkind: Leslie's car, hard-used in the exploration of rough ground, first gave trouble and then broke down altogether. The rest of the reconnaissance had to be carried out in discomfort and, to Rik, with the almost intolerable slowness of public transport in the Gallic countryside.

Overall, the prospectors were well satisfied, and during 1937 preparations were made for a British archaeological invasion of Gaul. The Antiquaries and other English academic bodies gave money and the Ministère des Beaux Arts gave its blessing. For a time it looked as though the insurance of Camp d'Artus was going to be an insuperable difficulty, for the French agencies quoted premiums running into millions of francs. Then Rik encountered a Lloyd's underwriter who was willing to use his independence to provide cover for something under one pound sterling. So it was that he was able to record, 'By the end of our last season's work at Maiden Castle the new enterprise was ready.'

It was during the summer of 1937 that Rik got to know Mavis de Vere Cole after her visit to Maiden Castle with Augustus John. She was then about twenty-nine years old, a woman of humble origins and Junoesque beauty: naturally fair with brilliant colouring and complexion and a fine, well-covered figure. She had made her way upwards, to marry Horace de Vere Cole, the famous practical joker, ring-leader of the Emperor of Abyssinia hoax against the Royal Navy. She had a small son, Tristan Cole, of whom she was fond, if careless. For some time she had belonged to what Rik, when he first saw them together, referred to as Augustus John's harem, and spent much of her time with him at Fryern Court. She was full of life, totally uninhibited, enjoying herself with universal amorality. This included a lack of concern for the truth that led to what should perhaps be called fantasizing rather than plain lying. She would, for example, on occasion claim the Prince of Wales as Tristan's father.

It was therefore quite characteristic that when, much later, Mavis was to sign a ghosted account of her life for the *Empire News* she declared that her earliest meeting with Rik was when she hailed a taxi near Warwick Street and 'a tall handsome figure with a clipped moustache' claimed it as his. 'His eyes met mine – they were dancing with mischief. "We must share it then. . . . No use quarrelling about it."' Rik himself said that this story was an invention – he often met Mavis in Warwick Street simply because she worked nearby. There is some mystery here, since in addition to his account of the well-authenticated Maiden Castle sighting, Rik told Molly Cotton that he first met Mavis when her hat blew off in Shaftesbury Avenue and he rescued it for her. Perhaps he felt he should cap her own fantasy with another, for in fact he had followed up that exciting first impression of Mavis skipping along the ramparts with a telegram from Maiden Castle, 'Do lunch or dine with me Jermyn Street tomorrow.'

They probably saw much of one another during the following months. However this may be, it is certain that when in the spring of 1938 Bill Wedlake was at Verulamium, digging with Kitty Richardson, Rik brought Mavis with him one Saturday, when he came from London to inspect the work. Wedlake writes,

I was particularly struck by this remarkably good-looking woman and her charming manner. She skipped like a goddess from wall to wall around the excavation. Her lovely blonde hair enclosed in a bright red handkerchief with white spots. It was quite evident she was more interested in R.E.M.W. than the excavations and he appeared to be completely enamoured with her and it was good to see him looking so well and happy.

Much of the rest of the story comes, patchily, from *Beautiful and Beloved*, a somewhat sensational book about his mother produced by Tristan together with Roderic Owen. It cannot have been very long after the time of the Verulamium visit that Augustus John wrote a letter of worldly advice to his mistress – who seems to have asked him to judge between Rik and a young man in whom she was also interested. He thought the youth's 'genteel mid-Victorian ambience' would prove insupportable.

But Wheeler is at any rate a distinguished personality, quite solvent and as it appears highly amorous where you are concerned – in fact a very eligible *parti* indeed. If he came up to scratch and asked for your hand I wouldn't turn him down in a hurry. Don't all the same . . . spread out your bacon for him on the spot.

'Highly amorous' he certainly was; he was infatuated with Mavis, not only physically but also psychologically. Hitherto all his women had been educated, belonging at least in part to the academic world and therefore reasonable, bourgeois, subject to restraints and scruples. It was a new excitement to engage in sexual battle with a beauty so intensely female and as unashamedly libidinous as himself. He was also attracted by the Bohemian, greatly talented circle in which she was living, and by the challenge of wresting her from the arms of Augustus John.

It was all very real, it fevered his potency, yet at the same time the actor in Rik Wheeler was aroused, leading to a performance that was not wholly serious. In June, when he went to stay at Fryern Court, he indulged his sense of drama by climbing up the wallcreeper to Mavis's bedroom. As he said, 'I was a conventional kind of Romeo to her Juliet, except that I hadn't got a fiddle between my legs.' He was always to remember this incident with pride and amusement.

There was to be an even more dramatic development during this visit. It was summed up in a typically succinct entry in the diary Mavis kept and liked to leave lying about for others to read. 'Stew. Fight with Gussus.' The upshot was that the painter, apparently in real rage, challenged Wheeler to a duel. In response Rik exercised the right of the challenged to name the weapons. As a field gunner he chose field guns.

Rik's jocular style contrasted with his opponent's, for John wrote to Mavis,

Darling Pirani, I am most awfully sorry for the incident on Sunday night. I got into a frightful state listening to the revelry in the dining-room and when I saw, on coming from the shit-house, Wheeler's countenance grinning through the haze, I felt still worse. The whisky I had been imbibing (secretly) doubtless determined my evil mood. I was wretched next day when I realized you had gone.

A little later he wrote again: 'Wheeler hasn't written or shown his grinning mask, so I take it the duel is off. . . . Very ungentlemanly conduct I call it. Perhaps his suggestion is right and he *is* a cad.'

Mavis on this occasion may have taken refuge with Charles and Cecily

St John Hornby in their country house, Chantmarle, near Dorchester. This relationship introduces another strand in her involved love life of those days. Earlier that year she had met Hornby quite by chance, in a railway compartment, and instantly captivated him. The founder of W. H. Smith, also a painter, connoisseur and fine printer, was then some seventy years old, ready to accept the role of gentlemanly worshipper. Mavis made use of him without scruple, but she probably gave him much more pleasure than pain, and always remained on good terms with his wife. Sometimes she addressed sentimental verses to him – free verse flowed easily from her pen. Rik naturally detested the association, but had to tolerate and even share in it.

Although Mavis had not taken Augustus John's advice of conserving her bacon, Rik was by now making frequent proposals of marriage. Yet despite this ardent pursuit and the wild doings at Fryern, he was not distracted from his usual crowded programme of work. During the first week in July he was in Belfast as President of the Museums Association and delivered what was widely publicized as 'a spirited Presidential Address'. Once again he was urging the importance of museums in education and the need of support for impoverished provincial collections. He also touched on a matter that he knew would soon become urgent: the safeguarding of museum treasures in wartime.

It was during this summer, too, that Dr Wheeler was briefly pressed into the service of Sir Winston Churchill. It began when he went to Bristol to take his first Honorary Doctorate – in the exalted company of Anthony Eden and T. S. Eliot. Churchill was then Chancellor of the university, and when Rik was kneeling before him to receive his hood the great man whispered, 'Want to see you. Meet me in the ante-room.' The upshot was that he soon found himself on the train to London in Churchill's private carriage. *The History of the English-Speaking Peoples* had just reached the Danes, and the author wanted help.

After that the two had a few sessions together, sometimes in the company of Professor Lindemann (Lord Cherwell). On one of these occasions Churchill asked, 'Who was the first Englishman?' and Rik, knowing that a rough question needed a rough answer replied, 'Piltdown Man'. It was only by great good luck that long after the war he was sent the proofs of Volume I and was able to strike out all reference to that Old Pretender, by then exposed as a forgery.

His main archaeological preoccupation was with making final preparations for the expedition to Brittany, which was to stage its first excavation at the Camp d'Artus. It was to be a large party, not far short of fifty, with many members of the Maiden Castle team and, as usual, students drawn from various universities. Kitty Richardson was now to be Wheeler's chief assistant in the direction, while Bill Wedlake was to take charge of the Breton labourers. Leslie Scott brought all her knowledge of the terrain, Huntly Gordon was the faithful surveyor, Cookie the equally faithful photographer, and John Ward-Perkins, a Roman specialist now on the London Museum staff, had been newly enrolled. Theodora Newbould, who had proved her organizing abilities at Maiden Castle, contributed not only these but also a large car and a Welsh-speaking chauffeur. Among Rik's students who had been at Maiden Castle was a very beautiful girl called Margaret Collingridge (usually known as Kim), a devout Roman Catholic, whom Rik had asked to marry him the year before and for whom he still had tender feelings, by no means nullified by his obsession with Mavis.

On 26 July Rik, together with many of his team, caught the night boat for St Malo, whence they drove by stages to Huelgoat, where they were to lodge in various hotels in the little town. The next day, somewhere en route, he found time to write a long love-letter to Mavis. It began, offensively enough to poor Hornby:

My Darling, I am scrawling this in the noisiest café in the world in a fog of smoke and peasant smells. You, I suppose, will be at Chantmarle, making all the right noises at the rock garden and lingering unduly behind the library door. Well, you'd be happy somehow anywhere, and Chantmarle is a lovely place to be happy in. ('How *glad* I am to see your dear face' – Shucks!) You'd be happy even here, although I've been utterly soaked, ball and tonsil, since I set foot on these shores yesterday morning. Gawd how its rained ('too wet for the rock garden today my darling. Come and see the library again.') No, I'm not a cad really, but I suppose life is slightly funny. I hope so because it was pretty grim these two days without you. Mon dieu how I want you.

The letter then warmed into the precise eroticisms Rik was always prepared to entrust to the post, but ended, 'Dearest heart – I am wholly and absolutely yours.'

A little later, on the last day of the month, when he was installed in Huelgoat's Grand Hôtel d'Angleterre, Rik dispatched another message, very different in purport and style:

Once more, will you marry me? As you know there isn't a deal that I can give you, except devotion and a good share of understanding, a moderate amount of baddish temper and quite a lot of that zest for life which is yours above all things. You know too that when my rather broken career comes to an end – shall we say at sixty-five – only an accident can preserve us from the poverty of the righteous.

Rik did not have to wait until his return to England to assuage his longings. Members of the expedition remember that he left them for a few days, going they knew not where. In fact, it must have been to Paris, where Mavis was on her way back from visiting Tristan. It was exactly the adventurous encounter to suit both of them. Mavis commemorated it in her diary. The two entries read, 'Wonderful Rikki ... Heavenly Three days.' Then 'Rikki. Oh Rikki mine. Rikki forever ... Wonderful R.'

Her habit of writing intimacies such as these, intending them to be seen, is revealed in an amusing passage of arms with Theo Newbould: 'I had a strong feeling Mavis meant me to read the postcards she used to send Rik. So although I would normally read other people's postcards I just wouldn't look at her ones. One day I told her so and she confessed "Of course you were meant to, Theodora. Now you've spoilt the fun!"'

Meanwhile the test excavation of the Camp d'Artus went forward. The atmosphere was cheerful, for the small hotels were pleasant and there was an abundance of food, all very cheap since the exchange rate was favourable. The Breton workmen, of whom some half-dozen were employed, brought large supplies of red wine up to the site and distributed it generously. The great granite ridge, strewn with elephantine boulders, on which the camp stood, was at least dry, the birches and pines smelt good, and, although a nuisance, had not grown too cumbersome on the poor soil.

The excavation of the two entrances and portions of the ramparts, and several soundings in the interior, yielded enough evidence to make it reasonably certain that the *oppidum* had been thrown up as a tribal rallying place against Caesar. It was briefly held in 56 BC by the tribesmen, but seems to have been stormed and its gates destroyed. The work had to be quickly done, but it was as skilful as ever. A minor technical triumph was the exposure of the *murus Gallicus* construction of the defences. This form, named after Caesar's own account of it, consisted of earth or rubble walls faced with stone and laced together with a grid of horizontal timbers. Rik succeeded not only in showing that these walls had originally been as much as twelve feet high, but also in exposing *in situ* the great iron nails that had held the beams together at their intersections. He had good reason to be proud when: 'At dawn one morning we met our vigorous friend Claude Schaeffer, who came to inspect us on behalf of the French government, and I think we were able to display to him an orderly British excavation in full blast, the first of its kind, I suppose, in the annals of Breton archaeology.'

Rik had one bad moment during the stay at the Camp d'Artus. Determined not to betray the trust of his benefactor at Lloyds, he had forbidden smoking, although he himself suffered 'the tortures of the damned' in forgoing his beloved pipe. One morning on arrival he saw a fire burning brightly among the trees. He 'broke into a frantic gallop' and found happy village children cooking bilberries. Picturing the forests of Brittany swept by flames, he 'leapt with a roar upon the fire and trampled it out'. He then had to calm frightened youngsters and indignant parents and persuade them to light no more fires while the dig was in progress.

While they were still based at Huelgoat a minor excavation was undertaken at Kercaradec, a small stone-built hill-fort near Quimper. It was multivalate, had already produced a pile of sling-stones, and lay near the tribal boundary of the Veneti, in whom Rik was so much interested. Leslie Scott was put in charge. She was probably not sorry to leave the main party for a while, since she must already have been aware of Rik's infatuation with Mavis, which naturally appalled her. Among all his friends it was to be Leslie who showed most courage in trying to save him from himself, if only by trying to break his incomprehensible determination to remarry.

The dig was successful in showing Kercaradec to be pre-Caesarian and to be structurally close to a Cornish form, but the evidence did not suggest any direct connection between its builders and Wheeler's Wessex slingmen.

The main party shifted eastwards to Avranches to tackle the second *oppidum*, Le Petit Celland, Theo Newbould managing all the problems of transport and lodging with unfailing competence. The diggers and plan-makers suffered as severely from the brambles as Ralegh Radford had anticipated, but the excavation went well. The story it revealed was similar to that at the Camp d'Artus: again, the fortifications were of the *murus Gallicus* type, but had not been quite completed before the stronghold fell to the Romans, its gates collapsing in flames. The dating was securely fixed to Caesar's campaign of 56 BC by the unearthing of more than a score of Celtic coins. An irony was here in store, for these coins were to play an important part in disproving Wheeler's date for the Maiden Castle take-over.

The effectiveness of rapid test digging was remarkable and renewed all Rik's old satisfactions. Yet perhaps an even greater achievement of his French expeditions of this year and the next lay in what he called the 'ground survey' that was executed simultaneously. He divided his forces into two sections, and these by turn either took part in the current excavation or formed motorized flying columns, whose purpose it was to seek out every considerable ancient earthwork in the region. For Rik, audacious as ever, had taken upon himself what should have been the Frenchman's burden, the archaeological mapping of most of Brittany and Normandy.

Each search party was a car-load of up to five, mostly young men and women but always with an experienced leader. They were armed with lists of sites and all available information, including that collected in the 1936 survey, for their allotted territory. The usual practice was first to consult the village *curé*, or, failing him, the schoolmaster or doctor. Living history asserted itself when it was found that Theo's Welsh-speaking driver could serve as interpreter with Bretons who had no French. Once the earthwork was located (and sometimes unsuspected ones were discovered through their enquiries) the party would make notes and a rough survey – then on to the next place on the list. Occasionally they had to stay out overnight, but it was more usual to return to base each day, late and weary.

The sheafs of reports were then submitted to Wheeler for him to decide which monuments were worthy of more thorough exploration and planning. This work had to be done after a full day on the current excavation, a regimen which even so sturdy a character as Kitty Richardson found 'very strenuous'. Rik would then visit the selected earthworks, usually taking Kitty with him, together with Cookie and his camera and two tape-holders (the archaeological equivalent of theatrical spear-carriers) for the planning.

Rik enjoyed these excursions, especially those from Huelgoat, which took them to cliff castles along the glorious coasts of Finistère. The weather was good, the work exhilarating.

It might have been thought that, with so much digging and driving during the week, Rik would have taken a day of rest. But, with thoughts of Mavis and rumours of war, he was wound up, his energy inexhaustible. At weekends he took all who wished sight-seeing, usually to mediaeval buildings, where he would extend his flock's historical appreciation with informal talks. He had never lost his love of Gothic architecture and all his life was indignant if excursions organized by more austere prehistorians passed by the monuments of civilization.

That September at Avranches rumours of war changed into manifest preparations. Day after day the cathedral bell tolled, summoning contingents of reservists to join their regiments. Bill Wedlake remembers standing with Rik outside his hotel while dozens of young men streamed past them. Before long Rik could stand it no longer, and, leaving Kitty and Bill to wind up the work at Le Petit Celland, rushed back to London.

From the day after Neville Chamberlain returned from Munich, Wheeler spent every evening touring the Territorial depots, seeking the promise of a commission. 'It was not merely that war seemed likely; I now savagely hoped for war, for a national opportunity to obliterate the disgrace of Munich.' For months he met with no response: he was forty-eight and had done no soldiering since being demobilized twenty years before. In the end it was not past military prowess that was to count but his reputation as an antiquary, which was known to a certain Colonel of the Middlesex Territorials. Through him Rik secured an order from the War Office to raise a new light anti-aircraft battery at Enfield, 'at a time to be notified'. With this he had to be satisfied – though his impatience for action was great; he saw as clearly as any of us that Chamberlain's shameful peace could not last. His zeal as Keeper was at a low ebb during this last year of his active tenure. This was made evident when, without any of his usual skilful preparation, without even informing his trustees, he abruptly handed over the administration of the museum to Margot Eates. Lord Harewood in particular was incensed by this high-handed indiscretion.

One cause of strain was undoubtedly Wheeler's anticipation of war, the other was Mavis de Vere Cole. His determination to marry her became even more compulsive, but for months she held out, recognizing clearly enough, for her female instincts were sound, that archaeology, and his passion for work, would always be her enemy. The pursuit was exciting and fanned his ardour, but at times became stormy. In the pithy entries in her diary for that winter she noted on 5 November that, after a display of actual fireworks, 'Quarrelled with Rik, who smacked me!!!' Then a month later 'Lunched with Rik. Dined with Gussus. Rik gave me a ring also thick ear! Brute!' A few days after this: 'Dreadful nightmare with ear. Saw specialist today – have to stay in. Rikki very sweet to me – almost worth the pain.' Rik himself seemed shocked into a new seriousness by what he had done:

We both of us – yes, you and me – managed the affair pretty disgustingly, but your admitted lies to me got beneath the skin. Why the devil you should lie to me in this stupid, half-witted fashion gets me. I daresay it's all my own fault on analysis, but that doesn't help much! Anyway, lies or no lies, I love you now and shall love you always.

Presumably the ring that accompanied the thick ear was a pledge of marriage, but the date to be fixed for it was not until March. Behind the scenes enough was known of Mavis for the press to delight in mentioning her relationship to the Prime Minister as news spread of her forthcoming union with another well-known character. The *Birmingham Post*, for example, on 1 February 1939, in an article praising the London Museum, mentions 'Dr Wheeler who is to marry a sister-in-law of Mr Neville Chamberlain'.

They were extraordinary months for Rik. Mavis herself was still far from certain about the prospects of wedlock. She wrote to Poppet John to say that she was contemplating 'doing a vamooz' as she was afraid of archaeology and had other misgivings about marriage – most certainly justified. She was therefore all the more erratic, making Rik wretched, enchanted and angry by turns. Then, exacerbating Mavis's own provocations, he was involved in the tragi-comedy of her relationship with St John Hornby, and, far more disturbingly, in the continuing entanglement with Augustus John.

Rik Wheeler had never been noted for discretion in his love affairs, but now he seems to have been so far off balance as to break even the most generous conventions. Aileen Fox (a Roman archaeologist whom Cyril had married after his first wife was drowned in a bathing tragedy) recalls an occasion during this period when John came to open an art exhibition in Cardiff. He arrived with his usual entourage, including Mavis, and Rik was present in what could have been an official capacity since he still had many connections in Wales. A formal luncheon had been laid on at the 'Mansion House' and in the course of it the whole party became excessively merry and Rik was so recklessly amorous in his attentions to Mavis as to cause serious scandal among the good Welsh hosts. Afterwards John wrote to her,

I can't see how I can run in harness with Rikki, it will be like an amputation to let go of you ... at Cardiff I felt you were a part of *me*, not of him, my lovely gyppo. Though I mayn't have shown it, I was a mass of nerves and brandy. Will it be possible to paint that supreme picture of you *now*? That picture which I *know* would come off at the right time.

The path to a marriage can seldom have been less smooth, for, if Mavis had not broken with a past love, Rik himself was still emotionally involved with Margaret Collingridge. A letter he sent her when she was going abroad for a time is indeed a surprising one. He said that he thought he ought to let her know that he was about to marry Mavis, yet begged her to come back as he needed her desperately.

No one who knew either Rik or Mavis could understand why he wished to marry her. The authors of *Beautiful and Beloved* sagely observed that he loved to show off so wonderful a creature, 'but by marriage to get her for himself he was bound to lose her'. Yet he could not possibly have thought he *would* get her for himself – he already knew her too well. He could hardly hope to take her away from John any further than he had already. He knew that as a wife she could not adjust to his way of life. He is said to have confessed to Theodora, 'You see some chocolates and you've got to eat them, even if you know you'll be sick afterwards.' Surely he had already enjoyed the best sweets Mavis had to offer? Just before the wedding a friend came across him in the Athenaeum, his head bowed on his knees. 'I am mad,' he said. 'I know what I'm doing is madness.' That seems a better explanation. He was undoubtedly in a state of total inner dissociation.

The wedding was to be at Caxton Hall, while the ever-complaisant Hornby lent the Chelsea premises of his Ashenden Press, Shelley House, for the reception. Rik left for the Registry Office from Lancaster House, very elegant and correctly turned out. He had asked Michael to help him with his tie, but the young man was so tense that, as his father said, it might be he who was getting married. Mavis (who had a stye in her eye) put on a jaunty hat and round her neck one of those odious fox furs, head biting tail, that we all wore just then. Her superb legs were well displayed.

One of the witnesses was Augustus John, the other A. P. Herbert. Inevitably there were photographers waiting at Caxton Hall. One photograph, said to have been taken before the ceremony, shows Mavis standing with John and Rik, the painter looking at her, the bridegroom, holding a cigar, looking away. The more conventional pictures of the wedded pair were to appear in a number of newspapers. Mavis, who was thirty, gave her age as twenty-eight – probably more for the fun of it than from any vanity.

The party gathered to take champagne and wedding cake at Shelley House included most of Rik's archaeological friends and acquaintances, among them Max Mallowan and Agatha Christie. Mavis's parents and brother were also there, and young Tristan scampered about. I remember feeling that the atmosphere was a little strained, with a sense of unreality, and it was impossible not to notice for how much of the time Mavis clung to Augustus John's arm. The most revealing memory of the hour comes from Rik's former secretary, Tommy. He went up to her 'in a distracted sort of way' and asked, 'Tommy, what am I doing? I am married, aren't I?'

A few days later St John Hornby wrote to Mavis,

You looked lovely on Thursday, darling. I felt proud to have you at Shelley House for your party. My heart was very heavy when the moment came to say goodbye and you made it a sweet goodbye which I shall never forget.... I suppose I oughtn't to write to you like this now that you are married, but after all, Rikki knows I love you and it's no use pretending that I don't! Give him my love. There are few men I would rather you had as a husband ... my loving thoughts are with you always, Mavis dearest.

The announcement had been made that 'the honeymoon would be spent travelling in the Middle East' and Rik had, indeed, made ambitious plans. Starting on 2 April, they were to visit Baalbek, Palmyra, Homs, Krak des Chevaliers, Ras Shamra; to stay a few days at Aleppo, then take the Taurus Express to Istanbul and return to London by Simplon-Orient Express. It was hardly a programme designed to please poor Mavis, who was not addicted to historical sight-seeing. Whether they kept to it is not recorded.

Back in London, Rik had an immediate opportunity to display his wife in public: he took her to the opening of the Royal Academy, then a great occasion for the exhibition of fame and fashion. She was duly photographed wearing 'a striking Arab hat'. It must have been at some time between the private view and leaving for the second archaeological expedition in France that Augustus John introduced Mavis to a tough, bold young man called Clive Entwistle, son of the photographer, Vivienne. They were immediately attracted to one another.

For this 1939 season, on 25 July, Wheeler, his wife and most of his team gathered at Newhaven to board the night boat for Dieppe – for now it was Normandy that was to be covered by the same combination of excavation with ground survey that had been followed in Brittany. The work was as strenuous as ever: indeed, the number of earthworks to be recorded was larger. The survey had satisfactory results in that it soon established that east of the Seine the earthworks were of quite a different type from those in Brittany. There was no difficulty in claiming that their builders were the Belgae, that, indeed, the expedition was on the southern border of the homelands from which the British Belgae had set sail. Rik felt great satisfaction in encountering them once again, and in being the first in France to recognize and investigate their distinctive fortifications.

Altogether no less than sixteen of these Belgic hill-forts were found and two, both to the east of the Seine, were chosen for test excavations. The larger and more promising was the Camp de Canada, two miles inland from Fécamp, and commanding a view over the port to the sea.

The second lay at Duclair, thirty miles to the south-east, on a chalk spur above the Seine.

All started well at the coastal site: the Hôtel de la Poste at Fécamp was exceptionally good and the conditions were pleasant – although, as ever, the hill was overgrown. Excavation soon revealed the massive earthen ramparts, with wide, shallow ditches so different from the *murus Gallicus* of the Breton forts. The archaeologists, whether of the digging or the flying column party, were at full stretch. Understandably, once the novelty had worn off Mavis was lonely and bored.

Then at last she bolted. For several days no one had any idea where she was until she rang up Theo Newbould, asking to be fetched from Mont St Michel. However, the meeting had been arranged, she was there with Clive Entwistle and the encounter had been so intensely enjoyable that even Mavis hardly knew how to cope with her torn feelings.

Rik was in turmoil, and when the message came dashed off with Theo, urging her to drive her new car at a fearful speed through the night. According to the story in *Beautiful and Beloved*, Rik finally found Mavis coming down the main street of Mont St Michel with that skipping walk that had attracted him so much when he first observed it at Maiden Castle.

This incident had been disturbing in itself and left Rik very much on edge. Naturally, it annoyed the women of the expedition, and most of all Kitty Richardson, who was to find working with Rik made more difficult – and who in any case had no sympathy with such doings.

Leslie Scott had a particular reason to look on with a sardonic eye. She had, after all, risked rows and unpopularity in her vain effort to prevent this preposterous union. Once again she took charge of a small dig of her own, at the Camp de César, a cliff castle on the Ile de Groix. There providence intervened, encouraging her to withdraw from Rik's immediate affairs. On her excavation she met a man as eligible as Thalassa's husband in being both well-off and handsome – though unlike him in being British, offspring of a military and landed family. Leslie was to marry this Peter Murray-Thriepland, the same young man whom Rik had encountered travelling steerage on the voyage to the Levant.

The digging team moved on to Duclair, the work at the Camp de Canada having been adequately completed. Rik, as he said, was there with no more than a half-mind, for (the fret of Mavis apart) he was preparing himself and his affairs for war. On Wednesday, 23 August, he wrote to Martin Holmes, John Ward-Perkins and Margot Eates with instructions about the evacuation of the most valuable part of the London Museum collections. Following plans drawn up two years before, the selected 'hardware' was to be packed ready for transport to the disused Dover Street tube station, while the best costumes were to go immediately to Ascott House, Buckinghamshire, where Mrs Leopold de Rothschild was providing storage. Costumes on display were to be rearranged to conceal gaps that might alert the public. In the event Rik's well-laid plans worked to perfection, all first- and second-line treasures being safely out of Lancaster House by the day war was declared.

As for his own movements, in this same letter Rik told his staff that he expected to return on the following Monday, but his impatience did not allow him to wait so long. He had, in fact, been daily expecting a call from the War Office to take up the promised command, but, when none came, on Friday, the twenty-fifth,

I suddenly handed the archaeological destinies of Normandy over to my partners, Miss K. M. Richardson and Miss Theodora Newbould, and took the night-boat from Dieppe. . . . The moment was exact; the War Office had just issued executive orders and my arrival was acclaimed. By lunch time I was in Enfield for the first time in my life, searching for a vacant house from which to recruit 'Enfield's Own'. I found one in the London Road.

So, while Major Wheeler was organizing his battery and his London Museum staff the evacuation of collections, Kitty, Theo and Will Wedlake had to organize a hasty return home. The unfinished excavation at Duclair was wound up, the personnel and most of the equipment were packed into all available cars and driven to Dieppe. The cars had to be left behind, but the whole party, with their bulky baggage, somehow got aboard an overcrowded and blacked-out steamer. On reaching London, they were startled to see barrage balloons riding the sky and mothers weeping over their labelled children. They, too, were being evacuated.

The story of Wheeler's French expeditions has to be completed here. Even in war Rik did not abandon his moral commitment to the prompt recording of archaeological fieldwork. Whenever he could, he dashed down from Enfield to collaborate with Kitty in preparing a provisional report on all the work done, in supervising the drawing of finds, and in other dutiful chores. The final Report was only to be published, under their joint authorship, in 1957, by which time they had made other brief sorties (1954–6) to finish the eastern part of the grand survey. It describes the five principal excavations and contains a gazetteer of nearly a hundred significant earthworks from the total of twice that number that had been explored. Molly Cotton contributed a study summing up all that was known of the *muri Gallici*. *Hill Forts of Northern France* remains a valuable contribution to French archaeology – and Wheeler's one important excursion into Continental European research.

CHAPTER 8

War: A Natural Condition
of Man

EVER SINCE THE Munich surrender Rik had nursed that savage hope
for war, and a determination, as he put it, 'to be in at the kill'. These
emotions were burning within him, adding to the passion with which,
all through the intervening years, he had served both Clio and Venus.
Now, when no one but Lord Beaverbrook could doubt that war was at
hand, he allowed them to take full command of all his energies, hurling
himself into his martial life as though every hour would affect the
outcome of the world combat.

With the sudden release of so much emotion, and with the nerve
strain of his recent life still upon him, all that he did tended to be
excessive. Yet because the ambience of those first weeks at Enfield was
one of improvisation and amateurishness the resulting incongruity was
bound to appear comical. The raising of the new battery, at first among
friends and relations, had something about it of amateur theatricals –
yet the final production was to be wholly professional.

On the afternoon of Friday, 25 August, Wheeler was at Fécamp; by
lunch-time the next day he was in Enfield and that Saturday afternoon
he had not only found the vacant house in the London Road but ordered
the estate agent off the golf-course to open it up for him. A highly
patriotic appeal for volunteers had been drafted, printed in red, white
and blue and stuck in shop windows before church-goers were home for
their Sunday lunch, while urgent telephoning had secured the legally
necessary medical officer and recruitment forms.

If his memory is to be trusted Rik had also, before Monday dawned
and the recruiting office opened, contrived to summon from London
his first volunteers, John Ward-Perkins and Michael Wheeler, now a
young barrister. During that week 'Enfield's Own', or the 48th Light
Anti-Aircraft Battery, attracted some remarkable officers and useful
men – although it cannot be said that they could immediately put

Britain's disgracefully neglected air defences on a war footing, since for some time they were not only without uniforms (except for one professional sergeant), but had for armament a few rifles and old Lewis guns.

Among the first recruits to arrive was a brilliant trio of lawyers, old friends who, like Rik the year before, had been having difficulty in finding a billet as volunteers. Now they heard that a new Territorial battery was being formed in Enfield and hastened to present themselves. One was none other than Arnold Goodman, solicitor, the future universal genius in our national affairs, Lord Goodman; the second, Dennis Lloyd, was to become Lord Lloyd of Hampstead; and the third, Jim (Laurence) Gower, though not ennobled, was to be an esteemed university Vice-Chancellor. These three clever and sophisticated young men were critically amused by Wheeler's high-pitched performance as their Commanding Officer – and Gower actively disliked him. All, however, recognized his qualities and (in time) his soldierly achievements.

There is a story, still told but always untrue, that Arnold Goodman, having been sent on a round of depots to find a uniform large enough to fit himself, learnt so much of army provision that he was made quarter-master-sergeant on the strength of it. In fact, he was fitted up by his own tailor, but he did owe his early appointment to that important office by the speed with which he mastered the mysteries of military supply. He served with Rik for nearly two years, until just before the Regiment went overseas, when he moved to Southern Command.

Yet another lawyer, destined for the High Court and already a KC, was Henry Wynn-Parry. He was promptly made a captain, for, as Rik was to comment, 'those were the days of wise if astonishing freedom in such trivial matters as rank and promotion'.

There was also a gifted contingent from the theatre, led by Bill O'Bryen, a successful agent and promoter, who had fought most gallantly in the first war. With him was his actress wife, Elizabeth Allan – and the chauffeur of their Rolls was also enlisted. Sir Ronald Leon volunteered, and added to the theatrical glamour by bringing his wife, Kay Hammond. Then Clive Brook arrived with his wife, and, although he failed his medical, they remained for a time to grace the scene.

Added to this sparkling company was a man from a very different mould, Nigel Wingate, the brother of Orde, who was gruff, unorthodox, adventurous and in time to rival Rik in popularity with the men. There can hardly have been another Territorial Battery manned by such an extraordinary group of people as that which Rik's magnetic energy drew to Enfield. No doubt, as he was to concede, the women of the Battery also exercised a powerful attraction, for, in addition to their endowments of fame, beauty, wit and wealth, these wives turned to and ran an excellent canteen for all ranks. There was one exception. Mavis was at Enfield, but took no part in the canteen work and was seldom to be seen, even with Rik. A reliable, if harsh, observer said that she was most often to be found 'sprawling in the Officers' Mess'. This was at a house known as Moncktons, near Epping – where she and Rik were probably billeted.

Professionals, tradespeople and workmen flocked to Rik's standard in such numbers that before very long the 48th Battery, officially commissioned to guard the local Powder and Small Arms factories, swelled into the 42nd Mobile Light Anti-Aircraft Regiment of four batteries – which its Commanding Officer was wholly determined to lead on active service overseas. With the formation of the Regiment, headquarters was moved from the London Road house to the Quaker Lane School at Waltham Abbey.

One small but painful setback in his recruitment Rik had to accept. On the day before Britain declared war he wrote to Bill Wedlake, saying that, now he was back from France, he imagined he would immediately 'be enlisted or conscripted into some form of military service', continuing, 'I should be very glad to have you in this unit at any time you care to present yourself during the next 48 hours.' Bill, however, 'for various reasons did not respond to this invitation', nor to the one that followed when the Regiment was being formed and Rik was able to urge that he would be of great assistance in the interesting tasks of digging and building gun emplacements. Henderson, of the London Museum, in spite of his one-handedness, was an early recruit.

In *Still Digging* the author was able to look back on the Enfield days with some lightness and humour, although he still cherished a memory of them as 'great days ... days of selfless effort and single-minded purpose'. At the time his state of mind was very different. He threw himself into the role of a military man, a bristling disciplinarian, with the exaggerated style that earned him the title of Flash Alf and the questioning and occasional resentment of the educated and individualistic among his volunteers. One small incident illustrates this excess, and the accompanying suspension of his natural humour. It was in the earliest days, when the Battery had no equipment and there was little that could usefully be done, or so it seemed to those still attuned to civilian life. Major Wheeler, however, insisted that strict stand-by guard duty should be maintained, and when one day a young man who was 'on alert' under this ruling was found doing a crossword puzzle Rik sought to dismiss him. Happily, in the end he was dissuaded, perhaps by that master of persuasion, Gunner Goodman himself.

A later instance of an excess of authority ended miserably. Rik, remembering experiences of his other war, was much concerned with the improvement of gun emplacements in the interests of both effectiveness and survival. When, therefore, a brilliant young architect who had joined him designed a most promising gun-pit he took it up with enthusiasm and submitted it to the appropriate higher command. He must have done it most forcefully, for a general was sent down to inspect. By bad luck the designer was in bed with influenza, but Rik ordered him to get up and demonstrate his design to the general. The young architect died and, rightly or wrongly, his death was attributed to his being torn from his sick bed.

When he got his Regiment Rik was able to exercise another characteristic form of his ruthlessness: that of disposing of individuals whom he found undesirable. On his own promotion he was succeeded in command of the 48th Battery by a regular soldier from the Indian Army, one MacWatt. Rik did not like him and was probably rightly convinced that he was wrecking his beloved Battery. The opportunity for dismissing him came about in a most amusing way. MacWatt had one great talent, that of drinking beer standing on his head. When at a party he displayed this gift he allowed a sergeant's wife to attempt an imitation. It proved that, in choosing her underwear, she had not anticipated being turned upside-down and in the excitement that followed the sergeant knocked someone down and there was an unseemly row. Acting swiftly, Rik contrived to use this affair to secure MacWatt's removal and his replacement by a printer-publisher called Steele, with whom he got on well.

After the triumphant formation of his Regiment the new Colonel was bitterly disappointed at the delay in getting overseas. A period of arduous training had, of course, been necessary, but when 1941 dawned and he seemed no nearer his goal his frustration was desperate. As the year went on he developed what he called 'getting mobile', a form of training that involved very frequent shifts of base, always taking over stations vacated by other troops going abroad. This was a most strenuous business, not least for the quartermaster-sergeant, who had to go in advance to the new station to organize the commissariat. During the spring and summer the pressure this 'mobility' put on the Regiment has been described by those who suffered it as 'ghastly'.

It was during this tense period, when the Regiment was stationed in Cumbria, that Rik was guilty of a failure in command that reflects his state of mind. He had ordered an exercise and was in his Lancia, leading a column of heavy transport and guns, when he suddenly turned up a rough track, giving a signal for all to follow. The track grew worse and the drivers were soon in hopeless difficulties. When one brave spirit among them refused to go further Rik confronted his men in fury, then, after a blazing row, climbed into his car and drove out of sight. The drivers were left to manhandle their vehicles back onto the road.

On another occasion the extent to which Rik was living on his nerves manifested itself in a very different way. A junior officer found the Colonel in tears: he had just suffered another setback to his plans for getting into the fight.

When he could, Rik went to London to attend to the affairs of the Society of Antiquaries, for in 1939, when Charles Peers retired from the presidency and Alfred Clapham succeeded him, Rik had taken his friend Clapham's office of Secretary. The following year Reginald Smith died, and Rik was advanced to Director, second in the hierarchy to the President. As duties allowed he took part in the work of officers and Council at the lecture meetings which were resumed, fortnightly, in 1940 after being suspended at the outbreak of war. I recall very clearly how he personally and privately admitted me a Fellow on the day the Germans moved against the Low Countries. Then, in addition to his work on the French material, he was completing the Maiden Castle Report for publication.

As for his personal life, it added most painfully to his other stresses. Clive Entwistle was still passionately engaged with Mavis and she made no attempt to conceal it – although this did not mean that she had ceased to love her husband in her own liberal way. Indeed, Clive paid Rik the compliment of intense jealousy, referring to him as 'that whiskered baboon'. He declared himself determined to win Mavis by fair means or foul. After the Regiment had left Enfield and was in training on Salisbury Plain she took a flat at 10 Chelsea Embankment, where her husband, her principal lover and any other favoured friend could be readily accommodated.

During these early years of the war Tristan was living most of the time at Fryern Court. Mavis was happy to encourage Augustus John's paternal feelings for him, but she did not want to lose him to Augustus and Dodo; moreover, she thought that he was being coarsened by the evacuees at Fryern and by attendance at the village school. Meanwhile St John Hornby and his wife had started a small school at Chantmarle for their grandchildren and others. He, of course, offered a place for Tristan and also provided Mavis with a delightful half-timbered Tudor house in the Wiltshire village of Potterne, within easy reach of Chantmarle. The Johns were both strongly opposed to the move and there began, early in 1941, what Rik was to call the Battle of Fordingbridge.

Mavis enlisted her husband's support in the tussle. He wrote her an affectionate letter of encouragement, telling her,

Go ahead with your plan even if it means extreme action. The violent offence which you will give thereby will disappear in time, and no lasting harm will be done . . . if the worst comes to the worst, I should not hesitate to abduct the lad and to take him straight to Chantmarle . . . the matter is not one in which I can help much, but I'm whole-heartedly behind you.

He followed this up with a telegram: 'Stick to your guns. Essential to win.'

Mavis followed Rik's advice: she abducted her son and took him to the Hornbys. Augustus was provoked into writing a letter of protest to the instigator of this outrage, to which Rik sent a most judicious reply, dated 31 January and from 'Upshire':

Your letter about the rape of Tristan has reached me after long lying on the floor of my vacant flat. From this remote spot it is easy to see *both* sides of the fence, and I must confess that the fence itself does not seem to me to be of great size or solidity. . . .

I do know this: Mavis has always regarded Fryern Court as her real home and you and Dodo as an integral part of her life, and it would be a thousand pities if it were magnified or perpetuated as a major offence. . . . Neither the Wessex accent nor the Lower Habits of the Lower classes are at the real basis of the trouble. The fact is, Mavis does not want to feel that T's destinies are completely beyond her control . . . do you blame her?

Rik sent his wife a copy of this letter, writing on the back,

Well, duckolorums, how's that? Will write to Tristan at first opportunity. Meanwhile here's Cicely's [Hornby's] letter – *charming*. It all goes to show what a good thing your action was. . . . And thank you for your 2 letters – also *charming*! More please.

In *very* great haste – all love R.

The Battle of Fordingbridge turned out as Rik had foretold. Within a month or two Mavis was again visiting Fryern, while Augustus went over to Chantmarle and 'liked the school and everyone in it'. On 16 March, her wedding anniversary, Mavis entered in her diary, '2nd year of Mrs Wheeler!' The union was not to survive for a third.

When Tristan was at Chantmarle Mavis spent a part of her time comfortably installed in Porch House, Potterne, and it was there that Colonel Wheeler's preposterous marriage was exploded on 18 May – surprisingly soon after his magnanimous and husbandly concern for his stepson. There are, as usual with Mavis, different accounts of just what happened. Undoubtedly, however, she and Clive were caught by Rik in *flagrante delicto* – or very near it.

Clive's account ran,

That pleasant idyll was suddenly interrupted by a boisterous banging on the oaken door. Peeping through the upstairs window, Mavis told me it was Ric Wheeler, furious, wearing side-arms, and with a batman. I dropped into the old graveyard on which the house backed and then ruminated on the sometimes intimate rapport between L'Amour and La Morte until I got the 'all-clear' signal.

According to Mavis herself, in an unprinted *Empire News* passage, Rik arrived with his batman, to find Clive in underpants and herself in bed; then:

Clive flew past him. . . . Ricky didn't say a word, nor would he listen to anything I tried to say. Brown [the batman] picked up the valise he had dumped in the hallway, and they drove off together, and there went my happiness, all the fun and love and gaiety I had known. Left alone in the house I wept and hated Clive as I have never hated anyone before or since.

Rik immediately started divorce proceedings, citing Clive Entwistle as co-respondent; the case was undefended and the decree nisi was obtained just three years after the marriage – in March of 1942, by which time Rik was in North Africa.

Unmarried and apart, they were again to be on most affectionate terms. On 19 July 1943, when he was near Tripoli, Brigadier Wheeler sent her photographs and a £100 cheque 'for grapes for you when you have your tonsils out'. He added that if she did not hear from him for some time it would be because 'as usual, my work is getting between us!' By then he was, in fact, much involved in strategic planning for the invasion of Italy. Mavis noted on this letter that Rik had written it just one week after their divorce had been made absolute. It was also a week after he had wound up a letter to Cyril Fox: 'On the board in front of me, next to a distribution-map of my brigade, I've pinned up a pencil portrait of Mavis by Augustus John. I came across it yesterday in an

Illustrated London News. Curious. Mavis was a devil. I like devils. . . .'
An illuminating comment on this relationship between two great
amorists.

The summer of 1941, with the divorce on his hands and his 'mobility'
exercises accelerated in an attempt to overcome his frustrations, was a
bad time for Colonel Wheeler. Then at last news of an overseas posting
for the Regiment reached him. What in fact was to happen was that Rik,
with three of his batteries, would be sent round the Cape to North
Africa, while his own old 48th, under Major Steele, was posted to Java,
where it was to fall into the hands of the Japanese and be decimated.

Some time after embarkation Rik began and kept a diary of the
voyage to Suez, with a slight retrospective account of the week before
sailing. The original was written very roughly, part pencilled, in one of
those Stationery Office exercise books with the Crown and 'G.R.' and
'Supplied for the Public Service' on the pale-green cover. In 1944,
before leaving for India, Rik was to have a slightly modified version
privately printed, together with several other war memories and some
verses, in a little book entitled *Twenty-Four Hours' Leave*. Together
with the letters to Cyril Fox it provides most of the material for what
follows.

The diary has the title of *The Hour of Fury*, from Robert Bridges's
lines

> But ye, dear youth, who lightly in the hour of fury
> Put on England's glory as a common coat.

It is written, too, in a somewhat high-flown literary style, but its
immediacy and the genuine excitement of the experience are enough to
redeem it.

The first inspection of the Regiment before sailing was in the Leeds
suburb of Headingly, on Rik's fifty-first birthday. The men, with their
heavy boots and huge packs, each with a solar topee attached, stood in
long lines up the 'tilted street', impassively awaiting his inquisition, but
most of them, he was sure, thinking about their girls. Suddenly he was
struck by the unreality of the new life they were entering. 'Those lines
of bipeds . . . those bodies, with mine, were circumscribed by battle
dress and their minds, with mine, were buttoned in and buckled up
with their bodies. Their supreme sacrifice in the fight for mankind was
the loss of their own personality.'

Colonel Wheeler received an urgent summons to the Mobilization
Centre, where the officer in charge carefully closed the door, unlocked a

drawer and in conspiratorial fashion passed him the sealed and secret Embarkation Orders.

The embarkation proved to be from Glasgow, and the day 24 September. The Clyde, a sad grey, was thronged with the steamers and warships of a big convoy, the tenders running between with troops and more troops. Altogether some twenty thousand men were put aboard: 'ant-like processions passed through the inhospitable sides and were engulfed.' Rik found himself on an ancient troop ship, the *Empress of Russia*, with a Chinese crew and two or three thousand fighting men.

The convoy sailed before dawn. The Atlantic was rough and persistently foggy as they ploughed westward day after day, some thirty troop-crammed steamers, escorted by destroyers, a couple of cruisers and a huge aircraft-carrier. On the *Empress of Russia* there were not enough lifeboats and not nearly enough latrines. Rik had to endure his one humiliating physical weakness: seasickness. So did thousands of others. 'The convoy vomited and stank to heaven.'

There were a few submarine alarms, accompanied by evasive zig-zagging and the dropping of depth-charges, but all went well and presently the misery on board began to lift. It was a little warmer, a band was formed, there were concerts, lectures and a film or two, the officers in their smoking-room could drink at all hours. Then, somewhere off the Azores, 'a cloud of small white specks scatter at the bows. Flying fish, like soapsuds among the waves. . . . They lend a gaity to the scene, and the scene reflects a lightening of the human heart.'

The convoy stopped at Freetown for coaling, most of the escort ships turning back as the rest steamed south for the equator, where, surprisingly, the weather was very cold for the usual ducking ceremonies. It was still chilly in the South Atlantic, but Rik was delighted, as he always was, by wild birds, when one morning he saw all about them 'broad-winged albatrosses, swaying above the wave tops and hiding in their recesses'. Table Mountain and Capetown they could only salute from afar, but at Durban the troop ships were moored at the quays and shore leave was allowed at last. 'It is a brave new world after five weeks of stench and cockroaches. Endless khaki-clad processions stream down the gangways.'

Here the Colonel made an amusing intervention, remembered by one of his sergeants as an example of his determination that his beloved 42nd must always have the best, be the best – and also look the best. An order had been given that all other ranks disembarking must wear topees, but these, when issued, were judged to be left-over stock from the Boer War. Colonel Wheeler (writes Sergeant Wheeler) was not going to have his men looking rather ridiculous in Durban, so he gave a verbal instruction that the men would go down the gangway wearing topees but carrying their side-caps. At the foot of the gangway the Orderly Sergeant of each battery with their staffs collected all the topees.

There were to be five days ashore.

Rik stepped into that brave new world of dry land with two fixed intentions: to see something of the countryside and its people and to find a sympathetic woman. *The Hour of Fury* is, I believe, the only place in which he put in print, though did not publish, a reference to his having a woman – and even here he was considerably more explicit in the exercise book than in the printed version.

The first day ashore was given to a reconnaissance of Durban and its hotels. Of Durban itself he found the architecture 'atrocious beyond description'; at the Royal Hotel the beer was good but the women unpromising. The Edward Hotel was a cosmopolitan place, fine for a meal but the haunt of those he would wish to avoid. Luck came on the second day, when he was invited to a cocktail party given by the Women Evacuees of Durban, a group of unfortunates, military wives from the Middle East, parked there with their children for the duration. From the exercise book it can be learnt that privately they called themselves the SSWEs, the Sex-Starved Women Evacuees. From among them Rik selected R, a lady from Cairo with almond eyes, a pleasant laugh and appealing outline. He carried her off to dine at the Edward and after her sex starvation had also been assuaged they sauntered along the seashore in romantic mood. It was an operation typical of him, with its combination of speed and appreciation of the whole woman.

It was on the third day that Rik fulfilled his other intention: with John Ward-Perkins, Nigel Wingate and his adjutant, Percy Stebbing, he drove up the northern coast road to visit native kraals. He noted all the details of the round huts and mealie stores in their circular enclosures – which made an interesting comparison with Iron Age settlements at home. From the local police, both black and white, he learnt of a social structure never likely to be suspected by archaeologists. Better-off farmers would have several wives and lodge each in her own kraal, where he would live with them in rotation – a custom, one cannot help reflecting, that might have been well suited to Rik himself.

That evening and most of the next day he spent with R, dining, talking, dancing, making love, on the last occasion in a shadowy wood. He found that she had grown on him and become very companionable and was 'a piquante listener'. For four days, as he observed, he had talked much nonsense and some sense with a gracious, intelligent woman. 'Now, light-heartedly, though also with the gentle sadness of finality, four days are torn off the calendar and cast away.'

The voyage up the east coast of Africa was very different from that down the west coast: day after day there was bright sun and blue sea, and even Rik cannot have found much that was purposeful to do. The *Repulse* was with the convoy until, on 13 November, in a sudden rain squall, she steamed up and down the lines of ships, taking farewell of them. 'The successive gusts of cheering from ship after ship across the misty sea, and the fine purposeful lines of the great battle-cruiser, are a memory that will remain.' It was a fortnight later that she was sunk by the Japanese.

It took another week to reach Aden, and there, after a long delay in entering the bay, it was announced that no shore leave was to be allowed. It is recorded that Colonel Wheeler played a leading part in the deputation that waited on authority to express the furious indignation of the troops, and demanded that the order be reversed. It was.

Once again Rik determined to see something of the country and took John and Nigel with him. They hired a taxi and drove first to the old shipyard near Aden town, where there were scores of dhows lying off shore. Rik's description of the place is not only a fair sample of the descriptive writing in the diary, but also expresses his vision of the material world in its historical setting with a romanticism he seldom allowed himself:

There is no more beautiful ship afloat than the dhow, with its cut away bow and square raking stern, carved and coloured, simulacrum of the great little ships in which Drake and Raleigh straddled the globe. Their twisted ribs, their clean carved sides, their carpeted decks, the floriated sun and crescent on the stern-board, the green, white and blue poops, the white-painted bow-waves, the stooping masts and noble bellying sails – they are a lively unaffected archaism in a world of ironmongery. Their traditional chaffering of silks alternates now with a trade in cement, but still, as of old, they set forth day by day on their coastwise voyages – three, four, five weeks at a time – to Kuweit, or Muscat or Bombay.

After more local sight-seeing and a frugal picnic the three men felt 'a Nordic restlessness' and made a dash to the Wadi el Kebir and the pinnacled, mud-brick palace of 'its Great Sheikh'. They were granted an audience and seated on European chairs until the Sheikh arrived, beautifully dressed and scented, most gracious, but without a word. The Englishmen felt shamefully clumsy and uncouth as they mouthed some inanities, to be translated by the taxi-driver and received in polite silence. Although the situation eased slightly with the arrival of several little sons and an even more scented brother, Rik left resolving to learn Arabic without delay.

The diary ends with the one word, 'Suez', and a harsh expletive. In the original manuscript version, in addition to *The Hour of Fury*, the diary is headed A DIARY OF A LIFETIME. I. BIRTH, and there is an opening sentence, 'I was born at the age of 51 in a respectable suburb of Leeds.' This, together with the elaborate writing, strongly suggests that Rik had intended to keep it going all through his born-again life as a fighting soldier. He must then either have repented of this resolve or the realities of war made it impossible. He knew that the letters to Cyril Fox would make a partial substitute.

With a few exceptions, these letters are in *Still Digging*, and although there are some cuts, transpositions and one substantial insertion, Rik's side of the correspondence is there for the reading. It contains some excellent descriptions of battles and deserts, less indulgently written than the voyage diary, and some personal reflections. It can serve as the main source for an outline of Rik's two years of war in North Africa and Italy.

After the long, agonizing delay over the foreign posting and six or so weeks in a crowded troop-ship, he still had to endure inaction – inaction made worse by the fact that in the ding-dong struggle against Rommel the Eighth Army suffered reverses in that January of 1942, the second Libyan offensive ending in failure.

After disembarkation at Suez Colonel Wheeler and the 42nd Regiment were stationed nearby on the shores of the Great Bitter Lake, exercising on the chilly sands of the Wilderness of Sin. 'One trains incredibly much for incredibly little fighting. . . . Waiting and waiting is inclined sometimes to weary the flesh.' He also suffered impatience of mind with the many 'fools' about him, ingeniously equating them with the equally numerous camels and looking forward to a far-distant time when, despite all folly, the war would be won 'and every camel will have an OBE'.

During this period of waiting Rik heard that Flinders Petrie, now nearly ninety, was dying in a Jerusalem hospital. He had not lost his reverence for this strange genius, and, taking one day off, drove across the Sinai desert to take leave of him. Lying in bed, 'His grey beard and superb profile gave him the aspect of a Biblical patriarch.' His mind, Rik felt, was racing faster than ever as he talked without pause on learned and abstruse subjects. 'I left the room quietly, my brain stretched by the immensity and impetus of a mind for which there were no trivialities in life and no place of respite.' So, uplifted, he returned to the fools and camels.

The spring went by and at the beginning of May, although his men had suffered some casualties, he was still in Egypt. He had enjoyed two breaks. One, of three weeks, was involved with the Higher Tactics, an 'interesting and intelligent interlude', when his billet had a view across the Nile to the pyramids. The second was entirely self-sought: convinced that, as an anti-aircraft gunner, he ought to have experience of being at the receiving end, he persuaded a group-captain to take him on a bombing raid against Rhodes. He was made the front gunner of a Wellington bomber – and enjoyed all the excitement he had craved. They were bombed on the ground when refuelling, losing an aircraft and having a risky take-off from the shattered runway; they were pursued by a fighter over the Mediterranean, when they dropped for cloud cover so fast that Rik felt that his body seemed to remain aloft while he observed 'the hands which grasped the two machine-guns in front of me as curious and alien objects'. After much searching of the Rhodes darkness they spotted their airfield target, were caught by searchlights, but bombed and machine-gunned the place as well as they could. Then, when they were safely out to sea, there was an incident comparable to that of the second gun at La Butte. They found they had forgotten to drop their propaganda leaflets on the island. 'Should we push the infernal leaflets into the sea and say nothing or should we go back and do our stuff? Cowardice prevailed: we turned back to the island. . . .' (It is here that the author did most editing of his correspondence. The account of the trip to Rhodes is an insertion in the letter of 2 May, while, less explicably, a short letter dated 10 May in *Still Digging* is an integral part of that of 2 May.)

During these months, when Rik remained unwillingly inactive, there was in fact very little fighting in progress. Since the British had abandoned their offensive the two forces had maintained an equilibrium, waiting while they built up their supplies; the British under Ritchie held a line to the west of Tobruk. Rommel was able to move first, launching his attack before the end of May. Although checked in the north, he successfully pierced the British line and soon put the Eighth Army in peril.

Just before the attack the 42nd was at last in the Western Desert east of Tobruk, behind the Gazala line, where its job was to defend forward fighter airfields against dive-bombers and Africa Korps tanks. For the first time Rik witnessed a massed air attack by the Germans, 'and, most moving of all, a modern armoured brigade moving grandly into action'. On 11 June there was lull enough for him to be able to be free at last to light a lamp and write philosophically on war as the natural condition of man, the stimulus of progress and even the necessary spring of poetry.

The next day he drove westward to visit some of his guns south of Tobruk, when he found he was running into waves of crowded lorries, tanks and guns, all surging eastward. There had already been British withdrawals, but on this day the great retreat that was to end at El Alamein had begun, and Colonel Wheeler, all unknowing, met it face-to-face. He continued westward against the tide, when, according to a poem he was to write, he encountered a wall of military transport and asked an officer, his face plastered white with sand, like a clown's, where the enemy might be. This

> Brings back the casual answer, 'Just behind that ridge,
> And coming along quite nicely.' The mass surges
>   eastward again in unanxious but unordered haste....
> Yesterday was heralded by achieved success:
> Today a great army
> Has snatched Defeat from the very jaws of Victory.

On 19 June Rommel captured Tobruk, but the time taken to reduce it helped the greater part of the Eighth Army to escape westward to Mersa Matruh and then to the El Alamein line, where Auchinleck made his successful stand. Colonel Wheeler was specially commended for the good order in which he and his men achieved the retreat. He had, in fact, always been the last to leave each evacuated area. Some regiments abandoned guns, but the 42nd, by means of a special squad of mechanics, actually increased its armoury as it fell back. John Ward-Perkins, and others who had known them, attributed success to those last ghastly months of training in 'mobility' which the Regiment had endured before leaving England.

At the end of the retreat they were put into a reserve position in 'box' formation. It was very hot and 'Everyone was pretty tired.' After that first week in July, when Auchinleck fought and won the first, defensive, Battle of El Alamein, Rik's spirits revived, he repented the last lines of his poem and declared, 'We are unbeaten....' He did, however, feel that there was need for a little heaven-sent impatience.

Although General Montgomery was not an impatient commander, Rik seems to have welcomed his appointment, when in August he took over the Eighth Army and Alexander became Commander-in-Chief, Middle East Forces. The first task was still to secure the El Alamein line against Rommel's expected drive for Cairo, but, once this had been accomplished by the victory of Alam el Halfa at the end of the month, Montgomery threw everything into re-equipping and regrouping the Eighth Army in preparation for a renewed thrust to the west, this time with forces superior to the German and Italian. By September Rik's part in this was, with the rest of the anti-aircraft artillery, protecting the landing grounds behind the line.

He spent much of his time in a lorry, surrounded by telephones, following the plottings as enemy bombers came in from the sea and ordering guns to fire if opportunity offered. He had bought a copy of Professor Gordon Childe's influential *Man Makes Himself* and read it whenever there was a sufficient lull in these activities. Conditions were not agreeable, with the heat, and heavy sandstorms every afternoon, and he found the job of taking occasional pot-shots at bombers trivial, but he was able to contain his natural impatience since he was confident that an offensive was pending. He wrote to Cyril (16 September), 'I hope and think we are on the verge of a more exciting destiny. What the hell of a time to live in! I wouldn't have missed it, would you?'

Shortly before this he had spent four days in Cairo – his first leave since disembarkation. He caught up with sleep, enjoyed many baths and some exalted social life. Nor did he neglect archaeology, for he went with 'the most treasured of his friends', the veteran Archie Creswell, Professor of Muslim Art and Architecture, to inspect the ancient walls of the City.

A month later, though still in a reserve position and often bored, Rik was inwardly excited and happy, for things were going his way:

Cyril, congratulate me. I'm now in the *crack Division* of the British Army! [The First Armoured Division.] This means a seat plumb in the front row of the stalls for anything that is going. . . . It's a grand and gratifying thought. My work now *is* nearly done. I boast that I've been able to lead this gang from the suburbs of northern London right into the very middle of the picture. The rest doesn't matter now. Almost for the first time a little sense of achievement has trickled into my consciousness. Forgive! It was better than staying at home with a red hat round my head.

In *Still Digging* Rik mentions letters written to Cyril during the Second Battle of El Alamein, which were not to be reproduced since they were fragmentary and contained unprintable verse. One survives (30 October) and was probably the only one written. It was penned in his jeep in the midst of a deafening barrage and includes a 'poem' that is not only unprintable but unspeakable. In apologizing for it, Rik says,

'One must do something to alleviate the sixteenth decisive battle in history' – which Montgomery had already announced it to be.

This letter mentions a battle diary that he has been keeping, so proving that this was written day by day. It has its place in *Twenty-Four Hours' Leave* and is in every way an admirable piece of writing, a truly remarkable composition to have come from a regimental commander fully engaged in battle by day and by night. Nor, so far as the course of the battle is concerned, does Colonel Wheeler's record conflict in any way with that to be written in the history books.

On the evening of 23 October Rik betook himself quite alone to the top of a low hill north of El Eisa, overlooking the sea and what he knew must soon be a vast battlefield. His own batteries of Bofors guns were there below among some 150,000 men waiting the hour of attack. It was a moment strangely reminiscent of that of August 1918, except that now the moonlight was brilliantly clear and contended with a desert after-glow. There were still two hours to wait, and the 42nd was not due to advance until daybreak.

Rik lay down to snatch some sleep and when he awoke nearly two hours later he found he had been joined on his vantage point by American war correspondents, an Australian colonel and a BBC man with a recording machine. At 9.40 pm precisely an almighty barrage began, relays of bombers went over and the infantry began their slow advance, clearing passageways through the British and enemy minefields to open the way for tanks and guns. In spite of the din, Rik slept again, then made his way down to the little heaps of rubble that was El Alamein to be ready for daybreak. It came, he drove forward a few miles in his jeep among a mass of vehicles and guns, then there was a halt and the sun rose.

It may have been at this hour that an incident occurred which was to be remembered and handed on to me by a man who is now a garage mechanic. His story is that he and some other raw young gunners very soon after their arrival found themselves engaged in the battle. They were badly shaken and almost demoralized by fear, when they saw their Commanding Officer, Colonel Wheeler, prop a looking-glass on a tank and slowly and carefully shave himself. The sight was enough to restore their confidence and morale. In his diary Rik records that during that first halt 'the Englishman shaves' and then how 'A few enemy shells burst amongst the guns and transport, happily no more than enough to give the newer soldiery their first faint experience of shell-fire.'

In fact, regimental casualties were soon to begin, but Montgomery's main attack along the coast had so far taken Rommel by surprise that he missed the initial chance of pounding the target of so dense a mass of men and what Rik liked to call ironmongery. The minefields proved deeper than anticipated and caused serious delay, but the Second Battle of Alamein had opened as nearly as could be expected according to the British plan.

Through all the ten days of the hard fighting, most of them spent struggling to break through the strong northern sector of Rommel's front, Rik divided his time between necessary visits to his regimental and other headquarters and visits to his widely deployed batteries, often, if things were 'sticky', staying with them for an hour or more and sometimes sleeping at their tactical headquarters. Once the move forwards began he was able to record that the 42nd had 'the foremost Bofors guns on the battlefield'.

Every day he ended the entries in his diary with a list of air attacks, the number of aeroplanes hit or brought down and his casualties. These were not terrible but severe enough, and several times on his forward visits he met with tragedies. On the 30th a shell had landed by one of his batteries, killing and mortally wounding several men. He attended the burial of Gunner Green beside his gun. 'The poor riven body, with its obscene aura of flies, the hard-bitten but strangely gentle companions of the dead, the drifting sand and the bursting shells are an oft-renewed battle memory.'

A day or so later one of his officers was badly wounded just as he came on the scene, while near the end of the battle he arrived to find that one of his best section commanders had stood on a retarded enemy mine which had blown off his legs and an arm. Rik wrote, 'Whether he lives or dies [he did not live] a cheerful, intelligent, sophisticated soul is gone.'

As a soldier, Rik always liked when possible to make himself an observer of actions in which he was not involved. On 29 October he got wind of an Australian attack to be staged that night. After so many days of hard fighting the breakthrough had not been achieved and Montgomery resolved to regroup the Eighth Army for a concentrated onslaught, code-named Supercharge; while this was in preparation the Australians were to make a thrust towards the sea. Under cover of darkness Rik drove forward to settle himself once more on the El Eisa hilltop. Soon after the British opening barrage the enemy sent bombers to attack the guns and one stick fell so close that Rik and his jeep were sprayed with mud. He watched the Italian aeroplanes involved with little respect, and was amused by one which made an inordinately long run-in, with a klaxon sounding the while, 'presumably intended to frighten the wretched Abyssinians but ludicrous to sophisticated ears'. The bomb, when at last delivered, proved to be a dud.

The Australian division succeeded in driving to the sea and cutting off a large German force, and when a day or two later an intercepted enemy message told that an attempt was to be made to relieve this force Rik decided to go forward, this time with a fellow-officer, 'to see the fun'. As they drove along the coastal track he rejoiced in the brilliance of the scene, the ultramarine of the Mediterranean framed in snow-white dunes. When they had gone as far as was reasonably safe they lay on their bellies below the crest of a dune, where they could watch enemy tanks crawling into action, while to their right a party of Australians were 'bathing nonchalantly in the bright green sea'. Presently a shell hit an ammunition lorry quite close to them. 'Burning ammunition, shell-fire, approaching tanks, bathers and the recumbent and idle spectators form a curious and contrasting series.' Just when very heavy fire had forced the tanks to withdraw, the bathers wandered slowly up the shore, gossiping as they went.

The Australians had, in fact, succeeded in weakening the resistance, and when very early on 2 November Supercharge was launched it went well – although this was not at once apparent to those in the thick of the fighting. For Rik it was 'A day spent about the battlefield', for some of his batteries were having a rough time of it from shelling. He stayed with them for long spells, just talking, and again spent the night at one of their tactical HQs. By the next day it was plain that the breakthrough was in progress, and Rik, visiting his divisional command, found the expected battlefield scenes: 'Burnt-out tanks – many of them ours – stray anti-tank guns, rifles, a line of enemy dead, their faces as livid as their green uniforms. The enemy shelling has receded. . . .' Vast numbers of prisoners, vast quantities of arms and other booty were being taken: the sixteenth decisive battle of history was a famous victory for Montgomery and a turning-point in the war.

On that last day somebody photographed Colonel Wheeler standing in front of a tank, his long legs in their baggy cotton trousers firmly straddled, hand on hip and pipe clenched between his teeth. His forecast had been fulfilled, he had enjoyed 'a seat plumb in the front of the stalls' and he and his Regiment, the gang from the London suburbs, had come through with credit. Rik himself had evidently impressed the High Command – what was to follow leaves no doubt of that.

Accepting his defeat, Rommel left his Italian infantry to fight to the last and turned to make a quick getaway with his German divisions. His escape was greatly aided by rain heavy enough to bog down his

pursuers: the planned advance to Tripoli was thus to be a fighting one
for most of its fourteen hundred miles. The weather became bitterly
cold and Rik rode in an armoured car, which was blacked out at night
with a roof light that gave him time for reading as various as Cobbett's
Rural Rides and *Moby Dick*.

By Christmas Day he was at his advance headquarters on the
borders of Cyrenaica and Tripolitania and, having sent back most of his
staff for festivities, was rejoicing in being alone, save for two signallers –
who had provided his own Christmas dinner, with a menu conspicuously less rich than those of 1917 and 1918. In peace, drawing on the
endowment given to him for life by his father, he wrote to Cyril Fox,

Are you good at flowers? I'm bad at them. Birds, fishes, butterflies, yes; but
not flowers. Through the open doorway of this steel curricle I look upon the
sandy deserts of Tripolitania, with its hummocky lumps of dingy camel grass
under a rushing wintry wind and a pale sun. There is no general sign of *colour*,
and yet, probing among the camel grass, I have found an astonishing number
of secret flowers: some I can only call daisy-lions, some small white poppies,
sprays of yellow and purple that are just *flowers*. Such is my learned contribution to the *Herbarium Tripolitanicum*.

Not that the long pursuit was a pleasure trip for the 42nd Regiment, for
air attack and ground strafing were a part of the Germans' tactics. Early
in January Rik described how he had harangued his men on the post-
war world: '"For the making of it, each individual man of you is
personally responsible," I shouted, glaring from one spade-like face to
another.' At this moment three ground-strafing planes rolled by and his
gunners brought one down, and were exploring its smoking ruin even
while he wrote. He was moved to apostrophize Cyril in high rhetoric.
'Are you alive, *really* alive, my dear Cyril, this brisk winter's day? Do
you hear the Middle Sea spewing and sucking along the foreshore. . . ?'
But then with a sudden volte-face he begged his friend to write to him –
'a letter from the real to the unreal, for this life of mine has no
tangibility. . . .'

Colonel Wheeler was restive after two months and more of 'west-
faring'. The Allies had a growing mastery of the air and many of his men
and guns were attached to other units, so that he felt under-employed
and his inturned energies were gnawing him. It was in this mood that he
determined himself to take command of a troop from the 42nd that was
to advance with the 12th Royal Lancers well ahead of their Armoured
Brigade (the 22nd). When it proved that the Lancers were failing to
remain in the van it was agreed that Wheeler's troop should move far

ahead to prospect for defiles along the main line of advance. This Rik earnestly sought to do, but, coming to the conclusion that his efforts were serving no useful purpose, he withdrew to Bir Dufan, a 'desert carfax', where he expected to rejoin the Brigade. He arrived there on 18 January, found it heavily mined and soon learnt that the Brigade had been diverted.

He had with him his wireless truck and three Bofors guns with their lorries and personnel – including two subalterns. Consulting his maps, he found that a bee-line to Tripoli was just a hundred miles and he instantly made up his mind to make a dash for it, following that line as nearly as might prove possible through country partly occupied by the retreating enemy. He sent word to his adjutant and they set off through the dusk, 'leaving the Army on our flanks and taking a path into the unknown'.

This extraordinary exploit is fully described in *Still Digging* and also under the heading 'Adventurous Journey' in *Twenty-Four Hours' Leave*. As a personal act of daring it must be likened to the capture of the guns at Sapignies, but it was even more of an escapade, for, although it involved more men and equipment and covered days instead of hours, its military objectives were intangible. Rik's own motives were that he wanted to be in the van of what he called the Rush to Tripoli and, surely, that he needed a vent for his restlessness and desire for the excitement of danger. He cannot, I think, have had any thought of it winning him any award, or even approbation from the High Command.

The journey was certainly adventurous, the hazards being those of nature rather than the enemy as they made their way across country seemingly far more impassable than any Cumbrian moors. They did encounter troops round the Italian colony of Breviglieri, but, although Rik led a daring sortie by night, they were too few to risk an attack. They had to make do with 'a minor achievement' in shooting down an Italian air force major and his driver encountered by chance on the roadway. In cold print this incident seems uncomfortably like murder, but it was war, an ambush, and the Italian soldiery were within earshot.

On the last days the bee-line led to mountain terrain that proved absolutely impassable and at last, on 23 January, hearing the way was open, the party had to turn on to the main road that would lead them to their goal, the harbour of Tripoli.

At 12.30 we stopped for a moment to dress ourselves in formal battle array. At 12.45 we entered the city, and at 13.00 hours the guns were in action at the harbour – the first A.A. guns in Tripoli by over an hour.

So ended our journey. Neither man nor gun nor vehicle had suffered any sort of harm from it. On the other hand, whether as a strenuous training under the urge of mild adventure, or merely as a carefree holiday, it wrought nothing but good to those who had the good fortune to experience it.

This is the ending of *Adventurous Journey*. Touching it up ten years later, he omitted the 'holiday' nonsense and was just sufficiently embarrassed by the exploit to add a note reminding the reader that it was undertaken 'before the author had attained to the responsibilities of brigade-command'.

The trek did, however, have one totally unforeseen result that shows Rik at his best: alert, decisive and forceful. In the wild country traversed he noticed many Roman remains, and on a night spent close to Breviglieri the party had boxed their guns within the ruins of a Roman shrine. It was then that an army's responsibility to protect antiquities 'thrust itself starkly' into his consciousness. He knew of the great Roman cities on the coastal plain already, or soon to be, fought over in the main advance. No one, so far as he knew, had given the matter a thought, and he resolved there and then that he must act.

It is now that Major Ward-Perkins re-enters the story. An early wound had kept John out of the El Alamein battle, but he had been summoned back to the Regiment as second-in-command. When he came up with the 42nd he found the adjutant in a state of bewildered alarm: where was the Colonel? In fact, of course, he was off on his 'crazy expedition'. The two men, colleagues and brother-officers, were re-united when John reached Tripoli soon after his truant Commanding Officer.

Rik lost no time: on that very first day he went to his Brigadier at Eighth Army HQ and persuaded him that they must concern themselves with the whole issue of the conservation of ancient monuments. It was an astonishing success for such a moment. Since there was to be a pause in the advance Colonel Wheeler had leave for a lightning reconnaissance to assess the situation. It was exactly the kind of undertaking he relished, with its combination of archaeology and soldiering, the chance to exert authority, impose order to get something important done, all under intense pressure. All, moreover, in the company of a good friend – for he took John Ward-Perkins with him.

While the hinterland was scattered with Roman towers, temples and farms it was the three great coastal cities (from which Tripolitania took its name) that must most concern them. Of these Tripoli itself lay at the centre, with Lepcis Magna to the east already over-run by two armies, and Sabratha to the west still in enemy hands. Tackling Tripoli first,

Rik was appalled to find that the Italian archaeological centre had been invaded, cameras stolen and records scattered, and that British soldiers were the worst offenders. Assuming an authority they hardly yet possessed, Rik and John found officers whom they could make responsible for the safety of the archaeological assets of Tripoli, before driving off to the far more important site of Lepcis. There the imposing ruins of the Punic and Roman city had been restored by the Italians in their usual spectacular if rather slapdash manner.

Rik and John had never seen Lepcis before and as they approached it were divided between admiration for its visible beauties and dismay at what was going on in their midst. The ruins were swarming with 'the momentarily idle troops of a famous division, with Satan in active attendance'. The museum had already been ransacked and rude graffiti added to the monuments. The RAF were preparing to build a large radar station among the venerable masonry. Perhaps most sickening of all, when the divisional commander was appealed to he 'turned upon his heel with the remark "What would it matter if the whole of these ... ruins were pushed into the sea?"'

In the day at their disposal they did wonders: out-of-bounds notices were posted, propaganda lectures given to the soldiery, the military police enlisted and the RAF persuaded to choose another site.

Rik enormously enjoyed this dashing excursion into rescue archaeology, but it could be no more than a prelude to setting responsibilities for the conservation of ancient monuments on a firmer and more official footing. Even before the army was advancing once more and he had to rejoin his Regiment, Rik made due liaison with the political and civil administration and drew up a sharp report which led, by means which even its author thought marvellous, to John Ward-Perkins being seconded for several weeks for further salvage work and organization.

During this period Colonel and Major were to come together again over archaeological affairs at the beginning of February, when Sabratha fell. They drove their jeep through mine craters into the ancient city, which appeared to be entirely deserted. Then all at once, as they peered about, noticing a white flag outside the museum, they were surrounded by voluble Italian civilians, men and women, led by a very little man who proved to be the Chief Inspector of Antiquities. The explanation was that 'Here at the western end of Libya, had accumulated the whole of the Italian personnel of the two provinces' – nearly fifty of them. They were eager to please, glad to be rid of their German overlords.

Rik immediately composed a set of regulations by which the Italians were made responsible for the safe-guarding of antiquities under the authority of the British administration. They were accepted by the Chief Inspector, read aloud to his underlings – and subsequently developed by John with great success. He gave up this work only to take over the temporary command of the 42nd until Nigel Wingate was ready to succeed him. Wingate was in charge during the final campaign, leading the Regiment among the first into Tunis.

In spite of all the exalted military duties in which he was to be involved, Rik had not quite finished with his archaeological crusade. Having been early admitted to the secret plans for the invasion of Sicily, he felt desperately anxious for the safety of the splendid antiquities of the island. In early June he flew to Cairo, contrived to penetrate the hush-hush headquarters where Montgomery and his staff were planning the invasion, and found an understanding listener in the person of Lord Gerald Wellesley, who was to command a large area in Sicily. As far as Lord Gerald knew, there were no plans for the protection of antiquities, but he promised to do all that he could, only regretting that he knew so little of their whereabouts, adding that 'Even a Baedeker would help'.

Rik had seen in the papers of the day that his old ally, Lord Harlech, had arrived in Cairo en route to London, so he rang him at Shepheard's Hotel and soon joined him on the terrace there. He wanted to secure his support for a much wider scheme for the protection of works of art and antiquity when the time came for the occupation of Europe. Sicily was also discussed and so concerned was Rik with the problem of Lord Gerald's ignorance of its historical topography that he even asked Lord Harlech if he could produce a Baedeker.

Some vague promise was made but it did not have to be fulfilled for Rik's next move was to call on his learned friend, Archie Creswell. The Professor let him in with habitual welcome – 'Take off your coat if you're not wearing braces' – and disappeared to brew some tea. Rik made a quick survey of the bookshelves, spotted the much-needed guide book and slipped it into his pocket, official secrecy forbidding any admission. Soon he was able to pass on the stolen volume to Lord Gerald 'with a lively mental picture of his lordship descending upon the shell-stricken beaches of Sicily, Baedeker in hand'.

That autumn, flying back from Naples after the Salerno landings, Rik was surprised to see Wellesley board the plane at Catania – still more surprised when he immediately returned the little red *South Italy and Sicily*. It came back from the person of the Duke of Wellington, for he had inherited the title on the death of his nephew at Salerno. 'Eight years later, Creswell was my guest . . . in London, and after dinner I formally handed the stolen Baedeker back to him. . . . He had not missed it from his shelves.'

There is no question at all that the first thoughts for the protection of antiquities in North Africa stirred in Rik's head in the shrine above Breviglieri; this was on 19 January 1943. Nor is there any doubt that it was he, assisted by his second-in-command, who put them into action. It is, in fact, a notable example of Wheeler's quite exceptional capacity for getting things done. It is therefore understandable that when the facts were by implication officially contradicted, he was provoked into one of his few published attacks on the Establishment.

In the autumn of 1943, in reply to a written Parliamentary Question, the Secretary of State for War replied, 'When the British Forces advanced into Libya in the autumn of 1942 immediate steps were taken for the preservation of any archaeological monuments which might come into our possession during the course of occupation.' Wheeler commented, 'In these righteous words . . . the Secretary of State had unhappily been misinformed: not to put too fine a point on it, his office had been guilty of communicating an impudent lie.'

After Rik had parted from John at Sabratha and the Eighth Army was fighting its way north towards Tunis his military career was to flower. On 19 March, when the Allied advance was still being held by Rommel along his Mareth line, he wrote to Cyril from Medenine. He was able to announce to his friend that he was now an acting Brigadier, having taken over the command of the Eighth Army's Anti-Aircraft Brigade – which had hitherto been brilliantly and unconventionally led by one Calvert-Jones and included a battalion of Free French. 'My age', he wrote, 'bars my formal promotion, but that doesn't matter – I'm doing the job. After Tunis I imagine that I shall go home. Probably it's time. It's been a long journey.'

Two days later Montgomery opened his main attack on the line but was repulsed, and it was not until the first week in April that it was carried – by which time Rommel himself had returned to Germany and Von Arnim was in command. Thereafter the Brigade was involved in the complicated and often uncertain fighting as the Allies, now including the American forces from the north, strove for Tunis against Italians, Germans and Vichy French. When Rik wrote to Cyril on 8 May, he was still at Monastir, near Sousse. He was, nevertheless, in jubilant mood.

... the military life has been pretty strenuous in these parts. I've left my regiment, bless it, and have been wielding a full-size brigade – I was, in fact, formally made a brigadier this afternoon. Don't laugh! Instead of sending me home, they've made me a full-blooded bouncing brigadier, all dripping with red tabs and platitudes and well on the way to Cheltenham. In future I suppose I shall be regarded as a 'retired brigadier who dabbled a little in archaeology.' It's a funny world, excessively unreal.

His military role might sometimes seem dream-like, yet once again, as in his search for wild flowers, he showed himself well-rooted in his past. That evening he had been out at dusk, lurking among the olive trees with his shotgun. He brought down one pigeon for the pot.

Although Rik could not know it as he sat by night in his caravan writing to Cyril, on that same day the 9th Corps, under General Horrocks, had made a swift assault and the British were in Tunis. On 12 May Von Arnim surrendered.

So the North African campaign was won at last, having cost the Axis nearly a hundred thousand men and eight thousand planes – to which the 42nd Light Anti-Aircraft Regiment had contributed its share. Rik had been in continuous action of greater or lesser intensity for just a year. Now he was to have a few months' break. His Brigade was soon withdrawn to Tripoli for special training, and he spent much of his time at its headquarters. Writing from there one excessively hot July day, he was in reflective mood. 'Looking back, I can only confess, Cyril, that I have profited by my wars. I should have been a fretful and restless man without them. Caught up in them, I have at least enjoyed something of the anxious stability of the whirling top. . . .' In the heat he allowed his mind to turn to another kind of war, for it was in this letter that he confided his liking for the devilishness of Mavis.

Even now, during what he plainly recognized as a 'lull between episodes', Brigadier Wheeler had another important military commitment, for he had been put on the staff committee planning the invasion of the Italian mainland. This involved thousand-mile flights over mountain and sea, often distressingly bumpy, to attend sessions in Algiers.

It was in late July, when Rik was in Algiers for one of these meetings, that a message reached him, crucial in itself, and delivered in such a way that the incident was to become famous in the annals of archaeology. It cannot be better described than in the letter he wrote to Cyril on 7 August, soon after his return to Tripoli. Beginning with a passage about affairs of the Antiquaries, he went on,

I hope to be with you all in December. . . . It's this way. The other day I was [at Algiers] returning to my tent in the evening sun when my Corps Commander

[General Sir Brian Horrocks] dashed along with a signal in his hand and the remark – 'I say, have you seen this – they want you as (reading) "Director General of Archaeology in India." Why, you must be rather a king-pin at that sort of thing! You know, I thought you were a regular soldier!' If the General ever paid an extravagant compliment, he did so then, although there was, I thought, a hint of pain and disillusionment in his voice. Apart from that, the proposition was a complete bombshell to me. Without any sort of pre-warning, the India Office was asking for my release to take up a key post in a country I had never been to in my life! However, I gathered my wits and said I'd accept the offer after the next battle but *not* before. It would obviously have been regrettable to miss all the carefully planned fun at this rather exciting juncture of the war. So I'll join you for a couple of months later on, with the snowflakes and the robins, before going East. Meanwhile I have some very active, tricky and interesting work to hand. And by the way its only fair to the Honourable Mysterie of Brigadiers to say that your kindly reference to my now having 'less personal risk' does them less than justice!! They're no heroes, but a red hat on a hostile beach isn't really much safer than a khaki one!!! However, I'll see you at Christmas.

I have to record that when I asked General Horrocks if he could add anything from his side of the story his reply was that he had no recollection of the happening whatever, and, indeed, appeared to be unaware that Mortimer Wheeler had ever served under him.

Rik kept unwaveringly to his intention of staying with his Brigade until 'after the next battle' – which, of course, meant the invasion of Italy. Indeed, before sending the news to Cyril he had already composed a signal for Corps Headquarters (with copies to the India Office and others) which read, under the heading 'Appointments, Officers',

I have the honour to accept the post of Director General of Archaeology INDIA which the INDIA OFFICE has offered me, if my release from the Army be sanctioned in due course. I do not desire that my release shall take effect before 30th Nov. 43 provided that until that date I am retained in a theatre of active operations.

It was at this time or a little later that Rik had a chance encounter in Algiers with several of his younger colleagues in British archaeology – this in addition to Ralegh Radford, who was himself on the planning committee. Although it was unlikely that familiarity with antiquarian air photographs added much to their ability to read the military variety, a number of archaeologists had been recruited into this branch of the service. Rik took a low view of their employment, for, although it put them into uniform, he regarded it as little if at all better than the civilian

jobs preferred by other despised peacetime colleagues. Now a conference of British and American specialists had been summoned to
Algiers, among them Stuart Piggott and Glyn Daniel, who were in
charge of Air Photographic Intelligence in India. Glyn, destined to be
Rik's future collaborator in television success, knew him only slightly in
those days, but treasures the memory of an evening party when Stuart
and he,

> looking across the crowded room saw Wheeler talking to Harold Macmillan
> then Minister resident at Allied HQ in Africa. Wheeler saw us and came over to
> talk. He asked us what we were doing in Algiers and we explained. 'Air Photo
> Interpretation' he said, his eyes flashing and moustache bristling, 'Women's
> work. I hope to find you something better to do.'

The something better he had in mind was, of course, to join his staff in
India. The hope was not to be fulfilled.

By early September the weeks of planning were over, Sicily had been
occupied and various operations were going successfully forward in
both the toe and heel of Italy. The main invasion, intended to lead to the
rapid occupation of the whole country, was to be launched against
Salerno, lying at the head of its Gulf, where the mountain roads over to
Naples were not too formidable. The invading forces sailed from
Bizerta, the fleet of landing-craft accompanied by larger warships and a
screen of destroyers, minesweepers and other small fry. Brigadier
Wheeler was on the bridge with the Commander of the landing craft, its
hold packed with guns and vehicles. His 12th Anti-Aircraft Brigade
numbered some eight thousand men, and now included three regiments
of heavy artillery as well as an equal number of light batteries. That
night an air raid on Bizerta gave them 'a noisy and spectacular farewell
to Africa'.

The next day, 7 September, was a fine, cool Sunday; the Brigadier
and the Commander staged a brief ship's service on the forepeak.
Rik chose to read from Joshua for the lesson, 'Be strong and of good
courage . . .', commenting, 'The fine resonance of the Old Testament
had ever the stuff of battle in it, with just that hint of the theatre which
helps a man through the first impact.'

Presently a signal was put up by the leading ship and Rik seems to
have been entirely taken by surprise when he decoded, 'Italy has
surrendered'. The truth was that Badoglio had capitulated a week
before, but the news had been held back. Unhappily the German High
Command was alerted and General Hube, commanding their southern
forces, was able to disarm the Italians along the Salerno coast and

replace them with Germans. As a result the Allies' landing was far more strongly opposed than it would otherwise have been.

As it was, the resistance could not be called severe, but going ashore was no picnic. Rik was woken from a nap by violent jolts as bombs straddled the boat; then, though the warships laid down a tremendous barrage, the craft waiting their turn for disembarkation, while dawn broke, came under shell fire from a shore battery: the captain of a neighbouring craft was killed and a tank-landing vessel sunk. This battery was knocked out by the Navy, but later another got their range to a nicety, and as Rik and the Commander took it in turn on the bridge, sharing a single tin hat, their joking was somewhat forced. At last their turn came and they were relieved to run full speed ahead onto the beach.

The assignment of the 12th Brigade was to defend the British 10th Corps on the left flank of the Americans, a responsible job since this position was largely beyond the range of fighter protection. Soon the invading forces were dug in along a narrow strip of shore, where they were to be held for several days. It was packed with guns, light and heavy, and with all ranks and conditions of men, 'all alike dependent on one another, spattered by the same high explosive, the same machine guns, brewing the same rich tea....' Comparing Salerno with 'the misery of Passchendaele, the intermittent strain and triumphant reaction of the two battles of El Alamein', Rik felt a strange kind of freedom, in contrast with the regimentation of individual action experienced in those other battles.

One initiative wholly characteristic of Rik was taken the day after the first landing. He detected among his highly trained and experienced batteries one, posted to him only recently, with such 'primitive ideas of speed and mobility' that it was not fit for action. He at once withdrew it, 'turned it into a field scarcely more than a thousand yards from the enemy', and ordered it three strenuous days of instruction. All ranks worked like slaves and on the third day returned to action fully competent.

'Thereafter the battle was a trifle stiff', as Rik wrote to Nigel Wingate, now commanding the 42nd Regiment, adding that he 'more than once wished the old 42nd had been there' since he believed its skilled 'layers' would have doubled the number of enemy planes brought down. The letter continues:

The most critical moment of the whole business was four or five days after the initial landing. At that time our right flank was definitely broken, and I was called out at midnight to raise a force of infantrymen from the gunners of my Brigade.... I shall not forget the spectacle in the moonlight when at two o'clock in the morning we lined up four hundred well-armed gunners in a hollow square, told them what it was all about, and marched them to a forward concentration area.

The Brigadier remained in command of this force until American parachute troops arrived by air to fill the gap.

By mid-September reinforcements had arrived and British and Americans broke out from their coastal confinement. Soon they were across the spur of the Apennines and were approaching Naples. That night (of 30 September) Rik spent encamped at Pompeii, and found time to write Cyril Fox his last war letter. (The following extract is taken from the original letter and shows some differences from the published version – notably in the unexpected final line.)

I've just turned up the light in my caravan and have shut the door. Before that I had been sitting here and smoking in the darkness. High up in front of me, the inflamed eye of the Volcano blinked at me beneath the Plough. Now and then the flash of a gun and the leisurely whine of a mortar shell. At the foot of my steps is a bomb crater, and a hundred yards away in the darkness is the amphitheatre, more ruined now than in AD 79. Its all astonishingly unreal. But its now many months since I had any close contact with reality. For 'reality' should be read 'accepted things'. Its been a stiffish battle, but full of new interest. For the first time I've been really *busy*, as distinct from being merely occupied. Its a good ending of the chapter....

Thank you for all you say about my new adventure in the East.... In cold blood I'm sometimes a little terrified when I think of the immensity of the new task. Then my blood warms up and the giant shrinks. I think that what I'm most terrified of is the loneliness of it all. But then I always was a woman!

In this same letter Rik expressed his delight, with an enthusiasm that was wholly sincere, that Cyril was to be the next President of the Society of Antiquaries – he was, he assured him, the only man with the creative imagination to lead the transition from war to peace. He also said he hoped to be back in London by mid-December.

Naples gave the conquerors, or liberators, a good welcome, although there were a few snipers and bombers to be avoided. Rik had always had a keen eye for the best billets or headquarters, and on arrival in the city he drove straight up to the Aosta Palace of Capo di Monti, taking it over from the Commander of the Hermann Goering Division, who had recently left after shooting five civilians and trying the effect of tank fire on the front of the palace. Rik got on excellently with the Dowager

Duchess of Aosta – who could hardly fail to be prejudiced in his favour. He found the old dowager, who had been a game-hunter in her day, 'utterly charming and bravely sad'.

As a conqueror-liberator with a red hat, Rik kept some aristocratic company while he was in Italy. He may still have been lodging at the Aosta Palace when he made the excursion to Capri, in the company of his Brigade Major, Dick Stratton, that is described in the little tale that gave its title to *Twenty-Four Hours' Leave*. Major Stratton also wrote an account of this trip, a factual, everyday version, contrasting with Rik's high-flown one.

It is Major Stratton who records how the day before the twenty-four hours in question they set out for the island in a wretched boat provided for them by the Navy and ran into very rough weather. Everyone except Stratton was sick and the Brigadier, his Achilles heel exposed again, was 'very ill'; they ran for shelter at Pozzuoli. The next day, 18 October, they set out again in a stout trawler and on a lovely morning, reaching Capri in a couple of hours. Stratton also tells how they spent most of the morning shopping before Rik encountered his Duke, the Duca Camarini, and got their invitation to the evening party and its aftermath which are the main subject of *Twenty-Four Hours' Leave*. In the afternoon they hired a car, visited Anacapri and spent a long time enjoying the collections in the Villa San Michele, where Rik proved to know very much more than their guide did. The crusader castle was next, after which Stratton rested while 'the Brigadier, always very energetic', insisted on walking to the Chartist Monastery.

When it comes to the Duke's party, where the company were entertained by a pianist, a fiddler and a singing fisherman, Stratton records the names of Rik's anonymous Dramatis Personae. In addition to their host, Camarini, and his mistress, the daughter of the Samboni who had tried to assassinate Mussolini, the Prince was Carachioli, the Marquis, de Bracco, and the Countess was the Contessa Maria de Lazara – whom both men called 'a dangerous woman'. All were anti-fascists and in their various ways had suffered for it.

After the whole company had been led on by the musicians to dancing and singing together until well after midnight Stratton's account suggests that it was already known that the Duke wished to appeal to Rik for help in realizing his patriotic dream of a force built from the shattered Italian army, which could fight with the British to liberate the country and restore its honour. The Major, however, was not included in the select party invited by the Contessa to move on to her villa. He was content to leave it to the Brigadier 'to put the British point of view', as he saw the Contessa seize his arm and lead off the procession to her house.

Rik's picture of the doings up at the villa reveals only social and personal trivialities, and he sets the scene of the Duke's eloquent appeal for his movement in a moonlit lane as the party is walking home. It is probable that the Duke, supported by the Marquis, did make such an appeal there in the moonlight, did beg Rik to take him to Montgomery. The fact is, however, that most of the actual words put into their mouths were written down by them the next day, and, as Major Stratton describes, handed over to Rik by the Duke at an appointed meeting-place. The two documents, each one signed by Carachioli, Camarini and de Bracco, and touching in their noble hopefulness, survive as mementoes of a curious evening, a picturesque cul-de-sac near the ending of Rik's military way.

Brigadier Wheeler left Italy on 8 November, a month sooner than he had planned and in such haste that he had to say farewell to his staff by letter. Back in London, and in archaeology, he had many things to see to during the few months before leaving for India. Foremost of these concerns was the future of the Institute of Archaeology, of which he was still honorary Director. An important advance had been made during the year when Lord Harewood, then Chancellor of the University of London, in a speech delivered at the opening of an exhibition at Lancaster House, 'The Present Discovers the Past', declared that the University must make itself fully responsible for the Institute. This crowned the efforts in this direction led by Stephen Glanville, the Egyptologist, an energetic member of the Committee of Management, ably abetted by Margot Eates. The Wheelers' hope that their foundation could be self-supporting had proved vain, and its poverty during these early years is exemplified by the fact that Margot Eates, as assistant secretary and maid of all work, was paid £3 per week.

London University found difficulty in taking over the Institute, chiefly because of the amount of non-academic practical work involved. Rik was able to attend meetings of the management, at one of which, perhaps because he felt time was so short, he is said to have 'stormed around and annoyed everybody'. However this may be, Stephen Glanville used all his talent and magnetism then and afterwards to solve problems and ease the Institute into the bosom of London University. So, by the end of the war it was ready to appoint Gordon Childe as its first paid Director and begin to fulfil, in part at least, the ideal for which the Wheelers had worked so hard.

Another concern of Rik's was to renew his many involvements with the Society of Antiquaries. He was still its Director, an office he had filled mainly *in absentia* and which he was now to resign. The Society appointed him as its representative on the new Council for British Archaeology, an institution set up after much travail during the past year to represent all archaeological interests, particularly in dealings with the government. He also had the pleasure of receiving the Society's Gold Medal – the award to which he and Tessa had secretly contributed what seemed so long ago. Then there was the question of his position as Director of the London Museum: was Wheeler to have a further secondment for the four years of his Indian appointment or to resign outright? The Trustees decided at their January meeting to accept his resignation.

Rik also found time and energy to devote to a selfless matter still dear to him, the wartime protection of monuments and works of art. James Mann, who was to succeed Rik in the directorship of the Antiquaries, had been agitating in the matter and the interest of Lord Crawford and the Archbishop of Canterbury had been secured, but it was recognized that only Wheeler and Ward-Perkins had as yet acted. From Africa Rik had written a powerful letter to Clapham, as President of the Anti-quaries, setting out his ideas, and now he delivered to the Society 'a forceful and constructive paper' on 'Archaeology in the War Zone: Facts and Needs'. There were Members of Parliament present and they, together with a House of Commons Committee, backed his urgent appeal, while Rik himself saw a high official at the War Office. There is no doubt that this effort gave impetus to the setting up by the Prime Minister of an official committee, and so to the appointment of none other than Lieutenant Colonel Sir Leonard Woolley as head of an organization within the services.

Another preoccupation, and one to which he devoted much of his time, was to equip himself to take charge of archaeology in India. He used his prodigious memory and his ability to work at all hours to get a grasp of the history, historical geography and archaeological problems of the subcontinent.

During his four months in London Rik had private affairs to contend with that might, and indeed ought, to have demanded his undisturbed attention. They concerned the beautiful girl, Kim Collingridge, last heard of when Rik told her how much he wanted her to return in the same letter in which he announced his imminent marriage to Mavis. Since then her own life had not been unadventurous.

She had been on the 1939 Normandy expedition (and must therefore have had at least some inkling of Mavis's escapade and Rik's reactions), but was with a party that had gone to the south of France when the rest rushed home at the outbreak of war. Soon afterwards she joined the ATS and was trained for range-finding on anti-aircraft gun sites – possibly thus feeling a bond with Rik. On leave at Rosyth she met Robert Norfolk, whom she had known in childhood and who was now in command of a submarine. He went in hot pursuit, married her and, so the story goes, refused to let her rejoin her unit. For this she was court-martialled for desertion, but later exonerated. Kim was pregnant and stayed on at Rosyth when her husband sailed. Her baby was born in the spring of 1941, only a few months before Norfolk's submarine was lost with all hands in the eastern Mediterranean. She left Rosyth, the scene of so brief a marriage, and went to live in London with her infant daughter.

Rik had begun to think of a third marriage while still in North Africa, for Thalassa Hencken, replying belatedly to a letter he had sent her in August to tell her of the Indian appointment, said, 'By the way, about this scheme of remarrying, for heaven's sake, take your time this time. You don't need to leap into marrying the first attractive blonde with good legs who comes your way, when you return. The trouble with you is you always want to marry them.' Whether he was in fact already thinking of Kim cannot be told, nor just when it was that he saw her again. He certainly made one visit to London before the Salerno landings, possibly more than one, and it seems it must have been then that he made a whirlwind courtship (which is remembered) and Kim proved very ready to accept him if he could secure an annulment of his marriage to Mavis.

Back in London that winter, then, his objective was to win the annulment; there was, of course, no question with Kim of any forestalment of marriage, and he did in any case wish to have her as his wife. The most immediate step towards this goal was for his own reception into the Catholic faith, the annulment meanwhile being sought on the grounds that as Rik himself had never been baptized into any church his marriage to Mavis had been invalid. He arranged to receive instruction in the faith at Westminster, and had a number of sessions there, inducing his two closest friends, Alfred Clapham and Cyril Fox, to stand as his sponsors.

None even of Rik's stoutest supporters, all those who were able to understand and forgive his sexual excesses and emotional cruelties, have ever been able to accept his conduct over this supposed conversion. Fox was deeply shocked, and even the worldly Clapham was a most reluctant participant. Beatrice de Cardi, then his secretary, recalls that he said, 'If you're going to have religion at all you might as well go the whole hog.'

It can be said that with the strain and 'unreality' of a year of battle just behind him and the all but overwhelming prospect of India ahead, he was even more than usually tense and living on nervous energy. Also that the pretence of the ecclesiastical side of the annulment plea and the formal moves involved – such as inviting Mavis to return to him – would have struck him as farcical, making it possible for him to see his Westminster exercises as a part of the same farce.

This, however, does not absolve him from failing to imagine what Kim's feelings would be when she realized, as she was bound to do, that his conversion was no more than a move in the contest with Rome. Perhaps, too, he was so much a pagan (as he had always proclaimed) that he was incapable of imagining the reality of faith in another. Kim's own eagerness offers another small excuse. Yet the whole undertaking remains wrong and essentially an irresponsible abuse of love.

For the time being, however, both were happily confident of success in the courts and of their future union. It was agreed that Kim should go back to her comfortable family home in Australia to await the annulment. It was to be nearly two years before it was granted.

In February 1944 Rik sailed in the *City of Exeter* and found himself once more in a slow-moving convoy – this time, however, able to pass through the Mediterranean and the Suez Canal. The sea road was not yet quite free of danger; when the convoy was off Algiers it was attacked for an hour by waves of low-flying German torpedo-bombers. 'With Alamein and Salerno fresh in the memory, my inglorious task was now to amuse the large number of small children assembled below deck; where, by rationalizing the attack as a bang game, we weathered the little storm successfully and almost regretted the succeeding calm.'

It was Rik's last taste of war, for the rest of the long voyage to Bombay was uneventful. Rik spent some part of it shut in his tiny cabin, drawing up a scheme for fieldwork and excavation ready to be launched as soon as he set foot in India.

CHAPTER 9

India

IT WAS AN initiative by Lord Wavell, as Viceroy of India, that lay behind the invitation to serve as Director General of Archaeology for the subcontinent so dramatically delivered to Rik by General Horrocks. In June of 1943 Wavell had cabled the following message to Leo Amery, then Secretary of State for India:

Post of Director General of Archaeology falls vacant next year and the Member for Education, after discussion with me, is extremely anxious to get a man . . . from home for succession. I fear condition of department is quite lamentable. It contains no one of any quality and level of its work is low. . . . I do not know if Mortimer Wheeler who I understand is at present serving in the army would be possible. . . .

The story as to why the department was in such a wretched state is one of decline and fall, for, as in so many parts of their empire, the British had in the past shown admirable concern for the Indian heritage. The first man to hold the title of Director General was General Cunningham, who was put in charge of the Archaeological Survey of India in 1871. As the name shows, the purpose of this body was to search out and record ancient monuments of all kinds rather than study or conserve them. For some two decades good work was done, but by the time Lord Curzon was made Viceroy the Survey was moribund. Curzon cared about India's marvellous historical and artistic riches, and he it was who revived the Survey, sent for a young classical scholar from Cambridge to run it, and gave him full backing when he arrived in 1902. John Marshall had studied archaeology in Greece, but, as Wheeler observed, had 'taken office at a very early age and at a period when modern archaeological technique (outside Cranborne Chase) was in a rudimentary stage'.

Enthusiastic and energetic, Marshall accomplished much: among other things conserving historic buildings, drafting an Ancient

Monuments Act, excavating for twenty years at Taxila and discovering for the world the existence in the Indus Valley of a Bronze Age civilization to be compared with those of Egypt and Mesopotamia. Yet within a few years of Sir John Marshall's retirement in 1929 the department had lapsed into the lamentable condition alluded to in Wavell's telegram.

Wheeler has been accused of being harsh in his judgement of Marshall, yet he fully recognized his achievements. If there were any bias at all it was because Marshall was weakest in two areas in which Wheeler was strongest and which he considered most important: in technically skilled and purposefully selected excavation and in the training of able lieutenants and successors. Cut off and overburdened with his vast responsibilities, Marshall had not kept in touch with advances in scientific method, while he was also one of those men who did not like to delegate responsibility. As someone said of him, he was like 'a beech tree under which nothing grows'. When he retired, therefore, all about him were old, backward-looking and soon to retire themselves. There were four Directors General within a decade. Collapse was inevitable.

Yet the organization of the Survey and its commitments remained as vast as they were feeble and neglected: something had to be done. It was decided to invite Sir Leonard Woolley, whose great career as an excavator was then slowing down, to advise on what that something should be. He arrived early in 1938 and in three months he and his wife were able to inspect all considerable museums, monuments and excavation sites – a feat worthy of Wheeler himself, as was also the promptness and clarity of his report.

Woolley's findings were keenly critical, particularly of museums, aimless and amateurish excavation and expensive, positively harmful restoration. Among his many very precise recommendations one was put forward as an essential priority: as the staff consisted of men so inexperienced and justifiably lacking in self-confidence that standards could not be raised from within he recommended the appointment of a European Adviser in Archaeology for a limited term of years.

This recommendation, even more than the generally critical tone, roused a storm over the Woolley Report, Indian self-esteem being then a most delicate plant. It was withdrawn for a time, then war came; it is remarkable that Wheeler's invitation was delivered within five years rather than that it was so long delayed.

There is no doubt that Leonard Woolley had privately recommended that Dr Mortimer Wheeler should be offered the role of European Adviser – to be the deus ex machina descending to rescue the Survey.

This leads on to a puzzle of no importance but some interest. About a month after his acceptance of the post Rik wrote to Thalassa Hencken in Boston to break the news. In her reply she said,

First, about your news. You know, it is an odd thing, but I had some kind of wind of that right back here some time ago. Do you remember, you probably don't, telling me about the possibility, well before the war started? I had forgotten all about it until I had dinner here one night with the Indian Agent General in America.... He had been Minister of the Interior in India ... talk somehow turned to archaeology and he told me that you had been going to be invited to the post, but that, owing to the war, you had changed your plans.

Rik had told Cyril Fox that the signal had come to him as a complete bombshell – and he was usually quite frank with his friend. It is true that four years of most strenuous soldiering had intervened, yet it seems hardly credible that no memory of these earlier negotiations (dating presumably from soon after the appearance of the Woolley Report) was stirred by the renewed invitation.

When in the spring of 1944 Dr Mortimer Wheeler landed at Bombay he was stepping into an archaeological kingdom covering one and a half million square miles, with responsibility for 2700 monuments, ranging from rough megaliths to the Taj Mahal, seven considerable museums – some urban, some remote – a huge and significant collection of Hindu and Muslim epigraphs, and all discovery and excavation that could be attempted throughout his domain. There was also, of course, the great administrative machine, divided into regions (or Circles, as they were called), each supposedly under a Superintendent and with a large, more or less demoralized staff extending down to an innumerable host of humble clerks and servants of every kind.

The memorable achievements of Wheeler's few years in India lie in his archaeological research, in his training of young men in its modern ideas and methods, and in the rousing in government, universities and the educated public of a proper appreciation of the subject and its enrichment of Indian history. Yet in everyday unrecorded fact a large part of his time and energy had to be devoted to the direction and improvement of this machine and all the paperwork and travel it entailed. During his first summer he was spending an average of seventy hours a week in railway trains and it was probably seldom very much less. In addition to routine travel, as between Simla, Delhi and Taxila, and his archaeological expeditions, he was always ready to make long, hot journeys to attend committees or meet individuals considered important for the furtherance of his plans.

The Director General's first train journey on Indian soil was to be a comfortable one, for, having been made welcome by the Governor of Bombay, Sir John Colville, he took the Frontier Mail for Delhi and Simla. He paused at Delhi to make contacts with the presiding authorities and announce his plans. On being warned that he must not be in too much of a hurry, since oriental habits and the climate demanded a more leisurely tempo, Rik replied that he *was* in a hurry and that he 'proposed to ignore the hot weather'. It was also during this brief stay that he sent for Glyn Daniel and Stuart Piggott and sought to relieve them from their 'women's work' in air photography by enlisting them in his staff. Both declined, Glyn because he had a Cambridge Fellowship waiting for him and Stuart from disinclination – although Rik was told that the Army could not spare him.

The headquarters of the Archaeological Survey were at that time on the top floor of the Railway Board premises in Simla. It was a gaunt, unlovely building, but the Director's office, often invaded by monkeys, had a view over wooded slopes to a superb panorama of mountains.

In *Still Digging* Rik left an account of his first intrusion on that top floor which is well known in the annals of archaeology – and closer to the truth than could be supposed:

I stepped over the recumbent forms of peons, past office windows revealing little clusters of idle clerks and hangers-on, to the office which I had taken over that morning from my Indian predecessor. As I opened my door I turned and looked back. The sleepers had not stirred, and only a wavering murmur like the distant drone of bees indicated the presence of drowsy human organisms within. I emitted a bull-like roar, and the place leapt to anxious life. One after another my headquarters staff was ushered in, and within an hour the purge was complete. Bowed shoulders and apprehensive glances showed an office working as it had not worked for many a long day. That evening one of the peons (who later became my most admirable Headquarters Jemadar) said tremulously to my deputy's Irish wife, 'Oh memsahib, a terrible thing has happened to us this day. . . .'

Had Jemadar Bagh Singh known the Revelation of St. John he might aptly have recalled the prophetic words: 'The Devil is come down amongst you having great wrath, because he knoweth that he hath but a short time.' The Devil had in fact a four years' contract from the Viceroy in his pocket; though, as events shaped themselves, only three of those years were to be effective, the fourth being submerged in the turbulence and bloodshed of Partition.

Though that ending was not foreseen, even four years then appeared devilishly short, and Rik was always conscious of galloping time.

In a letter to Cyril Fox (he started writing to his friend again within two months of his arrival) he declared,

The one redeeming feature of my task here, Cyril, is its utter impossibility under present conditions. In ten years of peacetime I – or anyone of my experience – could set it right. Now there isn't a car, there's *no* printing whatever, no plates or paper for your photography *and of course no money*. It's grim, and inexpressably lonely. But we'll make something of it in a sort of way. We're back in 1850.

There were ways in which Rik profited greatly from this backwardness, most importantly in archaeology itself, where, as we have seen, it suited his inclinations and methods to return to a pioneering stage of the subject. It also suited him to have authority among people who were not ashamed to accept and admire authority. His attitude towards Indians was ambivalent, and there is no doubt that in these days of 'anti-racist' obsession he would be condemned for racism. He wrote, 'I am constantly amazed by the glory that is India – and by the mental and physical flabbiness of the Indians . . .' and again,

. . . this is an astonishing country, rotten with the vilest intrigue, riddled with inferiority, lacking everywhere in *virility*, physical and mental; they feed wrongly and think wrongly and live wrongly – wrongly not from our point of view but from that of their own real needs. . . . I already find myself regarding them as ill-made clockwork toys rather than as human beings, and I find myself bullying them most brutally. Then suddenly you come upon a human streak, and are covered with shame. My students at least I am fond of. . . .

His 'brutality' could even be physical. In Delhi I met one of Rik's old pupils – who had become an antique dealer. 'I shall always be grateful to Sir Mortimer,' he said, 'because he taught me how to work. He beat it into me. Before that I could only be idle.' When I suggested he was speaking metaphorically the antique dealer happily declared, 'Oh no! He beat me, whack, whack.'

As time went by, greatly aided by ruthless selection and expulsion of staff, and by the admirable response of his students to teaching and example, he became more appreciative – perhaps even understood the possible strength in 'feebleness'. Certainly, on their side, those who worked for him not only responded to his dispassionate authority, many of them revelling in it, but came to recognize his frequent kindness and concern, and the fact that, if he drove them to sweat and even to tears, he drove himself harder.

After that first terrible descent upon his headquarters Rik threw himself into what he saw as his immediate tasks, the practical pre-liminaries to his higher ambitions. These were to set his headquarters in hard-working order, tour the whole of the subcontinent to see its problems for himself and, while doing so, to meet every member of his staff 'from Peshawar to Madras'. This programme he was to carry out, the first item within barely ten days of his arrival.

Although he gave priority to more practical duties, from the very first he was also working towards his cherished aims of excavation, research and training. The archaeological prospectus which he had drawn up on board the *City of Exeter* was divided into two parts, corresponding to the main geographical provinces of the great plains of the north and the plateau and coastal strips of the south. For the north he saw that the most urgent questions to be answered concerned the wide gap in knowledge between the end of the Indus Valley civilization and the dawn of history with the Achaemenid empire a millennium later; the background of the Vedic hymns; the date and the nature of the Aryan invasion; whether the Indus civilization left any detectable inheritance to later Indian civilization. For the south, where the material was abundant but historical references very sparse before the sixth century AD, he saw that a firm datum line could be provided by the scatter of datable Roman coins and coin hoards that might be related to contemporary Indian cultures.

The prospectus ended with a weighty paragraph.

Here, then, are two great problems which demand attention. In tackling them, I propose to work on a restricted and economical scale, with a view to develop-ing the technical side of our work and to training the younger generation who will succeed us. The work may not be immediately spectacular in the popular sense of the term, but, properly planned and controlled, it is capable of adding notably to our knowledge of the components of Indian civilization. And that is a basic function of the Archaeological Survey.

During the ten strenuous days at Simla Rik contrived to list all the recorded finds of Roman coins in southern India, and send two chosen officers to the south to select one or two from the listed sites where digging might be profitable.

Rik started his grand tour by heading for the North West Frontier Province and the Indus Valley. It was his first contact with the frontier country, which he was always to love, just as he was to admire its people, those 'virile toughs', the Pathans. For a time he was based, and lavishly entertained, at Peshawar. He was enthralled by its bazaar, and it was here, in such early days, that he bought 'two little pairs of Bokhara rugs – delectable things'. He treasured them all his life and they were to be on display at his Whitcomb Street flat till the last.

Rik penetrated as far north as Charsada, a huge city mound rising from the Peshawar Plain, where he was shocked to find it being carted away for fertilizer by 'great convoys of basket-laden buffaloes'. While fascinated by the possibilities of a renowned city visited by Alexander the Great, he put it low on his list for excavation since it was founded no earlier than Achaemenid times. It never lost its allure for him, and he was to return to dig there in the late fifties.

Taxila, a contemporary ancient city of many mounds lying to the south-east of Charsada and at the very foot of the Himalayas, was to be of immense importance for Rik's immediate plans. John Marshall had left many sound buildings behind him there, including a museum and a comfortable bungalow, and as soon as he saw them (it was in early May) Rik knew that mounds and buildings together would provide an ideal setting for the student training school he was resolved to open in the autumn.

With his training problem solved, the Director General set off for an inspection of that major concern of his archaeological thinking, the Indus civilization. This civilization, at its height in the third millennium BC, had been discovered by John Marshall through excavations at its two capital cities: Harappa, on a tributary in the upper valley to the north-east, and Mohenjodaro, on the banks of the Indus itself in the region of Sind. Marshall had been convinced that these cities were unfortified and lacked palaces and temples – with the obvious inference that, unlike the contemporary Bronze Age cities of Mesopotamia, they were not ruled by ambitious and militaristic kings. The Marxist-minded Gordon Childe had gone much further and taught us to believe that the Indus citizens had enjoyed the, to him, dubious blessings of 'a democratic bourgeois economy'. Gordon was to accept the reversal of his theory with good grace.

Having arrived at Harappa by train, Rik rode by tonga with his local official to the 'little bungalow beside the moonlit mounds'. He made no comment when his colleague assured him they would have to set out early the next morning, since after 7.30 the heat would be unendurable. They duly approached the site soon after the sun rose, and in its sloping rays Rik saw at once that the yellow mud encasing the highest mound could only be an eroded but still massive mud-brick wall: in fact, the fortification of a citadel which had dominated the city. It was the work of a few minutes to reveal the mud-brick construction, but Rik kept his staff toiling in the mid-day sun to establish other features. It must have been the first time that he put into practice his principle of ignoring the heat.

Having reversed the accepted interpretation of a great civilization with one glance and a morning's work, Rik went on to Mohenjodaro, over three hundred miles down river, and there found similar evidence. By the middle of May, back in Simla, he was able to tell Cyril Fox:

At Harappa the wall . . . is 50 ft wide with towers 30 ft high, and the bally thing can be traced all the way round!! In one spot the excavator (of Marshall's day) cut right through the rampart and called it a platform. The whole thing is pure feudalism: the heavily fortified citadel . . . overlooking industrial barracks, ordered rows of millstone emplacements and parallel lines of barns. . . . At Mohenjodaro was a similar citadel, here of baked brick . . . the quality of all past digging is *execrable*.

All these features and many more were to be more fully exposed when Rik returned to excavate at Harappa in 1946.

Only a few days later Rik sent his friend a long, facetious account of a visit to a Moghul tomb to illustrate the idea 'Yes it *is* a little different out here.' The opening paragraphs reveal his attitudes in these early days and also give an impression of some lasting aspects of his life as Director General.

At 9 o'clock in the morning, i.e. when the cooler and better part of the day is over and the unbearable hot-house period is just beginning, there's a loud explosion outside the door of your hotel. Striding through the dust and garbage, you find that the centre of the explosion is the remnant of a cloth-hooded Morris of protohistoric shape – by no means to be sneezed at in a country where a second-hand car costs 2 to 3 times as much as a new one and there aren't any new ones. In the act of dismounting you find Dr. Mohammad Nazim M.A. Ph.D. (Cantab.), the Superintendent of the particular Circle, i.e. in your dialect, Inspector of Ancient Monuments. His Circle is larger than the British Isles, but that doesn't worry him a lot, because he knows the problem is beyond him and that it's hopeless even to try. That, by the way, is all he does know. He was once a student of Persian epigraphy but many years ago. He now spends his time in persecuting his junior staff, from whom he occasionally accepts gift in lieu, and in writing anonymous letters about his colleagues to me. . . .

Well, through the dust the eminent Ph.D. Cantab. approaches, topi in hand and an ingratiating smile round his ferrety eyes. Bowing he takes your dispatch case and walking stick from you and hands them to your clerk who hands them to your jemadar who hands them to your peon who, finding no one else to hand them to, places them in the back of the car. We then bundle into the bulging vehicle. As you have gathered, we are quite a party.... It isn't done for a Director General to travel without a clerk (babu) to buy his railway tickets and to take down in a note-book all those pearls that are constantly falling from his lips. Also he must of course have a gold-braided jemadar to clear away any idle Indians who might obstruct the D.G.A.'s progress. And at any moment the peon might be required to run a message or lift a fly-curtain or fetch a bottle of lemonade. And how can you get into your trousers or dust your shoes without your bearer or valet?

With every reason to be well-pleased with his tour of the north-west, the DGA and some part at least of that entourage set out to survey the east and south of his domain. Staying long enough in Patna to harangue the nineteen university vice-chancellors he found conferring there, he went on to stay with an old acquaintance, R. G. Casey, presiding in Government House at Calcutta. Plans for his Taxila school were never far from his thoughts and while there it suddenly struck him that the Governor's younger brother, Dermot, who had dug with him in England, would be an ideal person to help run the school. No sooner thought than done – at the highest level. The Governor cabled the Viceroy who cabled the Australian Prime Minister and Dermot was plucked from an obscure military posting in Tasmania and flown to India. He was to prove an invaluable friend and aide.

Meanwhile Rik continued his advance to the south. When he wrote to Cyril in June he was in Orissa and had inspected the Pagoda of Konarak. It has to be recorded that Rik (of all people) referred to its erotic carvings as 'dirt' and 'smut'. When his Brahmin companion suggested that they represented worldliness, in contrast with the unworldliness and peace within, he peered inside the temple and was astonished to see 'that the cult object was a mighty phallus, as erect as Nelson's column and capped by a fresh offering of melted butter'. One wonders whether he had not yet heard of this aspect of the worship of Siva, a god whom, with his emblem, Rik was later to encounter in embryonic form at Harappa.

This same letter reveals a more important preoccupation: 'I'm going round India with half my brain; the other half being concentrated on Delhi. I expect soon to have my first clash with Government.' Already he was laying the plans for a drastic reform of the Survey that were to demand much of his energy during the rest of the year. Happily, despite the summer heat, this was now in full flow, with plenty to spare for a purer archaeology.

It was at Madras that he made a discovery of the utmost importance for tracking down the Roman presence in India. The assistants he had dispatched from Simla were doing useful work with the coin finds, but inevitably it fell to Rik himself to make the dramatic scoop.

He had been given the run of the Government Museum, and, well-versed in the dark secrets of museum storage, he was exploring the cupboards in a workshop when he drew out the unmistakable neck and handle of a Roman wine jar. It was a moment of vivid excitement, for Rik knew he was holding what could prove to be a key to the chronology of the later prehistory of southern India. Coins are useful, but they can remain long in circulation and travel too easily. An amphora (readily dateable) could not have travelled from the Mediterranean alone: it represented substantial trading contacts.

Happily the provenance of this precious relic was known: it had been found during trial excavations on what appeared to be an ancient port just to the south of Pondicherry, the capital of French India. Nothing could be better suited to Rik's hopes and he went in swift pursuit.

Pondicherry was at that time moribund: to Rik it seemed like 'a French provincial town gone to seed and to sleep'. However, he was well received at Government House – with cognac and other survivals of French civilization. The Public Library, he learnt, was the most likely place to find the source of his wine jar, and there, sure enough, in an inner room he caught sight of some museum cases, dirty but promising. Rik was never to forget his sensations, physical and mental, when he wiped the glass top with a sweaty forearm and saw in the case below quantities of Roman remains: many more amphorae, a lamp, an intaglio and, best of all, sherds of that glossy red Arretine ware that he had come upon during his search for the Belgae in Hertfordshire at the opposite extremity of its range. It was a moment of the kind of excitement that is the gold of archaeology. Arretine can be very accurately dated, and to find it here, five thousand miles from the Arezzo potteries in Italy, was a stirring proof of the wide reach of Roman commerce and at the same time of the existence of a Romano-Indian trading post where civilized households could eat from good tableware while they enjoyed their Mediterranean wine.

The site of that trading post, known locally as Arikamedu and lying two miles down the coast of the Bay of Bengal, proved to be an agreeable one. It had been built on the outlet of a river, now locked behind a sand-bar to form a wide, palm-bordered lagoon where villagers waded to fish gracefully if inefficiently with their long rods. On the bay side the accumulations of the ancient port rose above the water, with brick-walls protruding. The rough diggings where the Roman finds had been made, but not identified, were still visible: Rik resolved at once that he must return to conduct a model excavation the following year.

Having set those archaeological schemes that were nearest to his own heart so successfully in train, he was ready to turn to the other continuing issues that concerned him most as Director General, the Taxila training school and the struggle for reorganization. He was also being urged by governmental authorities with political ends in view to lead a cultural mission to Iran.

One small preparatory step for Taxila was made in July, when, largely for fun and to vitalize his communication with Cyril Fox, he sent his friend a telegram (from Hyderabad, where he was on an official visit): 'Please send two copies Personality for salvation of India.' This referred to Fox's famous *Personality of Britain*, with which Rik hoped to introduce his students to archaeo-geography and the use of distribution maps. By August he was able to report that students from all over India were applying for a six-month course at Taxila. Yet no one could fairly accuse him of showing too much favour to field archaeology, for at this same time he was giving public lectures in Calcutta, visiting Bombay to see Jesuits about seventeenth-century churches and Buddhists about sculptured caves, and 'lecturing to the soldiers at Poona'.

The school opened on 1 October 1944, with Dermot Casey as chief teacher of the mysteries of stratification and Gerard Mackworth Young, former Director of the British School of Archaeology in Athens and a fluent Punjabi speaker, in charge of administration. Rik himself, well-housed in the Marshall bungalow, wrote to Cyril a few days later:

I'm scribbling this late at night by the wavering light of an oil-lamp between bubbly pulls at my hookah whilst jackal shrieks to jackal beyond the garden hedge. My training-school has begun, and will shortly include 55 students of all faiths and origins. Out on the Mound the top of a building of the Taxila where Alexander the Great was entertained by the local king is beginning to emerge – or rather *was*, for a sudden cloudburst has just drowned everything and, incidentally, has floated away my students' camp. . . . I've already run my Department into debt over it [the dig] to the tune of 14000 rupees, and must go to Delhi (24 hours in the train) next week in an attempt to put it right.

The technique of excavation and its proper recording were, of course, the main subject of instruction, but there were also classes in more specialized topics, including surveying, draughtsmanship and even administration. By great good luck Cookie, who by then had quit the London Institute for the Royal Air Force, was posted to India and spent his Christmas with Rik, staying on long enough to give an intensive course in archaeological photography.

The daily regime was strenuous and strict. All students had to be at their work place by 8.45 and knocking-off time did not come until 6 pm; at 9 o'clock students came together again for a lecture – given by a member of staff, an eminent visitor or occasionally by one of themselves. Rik regarded most of them as 'good-natured children' who needed and responded to discipline. Nevertheless, he was fond of them, and, according to his habit, devoted to the interests of those whom he judged worthy. From among these emerged the men who were to prove capable of succeeding the master and fulfilling many of his hopes.

One of them was B. B. Lal, a future Director General. For him it was at once obvious that 'behind the gruff exterior, Sir Mortimer had a very kind and sympathetic heart'. Moreover, to his very great surprise, he found that Sir Mortimer was willing to admit to him, a stripling student, when he was wrong. After work one evening at Taxila Lal saw Rik scraping away to clarify the stratifications (at the bottom of a trench) of his sectional drawing.

Although my training in 'layerology' was only a fortnight old, I dared to pronounce from the trench-top: 'Sir, you seem to be wrong.' 'What nonsense,' came the reply from the deep trench. 'Shall I come down and discuss?' So saying I went down the ladder and tried to show the *guru* where he was wrong. . . . Sir Mortimer did not seem to agree with my explanation. Anyway, we broke off for the night. Next morning, within minutes of the starting of work, he came to my trench: 'My boy, you were right.'

Nor was this the only time that young Lal, already of the metal from which Directors General are made, was allowed to win such an argument.

Looking back in *Still Digging*, Rik saw the six months at Taxila as 'one of the happier periods of my life' and felt a certain sadness when he recalled the community of learning uniting the students

who flocked to me from the universities of India and the archaeological departments of the Indian States: swarthy Muslims from the North-West Frontier and the Punjab, little round-faced talkative Bengalis, quick-witted Madrasis, dark southerners from Cochin and Travancore. Alas, today . . . such an assemblage of races, tongues and creeds would no longer be feasible. Religious and political barriers have split [them] asunder.

The variousness of the students at Taxila produced incidents that became a part of tradition: there was, for instance, the young man from the south who was seen slipping ice into his pocket with the intention of sending it to his parents, who had never known such stuff. On another occasion Rik was walking in the evening sun with an Indian companion when 'a bird flashed by, turning its emerald wings into the sun'. When asked what it was the companion replied, 'Probably, sir, it is a bird.' This provoked Rik, in writing to Cyril, into a rather disproportionate outburst. Indians, he declared, had no appreciation of life, beauty or the joys of analysis, and so were incapable of naming each bird, flower or tree. 'They fill their nostrils with flatulent theory and forget to live.'

All through the latter half of this year the Director General had been developing his schemes for the reorganization of the Survey, submitting greatly increased budgets and battling with the authorities – often with the help of Oulsnam, the Secretary for Education. In October in reply to news from Cyril that he was meeting opposition at home he wrote,

... what a pair of idiots we are. We both allow ourselves to be bucketed into totally impossible jobs without a tittle of the equipment, money or personnel necessary for them. There are you, running Europe, and here am I, running India under the most fantastic conditions, 'backed' by governments that are either indifferent or actively hostile.... You're a large bit of a hero, Cyril, (and, damn it, I sometimes think that I am too), and heroism has its own reward.

Then in November he was able to announce an important success. He was still suffering from a bad bout of malaria when he made a hideous three-day train journey to address vice-chancellors once more before going to Delhi

to fight Finance about my budget, which had been drastically cut. Walked in with my resignation in my pocket and fire in my heart, but suddenly, on seeing the man, decided to try oil. Poured oil all over him, smothered him, pinioned him, and, to my utter surprise, he suddenly restored the cuts!!! ... So the first round's won. But there's another coming.

On his return to Taxila from this mission a small event occurred which once again brings out Wheeler's feelings for his students, the one force that always supported him when he would otherwise have been inclined to despair of India and Indians.

We [the school] make quite a good family, and I was rather touched the other night when the Frontier Mail brought me back at ten o'clock at night, four hours late, and I found every student waiting for me on the little chilly station a

ABOVE: Colonel Wheeler standing in front of a tank during the Second Battle of El Alamein, November 1942.

Kim (Margaret), Rik's third wife.

Rik talking to his Indian students at
Harappa, capital city of the Indus
civilization, 1946.

With the Governor-General of Pakistan at
the opening of the Pakistan National
Museum, April 1950.

The Archaeological Section of the India Museum, Calcutta, 1948.

'Animal, Vegetable, Mineral?', 1953. Left to right: Glyn Daniel, the Chairman, with the panel of experts Sir Mortimer Wheeler, Dr W. E. Swinton and Professor Thomas Bodkin.

Punch cartoon for the 'Buried Treasure' series, 1954.

Rik visiting an excavation site on the Wye Downs, Kent, 1954.

In conversation with Elizabeth Allan at the Foyles lunch to celebrate publication of *Still Digging*, 14 January 1955.

In Egypt.

Lecturing at Delphi during a Swans
Hellenic cruise.

Confronting one of the carved birds from
Zimbabwe.

A problem in stratification, India,
1959.

Talking to President Ayub Khan of Pakistan, 13 July 1964.

Sharing a joke with Barbara Cartland (left) and the Duchess of Bedford, 1965.

With Magnus Magnusson during the filming of 'Sir Mortimer Wheeler' in 1971.
The pub covers a large section of the Roman Balkerne Gate where in 1917 Captain
Wheeler with volunteers from his battery dug by candlelight to establish the original plan.

A reminiscent drink after filming. It was in this bar that the diggers had gathered
nightly to wash the ancient dust from their throats.

At a reunion of the 42nd Light Anti-Aircraft Regiment.

In 1971.

mile from their camp. To a silly sentimental bloke like me, that was the finest reward a man could wish for.

With March 1945 the six-month course was over, and had indeed, as Rik said, done something to reorientate Indian field archaeology. Although Taxila grew directly from that combination of excavation with instruction that the Wheelers had created in Wales and England, the large number of students involved and the routine of classes and teaching justify the claim that it was the first true training-school in world archaeology. Since then they have been widely adopted, with the growing academic acceptance of archaeology itself.

Already it was time to head south for the opening of the excavations at Arikamedu. They were to be, in part, a continuance of the training programme, for a fresh batch of students had been enrolled – drawn mainly from the peninsula. Rik selected a few of his best trainees from Taxila to pass on their newly acquired skills to the novices, then, after the briefest of stays in Delhi, entrained for Pondicherry.

The conditions at Arikamedu were very different from those in the north: there was the tropical heat to endure, with none of the amenities of Taxila, a part of the digging was below sea-level and the first two weeks were blighted by unseasonable rains.

Rik established himself in a bungalow about a mile from the site, where he could feel lonely in spite of his jemadar, manservant, Gurkha guards and a number of 'naked gentlemen' self-appointed to menial tasks. After working stubbornly through the heat of the day, refreshed only by coconut milk, he would return to his bungalow 'to struggle with my endless postbag. Then a cold bath, dinner, and the day's work begins.' It was a hard life, made more difficult by the need to keep in touch with Delhi, and with his Simla office twelve hundred miles away.

Indeed, the opening fortnight was really difficult, for while the rain came down in sheets nothing of interest came from below ground. The raw young southern students, resentful of physical labour in muddy trenches, might have become more restive than they did if Rik had not been inspired by providence to warn them in advance that they might have to work for a fortnight without reward. Just before that time was up a student emerged from the mud, holding the base of an Arretine dish stamped with the name of its Roman maker.

After that all was well, and the results turned out exactly as the Director would have ordered. It proved that round about the year o there had been a fishing village there by the river. Its timeless peace was quite suddenly broken by the arrival of the foreign traders, probably seeking gems from Ceylon, silk and spices from the Ganges, and the village was superseded by their emporium – which was at its height by the middle of the first century AD. Rik knew that both the pottery made by the villagers and the pottery and other Indian artifacts that continued in use beside the Mediterranean imports had been found over much of southern India. So here already he had established that all-important datum line for the south that he had hoped for when drawing up his plan of research on board the *City of Exeter*. Writing to Leslie Murray-Thriepland on 24 April, exactly one year after taking office, he was justified in calling it 'really rather a scoop'.

It was at about the middle of the three months of the Arikamedu excavations when news came of the end of the European war. Rik was flying back from a committee meeting in Delhi, and so was able to enjoy the festivities spontaneously offered by the Governor of Pondicherry before returning to his bungalow by moonlight.

His own form of celebration was to give all his local work people an extra rupee in their pay packets. This was well received, but it had to be explained that there had been a great war which had now come to an end. Their ignorance made the sequel all the more remarkable: his workers were resolved to give him a party, and Rik discovered by private enquiries that every one of them had surrendered one quarter of the extra rupee to pay for it. As he wrote, 'Never have I been more touched than by this gesture of the humblest of folk; folk known to me well enough indeed individually by sight and prowess but barred by every barrier of language and custom.' It was a tremendous party, with resounding brass as well as flute and drum, and delightful dancing that included a traditional hobby-horse dance performed by lantern-light under the greater light of the moon. In the end, seated on a gilded French chair, the guest of honour was duly loaded with flowers and fruit.

By the end of his three months at Arikamedu Rik had established the history and pottery sequence of the place, uncovered a large warehouse and other practical installations of the later phase of the Roman trading post – and taught another large batch of young Indians the rudiments of excavation. He then made a tour of museums and sites further north in the peninsula, preparing the way for further digging that would extend the Arikamedu dating evidence to the greater part of his southern province. By mid-July he was back in Simla after an absence of ten months from his headquarters.

The Director General had kept in touch with Dr Chakravarti, his good Deputy Director, who had been holding the fort at Simla, but there was a mass of administrative work awaiting him. He had won a twenty-five per cent increase in his budget and was trying to establish lines of promotion by appointing junior assistants to the Superintendents of Circles; he had also succeeded in reducing the most oversized of the Circles by demarcating a new one in the south-east – which had to be staffed. Then there was the organizing of the All India Advisory Board for Archaeology (or, as he privately put it, 'the Board to receive advice'), which he had induced the government to establish.

The jobs were endless, but the one that was dearest to Rik himself was to bring into being a new journal in which the work of the Survey and related archaeological matters could be promptly and decently published. At an early stage he determined the name, *Ancient India*, and that it should appear twice a year. The old Annual Reports of the Survey had petered out long since and there was a wartime ban on new departmental publishing; Indian printing was notoriously abominable and at this time there appeared to be no suitable paper to be had throughout the entire subcontinent. Undeterred by such obstacles, Rik had been preaching his gospel of the absolute necessity of prompt publication from the outset and felt deeply committed to securing it.

Supported only by the Minister of Education, he waged a hard but finally successful battle with government to get the ban lifted, and by the time he went to Arikamedu had somehow obtained five tons of tolerably good paper. Then, after a hunt as desperate as that which had led to St John's Lodge, he got wind of a small but capable press. No one would have supposed that the best printing in India was then being done by the Baptists, but so it proved to be. Their press had long ago been set up in a mission house on the outskirts of Calcutta. Rik established an excellent relationship with the management and so secured at least a considerable future for what was the first well-produced and illustrated learned journal in India, and one which appeared almost on time so long as he was in control. He laboured over every detail – blocks were sometimes remade three times – and in fact wrote or rewrote a large part of some numbers himself. It was a work of love that could often be done on railway journeys.

Inevitably the fact that *Ancient India* came from a British-controlled press provoked ill-will in ever-more-touchy government circles, and the complaint could be made that it was too expensive.

It was for this reason as well as his own feeling for conciseness and clarity that Rik was severe with some of his Indian contributors who were unused to such discipline. B. B. Lal has given an amusing account of his editorial style. Following the comment on Rik's concealed kindness of heart, he continues,

It is rarely that his anger and shouts were meant to harm a person. 'Bring that back,' said Sir Mortimer to me, 'I will tell you what to do with it.' This was in his office-room in the Curzon Road barracks New Delhi in 1947. Tears were trickling down my cheeks, for the taskmaster had unceremoniously thrown away the ten-page draft of a report on finds from the 1946 excavation at Harappa.... An 'officer' should not have been humiliated like that, I felt. However, having been so directed, I collected the sheets strewn on the floor and putting in a serial order placed them on the table in front of the boss. 'My dear boy, you must write always keeping in mind that each word is going to cost you a pound for printing. If you do this you would learn to be precise and straightforward.' My padded draft was slashed down by Sir Mortimer to a little over four pages and there was no omission of anything that mattered.... Sir Mortimer did not spare even his English colleagues in this regard.

The first number of *Ancient India* came out on time in January 1946, but the second was held up by postal strikes and by the severe rioting in Calcutta, a presage of disaster to come. Rik told Stuart Piggott how, on hearing that the streets near his press were burning, he had dashed up to Calcutta not from heroism 'but simply because so much blood and sweat have gone into the making of this issue that I couldn't sleep while Free India let off bombs and popguns all round it'. The situation at the press was restored for a while, but the production of the fourth number of the journal was to be one of Rik's last tasks in India. After Partition his successors got it going again, but delays increased and the last number, for 1966, was not published until 1973. Rik had apologized to Stuart when Number Two was six weeks late.

On his return to Simla from Arikamedu in July 1945 Rik wrote to Cyril in a reminiscent mood. However vile the cities, he had come to the conclusion that the country was stupendous. 'I've been round it twice in the space of a single year, sleeping alternately in the palaces of Dewans and on the earth floors of remote village schoolrooms.' By the end of August he was on the upper mark of this scale, staying with a progressive Harrovian maharajah, when he wrote once more to his friend, obviously in tearing high spirits, claiming to feel ten years younger every week. He said that he had three adventures ahead, one of which was the cultural mission to Iran, now arranged for October. It can hardly be doubted that another concerned plans for Kim Norfolk to come from home to marry him. In a letter to Leslie Murray-Thriepland, he said, 'by a piece of luck' he had 'managed to get Kim out here from Australia just in time to act as hostess to the Viceroy at Taxila before starting out for Persia'.

The annulment had gone through and Rik was an accepted convert to the Roman Catholic faith: at last he could claim possession of the beautiful young woman to whom he had first proposed six years before. She came out with her four-year-old daughter, Elizabeth, whom Rik found charming and who, having only seen him before in uniform, solemnly addressed him as 'Brigadier'. They were married in Simla, and soon afterwards the little girl and her nurse were comfortably lodged in the bungalow at Taxila, while Kim plunged at once into the adventurous journey to Teheran.

The Indian Cultural Mission to Iran was a return visit after an Iranian mission to India of the previous year. Officials of the External Affairs Department had accepted the invitation with alacrity since it was their policy to foster good relations with the Iranians. They had recognized very soon after his arrival that the Director General for Archaeology would be the ideal man to lead the mission. Rik and Kim made the three-day train journey to Quetta, where they were joined by Dr Nazim (so unkindly described by Rik on an earlier occasion) and took the staggering little train to the Iran border town of Zahidan, crossing the frontier on 25 October. There the Indian authorities supplied them with transport, and with sepoys and escort trucks for the crossing of Baluchistan. They set off, with Rik driving one truck, Kim another, and armed sepoys sitting behind them. Poor Dr Nazim seldom spoke, except to murmur of hardships.

Hardships there certainly were on their tour of Iran, and the bride must have been severely tested. Yet an expedition of this kind, free at least from routine work, was probably as near to a honeymoon as Rik would have tolerated. There were wonderfully romantic moments – as when an escort broke down and they 'slept on the desert with an incredible firmament over head', and again when they slept under a fig-tree in an ancient garden with water rippling beside them all night, and when they listened to bul-buls singing over moonlit Persepolis. On the other hand Rik had not been shaken out of his belief in the hard-driving of a wife. The unfortunate Kim went down with malaria, presumably infected at Taxila, where Rik had suffered earlier, but, as he nonchalantly told Leslie, 'we only allowed it to hold us up for one day'.

A week's driving by way of Isfahan took them to Teheran, where they stayed with the British ambassador. Rik was immediately envious of the archaeological museum and library, designed by the French, which he considered much superior to any in India. (His mention of this fact in the Report may not have been unconnected with the need for an Indian National Museum, which he was already urging.)

The mission did not stay long in the capital but set off on a tour of western and south-western Iran that included a longer stay at Isfahan, also Persepolis, Shiraz, Pasargadae and Kashan – from where Rik saw to it that they left architectural glories for a while and visited the great prehistoric *tell* of Sialk. In spite of the necessary round of formal visits and hospitality, Rik, with his genuine love of both architecture and wild country, certainly enjoyed this trip – and the expected brigands did not trouble them. Back at Teheran trouble of a slightly different kind awaited them.

The Russians were at this time in military occupation of northern Iran and their permission had to be obtained for the scheduled visit to the Caspian and Meshed. Anyone who has attempted to deal in such matters with Soviet authorities will understand the frustrations suffered by the mission and their Iranian and British hosts: long delays, promises made and withdrawn, loss of papers, long silences, ending in the announcement that the visit was not opportune. Rik, of course, was furious and was to declare in his Report that the situation was out-rageous in itself and 'aggravated by the dishonesty and prevarication of the refusal'. He also appended a fierce section on 'The Russian Menace' in the economic and political fields.

The cancellation of the northern tour upset their programme com-pletely, and rather than loiter in Teheran the mission left immediately for the final phase of their tour. With two trucks and their sepoys they headed west again, towards Kasvin, Rik driving the first of the closely hooded trucks with Kim beside him. Just short of the town they encountered three Russian tanks barring the road and although Rik had been instructed before leaving India that if he saw a Russian he must run away, he was resolved to suffer no further obstruction. Inspired, he told his wife to apply more lipstick, to take over the wheel and advance slowly. A Russian officer approached them, holding up a large hand. He was evidently puzzled by two lonely trucks with strange markings but, 'At length he cautiously raised the flap by the driver's seat and peered in.' Whereupon Kim 'smiled at him with coral lips and wished him a very good morning. The poor fellow started back into the snow.' Presently he tried again, his 'round peasant face resumed its puzzle-ment; evidently there was nothing in the book about a situation such as this.... Slowly and circumspectly he walked round to the back of the truck, gazed with patent disbelief at the shivering sepoys and turned towards the second truck.... Then he committed a most unsoldierly error. He continued to the rear of the second truck.' Both vehicles now cut him off from his own guns. Rik told Kim to head for the narrow space between two of the tanks. 'With admirable skill she squeezed our truck into the gap, and, praise be, the second truck closely followed.' They were on their way – and although Kasvin was swarming with Russian troops they met no further impediment.

After a few days at Hamadan and seeing the famous rock inscriptions of Bisitun, they left Iran exactly one month after entering it, and were soon in Baghdad. This was Rik's and Kim's first visit to the archaeological Mecca of Mesopotamia, but they had time only to see Babylon and other archaeological sites near Baghdad before flying back to Delhi.

Wheeler had returned to a winter of administrative chores and fighting for more money, broken by a lecture trip to Bangalore – five days and nights each way in the train. He now took a decision to save travel and bring himself close to the seats of power. He moved the headquarters of the Survey from Simla to the Central Asian Antiquities Museum in New Delhi.

Meanwhile Kim had suffered another attack of malaria and went away for a while, but in February they had a week together in Taxila. Rik went partridge-shooting in the hills; they could enjoy an agreeable house and the company of Elizabeth. It was, Rik sourly told Cyril, 'a week of the kind known as "idyllic"'.

This was in a letter written late at night in his museum office in Delhi, having left Kim at Taxila while he returned to the city to run a staff course on conservation. He was in a rare mood of utter depression and a kind of angry self-pity. True, he began, as though countering Cyril's misgivings, by declaring 'The marriage is a Good Thing – Kim is the staunchest friend a man could have.' Then, after describing the course and his other work, he goes on,

But, Cyril, I'm ploughing the sands. Nothing that I do or can do here will last. The country, I mean the people, *are basically* rotten. Some of my own young students are faithful to me and understand me, up to a point ... the older people are set and utterly hopeless, incapable of acquiring knowledge or anything resembling a sense of duty.... In a few months' time I've no doubt that we shall be living at the revolver point. Anyway, I've been dusting mine and it would give me a comfortable vindictive feeling to use it. You see, demoralized!

The letter ends with gloomy speculations as to how long the government would allow an Englishman to remain as head of a department: 'I may not get more than two more years from the politicians. So if you have a spare Keepership going, remember me!' This was Rik's first mention of thoughts about his future. Although jocular, it was a presage of the serious correspondence on the subject that was to come.

Why he was in such an ill mood that February night can only be guessed at. Evidently he had not found the week at Taxila the idyll that it should have been. Perhaps after the exhausting month in Iran, Kim's bouts of malaria, their brief parting and relatively quiet time together in Taxila, Rik may, in spite of his protestation, have been feeling uneasy about their marriage. Kim had certainly begun to doubt the sincerity of her husband's conversion to the faith that meant so much to her, and the shock of this realization was to play an important part in the failure of their relationship.

Whatever the cause was, work and more work was bound to be Rik's antidote. This spring, too, there was something to look forward to: the return to Harappa to follow up his astonishing discovery of two years before. Having had such success in launching his programme for the south, he was now ready to turn to his northern province and the Indus civilization. He and Kim set off with some thirty students and with a junior staff now experienced and hardened in the Wheeler Method and the Wheeler standards of work. As other commitments had delayed the start, the Punjab plains were already hot and were soon to be torrid. Indeed, the heat was so great that even Rik could not ignore it, allowing a long afternoon break and iced drinks.

This was a rare weakening: he had not altogether relaxed his rule of defying the climate, as three accounts of the dust storms that swept Harappa make clear. In *Still Digging* the author merely recorded how an occasional storm would advance 'like a solid moving cliff', smothering everybody and everything, and went on to say how well his team had endured all trials. In a letter written to Cyril Fox in May he gave a fine description of the 'wall of turbulent sand standing hundreds of feet into the air' and of the measures he himself took to close shutters and protect a newly discovered burial. Then:

I went out to the various digging-sites. At one, and one only, was work continuing. It was under the charge of an Indian student who had just come back from Oxford! On every other site, students and coolies alike were squatting about like static frogs waiting for the storm to pass. What leadership! Ye gods, there wasn't a man amongst them. I went into them with my stick and lashed them back to work and they had the grace to run. But oh Cyril, what miserable bifurcated radishes these folk are.

The third account, of a later storm, comes from B. B. Lal (whom Rik had by now made one of his new Assistant Superintendents, although he was under age). He was in charge of an area where Kim was drawing a plan and section. The temperature had been up to 118° before the storm came.

It was blinding. The visibility was hardly a couple of yards. The poor lady could not proceed with her drawing and sat down in a sheltered corner of the trench. Suddenly we heard a roar of the moustached man-lion. He was shouting at his wife for not having completed the drawing as per schedule. When I tried to intervene, pleading that the delay was on account of the bad weather, I was given the rebuff: 'It is your own weather. I have not brought it from England. If I can work in it, why can't you people.'

Lal told this story in wry admiration of the fact that Rik would not spare his wife any more than himself. As has already appeared, he fully understood 'Sir Mortimer's' tyrannical ways. Indeed, he expressed it well: 'Work was worship to him.'

The Harappa excavation was well executed and archaeologically successful. Most of the digging was concentrated on the great walls of the citadel that had been so strangely missed by Marshall's excavators. They and their baked brick revetments were exposed to their full surviving height and pursued down to their foundations thirty feet below ground. Much work was also devoted to establishing the stratification, to uncovering a known but unpublished cemetery and generally extending and clarifying the structures found in Marshall's day. The old mistake of the 'bourgeois' nature of the Indus civilization was even more thoroughly demolished by Rik's recognition of the rows of tiny standardized dwellings as the equivalent of 'coolie lines', and the grinding mills and huge granaries as further evidence of a powerful authority in command of slave-like labour and of the centralized collection and distribution of grain.

Rik was well satisfied with the results of his dig when it ended at last in the frightful heat of late June, and he wrote them up with his usual dispatch – in time for them to be published in the third, January number of *Ancient India*. More immediately, however, he was able to take Kim from her various grillings on the plains up to Kashmir, with the intention of inspecting its architectural monuments. While among the mountains they snatched three days of holiday – Rik's first since coming to India. This was pure enjoyment for him. There were trout in the mountain torrents, and, having initiated his wife into his favourite sport of fly-fishing, he rejoiced to see her land far larger catches than his own. They lived on a diet of trout, cooking and eating them on the river banks.

From Kashmir there was a quick dash to Taxila to receive Prince Peter of Greece before Rik and Kim set off in full monsoon for a tour of inspection down the Ganges. The river was a brown torrent and they were moved by the spectacle of 'the beautiful archaic river craft with their high, square sails' and by the doings of holy men. They stayed at Benares and then went on to Patna, where they lodged in the guest house of an Indian magnate, with flood water up to the window-sills. There Rik had to leave his luckless wife in the care of a doctor, as she had just gone down for the seventh time with malaria.

Calcutta, when Rik returned to it in late August, was in the grip of the rioting that held up the appearance of *Ancient India*. He sat one night writing to Cyril Fox in the silence of a city under curfew. Several people had been shot in the compound of the building a day or two before and he was 'flanked by a cup of tea (essential) on one side and a loaded revolver (quite unnecessary) on the other'. None of his local staff had been seen for a week, he was quite alone, 'and now in the warm night revelling in the bliss which only complete solitude can bring. . . .' He had one piece of good news to tell: for a very long time he had been badgering everyone from the Viceroy down to accept the necessity for an Indian National Museum. Now at last, in the face of stiff opposition from Finance, he had succeeded in getting it included in the next Five Year Plan. There were, of course, to be many delays, but by the time the Director General wrote his final Report in 1947 the Cabinet had just agreed to go ahead, though gradually, with a National Museum for art, archaeology and anthropology. Today it is one of the prides and pleasures of New Delhi.

The chief event of the autumn of 1946 was a second Cultural Mission, this time to Afghanistan. Once again it was a return visit, but its purposes, though similar to those for Iran, were rather more narrowly limited to archaeological and historical interests. Rik had been contemplating the visit with some eagerness since soon after his return from Teheran. He was always fascinated by Greek influences in India and neighbouring lands and longed to see Bactria, particularly Balkh, 'Mother of Cities'. The French had been granted special rights for archaeological exploration in Afghanistan, and Rik hoped to persuade Daniel Schlumberger, the excellent new head of the French mission, to excavate at Balkh.

This excursion was to be a far less exhausting one than its predecessor, with a single sweep of eighteen hundred miles in place of the four thousand covered by the Iranian tours. In addition to Kim, Rik took with him Mr Justice Edgely, President of the Royal Asiatic Society of Bengal, the oldest learned society in Asia, and M. A. Shakur, curator of the Peshawar Museum. There being no threat either of brigands or of Russians, they travelled in a personnel-carrier and a jeep with a few Indian drivers and attendants. They left Peshawar on 25 September and reached Kabul within two days. Nevertheless, on approaching the capital the leading driver became hopelessly lost; Kim was impressed when her exasperated husband took the wheel and delivered them at the British Embassy without further delay.

The party was royally entertained by the government and palace officials, culminating in a banquet at the Ghihil Sutun Palace. What Rik relished even more was an inspection of the recently discovered Begram hoard of metalwork and Indian ivories, with its evidence of the cultural links between Afghanistan and India and the presence of imports from Alexandria.

The mission went first to Begram, then drove through the mountains westwards along the most important of the ancient caravan routes to India before descending the valley of the Kunduz, the one river from the Hindu Kush that still flows into the Oxus. Daniel Schlumberger had now joined them, so Rik had the advantage of his learning and local knowledge as they descended onto the river plains of Oxus, ancient Bactria. They had seen many undated town or village mounds on the way down and now, near Kunduz, Rik was struck by a 'great irregular fortification ... astonishingly similar to that of an Early Iron Age *oppidum* of the Caesarian era in north-western Europe'.

They drove down the valley through desert and steppe, inspecting various mounds from the point of view of possible excavation, until they came, by way of the curious nineteenth-century royal ghost city of Takht-i-Pol, to Rik's especial goal, the vast ruins of Balkh.

Probably no site in Asia surpasses Balkh in its appeal to the historical imagination. Here the main trade-routes from China, the Mediterranean and India met. From the battlements can be seen ... the gap through which caravans carried some part of its commerce to Taxila and beyond. Here ruled the Graeco-Bactrian kings. ...

Schlumberger had assured Rik that when there was a trained staff available the French mission would undertake excavations, and he therefore made a survey of the place, particularly of the seven-mile circuit of the fortifications, where, he was sure, digging should begin in order to delimit the pre-Islamic city.

Balkh was the climax of the tour, but there was much of interest to see nearby and en route back to Kabul. Since Rik's mind was preoccupied by the problems of Greek influences in the region, it was a happy chance that on a site not far from Balkh Schlumberger picked up a potsherd with a Hellenistic graffito, the very first Greek inscription, coins apart, to have been discovered in Bactria. After three weeks in Afghanistan the mission left by way of Kandahar and Quetta.

Rik had found it a relief to be out of India for a few weeks, and on his return his profound dissatisfaction with Indians other than his own selected and trained young men became more pervasive. From this time and all through 1947 his letters to Cyril Fox were laced with the most harsh, and sometimes bitter, criticisms of their slackness, treachery and corruption. On rereading them many years later, he himself was shocked by 'a recurrent note of anger and despair, which jar a little upon my kindlier memory'. It is not surprising, for he was more than ever haunted by the fear that he was 'ploughing the sands', he was worried for his own future and everywhere uncertainty, lawlessness and riot were threatening the hard-won achievements of the Survey. The award to him of the CIE was no great recompense.

His own days were not encouraging: Kim had escaped to Rawalpindi to spend some time with her daughter, who was now staying there, and he was almost alone at his Delhi headquarters, handling all levels of administration and finding evidence of nothing but 'Incompetence, incompetence and more incompetence.'

Still, there were compensations. Digging at Harappa was continuing on a smaller scale and the results were important enough to draw him there for a few days, while he and his small family were reunited for a Christmas party at Taxila which included French and Arab acquaintances from Afghanistan. Rik was expected to dress up as Father Christmas – 'a bit of anthropology for the Arabs'. Soon after they left, the Taxila Museum was broken into by a score of armed Dacoits, who speared a police guard and did considerable damage.

In the New Year there was a visit to Rajputana to stay with a young rajah, which Kim enjoyed and which was an amazing demonstration of the extreme contrasts of Indian life in that time of transition. There were panther- and wild-boar shooting and game-drives with gorgeously caparisoned camels and beaters with trumpets, while everywhere they went in the desert servants were ready with elegantly served teas, cocktails and luncheons. The rajah himself was made of contrasts, for while he held durbars of mediaeval splendour, he was a Cambridge man and a professional communist who – genuinely, Rik judged – was anxious to surrender all. After midnight dinners they would argue the question furiously into the small hours.

After this exposure to princely luxury, a tour in the jungles of Assam added to the diversity of life-styles which Rik always savoured. Yet the real redemption for him came as ever from active archaeology. The previous year, when he scanned the southern peninsula for sites where he might be able to apply his Arikamedu datum line, by far the most promising was in the wild granite hills of north Mysore – some three hundred miles from Pondicherry. He had spotted in the state museum a distinctive type of rouletted pottery, associated with the earlier Roman settlement at Arikamedu, coming from an ancient town site known as Brahmagiri. When he visited the place it proved to have a large cemetery of megalithic tombs set close beside it.

Rik had long hoped to be able to date these megaliths, so common in south India. Some such tombs had been known to contain iron objects, and pottery very like the vessels used by the pre-Roman villagers at Arikamedu, but there was no sound evidence of their age. This was of a wider interest since it was an old topic of archaeological debate whether the Indian tombs could possibly have any significant connection with the megalithic burial chambers of western Europe (including Britain) – which they resembled down to the detail of sometimes having round holes cut through the entrance slabs. Now there was a very good chance that the stratification at Brahmagiri might date the cemetery itself and also carry the Arikamedu datum line thus far to the north of the peninsula.

This part of Mysore was terribly poor, a 'famine area', and water and even food were scarce for the invading archaeologists. They were installed by early March, the thirty-five students near the site in their customary neat lines of tents, and the Director in a very cramped village house, where the insects swarmed by day and by night. It was probably here that Kim recalls shooting pigeons off the roof, while the two of them rationed themselves to one can of beer a day, drinking Enos first so that they were not too thirsty to enjoy it. Rik allowed himself a small basin of water in which he 'swished out his hair', demanding, as a variant on ancient usage, to have it towelled dry.

The excavation was successful, and Rik was cheered by the performance of his newly formed Excavation Branch. Some half-dozen megaliths were thoroughly explored and sizeable cuts made through the well-stratified accumulation of the town site. The town proved to have had three distinct but continuous periods of occupation, of which the latest yielded the Arikamedu rouletted ware and could therefore be dated to the first century AD, while the second was unquestionably contemporary with the cemetery and could be judged to have begun in about 200 BC, iron being in full use throughout. Before that the site had been occupied by people still essentially in the belated Indian Stone Age tradition, although using a little bronze. So here at last was a firm date for the megalithic tombs of south India (incidentally too late for any kind of diffusion from Europe) and here was the datum line stretching as far as the Deccan.

Could one be certain of that? Rik began to think there could be a considerable time-lag between the use of rouletted dishes on Romano-Indian tables at the trading post and their introduction so many hundred miles to the north. He recalled another site forty-five miles away where in the past rouletted sherds and some early imperial Roman coins had been unearthed during haphazard digging. A competent team was sent to make scientific soundings there at Chandravalli, but when Rik went over to inspect he found his young men much cast down, for, though the pottery was there, well-stratified Roman coins were what was needed and none had come to light.

There followed a third dramatic incident to set beside the discovery of the amphora handle at Madras and of the Arretine sherds at Pondicherry. Going through all the Chandravalli finds, however unpromising, Rik's eye was caught by 'a little lump of purple oxidization' which his experience on Romano-British sites told him might contain a silver coin. It did: a denarius of the Emperor Tiberius, struck between AD 26 and 37. Synchronism with Arikamedu had been confirmed and the foundations of a chronology for the whole peninsula established.

I freely confess that as I stood there on the Indian plateau, far from any landfall for overseas traffic, with that crucial coin in my hand, I marvelled at the romantic chance that had brought me to it at the desired moment and in the desired setting. It was the crowning fortune of three years of steady planning and steadily attendant luck.

This was, in fact, to be Rik's last large-scale excavation as Director General in India, which made the fulfilment of his original prospectus for the south especially fortunate. He was not, however, quite satisfied. He thought it should be possible to link the dates established for the southern cultures with those still floating unanchored on the wide plains of his northern province, and so secure elements of a unified chronology for the subcontinent. He saw that the most likely line of contact between the two would have been by way of the eastern coastal lowlands, and, with his unfailing sense for a likely place to dig, he chose Sisupalgarh, a fortified site in Orissa lying just about half-way between the Mysore region and the Ganges Valley. He appointed his now trusted colleague, B. B. Lal, to take charge of excavations there, and on his own final tour, just before quitting India, he visited Sisupalgarh and had the very great satisfaction of learning that Arikamedu pottery was here lying in association with Gangetic wares: 'The twain had met in decent and orderly fashion.'

Meanwhile almost all aspects of life in the India of 1947 were falling into increasing disorder as the country moved towards Independence Day and the horrors that immediately followed.

Already while still in Mysore Wheeler had written,

Here political conditions are increasingly impossible, although I like Nehru personally and have seen a fair amount of him. His henchmen on the other hand are mostly quite impossible ... and I cannot help looking forward to April 1948 [the end of his four-year term]. It is natural that India at the present time should intrude its politics into every branch of life, but I am the least political of mortals and will not tolerate political intrusion into my science. This obstinacy of mine does not conduce to an easy life.

In early August, although he had just been to Goa, enjoying its ancient civilization and the lotus-eating ways of the fashionable and well-to-do, he told Cyril that life in Delhi was now hell, that all the evils of the East were 'abroad in the land unfettered' and that through Partition he was losing to Pakistan a number of his best young men. 'And so my work dissolves, after three years of hard labour!'

Much worse was to come. After 15 August, when the Union Jacks came down for the last time outside the Secretariat in New Delhi, the Director General and his staff were immediately involved in what, as he said, was essentially a Hindu–Muslim war. Wherever he went corpses lay in the street and there was firing and looting. One of his Muslim drivers told him how his wife, mother and whole family had just been slaughtered, while his other driver was in hospital with a knife wound. No wonder that his entire Delhi staff was 'in a state of abject terror' – far too abject, he felt: 'they just *ask* to be knifed'. He used such words but already he was taking time and some risks for his Muslim staff, helping a few to escape from the city and taking milk and vegetables to those who were among the many impounded in the Purana Qila fortress for their own safety – where 'they continued to die of their own volition but at a retarded rate'.

For Rik it was just as bad to imagine the agonies in the north-west, where streams of Hindu refugees from Pakistan were dying by the roadsides as they fled, while in the Punjab Muslims again were the victims and several members of his staff had lost their families and their homes. For him, too, it was a matter of intense professional regret that conditions in Pakistan made it impossible for him to carry out his favourite project: the excavation of the great mounds of Charsada. 'It was to have been my crowning dig in the North West Frontier,' he confided to Cyril. 'Now the little arch will lack its keystone.'

Towards the end of September Rik wrote to his friend again: 'outside India it must be difficult to understand the present filthy mess here or to foresee the filthier mess that is to come'. He felt totally isolated; almost all the English had gone and anyway no one at all had any inkling of what he had been trying to do. One incident he had obviously enjoyed, even though it exemplified evil times.

The staff of one of the Delhi hospitals had been threatened with murder unless they turned out their Muslim patients; relatives of a Muslim colleague begged Rik to evacuate members of the family from the wards. On arrival in his jeep he found the hospital gates locked and an unpleasant little crowd gathered outside. When at last an English sister let him squeeze in he learnt that already that day two Muslim families had been shot by the crowd as they left the gates and it had been decided that evacuation should only be attempted by night.

However, I eventually persuaded the matron to let me and my jeep up to a side door, and, since I had no escort (*very* dangerous and ostentatious things, escorts!) got there without attracting attention. Then it was easy enough – packed the Muslim family tightly into the jeep, had the gates quietly opened, and drove out at full speed before the neighbouring crowd realized! Not a shot was fired and we got to the refugee camp without incident.

By the end of October Wheeler was almost the only remaining Englishman of any position in the Delhi administration, and although he daily flogged himself to work, he felt it was quite vain and that Indian officials would 'much rather have my ugly white face off their land-scape'. He feared that archaeology in India was coming to an end, and continued unhappily,

About four months of leave are due to me ... so I'll take ship as soon as I can get *Ancient India* No. 4, my swan song, off my chest. Perhaps about the beginning of February. Nothing else would keep me. And then hey and ho for my jolly old pension of £280 a year – reward for a lifetime in Government service! Oh hell. How I wish sometimes that I were a gently declining don in one of the quieter college quadrangles.

However, life isn't over yet. Perhaps we'll bluff it through!

Rik's sense of disintegration all about him was exacerbated by another breakdown in his private life. Kim had left him and retreated to England. Perhaps, as her friends believe, her distress on realizing that his conversion to her faith was not even skin-deep was at the root of the trouble. Again, it has been said that she was often frightened of him, but this could not possibly have been true unless there was something radically wrong. Immediately, of course, it was the endless work and restlessness. Also the lack, after marriage, of 'lovey-dovey' – presumably the tenderer moments she had known before. So she escaped. As at this time Kim had considerable private means there were no financial obstacles to her flight.

For a long time now Wheeler had been troubled about his own future: he had been out of British archaeology for over eight years, effectively out of Britain for six years and had no job being kept open for him. As early as June 1946 he had written Cyril Fox what he called a business letter, asking him to find out if there was likely to be a place for himself in the newly established UNESCO – of which he had just heard through an ICS circular. At that time he thought India was to suffer provincialization rather than partition and that he might soon be thrown out along with the central government. He was 'far too full of a devil-sent energy to take kindly to a third floor back'. Surely the infant organization must include archaeology and perhaps the experience of a Director General of Archaeology in a subcontinent could be usefully employed. That was the gist of his letter, but Rik insisted that he would continue to work for India so long as it was at all possible.

At the moment he wrote I was being made United Kingdom Secretary for UNESCO within the Ministry of Education and it seems that Cyril and I sent Rik all the information we could. There was, however, quite a scramble for appointments in Education, Science and Culture, so that, with his decision to serve as Director General as long as possible, thoughts of UNESCO faded from his mind.

Not quite a year later Cyril tried to secure him a professorship in Indian archaeology, but it went elsewhere; Rik was mildly regretful, saying he would shed no tear. By the autumn of 1947, when the end of his term was in sight and he felt the 'oppressive economic uncertainty' weighing upon him, he regretted the chair quite sharply: 'I've seen more Indian architecture and sculpture than most people. What a curse a potsherd reputation is.'

Soon something had to be settled, the more urgently since Wheeler was making up his mind to leave India well before the April terminus. On 28 November he wrote his last surviving Indian letter to Cyril and devoted it wholly to the question of a job. The position then was that Cyril, working with that eminence grise, Tom Jones, had virtually secured him the offer of the Secretaryship of the Royal Commission on Ancient Monuments for Wales. The Treasury, it seems, was refusing to increase the salary above £1000, but Rik insisted that 'under modern conditions' this was unacceptable and that the Treasury should be asked to add £200 of 'personal pay'. So, the former Brigadier Wheeler, after high position and quite extraordinary achievements in India, was fighting for almost exactly the same salary that he had contested with the Treasury nearly twenty years before as the young Keeper of one minor museum.

He went on to argue that, whoever became Secretary, his head-quarters should be in London, since experience had taught him that the machine could only be run 'by *constant and informal contact* with the Treasury folk' – a practice that he was to develop to perfection when Secretary of the British Academy.

The letter then takes an unexpected turning:

Lastly, it is only fair to say that there is . . . a faint possibility of a part-time chair in London. This has only just arisen, and is very uncertain. Although such a chair would be a close call financially (very close, in fact) it would enable me to write and lecture and maintain some of my overseas contacts. I feel sure, my dear Cyril, that you would understand if, after all your generous efforts, I should let you down. . . . I still regard the RCAM as the more likely solution. Please don't regard me as a waggler – the position *is* a little difficult!

His own preference for the academic post emerges clearly enough and is not surprising. It would surely have been almost intolerable to find himself back with the Commission, back in Wales and with limited authority in so small a field. That was the way it went: Wheeler was to return home with a part-time professorship in the Provinces of the Roman Empire in what had once been his own Institute of Archaeology, to provide him with bread and butter.

It remained only to tie up as many broken ends as possible and to make final tours of inspection and farewell. In Orissa, as we have seen, Rik had the parting gift of Lal's success at Sisupalgarh. He must already, as memory of the autumn receded, have begun to hope that he had been too gloomy when he foresaw the dissolution of all his work, the end of archaeology in India. He was to receive further, and quite unexpected, encouragement when he went to make the last of his farewells. This was in Karachi, capital of the awkward new state of Pakistan. Seven Muslim officers of the survey, including some of the brightest, had by now withdrawn there to form an Archaeological Department that was bound to be ragged and lacking direction. In Delhi it had always been Muslim politicians who made most trouble for Wheeler, but now, to his surprise, the Minister of Education sought him out and invited him to return to Pakistan as Archaeological Adviser to the Government, particularly charged to set the department on its feet. Rik was pleased and amused by this change of heart, but, not wishing to be deeply committed, agreed only to serve for a few months during each of the next three years. So it was that he left the land that had so greatly fascinated and enraged him with the certainty of an early return.

Before quitting Delhi Wheeler had written an admirably concise Director General's Report on the development of the department under his management, not omitting what had gone before and what he hoped for it in the future. He set out with concentrated modesty what had been done to secure the renaissance of the Survey in such things as staffing and staff training, conservation, museums, publications and, of course, excavation. He did not touch upon the results of those excavations, on the striking success of his archaeological research, but he must have looked back on it with satisfaction. He had, after all, more than fulfilled his original schemes for the south, and if in the north he had failed to track down the Aryan invaders themselves or bridge the gap after the fall of the Indus civilization he had both vastly increased and revolution-ized knowledge of that civilization itself.

He ended the Report with a more personal summing-up. Under the heading of 'The Need for Hard Work' he hinted mildly at the criticism that he had often expressed so vehemently in his letters. He then praised the quality and immense potentiality of his students, declared that in the Archaeological Survey India possessed a machine that could be 'without parallel in the world' and ended with his favourite quotation from Asoka, 'Let small and great exert themselves.'

CHAPTER 10

The British Academy

FOR FOUR YEARS Dr Mortimer Wheeler had been the absolute ruler of the largest archaeological organization in the five continents. He had to battle ceaselessly with government, he groaned under a daily burden of inefficiency, he had encountered chaos – all that is true. Yet as Director General he was honoured as the Big Man and at every level from punkah boys to his superintendents and deputy he had lived with people eager to serve him. Indeed, in the whole of his long civil career it was only India that gave him an office equal to his natural stature as a leader. When he had written to Cyril Fox about the UNESCO appointment he had said, 'I have an urge amounting almost to a fire within me really to do something worth while in a reasonably wide field.'

It was not unreasonable. Yet, when he returned to London in the early summer of 1948 his own country offered him nothing better than a part-time professorship, which, as he said, 'my friends had discovered for me', in the Institute he had founded. If he did not repine or feel the pangs of a deposed monarch it was partly because of the new command in Pakistan, partly because, with his energy and self-confidence unabated, he knew that he could shape his ends without help from the stars.

If 1948 was in some ways a low year in Wheeler's fortunes there was much to catch up with and to prepare for. His most immediate concern was with the Institute of Archaeology, where his chair supplied him with an office and a working base. He could be moderately well satisfied with the growth of his foundation during his absence. When, three years before, he had heard in advance of Gordon Childe's adoption as its second Director he had greatly welcomed it as a fulfilment of his own wishes. (It is curious that Max Mallowan in his autobiography refers to Childe as the first Director: did Wheeler's term not count because he was unpaid?) If he was so bad an administrator as to be vexatious to the university bureaucracy, and a poor lecturer and excavator, as a world-famous prehistorian, an excellent teacher of the intelligent and a philosopher of history, Childe gave lustre to the Institute and drew many distinguished visitors to it. Different as they were, he and Rik respected and did not dislike one another.

Wheeler's return added to the already burgeoning oriental side of the assorted workers at St John's Lodge. The year before, Max Mallowan had been installed in a new Chair in Western Asiatic Archaeology – largely through the good offices of Stephen Glanville, who had done so much to further the Institute during and after the war years. Max taught, gave public lectures (for Childe encouraged his staff to draw in a wider public) and was soon to launch his fascinating excavations at Nimrud. Rachel Maxwell-Hyslop, the chief assistant in his department, was able to keep at a sufficient distance from Rik to avoid friction. Kathleen Kenyon was just surrendering her rule as Secretary to become Lecturer in Palestinian Archaeology and to dig briefly at Sabratha before going on to her epoch-making discoveries at Jericho. St John's Lodge was certainly a hive of archaeological activity, and if Gordon Childe was not the Director to impose order upon it the place was still small and intimate enough to do very well without. As Max observed, 'Never before had I realized the advantages of living under a rotunda: the great dome over the central hall held together the society living under it and as most of us taught with open doors, everyone knew what was going on.'

In term time Wheeler lectured to his students almost every day, walking up from Piccadilly, but he probably never intended to give more than a very limited part of his time and energy to instructing the young in the Archaeology of the Roman Provinces, and with the new responsibility that he was to accept soon after taking up the chair he had no more than a decent minimum of either to spare. He was, however, still deeply concerned with the general development of the Institute and as a powerful member of the Committee of Management still played a considerable role in its direction.

One difficult adjustment Wheeler had to make on re-entering the British archaeological scene. In spite of the wartime check, this was spreading and diversifying quite fast. His old sense of lonely leadership, already questionable in 1939, was being dispelled by events. A new Chair in European Archaeology had been set up for Christopher Hawkes at Oxford and many of the newer universities were making some provision for what was now a respectable academic subject. In particular, Wheeler had to recognize that Cambridge was tending to dominate in the more scientific aspects of research, where he had hoped that his Institute would particularly excel. Although the technical laboratories at St John's Lodge were doing very useful work, the more ambitious use of the natural sciences in archaeological research was for some time to find its leading exponents at Cambridge. (A powerful time-bomb had just been planted in this field by Willard Libby's idea for radio-carbon dating, first being rumoured in 1947.)

After one term in which to settle into London life and his part-time teaching Wheeler turned eastward once more and spent three months at the beginning of 1949 in striving to organize an efficient Pakistan Archaeological Department. He had a nucleus of some dozen trained officers from the Survey days and round them he now gathered promising university students, with the aim of making an all-purposes archaeological staff. Once again he intended to resort to his well-tried method of combining a training school with an excavation policy. Mohenjodaro was there within the confines of the new state: a most tempting site, with every probability of throwing further light on the Indus civilization and every possibility of unexpected discoveries. For the moment the temptation had to be left to the desert air: Mohenjodaro was a project for the next season.

Most of Wheeler's work during this first term as Adviser was of a preparatory and foundation-building kind. His relations with the government he was advising were fair, and he had direct access to the sympathetic Minister of Education, Fazlur Rahman. Inevitably, in the post-Partition climate there was much intrigue and contention both internally and in relations with India. Rik thought that 'the living contest of ideology *versus* geography on so vast a scale is an enthralling and significant drama to any humanist'. More than once he was present to witness the battle of wits across the Indo–Pakistan conference table. One small part of this contention concerned the division of museum collections between the severed states, but the most absurd of these Solomon-like judgements was awaiting him in London.

Wheeler was concerned with museums for what they could do to rouse some interest in their past among a shaken, hardly educated public needing a sense of nationhood. In this the authorities gave willing support; Frere Hall in Karachi was assigned as a national museum, a project the Adviser was determined to carry out, despite an insufficiency of both staff and exhibits. Then Rik's friend, Shakur, of the Peshawar Museum (his companion in Afghanistan), made him first President of a new Pakistan Museums Association, installing him at an open-air meeting in the presence of the provincial Prime Minister. It was a memorable occasion, for after the formal meeting (attended by Afridis and other picturesque border folk) they all embussed, leaving Peshawar in a long file. The buses 'crossed the plain and zig-zagged up the Khyber Pass – surely the most remarkable outing in the world history of museums associations'. As Pakistan was not on friendly terms with its neighbour it was not surprising that the sight of a party of men swarming up towards his gate caused the Afghan sentry to take up his rifle. However, Rik 'hastened towards him with an open cigarette case, and shortly both sides of the frontier lapsed into noisy merriment'. Afterwards a huge repast was eaten at tables set up with superb views of the mountains, the pass and the famous poplar-lined road. Museums could be happily forgotten.

Among all his official duties, pleasant and unpleasant, Rik had to fit in more personal matters. He was assembling material for the propaganda book, *Five Thousand Years of Pakistan*, to be published the next year, writing articles – and taking pains to help many of his old staff whom Partition had left in distress. All these concerns, together with personnel problems at Karachi and arrangements for the Mohenjodaro dig, continued to fill Rik's postbag after he returned to London in early May. Meanwhile, during his absence in Pakistan, Wheeler had been involved in one of those sudden storms that can arise within learned societies. Cyril Fox was to retire from the presidency of the Society of Antiquaries in the spring of 1949. In February the Council had nominated as his successor Sir James Mann, aesthete and mediaevalist. The choice had been approved by a large majority, and moreover was in line with the accepted practice that as far as possible antiquaries and field archaeologists should alternate in the President's ornate chair. It was, however, strongly resisted by certain archaeologists, most vehemently by O. G. S. Crawford and Gordon Childe, who believed that with the boom in prehistory and excavation the presidency should remain with their party. They also felt that Wheeler, who in some ways had suffered from his long absence in the service of his country, deserved the honour. They refused to retract, passionate feelings were aroused and Rik was nominated, so necessitating an almost unheard-of contested election.

This was held at the Annual General Meeting in April, when the usually calm, pillared hall and lecture room of the Society were crowded and seething with half-suppressed turbulence. Both sides had been canvassing to get out their supporters however old or ill. I do not think I am falsifying my memories of the scene when I say there was at least one wheelchair and many bent figures and rubber-tipped sticks in the long line of Fellows shuffling along towards the ballot boxes.

The antiquaries won the day, Sir James was elected and Professor Mortimer Wheeler made Director for the second time. Gordon Childe and Crawford resigned, but otherwise the storm subsided, Rik soon returning to assume the directorship which he was to hold until 1954 – when the presidency was his at last.

Back in London Rik was immediately embroiled in another troublesome affair, a small extension of the problems of Partition. In 1947 he had written to Cyril Fox, 'Just waiting for the arrival of the Royal Academy mission sent out to choose stuff for the Indian exhibition at Burlington House. I have declined to have anything actively to do with this, for the good reason that I sense muddle ahead. . . .' His prescience, as so often, was remarkable, for now, two years later, trouble was a rising wind.

The exhibits had been chosen from the entire subcontinent: with the close of the exhibition they had to be split and restored severally to India or Pakistan. At first all was sweetness and light. In April, just before Rik's return, not only had the division been agreed in principle but lists of the antiquities and works of art had been prepared and it was further agreed that Dr R. E. Mortimer Wheeler 'should carry out the division on behalf of the two Dominions'. Then mysterious delays began: it seemed that India was refusing to implement its side of the agreement. Letters went to and fro between High Commissioners in London, between government departments and archaeological directors in Karachi and Delhi. In time it emerged that Indian authorities were withholding consent because they declared that the Pakistan authorities were dragging their feet over the division of museum collections within the states – particularly that the West Punjab government had denied to the East Punjab 'the agreed portion of the Lahore Museum collections'. It was a sad, comical example in microcosm of the disasters of Partition.

In July Rik wrote to Chakravarti in Delhi, '*Please* can you do something to stir up your Government to action in the matter of those Royal Academy things? The situation has really become completely absurd.' He went on with increasing severity, urging the very bad impression 'which dishonesty or incompetence of this kind' was making upon the minds of others.

Chakravarti replied, but not until October and then in terms of Sibylline obscurity. By this time Rik was not only exasperated, but becoming anxious lest the important Pakistan collections would not be returned in time to help fill the great open spaces of Frere Hall for the opening of the National Museum. Chakravarti came to London, Rik took effective action with the eminent legal adviser to the Indian High Commissioner and at last some trust was restored. In November Dr R. E. Mortimer Wheeler supervised the division according to the April agreement.

During the wearisome course of these negotiations a happening at the heart of the learned world in London was to lead to a revolution in Wheeler's plans for the last phase of his professional life – and to an incalculable gain to British scholarship. This was his appointment as Honorary Secretary to the British Academy. But before starting on this new course, which was to stretch twenty years into the future, there are others leading from the past that must be completed.

One modest and little publicized undertaking is still of some significance. In the summer of 1949 Wheeler returned to Verulamium to conduct an excavation school on a site adjoining the west corner of the forum. This was a true training school in the sense that Taxila had been and the Wheelers' pre-war excavations had not: that is to say, there was a wide range of lectures and technical instruction as well as the practice of excavation. It was, indeed, the first of its kind to be staged in Britain. As well as training students drawn from many universities, Rik was also offering some older practitioners the chance to rub up their archaeology after the break of the war years.

For his staff, Rik enrolled some of his supporters of pre-war days, including Molly Cotton, Kitty Richardson and the ever-willing Huntly Gordon. Both as a school and excavation the project went well: a number of those who started or advanced their training went on to successful careers, and their efforts uncovered a second-century temple that must once have added to the dignified, Italianate style of the forum buildings.

The most important commitment outstanding from the past was, of course, the excavation at Mohenjodaro. In July word had come from Karachi that the government had approved the training school to be held there early in 1950. It was to be similar to that at Taxila, but on a smaller scale and 'intended primarily for officers and subordinates of the Archaeological Department', with a few 'senior students of Pakistan Universities' to be admitted. A grant of up to 25,000 rupees had been made, and camping equipment was being assembled there from Taxila and other places. On his arrival in the capital the Archaeological Adviser found preparations well in hand.

He had to spend his first month in Karachi, mainly engaged in turning Frere Hall into the likeness of a National Museum. 'In the absence of other exhibits,' he wrote, 'the building will have to be filled with flowers and the Diplomatic Corps.' Then, about mid-February, he made the twenty-four-hour train journey and the bumpy drive to the mounds of Mohenjodaro, where his trainees were encamped in readiness.

Much of the ancient city lay exposed by the Marshall excavations, dominated by the tank, or Great Bath, on the highest mound, which, with surrounding buildings, had been cleared without any realization that it was part of a fortified citadel. Some part of the lower town had also been uncovered, exposing the remarkable grid plan of the residential streets, with their excellent drainage system. Rik's intention, as at Harappa, was to concentrate work on the citadel, and particularly on a high part of the mound to the west of the Great Bath.

In *Still Digging* it is recorded that the work was done in March and April, but Rik had written to Stuart Piggott on 20 February, under the heading 'Bulletin I',

The M.D. citadel has surrendered to our first chaotic assault – 100 yards of burnt-brick fortification-revetment on our first morning. ... A sufficiently auspicious start, but ye gods! an entirely untrained oriental staff. Making preparations to pump out the 3rd millennium. Archaeological Adviser already pumped.

> Yours (just after lunch)
> Rik

After that dashing start the work of clearance, of returning sand to the surrounding desert, went methodically forward, as befitted a training school. Stratified pottery was found, and Rik began to recognize the possibility of setting up a chronological sequence. After four weeks twelve wagon-loads of pottery, already selected as worthy of study, had been removed, but there were very few small finds to add to the beautifully cut seal stones or the statuettes of men, women and bulls for which Mohenjodaro was already famous. After days spent sweating on the site evening classes were held under canvas by the light of a pressure lamp. Rik took satisfaction in the good progress made by his raw trainees.

By this time the staff had been reinforced by the arrival of a young man from Oxford, one Leslie Alcock, who had travelled out by cargo boat. In *Still Digging* Rik romanticized his appearance by suggesting that Leslie came as an unexpected volunteer. In fact, the young man, having had some archaeological experience and wanting more, was advised to consult Dr Wheeler 'because he always encourages young men'. They met, and when Rik discovered that Leslie not only had some knowledge of archaeology but of Urdu and Punjabi as well, immediately invited him to serve at Mohenjodaro. He was to prove an invaluable lieutenant, and this collaboration begun on the deserts of Sind was to reach another climax nearly twenty years later in the search for King Arthur's Camelot.

Leslie Alcock was made supervisor of an important part of the dig: the exploration of the base of the citadel and the sinking of a still deeper shaft to discover any evidence there might be of earlier settlements. The cultural origins of the high civilization of the Indus had long been a subject of archaeological debate, and here some partial evidence might be found.

Like other river valley civilizations, that of the Indus had been related to annual floods (sometimes violent) depositing fertile silts, and these, together with a certain ponding back due to a rise in land level towards the river mouth, had led to a continuing rise in the water-table. Excavation showed that the citadel had been built on a huge mudbrick platform, reinforced from time to time against the floods. Remains of earlier settlements there certainly were, but lying well below water-level.

With the help of motor pumps and baling by night and day, the exploratory shaft was sunk some ten feet below the water line, but time was short and equipment inadequate, and at that depth the sides of the cutting 'spurted a myriad of jets of water and then, in the dark hours of the night, streamed noisily inward like a mountain landslide'. The likelihood of such a collapse had been foreseen and all the sections drawn, but it was a blow that the pre-Indus horizons could not be sampled. Enough had been found to suggest that there had been no sharp cultural break when the citadel was first built. Rik interpreted this to mean that if any foreign intrusion was involved it was only that of an invading dynasty.

Some light relief during the strenuous digging was provided by two popular excursions organized by the Karachi authorities. On each occasion a trainload of townsfolk, men, women and children, gladly endured the journey and tramping round the dusty ruins while being lectured on the wonders of their past. Some came armed with shotguns and pistols, and Rik declared in the one letter he wrote to Cyril Fox from Mohenjodaro,

It was quite a normal thing during a conducted tour to be interrupted momentarily by a sudden explosion in the outskirts of one's audience and to find a
mangled dove descending in our midst. Anyway, a good time was had by all
and the Government's enterprise was, to say the least of it, remarkable.

When on 28 March Rik wrote to Cyril Fox he still believed that the
massive brick building they were uncovering on the west flank of the
citadel must be a fortress. He still thought so a week or so later when he
had to go to Karachi for the opening of the National Museum. This was
performed by the Governor-General of Pakistan, an unimpressive-
looking man, like an amiable humpty dumpty, whose legs seemed bent
under the weight of his presence. There were enough exhibits in Frere
Hall to carry off the day.

Perhaps it was during the long train journeys which his trip involved
that Rik pondered over certain curious features that had been emerging
in the 'fortress' and came suddenly to a new conclusion: surely the place
was another civic granary, different in appearance from the one at
Harappa, but to be equated with it. So it proved to be; the mysterious
'passages' within were air ducts to ventilate a wooden building above,
while the 'towering, grim and forbidding' wall that faced the plain from
the periphery of the citadel, though meant to be impregnable, was also
designed for the loading and distribution of the public grain supplies.

Although this excavation at Mohenjodaro was in general quite successful, it was affected by two of Wheeler's rare failures. One was the
technical failure of the collapsing shaft: he took a gamble and it did not
quite succeed. The other was far more serious: for the only time in his
career he failed to produce a full publication of an excavation. For one
who had preached against this deadly sin with something like fanaticism
and who had always most strenuously practised what he preached, this
remains an astonishing lapse. Leslie Alcock can only account for it by
Rik's disillusion with 'state organized archaeology in Pakistan', by all
the other work that claimed him back at home, and perhaps, too, 'the
dull competence of Indus architecture . . . left him with a kind of ennui
which he once professed to feel for Roman towns in Britain.'

He could exonerate himself to some extent since he was able to
summarize his principal findings in *The Indus Civilization*, his supplementary volume to 'The Cambridge History of India'. This includes
one of his finest sectional drawings, a cut through granary, reinforced
platform and the ill-fated shaft. The human figures drawn to scale that
Rik always lovingly added to his sections are here muscled and turbanned specimens of the local manhood.

The story has a happy ending. By far the most serious loss would have been the lack of any publication of the stratified pottery sequence. Leslie Alcock and a collaborator, however, have worked for years on the vast quantity of material involved and intend to redeem Rik's one fall from grace by publishing it at last – three decades late.

On leaving Pakistan in that spring of 1950, the Archaeological Adviser had made no definite plans for the third and final year of his appointment, and when duly invited to return for it he declined. He had not had altogether satisfactory support from the Department of Archaeology, and he came to the conclusion that as soon as he left 'progress ceased and was replaced by sterile intrigue'. Friendly relations were not, however, altogether lost, and later he was able to accept an invitation to fulfil his cherished plan to dig at Charsada that had been frustrated by the troubles of Partition.

Rik Wheeler returned to a London where he had no settled home. Two years before, on coming back from India, he had lodged for a time with Michael and his wife, Sheila, in their house at the end of Hallam Street, a quiet and solid cul-de-sac. Michael was beginning to do well as a barrister and his wife had a flourishing practice as an orthoptist – with her consulting-rooms in the Hallam Street premises. Rik's relations with his son were still uneasy, and were not made easier by the antipathy which grew between himself and his daughter-in-law. In-law relationships are usually toxic, and in this case Sheila had a temperament that would not allow her to accept the vagaries and inevitable dominance of a great man. She detested his fondness for showing off. Carol Wheeler recalls (though presumably from a later time than this) how her father, torn in his loyalties, would announce that Rik 'was behaving outrageously again'. Rik may from the first have been disappointed that Michael had not chosen a woman more after his own tastes, perhaps more dashing, elegant or otherwise head-turning. When to this was added her resistance to him, mounting into evident dislike, he made no real effort at understanding, but turned his back and condemned her as a bore.

Now, in the summer of 1950, he took 'a highly expensive little flat' in Mount Street, just across the way from the Connaught Hotel, in one of those terracotta red buildings with ornate mouldings. It was the smartest address he ever attained to, and although he knew he could not afford it for more than a year, he took a self-mocking pleasure in this flat, boasting that he 'hadn't an archaeological book in the place'.

It was an agreeable and convenient base for the bachelor life he was now leading. Kim Wheeler when she fled from India had gone to live at Thame. Although he also enjoyed his freedom, Rik was still strongly attracted to his wife, and had by no means given up hope that he could induce her to come back to him when he judged the time to be both ripe and convenient. Meanwhile he was busy, although still in a somewhat unfocused way, since his work as Secretary of the Academy was only just beginning and could not be developed until the necessary reforms had been made there.

In July and August he enjoyed a month's digging at Bindon Hill, adjoining the famous Dorset beauty spot of Lulworth Cove. Here a stony earthwork nearly two miles long ran from cliff to cliff, cutting off the Cove and the shallow promontory to the east of it. The fact that it had obviously been intended to protect the one good natural harbour along many miles of coast, its great length and complete ignorance as to its age made it an attractive subject, and the Royal Commission on Historical Monuments invited Wheeler to direct a trial excavation. Much of the work was done by members of the Commission's staff, but Rik also enrolled a few students and his tried assistants Theo Newbould and Huntly Gordon. The earthwork proved to have been built and occupied at a single period at the beginning of the Iron Age, perhaps rather earlier than the first settlement at Maiden Castle, twenty miles to the west. Rik judged it to be a beach-head where tribal invaders could secure themselves for a while before advancing into the hinterland. He commented, 'Military terminology in these matters is today somewhat less fashionable than it used to be, but is not on that account inapt.' It still appears apt, but has been mocked as an echo of 'Anzio and the Second Front' by a follower of the recent anti-invasion fashion of archaeological thought.

As the Lulworth dig was not too demanding it provided an agreeable working seaside holiday. Much of the site lay within a tank firing range which, since a little shrapnel was less disturbing than the general public, had become a strange kind of wild-life sanctuary. It also contained deserted farms and a whole village, where the church, the ancient manor-house and even a telephone box still stood little damaged and seeming to await the coming of peace on earth. Rik loved this place and one night picnicked there with some soldiers, enjoying its eerie, moonlit beauty. He was also delighted by a preposterous true story. One of the expelled farmers was allowed to keep a few cows on the range and when two mysteriously disappeared soldiers were called in to hunt for them. The pair were found at last upstairs in a farmhouse bedroom, the door fast shut.

In the following years Wheeler was to follow up this minor enterprise with his last important excavation in Britain. Even now his Academy work was not in full swing and he was still very ready to dig, not only for the sake of British archaeology and his own inclinations, but to continue in modified form his tradition of combining excavation with the training of academic students.

The extent to which public institutions and public money were now replacing private enterprise in archaeology is well illustrated by Wheeler's three post-war seasons in the field. Lulworth had been promoted by the Royal Commission, and now it was the officials of the Ancient Monuments Department of the Ministry of Works who took the opportunity to invite the best excavator in the country to undertake a dig on their behalf. Moreover, this was not to be one of the Ministry's usual salvage operations: it was an open invitation for Wheeler to select whatever site he wished.

With unfailing instinct he chose one ideally suited to himself, one where it might be said that he was to reveal the last figures of our British Iron Age retreating before the historic forces of Rome. The place in question was a unique network of earthworks in the North Riding of Yorkshire, lying (one cannot resist the poetry of the place names) within the parishes of Stanwick St John and Forcett-with-Carkin. These monumental ramparts, rising in places to twenty feet and enclosing 850 acres, had been known to the learned world since the time of John Leland, but their date was quite unknown. The authors of the 'Victoria County History' had been rash enough to suggest that they were mediaeval park enclosures, 'regardless', as Wheeler said, 'of their emphatically military character'. He himself could only be sure that they 'represented a major episode in the history or prehistory of northern Britain' and that he would be able to identify it.

While he could depend on the Ministry to put much of the organization in hand, Rik was able to gather many of his old team round him: Kitty Richardson was again his chief assistant and Theo Newbould the field administrator; Bill Wedlake was seconded from the Admiralty (which he had preferred to being a gunner) and Cookie was there to take the exceptionally fine photographs that adorn the Report; Leslie Alcock, now married, came with his wife.

Theo's management skills were severely tested, for in this post-war era students had displaced labourers on excavations and now they in their turn expected to be paid. They were numerous and discontinuous in their service and this, together with the varying exactions demanded in a post-Beveridge society, made pay days complicated and Rik was thankful for Theo's services. All the same they irritated one another and this was exacerbated by their lodging, with Kitty, in a small pub. At last the relationship became so explosive, with Rik usually the aggressor, that Theo moved out to rooms of her own, an immense relief to Kitty since she found 'people flying off the handle at breakfast time bad for the digestion'.

The digging was to last for some eleven weeks in the summers of 1951–2. It did not take long to discover that the fortifications dated from the first century AD, and as the work went forward it proved that their building had been in three phases, all within the period from the Roman conquest of AD 43 and the time some thirty years later when the powerful British tribe of the Brigantes was at last conquered by the governor Petillius Cerealis.

It remained to apply the archaeological sequence to the history of the Brigantes during these last thirty years of their independence, as recorded by Tacitus, to detect what 'major episode' would provide a fit. What events in the Brigantine resistance to the advance of Rome would account for the construction of such massive and extensive earthworks?

An all but certain answer was to be found in one of the most dramatic stories in our island history. (It is a matter of some reproach to us as a people that it has never been used for a great tragic play or opera.) It appealed to all that was romantic in Rik's imagination, and he was happy that his choice of sites enabled him to throw light on its material setting.

The story was that of the formidable Queen Cartimandua, who, with her consort Venutius, was ruling the Brigantes when the Romans were making their easy conquest of the south. The Queen was one of those Britons prepared to come to terms with the conquerors as rulers of friendly client states, and when the luckless Caratacus (Cunobelin's son), defeated in the south and in Wales, sought her protection she immediately handed him over to Rome. This was in AD 51. There followed a complete split between the royal pair; Venutius formed an anti-Roman party and went to war against his wife. When by 'cunning stratagems', as Tacitus put it, Cartimandua captured Venutius's brothers he was so enraged that he invaded her territory and with such success that the Romans had to send troops to her aid. Venutius had by now taken Caratacus's place as leader of the resistance, but seems to have been content to bide his time with his forces in the north. Meanwhile the Queen developed 'a wanton spirit', despised her husband and took his one-time squire as her consort – a scandal that shook her royal house and roused tribal sympathy for Venutius – while 'the adulterer was supported by the Queen's passion for him and her savage spirit'.

Then came AD 69, the Year of the Four Emperors, when upheavals in Rome, affecting also the legions in Britain, gave Venutius his chance. He summoned allies from Scotland, disaffected Brigantes rose in support, and Cartimandua was in danger of her life. Again the Romans had to come to her rescue, but the forces they could spare were able to do no more than snatch the Queen from her husband's vengeance, leaving him triumphant on the throne.

The triumph could not last, for Vespasian was now secure as Emperor and to have a strong, hostile power on the northern frontier of Britain was unacceptable. In AD 71 Cerialis, a bold soldier, was dispatched, with an additional legion, to crush Venutius and pacify the north. This he did, but only, it seems, after three bloody campaigns. It is not known just how Venutius died or what happened to Cartimandua (leaving author or librettist a free hand).

Once the age of the Stanwick fortifications had been even approximately established, Wheeler had no doubt that they related to this story, and by the end of the excavations he could claim that archaeology and history made a perfect fit.

The general evidence in favour of the identification was geographical and strategic. Clearly Venutius would choose a rallying point for his tribesmen and allies well beyond easy reach of the Roman forces and this site in the far north of Yorkshire would meet his needs – moreover, there are no other fortifications in all former Brigantia to rival those of Stanwick in appropriateness. Then their precise position, close to Scotch Corner, was already a strategic point where the main route from the south forked into two approaches to the Scottish lowlands: an ideal situation 'alike for tribal assembly and for anticipation of an enemy from the south'.

For more particular evidence the three phases of construction, dated by imported pottery from south Britain and Gaul, are equally well adapted to the story. The first ramparts to be built at Stanwick enclosed a low hill known as the Tofts, making a stout stronghold or hill-fort. This can be dated to a little before or immediately after the betrayal of Caratacus and the marital war of AD 51. The second phase saw the construction of a mighty stone-fronted rampart and rock-cut ditch, enclosing 130 acres watered by the Mary Wild Beck that had flowed past the north wall of the fort, now levelled to give access between the two. This was clearly designed to shelter considerable forces, together with their cattle, and was certainly made before AD 60 at a time when

Venutius had become leader of resistance fighters drawn from many quarters. The fortifications of the third period are more precisely and more dramatically identified with the historical events. Similar in construction to those of the second, they enclosed no less than six hundred acres to the south, evidently needed to accommodate the allies called in by Venutius in AD 69. There was to be an entrance on the southern rampart, but probably the place had to be put into a state of defence before it was completed. When Leslie Alcock opened it up he found no trace of gates at the rampart ends, the ditch had been dug to the rock surface but the cutting of the rock itself had stopped when only a few blocks had been detached (they still lay there), and the usual entrance causeway of undisturbed soil was missing.

Rik felt that the inference was not in doubt:

During the cutting and building of the principal surviving entrance into the vast enclosure of Phase III, when the cutting of the ditch was still incomplete and the erection of the gate itself had not begun, a sudden alarm stopped the work. As an emergency measure the causeway was cut away so that the ends of the unfinished ditches were joined up, thus isolating the intended gateway. . . .

The emergency was, of course, the approach of the Romans under the command of Cerialis: 'We can almost see the tribesmen toiling vainly at their gate, almost hear the Ninth Legion tramping up from its new fortress at York to one of its rare victories.' At Stanwick there was no equivalent to the Maiden Castle 'war cemetery': there is nothing to tell how the end came, except that the huge, laboriously built complex fell and afterwards a length of the north wall of Phase II was slighted by toppling the stone-fronted rampart into the ditch. In considering the tactical position, Wheeler allowed Venutius foresight in that he had the ramparts aligned in such a way that nearly all were in view from the Tofts, to secure his centralized command. On the other hand, it showed fundamental misjudgement to hope that he could hold so many miles of defences against a Roman assault. Wheeler concluded,

tactically the whole plan had by now monstrously overgrown its strength and must surely, in the ultimate trial, have dissolved into chaos. Its creator [Venutius], fighting as he doubtless did to the end, was pitting an embattled mob in unwonted conditions against an army engaged upon a normal manoeuvre. Stanwick is at the same time a very notable memorial to a heroic episode of the British resistance and a monument to its futility.

While Rik Wheeler had immensely enjoyed fitting together his historical jigsaw and reflecting on military strategy and tactics he had not been unmindful of social and economic considerations. Inside the Tofts

hill-fort he opened up a level area some sixty feet square by an impecc-
able application of his grid system, revealing the plan of a typical round
hut and drainage channels. The absence there of storage pits and
querns, together with the plentiful cattle and sheep bones found
throughout the site, supported the general historical picture then
beginning to be accepted by prehistorians, that in the north the Britons
were very largely a mobile, pastoral, meat-eating people, in contrast
with the arable farmers of the south. In harmony with this there was
some evidence that wood and basketry were mainly used for containers
and (Rik believed) that the very crude local pottery was made by menial
women for their menial cooking, while fine beakers were imported from
the south to serve the heroic menfolk with their ale.

Finds other than pottery were poor – with one notable exception. In a
section of rock-cut ditch adjoining an entrance to the Phase II enclosure, where watery mud had always provided a good preserving
medium, a lucky student digger found an iron sword inside its
bronze-mounted ash wood sheath. Nearby had lain a severed head, the
surviving skull showing terrible wounds. Both may have been trophies
adorning the gate above.

Bill Wedlake was charged to lift the sword. The temptation to
examine it closely was resisted; still coated in wet clay, it was shrouded
in newspaper, boxed and given to Kitty Richardson to rush to the
British Museum by the next train. This intelligent promptitude enabled
the museum laboratory to make an excellent job of preserving what is
quite a rarity, a Celtic blade complete with sheath.

Most digs have their ludicrous or disastrous moments, and Stanwick
was not one of the exceptions. The site abounded with pigs, both
free-range and tethered. When a man from the Ministry came to do
some surveying interested pigs ate his tapes, and when Rik tried to
move a tethered porker it ran away with him, a happening which, sad to
relate, did not amuse him.

Although the Society of Antiquaries had not been the sponsor of the
Stanwick excavation, it was to be published in 1954 as a Report of the
Research Committee. For this volume she was not a co-author, but
Kitty Richardson collaborated fully in the sections dealing with finds.
Set beside *Verulamium* and *Maiden Castle*, *The Stanwick Fortifications* is
a slim work, but Rik, as author, must have felt that it came close to his
own ideal for an excavation report. Finely illustrated in both half-tone
and line, the text was quite properly devoted in large part to the kind of
historical and military interpretation of archaeological evidence that he
loved to write and wrote so well. Nor have its findings ever been

seriously questioned. It makes a fitting termination to the career in British field archaeology that Wheeler had launched with such deep seriousness and missionary zeal after the First World War.

Looking back over the Antiquaries Reports, not even excluding Lydney, one is struck by the fact that, by a mixture of chance and design, all Wheeler's major British excavations had been more or less involved with the impact of Rome on the native tribes of Britain. Even in India, in his most significant dig, at Arikamedu, the theme had been of Romans imposing themselves on a prehistoric native population, although there the contact had been one of trade and not of conquest.

While Stanwick occupied a few of the summer months in 1951–2, Rik Wheeler had, of course, been leading his busy London life, which was very much as it had been before the war. In addition to his professor-ship, he was at that time Director of the Society of Antiquaries, Presi-dent of the Royal Archaeological Institute, and Royal Commissioner; these posts demanded his attendance at countless committee meetings, lectures and conferences. While he was often bored or irritated by lectures he considered trivial or badly presented, and said the harshest things in private about the lecturers, he found committees on the whole less irksome, since he was always an effective member and one who knew just how to use them for his own purposes. Another commitment of a very different kind that he was always to maintain was attendance at the 42nd Anti-Aircraft Regiment's annual reunion dinners, where Flash Alf was enthusiastically received as an honoured guest.

Honours were beginning to come his way: in 1950 he was awarded the Petrie medal and in 1952 the prestigious Archaeological Institute of America invited him to deliver the Norton lectures, while he also received the Lucy Wharton Drexel medal at Pennsylvania. This visit to the United States roused in Wheeler an unaccountable prejudice against almost all things American, and he would afterwards make strongly felt if conventional accusations of philistinism and brashness. Nor could he ever take pre-Columbian American archaeology quite seriously – it was something too remote from his classically based vision of the ancient world. This was a curious blind spot which also affected Gordon Childe.

In this same year he was knighted, and he who had been so long known in public as Dr Wheeler became Sir Mortimer, a fine resounding name for the hero of a new career that was soon to bring him a wider fame.

Rik's attitude to honours was ambiguous, some would say dishonest, or at least showing self-delusion. There is no doubt that he wanted them, intended to win them and was prepared to pull a few strings to speed their coming. This was certainly true of his knighthood – and he spoke openly of his satisfaction at getting it before his presidency of the Society of Antiquaries would have made it an institutional rather than a personal award. Yet he always mocked at his honours, and in days when the letters after his name extended to the edge of the envelope declared that he would like to do away with the lot. Perhaps such inward divisions are almost universal and Rik merely showed them in his own rather exaggerated style. He never tried to make use of his public distinctions, as his dealings with the Treasury will show, nor did they affect his outlook or habits.

In Rik's private life there were some changes at this time. His mother died in 1951, after living for many years with his sister Amy, whose marriage to Frederick Bailey in the 1930s had soon failed. The death of an old lady whom he had never liked and seldom saw, and who must have seemed to belong only to a remote past, meant almost nothing to him.

The important change was in his attempt to renovate his marriage. Kim had returned to London with Elizabeth and bought an agreeable house in Mallord Street, Chelsea, just across the road, as it happened, from Margot Eates, who was still working at the Institute of Archaeology. Although Rik had let some five years go by since his return from India, he still hankered after her intermittently. Indeed, when it is recalled how long ago it was that he had first asked her to marry him, however carelessly, it can be said that no one else ever maintained an erotic appeal for him over so great a time. Almost inevitably accounts as to just how they began to live together again differ. Kim's friends would say that she invited her husband to return, but Molly Cotton remembers how Rik had confided to her that he believed if he could as much as have lunch with Kim he could win her back, and that, when some such meeting was arranged, he proved to be right.

So, by invitation or enterprise, Rik moved into the Mallord Street house, and that in itself was a mistake, reducing such chances of success as there were. It was very much Kim's house, and her husband entered it rather on the terms that used to be called 'hanging up his hat'. Indeed, he even paid his wife for board and lodging, but at an inadequate rate – surely the worst possible compromise. Later, when this unpropitious arrangement was cracking, Rik was to take a room in London as a private retreat and a meeting place. Even those most convinced that their inability to settle down together or to build any kind of durable relationship were due to Rik's temper, his fanatical devotion to work and other familiar sins admit that Kim should have done more to let him make the place partly his own. As it was, Number 5 remained an artificial background for him, a place where visiting friends felt he did not belong.

Other difficulties on Kim's side were perhaps that she could never quite escape from the effects of having first come to him as a young student: she was always inwardly afraid of him. As with Tessa, he never spoke against her to others: all he ever said to me was that he found he could not talk to her. I took this to mean that her piety, her totally different idea of what life was about, was an obstacle, and also that her extreme femininity prevented any possibility of talking openly and honestly, as well as irreverently, on any subject under the sun. Underlying all such incompatibility was the shock she had sustained from the falsity of his conversion to her faith, and this was his one inexcusable abuse of her nature – though one he probably never fully understood. Their coming together had its rewards, but it never looked likely to last and, in fact, was to totter along an erratic course for only some five or six years.

By the time of his attempted resurrection of his marriage the demands of the British Academy were beginning to claim a large part of Rik's time, their increase having been very largely generated by his own efforts. This was, in fact, to be the last and longest of all his exercises in revitalizing a decrepit institution. Since it was founded in 1901, with the intention that it should serve all the humanities much as the Royal Society had long served all the natural sciences, the Academy had remained an undeniable failure. Beatrice Webb, in no way softened by the fact that she was, in 1932, the first woman to be made a Fellow, found the academicians 'a funny little body of elderly and aged men – the aged predominating' who 'gave a lifeless and derelict impression, devoting most of their energies to canvassing for rival candidates to fill vacancies up to the statutory limit'.

Another and related activity was the production of obituaries of its Fellows. Rik observed, 'from the deserts of Africa to the hills of Simla, those slim gravestones reminded me intermittently that, if the Academy no longer lived, at least it died with grace and honour'. These two forms of enterprise could keep the academicians quite busy, since, although they appeared to enjoy exceptional longevity, they were usually so ripe before the elective process could reach them that they were soon bound to fall from the tree and so make work for the obituarists.

Rik himself had, in fact, been chosen to fill a vacancy when he had only just turned fifty and was still objectionably active. Although he had willingly accepted election, since he always liked to win in competitive stakes and an FBA was worth having, he was telling the truth when he declared how little it had meant to him. Writing from India to secure Cyril Fox's signature on the nomination paper for their friend O. G. S. Crawford, he had added, 'Incidentally, does the Brit. Acad. do anything except issue tombstones, and do Academicians do anything as such, except die?'

Back in London in 1949, however, he was immediately involved, as we have seen, in a reform movement that was already stirring the dust in the cramped and awkward premises behind the grandiose façade of No. 6, Burlington Gardens. That this dust was not only metaphorical I can vouch for. I visited the Secretary at about this time in the most unrealistic hope that the Academy might endow a UNESCO scholarship, and although there were no cobwebs suspended from Sir Frederic Kenyon's venerable head, I did have to wipe the seat of my chair at the council table before risking contact with my best suit.

The first signs of revolution had taken place at a Council meeting early that year when Rik was in Pakistan. It was led by the historian Charles Webster, whom Rik described as 'an honest, sociable, fearless, scholarly, internationally-minded son of Lancashire'. Believing the Academy to be near death, Webster had demanded a change in its administration. Thus encouraged, the President, a learned but unworldly papyrologist, was moved to admit that the Academy was not fulfilling its functions: the premises were quite inadequate, there was no library, there were no funds for publications, there was need for a larger clerical staff (it consisted in fact of one good lady) and for a room where the Fellows could conveniently meet. All this and more he attributed to 'financial reasons' and with apparent justification, since after nearly half a century the Treasury had been induced to contribute no more than £2500 a year, while endowments remained low.

Sir Frederic Kenyon, though certainly one of the aged, was by no means dulled, and gracefully announced his intention to resign the secretaryship and to seek an immediate successor. He had known Wheeler before the war, appreciated his energy and was aware that he now had some time to spare and just enough to live on – very necessary, since the post was honorary, with an expense allowance of £100 per annum.

The choice was an obvious one, and acceptance of the invitation almost equally assured, since by now Rik could not fail to have absolute confidence in his creative powers as an administrator and money-getter and saw that by reviving the Academy he could do much for the humanities in general and archaeology in particular. He would also gain helpful scientific contacts through its powerful sister institution, the Royal Society, still at that time lodged close by in Burlington House. Events moved with such surprising speed that he had claimed the Secretary's office and attended his first Council meeting before the end of 1949.

Wheeler, of course, saw at once that a much larger grant would have to be wrung from the Treasury if the Academy was to play its proper role, but he also recognized that before this could be demanded with any chance of success it had to set its house in order. With his customary sense of forward planning, he decided that he must play himself in with the Council and help to ensure that the right man was elected to the presidency the next year before any major reforms were attempted. Meanwhile he could make a beginning with the management of his own office – which had appalled him by its inadequacy. As no files had been kept, 'the Academy's affairs were wrapped in mystery'.

In response to his appeal for an assistant, fate brought him one who was not only to do much to bring efficiency to Burlington Gardens, but to be Rik's staunchest support and friend to the end of his life. This was Miss Molly Myers, whom, having been offered her services for a few days a week, he soon stole away from her previous employers and caused to work in and out of office hours for very much longer than is normally meant by 'full time'. Her tall, severely soignée figure became a part of all Academy gatherings, seemingly detached among the scholarly rabble, yet in truth watching with an eagle eye for anything that needed to be set right.

I have always found rough justice in Rik's capture of Molly; he had made such a ridiculous mess of his later marriages, yet because he was capable of liking and appreciating women for themselves he did deserve to have one who would devote herself to his work and well-being. In Molly Myers he had found one at last. Not only was she the perfect private secretary and a chauffeur prepared to drive him to stations and airports at all hours, but more and more she took over wifely functions, or, as she puts it, 'became his female looker-after'. Rik, of course, accepted this, although he never drew her fully into his personal life or took her out to restaurant meals. When on some occasion they arrived together and a foreign receptionist referred to Molly as 'your vif' it appealed to them both, and thereafter Rik often addressed his affectionate letters to her as 'Dear Vif'.

At the Academy Molly knew his rages – although only once did they lead to violence. In private life she was always sure of his 'general sweetness and kindness'. Rik says they fought one another through the twenty years they ran the Academy, but it was the kind of contention he enjoyed and needed – and in which both were gainers.

While the administration was put in order Wheeler took steps to secure that the prime mover in what he called the Palace Revolution, Sir Charles Webster, should be made the next President. His old friend Clapham, now Sir Alfred, was an influential member of the Council and Rik had little difficulty in persuading him that a courageous yet shrewd innovator was the man the Academy must have if it was to advance. How far this scheming determined the result cannot be gauged, but Sir Charles was duly elected. The elders of the Academy knew not what they did, for in admitting such a Secretary and President they were as sheep opening their fold to a pair of wolves.

Rik had not known Sir Charles personally, but now they became friends as well as fellow-conspirators. 'Day-by-day, after lunch, we got together beside one of the gaunt fireplaces of the Athenaeum's drawing room and settled the affairs of the world with special reference to the Academy. We found that we shared revolutionary ideas and in argument we hatched dreadful plots.'

Their purpose was, of course, not only to bring in younger blood, but also to overthrow the gerontocracy which, through its dominance of the Council, imposed its dead weight of inertia upon the Academy. Many of them were in their later seventies or eighties and, once elected, naturally tended to regard their removal as 'a gratuitous indelicacy'. It did not prove too difficult to let in some younger (not young) scholars by increasing the permitted number of Fellows, nor even to win agreement for continuous membership of the Council to be limited to three years. These reforms Webster and Wheeler had achieved by 1951, but they were not enough: 'faithful and numerous ancients would not unnaturally combine to resist the loss or reduction of their accustomed kingdom'. Old men retiring could be replaced by others equally old.

The plotters agreed that the only sure way of deposing them would be, as Webster most discreetly suggested in his presidential address, 'to make a category of senior members, who, while retaining all their rights and privileges, will not be expected to take the same part in our administrative activities'. Set out more precisely, the motion was that Fellows over the age of seventy-five should not be eligible for the Council. 'The sequel was to be long and stormy. The Old Guard was not going down without a fight.'

The whole course of the conflict cannot be chronicled here. The

President's brutal proposal was defeated in 1951, allowed to lie quies-
cent while the ground was further prepared during 1952 and trium-
phantly carried the following year. The whole story is most amusingly
given in *The British Academy, 1949–1968*, which Rik published on his
own retirement, salt being added by the fact that the author was himself
by this time eighty years of age and of undimmed wit and competence.

While these internal reforms were being pushed through by a deft
mixture of persuasion and tactical skill, the Secretary began to move
towards that other essential goal – to secure more appropriate financial
aid from the Treasury. Rik, reared by a father who scornfully neglected
all money matters, had by now developed financial acumen and even
greater ability in extracting funds from reluctant governments and their
treasury officials. What had begun with his first foray from Cardiff to
Whitehall had recently been raised to a higher plane by his battles in
New Delhi.

As he saw it, the Academy's past attempts to raise more than a
pittance had failed because approaches had been made through formal
correspondence at the highest level – as, for example, when an application by Arthur Balfour as President had been turned down flat by
Neville Chamberlain. He himself had found a very different method all
but infallible, 'that was, to *interest* the middle or upper grades of the
Treasury personally in the business of the moment, to *consult* the officer
concerned face to face (of course along premeditated lines), to involve
him as one's partner, and, above all, *never to exaggerate* demands'. To
this recipe he would add 'sweet reasonableness' and honesty in all
transactions, and cementing the resulting friendly relationships by 'the
equally amicable discussion of luncheon-claret'. (Rik was in these days
becoming an habitué of the Athenaeum, the club where so many top
civil servants settled their affairs in the privacy of its dignified gloom.)

The Secretary soon recognized the best opening through which to
approach Treasury officials and feel his way into their confidence. He
would approach them not with an immediate demand for a larger grant,
but, on the contrary, to offer the Academy's assistance over an administrative tangle that had been embarrassing them for years past. This was
in the allocation of funds to the several British Schools and Institutes
abroad, of which there were now four fully active – in Athens, Rome,
Iraq and Ankara – while a fifth, at Jerusalem, had all but faded away.
There was also the Egypt Exploration Society, which, since so much of
its work was done overseas, fell into much the same category. They
were mainly concerned with archaeology and history and some to a
lesser extent with the fine arts and literature. In fact, these British

Schools were highly individual, according to the nature of their settings and of their idiosyncratic and sometimes amateur directors. While all, except the lapsed school at Jerusalem, were receiving monies from the Treasury, there was no agreed procedure for allocating these. The British Museum, the Foreign Office and the Academy itself were all involved and 'The unhappy Treasury, with no inside knowledge of all these institutions ... was at a loss and confusion reigned.'

So it was that in 1950 Wheeler and Webster sought an interview at the Treasury. They were received by the lively and brilliant Edward Playfair, who wasted no time in telling them that their Lordships would welcome the Academy's services as a well-informed and sympathetic agency in their dealings with the schools. Playfair hesitated only when it came to the question of a renewed grant for Jerusalem, since it had lapsed for so long. Rik, always alert, sympathized with his difficulty and suggested the alternative would be to hand over our cultural responsibilities in Jerusalem to the Americans. The modest sum which this quickness of wit secured, with the confidence it implied, was enough to get the school started again, and for Kathleen Kenyon to become its honorary Director and within a few years make the discoveries at Jericho that were to revolutionize prehistoric chronology. Rik's career as an administrator was studded with such valuable interventions, most of them unrecorded.

At this first meeting with Edward Playfair the Academy's own finances were also discussed and its income doubled: a satisfactory beginning for the Secretary, although twice £2500 was hardly wealth. Since his excellent relationship with the Treasury accounted for much of Wheeler's achievement on behalf of the British Academy, and since it was a manifestation of how an often stormy character could also be a discreet, tactful and inconspicuous strategist within the world of officialdom, it must be right to treat it as a distinct whole, especially since it is possible to present an inside view from a Treasury official. This will, however, mean looking ahead of events.

In *The British Academy* Rik describes how after the first encounter with Playfair he was equally happy in his dealings with other Treasury men, and singles out one in particular. This was Richard Griffiths, who 'in some of our most crucial years piloted our little ship with skill and ... uniform success through the various inshore waters of Whitehall'.

When Rik began his campaign Treasury grants to the arts and sciences were dealt with piecemeal through several divisions, but, with the growing public demand for more money to meet cultural needs, in

1957–8 a separate division was set up and Richard Griffiths was made its head. Among his many cultural charges were, of course, the Royal Society, which handled very large sums of money, and the British Academy, which, in spite of its rapid growth, still made demands that by Treasury standards were chicken-feed. Partly for this reason, and partly perhaps from personal sympathy, Griffiths and his colleagues were ready, almost eager, to provide all that was asked for scholarly research.

What Richard Griffiths told me of Rik's methods only confirmed and enhanced what he himself had written. In contrast with other representatives, including those of the Royal Society, Rik was very sensitive to Treasury structure and function, and so was quick to recognize key men: those who were high enough to take the decisions he needed, but no higher; he never went over their heads, unless it was agreed that to bring in Academy 'bigwigs' would be useful. When he saw Griffiths to be the key man for most of his purposes he made an ally of him, always visiting him to discuss problems, and particularly to tell him of new projects and their cost, well before the annual accounts had to be agreed. If Griffiths had to say he would have difficulty in getting any idea past his chiefs Rik would usually drop or postpone it without protest. All transactions were made easier and more agreeable since the Secretary handled Academy affairs entirely on his own – again in contrast with the Royal Society people, who usually arrived in large delegations.

Virtues shown in his approaches to the Treasury would have been of no avail if Rik had not been equally faultless in the management of the funds they helped to win. Richard Griffiths judged Rik to be a good administrator and an exceptionally effective financial controller. His accounting was always meticulous and the Treasury appreciated his frankness, how, for instance, he always 'turned out his pockets' – that is, did not try to conceal unspent money or occasional failures.

Griffiths also believed him to be outstandingly good at directing and scrutinizing research, whether by individuals or institutions, and this is corroborated by Lord Robbins, a President in office during the mid-sixties. Observing from the Academy side, Robbins was convinced that the organization for appraising requests for grants as between the special subject and research committees and the Council was so effective that few undeserving applications got through. All this was done with discretion, but Lord Robbins smiled widely when he told me how in private the Secretary often advised the President on the capacities of other Fellows and scholars 'very frankly indeed'.

During Rik's administration archaeology won a large share of grants, but Griffiths and Robbins were again in agreement that he maintained a fair detachment. Archaeology was then still young and expanding fast; moreover, fieldwork needed more cash than armchair studies. If anyone pushed the claims of archaeology rather too hard it was Kathleen Kenyon.

Richard Griffiths wound up his account of his fruitful collaboration with Rik by declaring that, for his zest and his combination of great archaeological achievement with sensitive understanding of administrative and other practical affairs, he believed him to be one of only three great men he had known.

While Rik's most happy relationship with the Treasury was the foundation for his twenty years of work to raise the Academy from 'a funny little body' of elderly scholars into the main source of official patronage for the humanities, help was to come also from private sources. It was very much needed, for although its responsibility for the British Schools' grants gave the Academy a better standing and more influence, its own purse was still pathetically small, while the need for help was very great in those post-war years. Even the British Schools themselves needed more support of every kind, and it was not the least of Wheeler's accomplishments during his secretaryship that he was able to provide it, taking a paternal interest in their affairs and helping to set them on their feet again.

At home the plight of the humanities was near crisis. The war had left learned societies impoverished and with their publications far in arrears, while young research workers were not only more numerous but more clamant for public funds as the era of private means faded away. Rik used all his ingenuity and his knowledge of the personalities concerned to make the Academy's halfpence go as far as possible, but it would have been a very little way had not a young man in the days of freer enterprise founded his fortune in a bicycle shop.

The tentative offer of help that came from the Nuffield Foundation late in 1953 seems to have been genuinely unexpected. The Trustees had become aware of the straits of British scholarship and had selected the particular difficulties of learned publications for their charity. A letter reached Rik's desk, asking if the Academy could supply information about the condition of 'journals concerned with the Humanities' – while a parallel message of hope was addressed to the Royal Society.

The Secretary moved with his usual speed to report on the harrowing facts, and soon he, together with David Martin, his 'opposite number at the Royal Society', were meeting with officials of the Foundation to agree a plan of action. The upshot was that each body should receive about £4000 annually for five years, to disburse to the most deserving periodicals, while the Foundation also undertook to provide experts in publishing to advise the societies concerned.

The scheme was launched in 1955 and even in that first year payments were made to as many as twenty-five journals. Wheeler put much detailed work into awarding the grants and the whole rescue operation was so successful that a combination of sound economies with increased subscriptions enabled some publications to become self-supporting. However, as the five years drew to a close it was evident that subventions were still needed at least for the most specialized publications. This time help came to the Academy from the highest peaks of Oxford. That ebullient and powerful plotter, the Warden of Wadham, Sir Maurice Bowra, was now the Academy's President and he appealed to his equally Olympian fellow-Warden, John Sparrow of All Souls, for the college to take over from the Nuffield Foundation. Rik could certainly be proud when Mr Sparrow replied that as the case seemed deserving 'and the appeal came from a quarter which recommended itself ... strongly to the College generally, All Souls was ready to find £3500 for three years.' The Treasury had been prevailed upon to pay up quite handsomely when that time was over. The Pump of State had been primed.

In fact, it was already being primed from another source, from another charitable foundation: that admirable instrument of Anglo-American friendship, the Pilgrim Trust. Just a year after the Nuffield approach, Lord Kilmaine, Secretary of the Trust, addressed a long letter to Sir Mortimer Wheeler, the gist of which was that his Trustees, having formed the impression that scholarship in Britain was starved for funds, wished to discover whether there were needs that might be met by quite modest grants to help scholars to travel, to take 'sabbatical' leaves, to pay for secretarial help and the like.

The trustees have felt that, if they could be convinced of the need, they might themselves establish a fund, placed for purposes of administration in the hands of some suitable body, from which grants might be allocated to deserving scholars ... in the field of Humanities and the Arts.

With what pleasure Wheeler read that letter can be imagined, nor could there be any doubt that he would promptly convince the Pilgrim Trustees of the need for such a fund and that the British Academy was the most 'suitable body' for its administration. Sir George Clark, the historian and Provost of Oriel, had recently succeeded Webster as

President of the Academy and he, Kilmaine and the Secretary formed a friendly triumvirate, working so smoothly that within a few months the Pilgrims had assigned the Academy a fund of £2000 per annum for three years.

The triumvirate remained active, helping itself forward not least 'by highly agreeable and profitable luncheons' in the style that Rik had now made his own. He did not fail, however, to set up an advisory committee with an outside membership and worked even harder than for the Nuffield Foundation to supply the Trust with detailed annual reports from the Academy and individual reports from the beneficiaries themselves.

It was fortunate that in this year of 1955, when both the Nuffield and Pilgrim grants began, Rik reached the age of sixty-five and retired from his part-time professorship. This enabled him to spend more of the ordinary working day at the Academy, where Molly Myers now had a few secretarial underlings with her in the little anteroom to help with the fast-mounting work and to guard his door. Although some visitors might be barred, many were admitted and the Secretary's room, the only good one on the premises, became at times a lively meeting-place for the exchange of advice, news, ideas and gossip.

The Pilgrim scheme had been running for a twelvemonth when Rik heard that the Trustees wished to express 'their great pleasure and praise at the way in which the Academy had administered this grant. . . . They considered that the money had been used for exactly the sort of purpose which they had had in mind. They would wish you to continue the good work on the same lines.'

He did continue the good work – and to such effect that the Pilgrims twice renewed their original triennial endowment. Rik was, of course, very happy that during the time when they ran concurrently the two charitable trust funds gave his foster child, the British Academy, some £6000 to dispense to research and publication, adding very considerably to its prestige and to the interest of his own job. Yet he never thought such temporary doles, necessary though they were in the conditions of the fifties, more than bridging funds to be used experimentally until the Academy could make its due claim on the public purse. Then and only then could he be satisfied.

He was clear that the Academy could not go to the Treasury to get the neglected humanities their due until it could present a picture of the existing situation which, as Sir George Clark was to declare, was 'truly Gothic in its wealth of irregular detail' and could formulate a reasonably precise plan of what had to be done and how much it would cost. That was his well-tried way of dealing with Treasuries and the only one likely to be successful on the scale he envisaged.

Already before the end of the first triennium of the Pilgrim scheme Wheeler and Lord Kilmaine had been nursing the idea that its results should be treated as a pilot-project to provide evidence to lay before their Lordships, and it was with this in view that the grants were to be renewed again and then again.

While much could be learnt from administering the Nuffield and Pilgrim funds, it was evident to Wheeler that the findings would have to be brought together and developed into a report authoritative enough to inform and convince the Treasury. Although he took care to keep in touch with Kilmaine and had the whole-hearted and able backing of Sir George Clark, it was he himself who took the initiative in securing the money and the organizational help that such a report would demand. They were to be won from yet a third of those admirable private trusts: none other than the great Rockefeller Foundation, with its vast resources.

Early in 1957 Sir George had a meeting with the Foundation's London representative and a plan was discussed for setting up a committee of enquiry, with a full-time secretary, to survey the 'truly Gothic' scene in Britain, seek comparisons abroad and report with recommendations to the Academy. It was surely Rik's notion of time-and-work that lay behind the hope that this committee could publish its findings by the summer of the next year.

In the late summer the Academy submitted detailed proposals to the Foundation for the work of the proposed committee and estimates for its expenses. The clarity and style of this document are a sufficient proof of Wheeler's authorship. So, perhaps, is the firmness with which the whole enterprise was to be kept within the grasp of the British Academy. It had by now been decided, a little unwisely, to widen the scope to include the social sciences, so that the project was to be entitled *Survey of Provision for Research in the Humanities and the Social Sciences, Rockefeller Grant*.

By the beginning of 1958 the Foundation accepted the proposals and put the estimated costs of £6000 at the Academy's disposal – originally for a period up to the end of 1959, but this had to be extended by two years as reality displaced optimism. The committee, consisting of seven Fellows of the Academy, all eminent academics (with Kathleen Kenyon as the only woman), under the chairmanship of the President, with Mr R. H. Hill as full-time Secretary, held its first meeting in April 1958.

Between then and the final, eighteenth, meeting nearly three years later the Survey worked hard, wide-ranging tasks, including visits to Europe and North America, being assigned to each member, and a vast correspondence, including questionnaires, being conducted by its Secretary. Quite early in the programme, with the main object of the operation clearly in mind, Sir George Clark, together with Sir Maurice Bowra, who had just succeeded him as President, went to the Treasury and secured its blessing on their plans. The final report, of 120 pages, entitled *Research in the Humanities and the Social Sciences*, was published by the Oxford University Press in September 1961. The first recommendation is a discreet murmur that 'The position in the Humanities and Social Sciences would be more satisfactory if there were some authority which could allot funds . . .' and the remainder set out just where the nameless authority could best distribute those funds. For archaeology an increase in university posts was urged, together with grants for excavation and publication, for capital development of British Schools and 'other projects of a less expensive nature', not forgetting the expenses of part-time and freelance archaeologists. Rik considered the report to be 'both informative and cogent' – and so it was.

In his formal account of the Rockefeller Report in *The British Academy* Wheeler is exceptionally self-effacing, barely mentioning his own part in it. Yet Lord Robbins and other surviving witnesses tell that it was his greatest service to the Academy and to human studies; that he put an enormous amount of himself into every part of the undertaking. In addition to his own labours, I see him as a skilled sheep-dog, driving along his academic flock, singling out leaders, rounding up stragglers, trembling with restrained impatience, but keeping them always on the move along his chosen track.

Once the report was out, and had been submitted to the Treasury, it was time for action and events moved with what Rik, still restraining his impatience, described as 'decorous promptitude'. An appointment for a delegation from the Academy to Whitehall was sought and finally granted – with the Financial Secretary of the Treasury, Henry Brooke. The little party of Fellows, led by the President, Bowra, and accompanied by the Secretary, was well received and the ensuing discussions, as might be assumed from the participation of Maurice and Rik, were lively and informal. When that first recommendation for 'some authority which could allot funds' came up the Financial Secretary read the message between the lines and at once announced that no new body should be created since the task could be performed equally well and more cheaply by the Academy. No one was surprised and all were happy. In general the main arguments of the report were accepted, with the exception of the inclusion of the social sciences in the scheme. There the Treasury gave warning that other plans were afoot and that the Academy should probably limit its responsibilities to the humanities alone. (These plans descended from recommendations made by the Clapham Committee. Although later Wheeler and Lord Robbins were to submit evidence to the Heyworth Committee that the Academy could very well handle grants for the social sciences, to their chagrin that Committee found in favour of a Social Sciences Research Council. It was given lavish funds, much of them to be wasted: Rik and Robbins had no doubt that the Academy would have done better.)

The delegation left Henry Brooke's room confident that the Treasury would move with all reasonable speed to implement the report. Rik may have been a little uneasy that, in contrast with his own procedures, no estimates of costs had been offered, but he thought this would be settled 'at a lower level'. He was anxious that an announcement of the acceptance of the scheme could be made by Sir Maurice Bowra in his last presidential address, due to be delivered in July of that year, 1962.

Weeks went by without a sign from Whitehall and July was at hand. Rik resolved to abandon restraints and Establishment formalities and behave in the way that was natural to him. It is to be wished that, having resolved on bold action, he could have galloped his horse across the Park or whirled the old Lancia round Trafalgar Square, but what happened was still worthy.

I hastened down to the Treasury and put the matter with force and urgency. It was now or never. Without a specified grant in his pocket, our President ... would be restricted on this cardinal occasion to the indignity of mere air and bathos. The dramatic moment had arrived to pin immediate and proper substance to the Financial Secretary's expressed goodwill.... I left the Treasury with an initial grant of £25,000 and the avowed intention of a rise to £50,000 at an early date.

Richard Griffiths's explanation of the delay was that precisely because the Academy's recommendations were uncosted they went no further: the wheels of the Treasury were not made to turn. If that is so then Rik must have produced his own estimate, and, with the high repute he had won at the Treasury, that was good enough. Sir Maurice Bowra was able to wind up his Presidency in triumph.

The production of the Rockefeller Report and this final dramatic raid on Whitehall were in a sense the culmination of Rik's inspired effort to raise the British Academy to the position originally intended for it. Meanwhile the Secretary had been busy with other enterprises which, although not so directly concerned with the Academy's own fortunes, were to enhance its standing and its disposable budget.

The most important followed from those first dealings with the Treasury when the Academy was made paymaster for the British Schools overseas: Wheeler far more than anyone else was to be responsible for founding two more of these admirable institutions, and to do it with a flourish that had not been possible for their predecessors.

As early as the thirties he had felt concern for archaeology in Africa. Considering his lack of enthusiasm for prehistory in its stonier forms this is surprising, but he was moved by his conviction that Britain was in this field failing in its responsibilities as a colonial power. Then came his war years, and, remote though Mediterranean North Africa was from the tropical continent, he was not unaware of it. He was to remember in particular an occasion when

in the Barbary town of Tripoli there emerged ... a motley, friendly crowd of adventurers, ranging from shining purple negroes to leathery Frenchmen ... a sudden sense of inner Africa, of remote and fishful Chad, of which we knew pitifully little, recurred to the mind of at least one observer.

After the war interest was stirring within Africa itself, and this led to an international pan-African conference, held in London in 1953. Wheeler was among those who spoke, urging the care and exploration of ancient sites, and who drew up resolutions that included one in favour of an Institute of History and Archaeology in East Africa on the lines of existing British Schools. He saw to it that the Academy gave a sympathetic response to this idea, and before long he and Webster went to see the Secretary of State at the Colonial Office and induced him to accept a committee to advise him on such matters.

The committee was a powerful one, and under Rik's influence concentrated on the plan for an institute to cover the needs of Kenya, Uganda, Tanganyika and little Zanzibar, but progress was slow. Rik himself was able to give it a fillip when, as its president, he delivered a severe address to Section H of the British Association, on 'Colonial Archaeology'. A step forward was taken a year later, in August 1955, when he had struck up a profitable friendship (very much like that with Reardon Smith at Cardiff) with Sir Eldred Hitchcock, the sisal king of East Africa, and was invited out to tour the four territories in conditions of comfort and high esteem. With him went a curious character, Gervase Mathew, a Dominican and a Byzantinist, whose brother had been

Roman Catholic Archbishop of East Africa. They moved from capital to capital, staying always at Government House and everywhere carrying their mission to governments and to all men of good influence. In Tanganyika they did particularly well, as it was Sir Eldred's home and the Governor, Sir Edward Twining, was both hospitable and sympathetic. After a fine party in their honour they sat up drinking with him, 'For that is the way in which good work is done; not by loads of memoranda but by talk and talk and a little listening, savoured with a sufficiency of laughter and of the soma of the tropics.'

In contrast, and Rik still loved such contrasts, he and Gervase went for a week to the island of Kilwa Kisiwani, where they lived in grass huts while making 'a small sample excavation on the approved principles'.

Nothing tangible came from this grand tour, and yet it accomplished much. The idea of an institute had been made acceptable, and, indeed, it became a kind of cultural prize which each territory hoped to win. On their return, the Advisory Committee submitted a detailed memorandum on the proposed institute which was well received by the Colonial Secretary and the Colonial Governors. By 1956 the path appeared to be open; the Academy approached the Treasury for an annual grant of £6000, with an expectation of contributions from the territories themselves.

It was now that wretched delays began. The East African Institute was that dread thing, a New Project, and their Lordships stalled for two and a half years. Rik, however, remained stubbornly determined to succeed: at the beginning of 1959 he wrote to Sir Eldred, then a dying man, declaring that he would make a sortie to Dar-es-Salaam in the spring for 'active work on the spot' and finishing, 'I know that you will be with me in my determination to go ahead.' This raid proved unnecessary; within a month news came that the long-awaited Treasury grant would be in the next budget.

With that seal of approval, funds poured in, from the territories and from trusts, Rik now having stout support from Maurice Bowra. There was still, of course, much to be done and in the summer Rik and Gervase Mathew went out to secure premises, once again doing the round of all four Government Houses. By 1961 the institute was fully established in Dar-es-Salaam, with British and African students and with an excavation programme at Kilwa Kisiwani. Later, headquarters were shifted to Nairobi, where the institute continued to thrive and to do excellent work.

Rik's second project for another British School overseas started well behind the first, but with so much dash and good fortune that it reached the finishing post at about the same time. The style in which a British Institute of Persian Studies came to be created was, in short, very much more to Rik's own taste. In *The British Academy* he begins the story in 1959, with the arrival in London of a dynamic Persian gentleman, Majid Movaghar, former member of the Iranian parliament and publicist, who came determined to induce the British to set up a cultural centre to rival the existing Institut Français in Teheran. In fact, however, many strings must have been twitched before this energetic campaign, for David Stronach remembers that when, as a young archaeologist, he joined Rik at Charsada in 1958 (as will be told) he came by way of Iran and brought with him a message from the British Embassy urging the case for setting up a British School in Teheran. Rik showed the keenest interest in these tidings, and it can hardly be doubted that some diplomatic lines ran between himself and the Embassy and Majid Movaghar.

Since the two cultural missions of his Indian days Rik had been personally very much aware of the French cultural, and especially archaeological, dominance in both Afghanistan and Iran and was eager for some (of course) friendly British rivalry. When, therefore, Movaghar went home, after a whirlwind tour of cultural summits, promising support from the Shah himself, and his mission was left very much in the hands of the British Council and the Academy, Rik was prepared to take the Persian seriously. He must at least have admired an energy almost equal to his own.

So another series of club lunches began, this time at the Athenaeum and the Guards' Club, as the Secretary of the Academy and the Deputy Director General of the British Council discussed the possibilities and the impossibilities of a cultural penetration of Iran. Rik was well aware of one total impossibility: the Lords of the Treasury would not accept another New Project when that for East Africa had just been agreed. He therefore thought up a compromise that he was reasonably certain could be made into the thin end of a wedge.

At Charsada he had taken a great fancy to David Stronach, with 'his quiet and cheerful intelligence' – perhaps once more recognizing good subaltern material. With the support of Bowra and the ready consent of the British Council, he proposed that the Academy should find the salary for a suitable person to be given office room and attaché status with the Council in Teheran. The suitable person was, of course, David Stronach, who at that time was with Max Mallowan in Iraq and winning golden opinions there. In his letter to David apprising him of 'the plot' he explained that the underlying purpose of his appointment for one year would be 'to warm up the nest for a larger project. . . .' The young man saw the possibilities and accepted, a decision which he was not to regret.

After that events moved with a speed that even Rik could not hope to exceed. By September of 1960 the British Academy Attaché was installed with the Council, the still active Movaghar was hunting premises for the institute, the Ministry of Education and the University of Teheran were proving most helpful and so, too, was the Minister of Court, who had the Shah's ear. A unique incentive for some fast work was the State Visit to Iran by the Queen and Prince Philip, expected the following March.

Rik judged that Teheran was ripe: 'it seemed to me that the moment had arrived to attack with all guns. And both Maurice Bowra and I had been gunners. We would open fire together.' So just before Christmas they set off with the Foreign Office at their back and the open arms of the British Embassy ready to receive them. There were dinners and speeches, they saw all the right ministers and heads of the university and 'struggled into morning coats, as into ancient suits of armour, and waited upon H.I.M. the Shahanshah, who had been suitably briefed . . . and blessed our enterprise'.

It remained only to win over the British Treasury for the British Institute of Persian Studies in Teheran, already existing in the spirit, to be made incarnate. Rik succeeded by a coup in total contrast with his normal Treasury methods, and which he enjoyed all the more because it broke the Establishment rules. He was at this time chairman of the committee set up for British collaboration with UNESCO in the rescue of antiquities in Nubia. Very soon after his return from Teheran a meeting of this very exalted committee was held in the room of Sir Edward Boyle, then Financial Secretary at the Treasury. As the party was breaking up 'some gadfly drove the Secretary of the Academy to corner Sir Edward about the Persian scheme and to indicate how much depended on an immediate government grant of £8000 to enable the Institute to be formally established. . . . The Royal visit was mentioned, and Sir Edward said "Yes". The whole interchange lasted about five minutes.'

So much was done during the following weeks that Max Mallowan, as the first President of the governing body, was present on 3 March when Prince Philip thanked the University of Teheran for providing the institute with a home and the Queen also made a graceful reference to this generosity in her state speech. The grand opening of the British

Institute took place only at the very end of the year, but meanwhile it already had its students and, in addition to his wider cultural duties as Director, David Stronach had taken charge of important excavations at Pasargadae, ancient capital of the Achaemenid Dynasty. The site had, in fact, been selected for the institute by Sir Mortimer Wheeler.

The opening of the two new British Schools near the beginning of Rik's second decade as Secretary was enough to make his one failure tolerable. During the sixties he worked hard for another new foundation, in Japan, but after high hopes the plan was killed by the British financial collapse of 1967. There were very many smaller services that he did for the Academy and the secretaryship remained his greatest commitment. Yet he was also to launch on a further career of a very different kind.

CHAPTER 11

Many Callings

IT WOULD BE understating the case to say that during the 1950s and 1960s Rik was leading a double life; rather, he lived as a brilliant juggler, keeping an uncountable number of multi-coloured balls in the air. There was the Academy; the professorship; excavations; presidencies and membership of very many boards and institutions, academic and public; authorship of a large number of books, specialist and popular; journalism; lectureships; television and radio broadcasting; Swans touring – these are only a selection of the more important of the tasks and concerns that he had on his hands during this stretch of his life, from his sixtieth to his eightieth year.

Yet perhaps the picture of the double life has meaning if it illustrates the contrast between all those activities, focused on the Academy, the Antiquaries, the Institute, the Athenaeum, in which he was engaged with eminent scholars and Establishment figures or with his own archaeological work, and that hurrying, extrovert, exciting but largely ephemeral world of broadcasting and touring where he was rushed by land, sea and air to so many countries and in the most various company. There can have been few elderly men (according to the chronologer) who did so much at the top of two such different trees.

It was late in 1952, during the battle against the gerontocracy of the Academy, when Rik stepped unknowingly on to the very short path that was to lead him into popular fame, to make him one whom every taxi-driver or shop assistant delighted to serve, one whom many turned to watch as he went down Piccadilly with that strange gait of his, well-tailored but (latterly at least) with hair flowing behind him.

Mary Adams, of BBC Television, saw the potentialities of an American programme broadcast as 'What in the World?' and resolved to adapt it for British screens. Paul Johnstone, a most likeable newcomer to television, armed with a First in History from Oxford, was selected as producer, and Dr Glyn Daniel, the Cambridge archaeologist, was recognized as a likely compère, capable, imperturbable, but far from dull. Although Glyn had met Rik in Algiers and Delhi, and occasionally at home, they did not know one another well when they met at the Lime Grove Studios for an experimental 'dry-run' of the programme.

Glyn Daniel has recalled how later that evening, when they travelled homewards together by Tube, Rik said, 'That is the last we shall hear of that. No possible good can come of it.' Only three weeks later they were facing the television cameras and 'Animal, Vegetable, Mineral?' was born.

The programme was given a competitive edge by the device of inviting museums to submit objects from their collections with a challenge to the panel of the night to identify them, the score being conspicuously displayed to the public view. By the end of the show the panel had invariably won, but with enough misses to keep the game alive. Glyn presided loftily from a desk, while the three chosen experts sat close together at right-angles to him. A girl assistant laid each object on a turntable, which was then revolved to display it to viewers, while a caption let them into the secret of its true identity. It was now ready for the experts, who passed it from hand to hand, each commenting on its attributes with as much knowledge and wit as they could muster, until a precise identification was offered – usually correct but occasionally so far wrong as to allow the viewers to enjoy their foreknowledge.

It seems a simple entertainment to have proved so immensely popular, to have roused so much enthusiasm for archaeology in men, women and aspiring children, and, through this success, to have affected the manner in which Rik Wheeler spent the latter part of his life. In part, the success was due to the ripeness of the hour: there was a growing interest in archaeology at all levels as a part of the reaction against the dreary practicalities of war. Moreover, 'Animal, Vegetable, Mineral?' gave the public its first experience of high expertise at work: in 'The Brains' Trust' audiences had responded to intelligent, well-informed talk, but now this ability to make exact attributions of curious artifacts from all times and places since the emergence of man astounded and fascinated them.

These things counted, but there is little doubt that above all the programme owed its appeal to Rik's masterly performances. He once said, 'It is no good picking up something and saying "this is a Samoan cake mould" – viewers want to see how you arrived at your decision. They are interested in watching your process of thought.' This was his principle, but, always something of an actor, he soon learnt to embellish it with artful devices of timing: the delayed recognition, the double-take, the appearance of being at a loss followed by the sudden kill. Then his enthusiasm and vitality, his popular humour and flashes of wit all radiated from the screen. Women, of course, responded to him simply as a man. Bernard Levin has recently recalled how one lady, having heard that Sir Mortimer liked sherry, always stood a glass of it on her television set when he was present in the box below.

Inevitably Rik dominated any of the rest of us appearing with him (only Thomas Bodkin was capable of rivalry), while Glyn Daniel provided the perfect foil. Nor was that dominance entirely due to personality and performing ability: he was in fact very good at the recognition game, having a vast range of experience and a remarkable visual memory. He delighted his followers by being so often right, and was prepared to take trouble so to please them. It is certain that he did sometimes glance through catalogues or journals connected with the challenging museum to spot likely specimens from their collections. He also grinningly admitted that on just one occasion, happening to visit the museum that was to be the next challenger, he scanned the cases to see where exhibits had been recently removed from their labelled boards.

Stories that Rik in particular, or the panel as a whole, knew in advance what to expect were quite untrue, as a memory of Glyn Daniel's must prove. It was the practice for the panel to have a rehearsal with a few objects not to be used on the air, then to break for a good restaurant dinner followed immediately by the broadcast. In one of the later series the programme was going out from the Musée de l'Homme in Paris. When the dinner break came Glyn observed that Rik had been taken aside:

There seemed to be an altercation and he suddenly turned round, came to me, his eyes blazing: 'Take me to the nearest café,' he said, 'and as quickly as you can.' When we were seated and he had a pernod in front of him, he declared that he had never been so insulted in his life, that he had been asked whether he would like to see the list of objects he was later to identify. I have seldom seen anyone more furious.

'Animal, Vegetable, Mineral?' was to have a long history, running for over six years. The first series of 1952–3 went very well, but it was with the second, a year later, when producers and performers had perfected their techniques, that the programme achieved supreme success with the British public. By this time young David Attenborough had been drawn in and in June 1954 he wrote to Rik,

There seems no doubt, if one is to believe the popular press and our Audience Research Department, that *Animal, Vegetable, Mineral?* has ended in a blaze of glory and I feel I must write to you, as one of the chief architects of the success, to thank you for all you have done for us. Paul [Johnstone], with his deplorable flippancy, seems to have cornered the television archaeological market but I shall hope to be a camp follower so that my archaeological education will not be halted too abruptly. . . .

Both Paul and I have enjoyed ourselves hugely with the programme and I hope that you have not suffered too much as a result. I myself am most grateful for having had the opportunity of basking in so much reflected glory.

Everyone involved enjoyed these programmes, and that was another reason why audiences enjoyed them also. Rik himself got on well not only with Paul and David, who became his young friends, but with all the production staff, while he was always considerate and charming to the technicians, from cameramen to the humblest assistants. Indeed, the only occasion when Rik's resources of temper were manifest was in his fully justified outbreak of fury when invited to cheat. This was all the more remarkable since after a time sessions were no longer confined to the Lime Grove studios, but might be staged in the museums themselves, both at home and abroad, bringing the viewers an interesting variety of settings but burdening all concerned with tiresome journeys and adjustments.

Standards were to be well maintained, but perhaps 'Animal, Vegetable, Mineral?' was never more sparkling than in the freshness of that second series in 1954. It was in this year that the critics chose Professor Sir Mortimer Wheeler as Television Personality of the Year. Shortly afterwards, in response to a newspaper questionnaire, very many readers voted for him as the man they would most like to meet. For the rest of the fifties he was the kind of popular figure to be bombarded by the editors of every kind of newspaper with requests for articles on every kind of subject, even to the point of a demand from *Sir* to give his views on Nightwear for Men, and from Marjorie Proops to nominate a woman deserving of a statue. These advances were usually ignored, though once, in his absence, Molly Myers replied to a question from a well-known daily newspaper that she was 'practically certain he has no superstitions'.

Wheeler did, of course, undertake some popular journalism and some lecturing for the substantial fees he very much needed at that time. (The fact that he was hard up and she relatively rich was proving one of the minor difficulties in his renewed life with Kim.) The boys of his old school, inspired by 'Animal, Vegetable, Mineral?', started an archaeological society, but could never induce him to address them, although a party did go to the St George's Hall in Bradford to hear him give a talk with that most non-committal of titles, 'Digging up the Past'. Nor did Bradford Grammar School itself fare better, for, when invited to lecture there, Wheeler asked what he must have known was the prohibitive fee of £150. This led some masters to think that, having left for 'the fashionable world beyond the provinces', Wheeler had grown ashamed of his grammar school background. There is little truth in the accusation: Rik wrote quite generously of the school he had left when barely fifteen, but was honest in saying that it had not meant much to him. He never went back. Yet if any individual boy had gone to him for help in archaeology his reception would have been very different.

Rik certainly wanted to make money out of his television fame, although he made it a rule, hardly ever broken, that he would do nothing outside his own professional sphere of interest. No opening of garden parties or luncheon club performances. That he was not making a fortune out of 'Animal, Vegetable, Mineral?' itself is almost touchingly exposed in a conspiratorial aside in a letter from Glyn Daniel written some months after the 'blaze of glory' of the second series:

I said to Paul when we were alone yesterday and had finished a good bottle of wine 'Now that AVM is starting again I think Rik and I must tackle Miss Knight for some more money, don't you?' He said, after some thought, 'I think that is very reasonable; for God's sake don't quote me, but I think Rik ought to put up his figure from 25 to 30 guineas.' This is for your private information. May we agree on some demarche?

This bold demarche was made: thirty guineas Rik's fee became – and remained. However, this was not the only income he drew from the BBC, for the triumph of 'Animal, Vegetable, Mineral?' led on to his engagement in a variety of archaeological broadcasts for both television and radio during the period when the original programme was still running. Often Glyn Daniel was the moving spirit, for he had discovered his gifts as a deviser and presenter of productions. One of the earliest and most popular was a series first running in 1954 under the title of 'Buried Treasure', which actually achieved higher viewing figures than 'Animal, Vegetable, Mineral?', although it had not the same lasting impact on the public consciousness. This theme involved filming on location, and when Rik was assigned to cover Tollund Man, the marvellously preserved two-thousand-year-old sacrificial victim whose body had been found in a Danish bog not very long before, he and Glyn enjoyed a convivial trip to Denmark. They were not only able to indulge the British public's taste for the macabre, but undertook to consume a gruel from a recipe based on grain and seeds in Tollund Man's stomach. They found it so disgusting that they thought it best to wash it down with quantities of decent Danish brandy.

One way and another broadcasting involved Rik and Glyn in much travel together, both in Britain and abroad – particularly in France. They came to know one another well, and formed a habit of giving one another lunch once a month, Rik being host at the Athenaeum and Glyn at the United Universities Club. It annoyed Rik that the food at his club was inferior, but then Glyn was far more of a serious gourmet. (Rik always apologized for the bad cooking at the Athenaeum, but continued to use it for most of his entertaining. His women friends, admitted to the Ladies' Annexe, were accustomed to his sending back the wine, a gesture he contrived to make while delighting rather than infuriating the waitress who ran to do his bidding.)

The two men were to see even more of one another when Glyn Daniel took over the editorship of *Antiquity*, but this connection, as will be told, was a little more stormy than was their happy collaboration in broadcasting.

Among the vast number of broadcasts that Rik undertook for the BBC during the fifties – all the more astonishing since most of them were scripted – were several contributions to John Irving's radio series, 'The Archaeologist', including talks on Stanwick and Maiden Castle. In another he took the chair for a programme on 'Roman Towns', in which Sheppard Frere described those excavations at Verulamium that were exposing faults in Rik's own earlier findings. He also allowed himself to be persuaded to edit and present a run of eight radio talks on Roman Britain, to which old colleagues such as Christopher Hawkes and Ralegh Radford contributed. Mainly out of good nature and a sense of obligation he several times took part in the 'Asian Club' programmes designed for immigrants.

Much of this broadcasting was quite small beer: while he turned down requests for articles by the dozen he did not much like saying 'No' to the BBC. After all, he enjoyed the work, it swelled his earnings most satisfactorily and radio at least carried the archaeological word into many homes lacking television sets. There were, however, television projects towards the end of the decade which were far more ambitious and in which Rik himself was virtually the sole performer.

Two were for the 'Buried Treasure' series, which was rivalling 'Animal, Vegetable, Mineral?' in the length of its run. First, in the early spring of 1957 he went with Paul Johnstone to Pakistan to film in his familiar haunts at Taxila and Mohenjodaro, the programme going out in June. The next furthered his growing enthusiasm for African archaeology: this was to be an expedition to Zimbabwe, plans for which were already stirring early in 1958. The intention was for Rik and Paul to spend some days filming among the famous ruins, and since he had never seen this still mysterious place he welcomed the opportunity to do so in agreeable and profitable circumstances.

As soon as word of his visit spread in Southern Rhodesia he was bombarded with requests to lecture, to meet old friends (including an architect who had been with him at Enfield) and eager schoolboys, and to identify dubious antiquities. All received charming replies pleading extreme shortage of time. To one boy he wrote, 'there is nothing I like so much as trout-fishing. . . . I will carry your letter in my pocket and hope for the best.'

Some advance publicity was inspired by the fact that not long before his arrival 'Sir Mortimer Wheeler, the eminent British archaeologist and well known broadcaster' was to open a series of eight talks for the BBC's Overseas Service on African prehistory, an enterprise not unconnected with his effort to rouse wider interest in the subject.

Rik and Paul Johnstone flew to Salisbury together at the end of August, spent the night with an old acquaintance, Brigadier Michael Collins, of the Department of Federal Surveys, before flying on to Bulawayo, where they lodged for another night with Roger Summers, an archaeologist who was chairman of the Rhodesian Historical Monuments Commission, and had recently been involved with Rik in a pan-African conference in London.

The next day Rik and Paul went on at once to Zimbabwe, and were joined by Roger Summers, who had been doing some digging on the site and who was now pressed into a supporting role for the film. It must have been a relief to Rik to have his company for the perambulation of the ruins, with all the informed wonder, the enthusiastic forays, the enterings and comings out, that such performances demand. They worked hard for the best part of a week, including an excursion to the related ruins of Nalatale; afterwards Paul boasted of having taken as many as fifty-seven shots on one outstandingly strenuous day.

Rik lectured on 'Modern Science and Archaeology' to Brigadier Collins's department when, in mid-September, he and Paul flew back to Salisbury. After that they do not seem to have delayed a day for the 'sundowner' party which, according to the Brigadier, half Salisbury was clamouring for, but took the long flight home. In London Rik was immediately confronted with a taste of the kind of publicity that is the penalty of popular fame: the *Daily Mail* printed a photograph of him in bush shirt and shorts, apparently gazing across at the legs of 'blonde Rank Star Belinda Lee', with the caption 'The knees are knobbly. The calves resemble a drainpipe from the 5th Dynasty of the Pharaohs. But 68-year-old archaeologist Sir Mortimer Wheeler, out in Central Africa to collect material for TV's *Buried Treasure* series, has had a chance to prove his pins are still in splendid shape.' Paul Johnstone was said to have declared that many of his shots 'showed Sir Mortimer scampering up and down a 350 ft. hill. But he never twitched a muscle.'

The Zimbabwe programme was shown under the title of 'King Solomon's Mines': Rik had never been shamed out of attracting interest through the deployment of romantic associations. The plan was first to talk of the legends that had related the ruins to Solomon's gold and the Queen of Sheba, then of the arrival of oriental traders – allowing Rik to show the pieces of Chinese and Persian pottery, the presence of which in Africa delighted him as much as the Arretine sherds in India. From there it was easy to pass on to the Portuguese and then to such information as had been won by modern science, which, since it had proved there was nothing at Zimbabwe more than fifteen hundred years old, was 'definitely against King Solomon and the Queen of Sheba'. The tour of the primitive Acropolis, the walls and towers, was lightened by clips showing a modern African village, complete with witch doctor, simple gold-working and the like. At the end of his commentary Rik returned to the theme that much remained mysterious about Zimbabwe. It went down well, helped to spread interest in the African past, and delighted those who, like Basil Davidson, were trying to prove that it was not so dark as it had been painted.

The third of these later ventures in television was also the most ambitious. This time it was not Rik's friend and familiar companion Paul Johnstone who was in charge, but a rising script writer and producer at the BBC, Stephen Hearst, whom Rik had met when he filmed a Hellenic cruise. Sir Compton Mackenzie had served as guide and historical interpreter of a series on 'The Glory that was Greece' and now Sir Mortimer Wheeler was to follow with three programmes pursuing 'The Grandeur that was Rome'.

The project got under way when at the beginning of 1959 Stephen Hearst wrote to Rik, telling him that he had put up a proposal for three half-hour programmes under this title, boldly outlining their purpose and content as well as a schedule for locations and dates of filming. He was fairly confident of acceptance from above, for he invited Rik to set down further ideas for content, or, if he preferred, 'to pace up and down in the British Academy' with a tape recorder. He ended, however, 'Let's hope that Higher Thought take half as favourable a view of me as a producer as of you as the greatest Roman of them all.'

After some earlier shooting at home, mainly along Hadrian's Wall, Rik flew out in mid-September to join Hearst and his crew in Trier. Rik had memories of the place, with its marvellously preserved Roman city gate, going back to the Rhineland researches of his youth. They filmed there for a few days and then the whole party drove at a leisurely pace down to Avignon, where they stayed at the Crillon while working among the theatres, temples and amphitheatres of Orange, Nîmes and Arles, the atmosphere of Provence making a happy contrast with Rome's northern territories. Rik had to return to London for a time, but rejoined the BBC team in Rome and was to be away with them continuously for over a month.

Under Stephen Hearst's leadership the pace was not too hot: they had a whole fortnight shooting in the imperial capital before driving down to Naples, where Rik wanted to film some of the mural paintings in the museum as well as the ruins of Pompeii and Herculaneum. The last fortnight was to be spent in Libya, where at Lepcis Magna and Sabratha they could catch something of the Grandeur that was Rome away from the encroachment of the modern world. For Lepcis the whole party was lodged at the Officers' Mess of the Royal Tank Corps in Homs – which for Rik must have called back with particular force his wartime experiences, and perhaps, excusably, led him to wonder how much more ruined Lepcis might have been if he and John Ward-Perkins had not made their lightning intervention. From the Libyan sunshine they returned to London in the gloom of November and, when time could be found for it, worked on three elaborate scripts.

They were to be entitled 'Skeleton of an Empire'; 'Gods and Men'; 'Roman Art and Architecture'. They followed the pattern, already laid down in Hearst's original letter, by which Rik gave a spoken commentary over silent film for the greater part of each programme, but occasionally talked to camera about the more abstract ideas that could not, or should not, be illustrated. The first programme opened with one of these talk pieces and it is so characteristic, such a deft essay to catch the attention, that it can be quoted:

In the beginning there was a patch of hill and valley beside the sea. That patch grew, through confidence, through ambition, through a sense of adventure. But chiefly as the trees grow or the sun shines, through a sort of obscure inevitability. Ultimately it stretched from the Atlantic to the Tigris; it reached the Emperor of China; it was the world; then it crumbled. Colony after colony fell away from it. It continued to win wars but more and more often lost the peace. Its citizens worked less and depended more and more upon welfare and having a good time. Its Civil Service grew larger and larger and interfered increasingly with everyday life. Taxation ate out its heart. . . . It vanished into history almost imperceptibly. I've been talking of an empire – but I wonder if you and I have the same empire in mind. Perhaps we have.

Then Rik went on over the first shots: 'I've been speaking of course of ancient Rome. . . .' This 'Skeleton of an Empire' is very good; it was Rik's kind of thing. 'Gods and Men', covering law as well as religion and town and country life for everyman, perhaps tries so hard to be popular as to have a hint of condescension. The third programme, in which the visuals were naturally very strong, again has a good commentary. Showing a lively selection of realistic portrait busts, Rik claimed that it was with the Romans that the individual arrived, and he saw them also as the authors of the first Romantic Movement in painting. He was on more certain, but no less interesting, ground in speaking of the architectural revolution that came with concrete and the ability to build great vaults and domes.

Both producer and performer had put much time and effort into 'The Grandeur that was Rome' and the expense must have been heavy. The results were honourable: these programmes were informative, never dull, had aesthetic appeal and ideas linking them to the modern world. I find that I wrote to Rik about them, for he quotes me to Hearst. 'My stern critic Jacquetta Priestley has written as follows: "I think *The Grandeur that was Rome* is a hundred times better than Monty's effort [Compton Mackenzie on the Greeks] – though as you know this is not a favourite form with me. I think you've done marvels with it." ' I do not think I was saying more than I felt. Yet the viewing figures proved disappointing and it seemed that no great impression was made on the public.

The truth was that the gamesmanship, the personal challenges of 'Animal, Vegetable, Mineral?' and the simple attraction of the idea of 'Buried Treasure' had led to an over-estimation of the appeal of a more academic form of archaeology for the mass viewing public. That was the main explanation for the relatively poor reception, but there was another. This guided tour form is a difficult one, the BBC at that time had little experience of it and Wheeler, so brilliant at a declamatory style on the one hand or the sparring of debate on the other, lacked the stealthy tactfulness, the selfless presentation of the self achieved by a Lord Clark or a Huw Wheldon.

He did occasional broadcasting during the sixties, but chiefly on radio and of an unambitious kind, although he did appear in 'Evening with [Ifor] Evans', during which they exchanged reminiscences about University College and especially about A. E. Housman. Among many other readings Rik seems to have slipped in his account of Passchendaele and his poem of El Alamein under the guise of anonymity. It can be said that as a broadcaster he was virtually 'out' until, after his eightieth birthday, his all but unabated powers were to be so happily rediscovered by David Collison.

Becoming a television celebrity, however, was largely responsible for introducing Wheeler to yet another enterprise that he was to follow for the rest of his life. In 1954, when he was Television Personality of the Year, he was invited by Mr R. K. Swan, who ran his own travel agency, to join a Hellenic cruise as lecturer in the coming spring. The passion for holiday travel abroad was then just taking possession of the British public as the restrictions of wartime were left behind.

Hellenic cruises had been established before the war, but now Swans were determined to revive and extend them, while maintaining the high academic standard of the guest lecturers employed for the edification of the other voyagers. For these were no ordinary holiday cruises for bronzing and drinking, with some sight-seeing thrown in. Hellenic Travellers were expected 'To begin a new interest or develop existing knowledge in the art, history and culture' of the Mediterranean world – and soon of the world far beyond as well.

For many years the ship used for these virtuous aims was the *Ankara*, a veteran of the Alaska run, now decently but far from luxuriously done up and under Turkish management. She took about three hundred passengers, and in vacation time knowledge certainly existed among them, for they included a good sprinkling of dons and school-teachers. That they also included some aristocrats became known when the Duke of Devonshire was among those left behind when a party failed to return from plant-hunting on Mount Parnassus. (The press inevitably associated Sir Mortimer Wheeler with this misadventure, but in fact he had no part in it.)

The schedule was for the lecturers to give hour-long talks on their special subjects to audiences on board ship and then brief introductory accounts of each site on arrival. Parties were conducted round the monuments by well-informed local guides. Most of the cruises were managed by Doreen Goodrick of Swans, who became a stout ally of Rik's. She had something like genius for the job: everything happened on time and in good order, yet her flock had no sense of being chivvied.

Rik duly went on his first Hellenic cruise in 1955 and was an immediate success. He was by now an immensely experienced popular lecturer for any genuinely interested audience, and he particularly relished speaking on site, when he could employ all his powers of eloquence. His addresses, delivered from the steps of the Parthenon and from the heart of ancient Baalbek, became his most admired performances.

In the face of occasional stories to the contrary, Rik was usually charming to everybody, showing no intellectual or other brand of snobbishness. He only reacted badly when pretentious, empty-headed people gushed over him, mingling the gush with idiotic questions. As at all times and places, he was always ready to take extra trouble for students. His wit could be a little unkind, as when he had to lecture in a storm, and a particularly stout lady in the audience was thrown to the floor. 'Not hurt, I hope?' he asked. 'Oh, no Sir Mortimer.' 'No damage to the ship, I trust?'

He did not immediately become a regular guest lecturer for Swans. Indeed, in the autumn of 1957 he even allowed himself to be enticed away by their then rivals, Fairways and Swinford. Glyn Daniel, always a shrewd businessman, was an adviser to Fairways and he it was who persuaded Rik to lead this, his earliest travel tour in India and Pakistan – and provided him with good company and a helpmeet in the person of his wife, Ruth. The brochure, which advertised it as 'A Tour with Sir Mortimer Wheeler', was embellished with an alluring studio portrait and insisted that this was no rushed tourist trip but a leisurely and luxurious 'expedition into time,' from the Indus civilization to Le Corbusier's Chandigarh. The charge for the four weeks was 770 guineas, quite stiff for those days, and it was presumably for this reason that it had to be postponed from spring to later summer for lack of subscribers. Rik had been at pains to secure the help of Indian and Pakistani friends, particularly of Shri A. Ghosh, his next but one successor as Indian Director General of Archaeology, with whom he was to have many future dealings as he resumed closer contacts with the subcontinent.

Swans now moved to secure Rik for themselves; he was made a paid director of the company and chairman of its Hellenic Cruise division, appointments he was to hold until his death. They involved him in a very substantial amount of work, for the committee met quite often, he undertook to select and secure all lecturers, and might write brochures and the like, as required. He also compiled and edited Swans Hellenic Cruises, a handbook containing brief histories of all the sites visited by Swans and plans of most of them, together with lists of dates, dynasties, deities and all manner of information invaluable to the more earnest travellers bent on self-improvement. Rik even kept an eye on the balance sheet, and did all these things with such efficiency that Kenneth Swan was ready to declare that 'he would have made a first rate businessman'.

From the year he became chairman Rik always went as lecturer on two cruises a year, in the early spring and late summer, and after his retirement from the Academy he might fit in a third. These were Swans' familiar cruises round the shores of the Mediterranean, each lasting two weeks.

Rik never lost touch with his Indian and Pakistani colleagues and former pupils, but with the unfortunate ending of his spell as Archaeological Adviser in Pakistan the relationship became a more tenuous one. Then the filming and the Fairways tour in 1957, followed by his major excavation at Charsada and shortly afterwards a lecture tour in India associated with the British Council, drew him back to the subcontinent, for which he still felt more love than hate. From that time onwards, as will appear, he was often to be in the subcontinent on various working missions.

At much the same period Wheeler was very much involved with Iran through his efforts for the foundation of the British Institute in Teheran. It was therefore a natural development for him to think of organizing Swans tours in Asia. He never himself accompanied a tour in Iran, but between 1967 and the early seventies he arranged a number, having in David Stronach an invaluable deputy. In later years he had another very able young man, prepared to serve as a leading lecturer – David Whitehouse, whom we shall encounter excavating at Siraf.

Rik's own most important undertakings on Swans' behalf were two very ambitious tours in India and Pakistan, when not only his own presence but the extraordinary esteem in which he was now held all over the subcontinent added greatly to their glamour and interest. His uninhibited letters to Molly Myers help to bring them to life.

The first was in November and early December of 1966, the route lying through Pakistan and northern and western India. From the first Rik seems to have been greatly, perhaps excessively, elated by the enthusiasm and hospitality shown to him. 'Garlands, garlands everywhere – it's astonishing.' He was, on the other hand, much disappointed in the quality of the party he was leading, which seems to have consisted mainly of elderly, and presumably rich, old ladies, relieved only by the presence among them of Anthony Powell and his wife.

Already at Peshawar he was complaining of old women 'without a spoonful of brains among the lot'. Then from Ashoka Hotel, New Delhi:

I have been on the go almost night and day without let-up. How the old man stands it I don't know – presumably he isn't quite so broken up as he imagined. The progress through Pakistan can fairly be described as triumphal. Everywhere I was welcomed as a returned hero (!), culminating in a grand performance of *son et lumière* in my honour in Lahore fort before 300 guests. And now in India all is breathless friendliness. I only wish these twenty followers were more rewarding. Except for the Powells all are senile half-wits with no sort of understanding of anything.. . . . It's a pity, because I doubt whether ever again there will be so well informed and organized a tour of the kind. There just isn't anyone else who could do it, and who can be greeted, as I have been, as an old friend by kings (the Wali of Swat!), by scholars and by little sweepers and gardeners who rush up to me and kneel to kiss my trouser-legs. All most humble-making. . . .

These remarks about his elderly charges, and others even more unkind, are clearly objectionable. Rik was not automatically cruel about aged females: on the contrary, he could be highly appreciative of them, all the way from the country archaeologist, Elsie Clifford, to Agatha Christie. His distaste on this occasion may in part be accounted for by a fact that also makes it all the more poignant. Among his flock was the actress Fabia Drake, who in her book, *Blind Fortune*, published after Rik's death, records that 'under his inspiring guidance only two or three were not visibly attracted to him'.

Fabia Drake herself was strongly attracted, making a practice of joining those cruises and tours where she could enjoy his presence. 'We had an *amitié amoureuse* which lasted for ten years,' she declares, adding that it saved her from losing her femininity and with it her powers as an actress. Her account of Rik and of their 'love-hate' relationship is decidedly embarrassing for anyone who knows more of his nature and history: 'By the time I reached him, he was set in an implacable hatred of women,' and this she attributes entirely to his marriage to 'a strange, fated and fatal Ninon de l'Enclos of a sprite, Mavis de Vere Cole. . . . She was insatiable and the traditional story of the soldier who comes home from the wars to find his wife in another man's arms came true. What that will have done to this proud man can only be imagined, but the scar did not heal.'

On this Indian tour Fabia tells how, when some of the party were to be flown to see the erotic sculptures of Khajaraho, Rik persuaded her to overcome her prejudice and go with them. Rightly finding the carvings to be joyful rather than pornographic, 'I was grateful to Rik for making me go and I wondered if it had done anything to ameliorate his own relentless attitude towards the opposite sex.'

It can easily be seen how travelling with eleven or twelve 'visibly attracted' females and with Fabia Drake, of whom, alas, he had grown weary (as an aside to Molly Myers reveals), Rik would have been in a state of intense suppressed irritation, released only in writing to his confidential secretary.

On 29 November, about a week after leaving Delhi, when Rik was staying in the famous Lake Palace Hotel at Udaipur he received urgent intelligence from Molly Myers. He had been awarded a CH. If before he had been euphoric over the warmth of his reception in India now he seems to have been a little shaken by this 'wholly unexpected recognition'. As though fearful of losing it, he immediately cabled his grateful acceptance to the Prime Minister, sent confirmation to the Private Office, then wrote two letters to Molly and had them delivered by hand to Delhi airport. He was afraid that his other messages, dispatched from this 'beautiful but benighted spot', might fail to reach Whitehall, and that she would have need of a letter signed 'Mortimer Wheeler' instead of 'Rik' to convince the Prime Minister of his readiness to be a Companion of Honour. There is an impression of an elderly man alone in a strange place getting uncharacteristically fussed.

His own response to the award, as confided to Molly, was reasonable enough. True that he thought fit to refer to it as 'the what-not', but then he went on, 'You know, the C.H. isn't bad – next to the O.M. which I can't imagine their giving to a mere me.' Then a little later he wrote again, 'On thinking it over I really am rather pleased about that C.H. – it's the first time it's happened to an archaeologist.'

The tour was still successful, 'though it's becoming excessively wearisome to its leader. The old dears are keeping up well and cheerfully, even if they do become more and more like a mixture of Walt Disney and the Retreat from Moscow.' The night before leaving Udaipur Rik took the Powells 'to dine with Maharana in the palace on the hill'. He was looking forward eagerly after a week in Bombay to making his escape to Teheran and freedom.

For, indefatigable as ever, on his way home Rik was to spend some days with David Stronach in Iran. There he had real work to do and, in particular, a visit to Siraf, where David Whitehouse had begun his excavation at the ancient port on the Persian Gulf, a site which Rik had long wanted to see explored. Stronach was to meet him at the airport in the early hours, and the journey to the Gulf promised to be rough, but Rik was always thankful to be back with down-to-earth archaeology.

The second ambitious Asian excursion that Wheeler was to lead for Swans, one of their Art Treasure Tours, lasted for four weeks in October and November 1969. He had seen to it that the party should be as unlike that of three years before as possible. When Swans had urged another Indian tour upon him he replied,

My only cause for hesitation is the fact (generalizing on previous experience) that these tours consist mainly of elderly ignoramuses who, however appreciative, contribute nothing from their side.... I am not prepared, therefore, without safeguards which I have not yet thought up, to spend a month or more of my life in their company.

Evidently safeguards had been devised, for Rik told Molly that he had 'not too bad a crowd'. He had also taken more pains than ever to secure a ready welcome by alerting well over a dozen Indian colleagues, including B. B. Lal, who was now Director General of Archaeology, to be prepared for his arrival.

Geographically, this tour was complementary to that of 1966, covering eastern and southern India, with Ceylon. Only round Delhi did the two overlap, for every tourist wanted to see the Taj Mahal and Rik himself reported that it was 'as perfect as ever, night and day'. Once again, following the Ganges route he had travelled with Kim, he was stirred by Benares, with 'its usual lively mixture of gaiety, filth, life and death – the early morning crowds happily washing away their sins whilst auntie burns merrily next door and a few yards away swollen bodies float casually down the river'; and once again he was rescued, though this time from a bad hotel, by his rich friend at Patna, who laid on dinner for them all by the moonlit Ganges.

He was well entertained at Patna University and had been received at the All-India Archaeological Society's first conference with 'really tremendous acclaim. In fact, not to exaggerate it, I am manifestly a god in India....' Later, at Hyderabad, the Nizam invited Rik and his party to great festivities at the Palace. Kenneth Swan and Doreen Goodrick, who were with him on this tour, were quite amazed by what they saw, fully confirming Rik's own assessment of his evident divinity.

Of course, Rik enjoyed it all enormously, but perhaps he got even more pleasure when, before flying to Ceylon, he guided his followers round Arikamedu and could give a dramatic account of how nearly a quarter of a century before, clue by clue, he had tracked the Romans to this spot.

In attempting to follow Rik Wheeler's multifarious life through his sixties and seventies, the years 1954–5 mark something of a turning-point: from that time onwards, through broadcasting and touring, he gave a very considerable portion of his days and his energy to what might be called the public relations side of archaeology – even while the British Academy continued throughout the two decades to be by far the most important and creatively satisfying culmination of his professional career. The broadcasting was a right and previously unimaginably successful development from his life-long belief in the need to popular-ize his subject. The touring, although related to this urge, is perhaps more difficult to justify, though not to understand: it satisfied his restlessness and love of places and of movement, it provided some agreeable and free living, enabled him to enjoy his new celebrity in quite congenial and ever-changing company. There was always a possibility of adventure, and he could sometimes see new sites and excavations and keep in touch with the doings of friends and colleagues. The Indian tours were perhaps sui generis in the adulation they generated – and which at first took him genuinely by surprise.

The Academy on the one hand and these exercises in public relations on the other have seemed sufficiently dominating and coherent to be followed through towards that last phase in Rik's life in the seventies. Meanwhile, of course, his days were crowded with other activities, some continuing, many new, of which an account must be rendered.

When Wheeler had left India, with no very brilliant prospects before him, he had given Cyril Fox his wish to have time for writing as one of the reasons for preferring the part-time professorship. Immediately on his return he plunged into book-writing commitments in a haphazard way, with a variety of publishers, and for several years without the help of an agent.

His first idea, which he had had in mind for a very long time, was for a work on archaeological techniques, intended to make available through the written word all the skills of digging, recording and publishing excavations that he had been imparting through practical demon-stration to so many students over so many years. It was obviously right from his own point of view that he should record his methods, and the book would be a witness to his belief in the paramount importance of student-training in scientific archaeology. As early as 1948 he was in correspondence with Faber and Faber about a work of this kind, but the proposal was presently shifted to the Oxford University Press. When at one point the Press asked him about the progress of the work he replied, 'Strange and outrageous as it may seem, there has been a certain amount of competition from publishers for this book – all very flattering and disturbing.' He remained with the Press, however, and in 1952 they accepted his text, the title being changed to *Archaeology from the Earth* from *Handbook of Field Archaeology*. Just a year later the author was enquiring, with excusable impatience, whether his book was 'alive or dead. . . . These things do not necessarily improve with keeping.'

It came out at last early in 1954 in a modest edition, but, being overtaken by Rik's spring to fame that year, did very well and was to appear in several languages. There had been an earlier work by a young archaeologist on field archaeology, and Kathleen Kenyon had produced one for the beginner, but there had been nothing to approach *Archaeology from the Earth* in authority and scope. Moreover, the Introduction contained his much-quoted dictum that 'the archaeologist is digging up not *things*, but *people*'. Finally, and unexpectedly in this context, Wheeler reveals how far, as a humanist, he has already taken alarm at the prospect of his beloved subject 'passing wholly into the hands of the biologist and the technician' when in truth 'man is in some sense the casket of a soul as well as five-shillings-worth of chemicals'.

During the leisurely proceedings of the Oxford University Press this book had been overtaken by the already-mentioned *Indus Civilization*, which had been started a year later and published a year earlier. *Rome beyond the Imperial Frontiers*, an excellent study, suitably related both to the author's Arikamedu discoveries and to his professorship, had also moved fast to appear in 1954. In dealing with Bell over its publication, Rik showed a new toughness; Penguin Books had made him a better offer for it, so he informed Colonel Bell that, while he felt a moral obligation to allow him to keep the hardback edition, he must insist that Penguin should have the right to publish after a short interval – and this came to pass.

Early in this same *annus mirabilis* of 1954 Rik took the next step towards professional authorship in accepting the services of an agent. The ambitious firm of Curtis Brown saw in a television idol who could write a likely bet, and with the ready help of Glyn Daniel a lunch party was arranged to introduce Rik to Juliet O'Hea of that firm. They had heard, perhaps through Glyn, that he had the material for a book of reminiscences.

In fact, Rik had written to Cyril Fox as long ago as when digging at Mohenjodaro,

In moments of solitude (bless them!) I've been foolish enough to scribble part of an episodic autobiography, of no interest to anyone, but I found myself wondering if by the remotest chance you had any of the letters I wrote to you during the war? Their only merit (?) was that they were written on the spot, and if you *do* happen to have any of them (probably not) I should like, if I may, to have a sight of them when I get back in May. This all sounds very foolish.

On his return he wrote to remind his friend of this request, but then must have let the idea drop from the pressure of events and other literary work. Now, with three books out or in the press, he could contemplate it once more.

Juliet O'Hea remembers going to the lunch reluctantly, for, 'not being a TV addict', she knew nothing of Sir Mortimer Wheeler and thought it unlikely that she would be able to place the memoirs of an archaeologist with a general publisher.

I was in fact determined to be as discouraging as possible, but after about ten minutes conversation with Rik I found myself urging him to finish the book, and was all enthusiasm. I asked him if he had chosen a title and he said it was to be called *Leaves from an Antiquary's Notebook*. Without considering his eminence I snapped back 'That is one title that will *not* be used.' For a moment he looked furious and then, bless him, burst into laughter and said I'd better find a title myself if I felt so strongly.

So Rik acquired an agent for the book which was to be by far his most popular and therefore, with her help, also the most profitable.

In fact, there was very little more work to be done, except for editing, arranging and writing the last little section, 'Twenty Years Asleep'. By this time further letters from Rik to Cyril Fox had been woven into an account of his Indian years, and the 'Pakistan Postscript' added. No attempt was made to cover the early fifties. It was to remain, as it had begun, an episodic autobiography.

Soon Rik was able to write to Juliet O'Hea that he was ready to deliver an ink-spattered version of the manuscript into her hands if she would lunch with him at the Athenaeum. 'What about Thursday April 1st? It seems to be the right sort of day for this kind of thing. . . .' The lunch, delayed by one day, went swimmingly, they were soon on first-name terms and Juliet experienced the sending-back of the wine, twice on this occasion and with the unusual feature that the waitress said at last, 'Sir Mortimer, you must realize that in the ladies dining room we only get the wine the gentlemen won't drink.'

Curtis Brown had a special relationship with the publisher Michael Joseph and Juliet was confident of getting good enough terms from them, through Robert Lusty, and so it proved. At this time the title being used was *Twenty Years Asleep*, but after a lunch at The Ivy with Lusty it emerged as *Still Digging*. Rik had recalled how, on encountering Augustus John in the Mall, the painter had said, 'Hullo, Rikki, still digging?' to which he had retorted, 'Hullo Augustus, still sketching?' So the problem of the title was solved.

Everything went swiftly and smoothly with the production. American and Readers' Union editions were secured, and two extracts printed in *Everybody's* before publication day arrived in January of 1955. This was to be celebrated with a Foyles Literary Luncheon, Rik pretending great nervousness over this to him novel form of 'jamboree'.

Still Digging in its English edition had sold over seventeen thousand copies by the end of the year, and on the greater part of these Juliet had secured a high-rate royalty. When to this is added the other books, various articles and interviews for the popular press, much broadcasting and, until the autumn, his professorship, it is evident that for the first time in his life Rik Wheeler was earning a comfortable income. There is no doubt either that this crop of books, produced during the first half of the fifties, included the best of his writing for the archaeologically interested public. They all came from the matured experience of his first sixty years; they were all books he himself really wanted to write.

There was not much time left for active archaeology, but even now Rik could not abandon it. The Stanwick Report came out in 1954, but the record of the important work on the French hill-forts, though virtually ready, had remained unpublished and must have been something of a burden on Rik's conscience. He judged some further surveying to the north of the main region was needed, and, still in that congested year of 1954, he led a small expedition to the Somme and Pas de Calais. It was as though in the midst of so much worldly success he wanted a reminder of former austerity. He took with him a part of his pre-war team: Kitty Richardson, Cookie – and Kim. The survey went as it should, Cookie being kept particularly busy since they were concentrating on a photographic record. Rik, however, wrecked all possible pleasure for the others by his constant attacks on Kim. It became so bad at last that Kitty threatened to leave unless he restrained himself. Since he was free of the difficulties of Mallord Street and his relationship with young Elizabeth, and since there was no question of Kim resenting work in which she herself was sharing, it was plain that their attempt to restore their marriage was failing hopelessly.

That summer Rik and Kim were obliged to live with most public reminders of his other failure to maintain the married state. Mavis, who had kept the name of Mrs Wheeler, had flitted through many affairs since their divorce and one, with an American airman, Stewart Bryan, whom she loved in her fashion, intermittently over many years. Then in 1953 she met Lord Vivian, at that time a theatrical impresario. She captivated him at once; although, since she was now in her mid-forties, her ravishing loveliness was past, she was still handsome and vital. Soon she was noting in her diary, 'Wonderful din at the Mirabelle. Tony *more* fascinating than I dreamed of.... I'm in LOVE.' The only obstacle to their marriage was, as with Stewart Bryan, a firmly attached wife.

That winter it chanced that Tony Vivian was offered a play that my husband and I had written together: we heard that it was Mavis who liked *The White Countess* and urged her lover to stage it. I saw something of her when the play was opened (unwisely) in Dublin. Although she was still very fond of Vivian, she could not resist the habit of seeking to attract any likely man. Rik attended the London first night at the melancholy Winter Garden Theatre, but behaved with perfect discretion, although Mavis noted that he said to her, 'My dear, what have you done to yourself, you look as radiant as a bride – remarkably so.' To which she added in her diary, 'tum-tiddly-um-pom-pom'.

The play was a flop and everybody lost money, Tony Vivian more than he could afford. Mavis remained with him, always dreaming of marriage. She had never liked the demands theatre made on her lover – although she preferred it to archaeological excavations. They were both drinking quite heavily.

It was in late July that Mavis took Tony down to stay at Potterne, in Pilgrim Cottage, which a legacy from Hornby had enabled her to buy, not far from Porch House, where Rik had found her with Clive Entwistle. For the rest of the day they ate little and consumed a weird mixture of drinks; Mavis lost the key of the cottage door and they used a low window instead. They were on affectionate terms. Then, at about eleven o'clock at night, when Tony came back from the local pub bearing bottles of stout, Mavis shot him in the lower bowels as he was climbing through the window, using a gun left with her by Stewart.

Anyone old enough to read a newspaper at the time will remember the vast outpourings of drivel, the flashy headlines in the popular press. No one ever knew why Mavis fired at her lover, but inevitably she told two stories as to what had happened, as false as they were contradictory. Tony, his life saved by an immediate operation, did his best to make an accident of the event, as in a sense it was, but it would have been useless to support her statements that he shot himself. He stood by her during the trial and her brief imprisonment and for a few months after her much publicized release, but by the spring of 1955 he had slipped out of Mavis's life.

Rik was not directly involved in any of these tragi-comic proceedings, but the press did not fail to draw him into the story as it dragged on, holding the headlines day after day. He was to be more embarrassingly exposed by Mavis herself when, after Tony Vivian had gone, she supplied her ghost writer with a version of her life story for a series of articles in the *Empire News*. She had held out against selling herself in this way before, when she was offered large sums, but now she was miserable and in need of cash. The account of her second marriage began, 'Thousands of women would, I suppose, love to be the wife of Sir Mortimer Wheeler,' which was probably still true enough, but what followed was gushing, absurd and much of it untrue. The ghost was largely responsible, but that was little comfort. Rik could only be thankful that it appeared in a paper his friends would not read.

The last meeting between Rik and Mavis was to be in 1965 at a reunion dinner arranged by Tristan and his wife Diana. These two, with their small children, had been wonderfully good to Mavis as she and her world of friends disintegrated. They would have done more, but, as Tristan wrote, 'she chose to live in loneliness with her dog and whisky and the depression of mounting chaos around her in a damp and crumbling house.' This was the Little House near Sloane Square which she had leased since the war and where she was now known to the neighbourhood as Lady Wheeler, a misnomer she did not correct and may have helped to spread.

Mavis arrived to dine an hour late but strikingly rigged out in tights, a red dressing-gown and over it a floating garment of red nylon. The four had an amiable meal together 'until Mavis became very carefree and flung wide her garments to reveal her still splendid shape. Rik remained master of the situation despite being pursued about the room and in his prompt and cheerful note of thanks he wrote, "I thought Granny was in riotous form."' She died about five years later in the way that could have been foreseen: a fatal mixture of whisky and sleeping pills.

When Rik attended this curious dinner party his own marriage had long died its second death. From its outset he had wanted Kim to maintain her own interests and particularly her continued involvement with archaeology. She had formed a working friendship with Kathleen

Kenyon and for three seasons (1954–6) was with her on her famous excavations at Jericho. Though during that period she had gone with Rik to France and then on his first Swans cruise, the relationship was disintegrating.

The end of this ill-judged attempt at living together was an abrupt one. There is no doubt that Kim took the initiative and turned her husband out of the house together with all his possessions in a way that caused him unaccustomed humiliation. The memory of it always rankled, and although Kim used to visit him occasionally during the next few years, sometimes taking Elizabeth with her, these meetings seem to have been awkward and fruitless.

After Rik's expulsion from Mallord Street in 1956, Molly Myers was in charge of his domestic affairs as well as his official ones. For some time he lived a shifting existence, his first move being to Clark's Mews, Marylebone. Molly had to give much time to house-hunting until at last she found a little house, 27 Whitcomb Street, ideally situated just behind the National Gallery. It had once been a brothel and was still very squalid, but, as we shall see, Molly put it in good order while Rik was digging at Charsada. There, although he always looked too large for the place, particularly when climbing the steep and narrow stairs, he was able to hang his oriental rugs, set out his Persian plates, and be as much at home as he wanted to be.

When the moment came for Wheeler to cease to profess the Archaeology of the Roman Provinces even part-time he had little to regret. It would, of course, be his last regularly paid job in professional archaeology, but, with valuable and challenging work to be done at the Academy and money coming in as never before for activities that busied and amused him, he could welcome the prospect of greater freedom and a precious saving of time. There was, however, another matter to do with the Institute of Archaeology that greatly troubled him: even as his own retirement was celebrated with a praiseful dinner, he was in the heat of battle over the appointment of the next Director. Modern premises, what Max Mallowan disparagingly called 'the new box in Gordon Square', were being built for the Institute at a cost of half a million pounds. To make the transition from St John's Lodge easier, Gordon Childe had decided to retire the next year, a little in advance of the appointed time, so that a new man could take over before the move was made in 1957.

Early in 1955 Rik had written to Stuart Piggott, asking him to consider the post, 'I should like to see at the Institute a man with the broad vision and the imagination that distinguishes your work, and there is none other than yourself.' Stuart, happily established in Edinburgh, declined the invitation as firmly as he had declined the Indian appointment, though he agreed with Rik that there was a likelihood that 'an industrious mole' would be appointed, while an 'eagle' was evidently needed.

In the summer a directorship sub-committee was set up, with Wheeler among the archaeological members and Professor Wooldridge, a sound and solid administrator whom Rik regarded as an honest but wooden-headed Yes-man of the university authorities, in the chair. By this time, after his disappointment over Stuart, Rik had no candidate he greatly wanted, but there was one he did not want at all. This was W. F. Grimes, once a pupil of Rik's, who had been Director of the London Museum since the war and whose name was now being advanced by Professor Wooldridge and others among the majority on the sub-committee who were not archaeologists.

It soon appeared that there was to be a deep split of opinion between the administrators and those who would put scholarly and academic values first. Rik had always relied on Cyril Fox's support at the Institute and now he sent him a long briefing letter on the directorship. 'The normal emphasis of the University on administration has, in the case of the Institute, been exaggerated by Gordon Childe's astonishing incapacity in this matter.' Childe's vacillation and general incompetence had, Rik felt, antagonized the Principal of the University, enabling him 'to weigh in heavily on the need for administrative ability. In other words, we have to deal with reaction from Gordon Childe muddle towards Gordon Square reform.' Rik went on to set out all the reasons why he felt Grimes should not be appointed. There is no doubt he was prejudiced against a man of a very different type from himself, but it was true that, following Gordon, he would appear undistinguished, that he was little known in the academic world at home or abroad and was perhaps lacking in imagination. Rik also condemned him for his tardiness in publication. 'He must have more than twelve years of excavation somewhere in his cupboard. What a shocking example to the young idea!'

In this letter Rik went on to turn down other possible candidates, including Christopher Hawkes, for his 'prolixity and tangentialism', and to prefer, though reluctantly, Dr Donald Harden, another museum man but one who had good connections with both Oxford and Cambridge.

The decisive meeting of the directorship sub-committee was to be held in early October. Rik had arranged luncheons and interviews for Wooldridge in the hope of winning him over, but then, not long before the meeting, wrote to him at length, regretting the 'unhappy dichotomy, with what I may call the University on the one side and the professional archaeological members of the Committee on the other' and seeking to heal it with a new suggestion. He put forward Glyn Daniel as a man who could satisfy both sides. For the first time he mentioned with approval Glyn's promotion to Group-Captain in 'the non-flying branch of the R.A.F.' as a proof of his ability to get on with everybody and to organize; 'he is indeed outstanding as an administrator and most unusually easy to work with'. At the same time he was 'a thoroughly sound archaeologist ... and a born teacher'. Even his 'judicious use of broadcasting and writing to popularize his subject could be of some value in a Director'. Finally Glyn Daniel was recommended as being 'exceedingly active, lively, and personable'.

It was all of no avail. When the sub-committee met the division between the two sides was deeper and more bitter than before; a vote was taken and the university party won. The next day the chairman sent Rik a very tough letter in which he said that if criticism of his conduct of the meeting was supported by the management committee he would have to resign. He had no doubt that Grimes was the best man for the job and that he would be able to work with him 'for the integration of the Institute with the University as a whole'.

Rik had to climb down over the resignation threat, and the man who had been 'wooden-headed' was now assured he was 'a main pillar of the Institute', but he still told Wooldridge that his 'exercise of the privileges of the chair was a little embarrassing' and urged him to reconsider the verdict and to select Harden or Daniel since 'to flout the considered opinion of the archaeological profession ... is academically a mistake of the first order'.

For once Rik was charging a stone wall. Grimes was appointed Director in 1956 and held that office for seventeen years, archaeological opinion being somewhat mollified by the foundation of a new chair in prehistory at the Institute. There is no doubt that Rik was mortified by his defeat. He could not fail to have proprietorial feelings for his foundation; perhaps few of those involved in the contest knew quite how much his creative dream of an Institute of Archaeology had meant to him, how much he had risked, and how hard he had fought for it. The actual Institute was to grow and prosper, but it may be that the long tenure of Grimes had something to do with its becoming more a centre of archaeological technology and expertise than of learning and humanistic research. But then, after all, there had been no eagle anywhere on the wing.

His failure to get Glyn Daniel the directorship was a part of Wheeler's general humiliation over this affair, but before long he was able to persuade him to take on another task of considerable importance in British archaeology. Late in 1957 O. G. S. Crawford died suddenly, in the thirtieth year of his editorship of *Antiquity*, the quarterly that had brought amateurs and professionals of the subject together. Just before writing his editorial for the December issue, he had heard of the death of Gordon Childe in Australia (a death that a few people at home already knew to have been suicide) and wrote that he would be 'mourned by archaeologists all over the world'. Rik was saddened by the death of two of his generation, both extraordinary men, but most deeply by Crawford's, since he was one of his true intimates, an independent man after his own heart.

He was among those determined that Crawford's creation should not die with him, and recognized at once that Glyn would be the best possible occupant of the editorial chair. Glyn recalls how 'Rik insisted that I should succeed as editor, would hear of no other name, and would not allow me to decline. I agreed only if he and a few others were advisory editors.' It was a private concern, so that action could be swift: already by mid-December Glyn had formally accepted the editorship, having come to an agreement with H. W. Edwards, the publisher and, since Crawford's death, the owner of the magazine. That Christmas Rik spent with Glyn and Ruth Daniel at Cambridge, and it seems to have been there, in the midst of much good eating and drinking, that he wrote 'Crawford and *Antiquity*', a memorial to his friend which was to appear in the March number. To my surprise and pleasure, he declared that a piece I had written for *Antiquity*'s silver jubilee remained 'Crawford's finest epitaph'.

Glyn made good use of the strong panel of advisory editors; to Rik he wrote almost weekly during the early years for his advice or opinions. The magazine went on at least as well as before until 1960, when Edwards made it known that he wanted to sell *Antiquity*. At first the problem was handled in a leisurely style, with thoughts of finding another publisher, perhaps Robert Lusty, but by November the editor and his advisers were already beginning to prefer the idea of setting up a non-profit-making Trust when Edwards, who had been becoming increasingly difficult to deal with, suddenly announced that he intended to withdraw immediately and not to publish another number after the

December issue. For a short time there was consternation and some fear that *Antiquity* might succumb, but, with so much energy and enthusiasm available, a drive for funds was quickly organized, archaeologists being expected to subscribe according to our means or generosity. Gifts flowed in and the few thousand pounds needed to buy out Mr Edwards was soon in hand: the list of donors was so comprehensive that it proved the coherence of the British archaeological world. There were a few dissidents: as Glyn told Rik, Ralegh Radford disapproved of a Trust and of advisory editors and would not give a penny, while Christopher Hawkes took many pages to tell Glyn that he disapproved of his running of *Antiquity*, that more executive editors were needed to get him on the right lines – and that he would not give a penny.

Antiquity was saved and has thrived ever since in the capable hands of Glyn and Ruth Daniel. There was, however, an explosive row between Glyn and Rik that led to the omission of the name of Sir Mortimer Wheeler from the list of advisers in two numbers of the magazine. Rik had wanted to pre-empt a particular book for review, and Glyn, perhaps always a little touchy when Rik's dominance was concerned, saw this as an infringement of editorial propriety and refused him. The resulting row was a hot one, and Rik seems to have been astonished at the editor's temerity in striking him off. When humour was able to win over temper he wrote a letter asking for the hatchet to be buried – and his name reappeared on the cover. He was in fact always appreciative of the Daniels' work and, as Glyn himself says, 'unswerving in his devotion to the journal, unstinting in his help. . . .' One of his last appearances in London was to be at a Trustees' meeting.

There was yet another of Glyn's successful enterprises that further involved him with Rik during the second half of the fifties. This was his editorship of the excellent 'Ancient Peoples and Places' series, launched with Thames and Hudson in 1956 and still sailing on today. He often consulted Rik on authors and subjects, and had little difficulty in persuading him to contribute a volume which appeared as *Early India and Pakistan* before the end of the decade.

The editor sent this book to B. B. Lal to review for *Antiquity*, and the upshot was to be of lasting interest. He began by praising the writing, form and up-to-dateness, but went on to say how difficult it was for any Indian archaeologist to find fault with Sir Mortimer, since he was bound to owe so much to him.

The present reviewer, one of the direct associates of Wheeler-in-India, has, however, ventured to overcome this handicap and the Indian's traditional reverence of his *guru* when he records the following criticism, which, he is confident, will be taken by the ever-magnanimous Sir Mortimer in the spirit in which it is meant. One of the points of criticism relates to Sir Mortimer's tendency to rush to conclusions, or throw out suggestions of far-reaching consequence, although in reality there may not exist any basis for them.

This was swingeing criticism indeed, and perhaps not fully justified, since, in the examples given, Lal did not allow for the permissibility of a hypothesis providing the evidence, or lack of it, is made clear. All is to be forgiven in the sequel. In his reminiscences of his *guru* Lal tells the story as a proof of 'the greatness of the man' in his magnanimity, for Rik had written to him at once, 'I am glad that I have lived long enough to see my student reviewing my work.' Moreover, he found that 'Sir Mortimer's affection for me did not decrease in any way on account of this dreadful review. If anything, it increased.'

Of all Wheeler's purely archaeological activities during this same period by far the most significant was his great test excavation at Charsada in 1958. It was the last ambitious dig he was to direct and one which he was eager to undertake and which brought him great satisfaction in its completion.

In spite of this, it was an enterprise that might never have come to pass if Wheeler had not been disappointed over another scheme that had been still dearer to him. Even before he went to Balkh (Bactria) with Daniel Schlumberger during his mission to Afghanistan he had longed to see it explored, and after stumping about its ruins the dream had intensified. Then in 1956 he had won from Nehru a promise of Indian participation in any excavations at the Mother of Cities and he had further corresponded with Ghosh and Schlumberger about the possibilities of collaboration in a joint British, Indian and French expedition – the British side to be represented by the Academy.

This exhilarating prospect faded before a total rejection of the scheme by the Afghan government. Instead, Rik was invited through the Pakistan Ministry of Education and its subsidiary the Department of Archaeology to revive the plan for an excavation at Charsada, which had been frustrated by Partition. Their thinking was stoutly nationalistic: the work was to be done in the name of the Department of Archaeology and to be funded by the government, and all finds were to remain in Pakistan. Its Adviser in Archaeology, Raoul Curiel, was to represent the government on the dig, an arrangement that caused no pain as Rik pronounced him 'a sweetie'. The Director of Archaeology, F. A. Khan, with whom Rik was to have discordant relations, looked after all practical arrangements, and there was a muster of Pakistani students, many of excellent quality but little experience.

Rik had only two experienced assistants, both of them Cambridge men. One was David Stronach, whom he had only recently met through helping him to secure an American appointment in China and then impulsively invited to Charsada. He came, it will be remembered, by way of Teheran, bringing the fateful message from the Embassy. The other was Roy Hodson, of the Geophysics Department, whom Rik condemned as suburban because of his longing for fish and chips and dolly ices. He had also been able to enrol his 'old friend and foreman of other days', Sadar Din Khan. Stronach was to be greatly impressed by what he recognized as the wonderful relationship between these two, Rik understanding Khan and his great dignity and receiving in response the foreman's 'unashamed loyalty and devotion'.

The expedition gathered together at the site towards the end of October (Rik, it may be recalled, having returned from Southern Rhodesia only the previous month). The little town of Charsada lies in the wide, level expanse of the Peshawar plain and not far from that city. The mountains of the Hindu Kush rise to the north and west, and at that season tribesmen, with their camels and other beasts, were passing by on the way to their winter pastures. Nearby are the mounds, a vast extent of them, dominated by the Bala Hisar (High Fort), only sixty feet high yet seemingly a mountain in the flat landscape, that are the ruins of Pushkalavati, ancient capital of Gandhara. This 'City of Lotuses', like Taxila to the south-east, was on the old trade route from inner Asia into the Indian subcontinent. Not very much was known of its history, except that it took Alexander the Great's troops a month to capture, and that, according to the Ramayana epic, it was founded at the same time as Taxila. John Marshall's soundings had been ineffectual: everything remained for the expedition to discover.

The three Englishmen were comfortably lodged in a rest house on top of a stupa – an exalted perch. At the centre was what David Stronach called 'a sort of English villa', Rik 'a fortified bungalow', which was kept spick and span. Every day save on their free Fridays they rose at 6 am and drove the four miles up to the Bala Hisar, to arrive on the dig by 7.15. The drive, in an old Jeep without doors, was bitterly, and increasingly, cold, but while the young men wrapped themselves up, Rik refused to put anything over his regulation khaki shirt, 'long shorts' and long stockings. His companions believed he kept his teeth clamped on his pipe to stop them chattering. (When not smoking he often tucked the pipe into a stocking top.)

On arrival at the tented excavation camp, always kept in immaculate order, with white-painted stones and other military touches, everyone stood together while the flag was run up. This ceremony, and all the spit and polish, were very much to the satisfaction of the chief guard, whom Rik respected and wished to humour. Work went on, with a break for a meal of the very hot curries that Rik relished, until 4 pm, when all lined up once more for the lowering of the flag. When the Englishmen went back to the bungalow there were baths, tea laced with whisky and a dinner that might offer another curry or perhaps a pilau. The nights were cold and the three might sit snugly by the fire. Evening meetings, when site reports were made and the day's work was discussed, were intended to keep the diggers in touch with the Director and his ideas. Sometimes, too, there were lectures for the student trainees, which Rik found very tedious. On one occasion there was a very special intellectual exercise. Daniel Schlumberger came on a visit to Charsada and he and Rik staged a grand debate on a subject of long-standing disagreement between them. As soon as he was introduced to Indian history Rik had become fascinated by western influences on India in classical times. He had made a particular study of Gandhara sculpture, and was convinced that the western element so conspicuously present was Roman. His opponent, with his long experience of this art, was equally convinced that the influence was Hellenistic. The two battled it out before an enthralled audience of students – who felt they had been admitted to the archaeological kitchen. (When in later days Schlumberger was proved right Rik handsomely admitted his defeat.)

For their Fridays off Rik kept to his usual custom of leading or sending his staff to see the local sights. One day he drove them through the Malaband Pass to the Kingdom of Swat, where an Italian expedition, led by Tucci, was digging. They paid their respects to the King (or Wali) and were royally entertained by the Italians. On seeing an hotel set among trees by a trout stream, Rik remarked, 'Just the place for my next honeymoon.'

The routine was, in fact, quite exacting, but not strenuous by the Director's standards, especially since there was no heat to contend with. In the series of letters that he wrote to Molly Myers he reported his increasing fitness and muscle – until towards the end, when his face swelled up with a dental abscess. In these same letters he reported briefly on the progress of the dig with a tameness of language he might not have shown to Cyril Fox or Stuart Piggott. Until the end of the third week the results were 'unexciting'; thereafter he was getting 'the main story' he wanted but they were still undramatic.

Yet, if there were no unexpected discoveries the nature of the digging itself was highly dramatic. This was essentially a test excavation, Rik knowing that in the seven weeks allowed he could not hope to do more than establish the chronology of the Bala Hisar. For this purpose he determined to cut a wide trench in deep steps down the precipitous east face of the mound, expanding it for a distance beyond the foot and to a depth that would reach the natural ground surface. This was a colossal and difficult, though not intricate, operation, the trench being thirty feet wide at the top and descending in eight-foot steps for a total drop of over sixty feet. This, with another trench in a little valley further to the east of the cliff face, was enough to show that the Bala Hisar was not an artificial citadel, like those in the Indus capitals, but the ordinary mud-brick accumulations of a city that had stood beside a small tributary of the Swat, until the stream had silted up quite late in the history of Pushkalavati.

The foundation proved to be an Achaemenid one, of the sixth century or a little earlier. This was perhaps something of a disappointment to Rik, who could have hoped for greater antiquity. The stratification revealed by the great stepped trench proved the city to have flourished for some five hundred years, after which it was impoverished. Early in the dig the whole mounded area was photographed by the Pakistani Air Force, 'which combed our hair with a jet fighter', as Rik put it. The pictures were unexpectedly significant, showing that one of the lower mounds represented a town with a regular grid street plan, suggesting that the main centre of Pushkalavati had been rebuilt on a fresh site by its Parthian rulers in about the second century BC.

So Rik had his chronological framework, but his keenest personal interest was in the Alexandrine siege of 327 BC – if the place had held out for a month it must surely have been fortified? Logic suggested that the defences would have run to the west of the river, and an extension of the main trench struck a considerable ditch in the expected place and, with luck as usual enhancing Rik's tactical skill, the site of a postern gate and bridge. The ditch was followed round the western fringe of the Bala Hisar and by inference shown to have been dug and then filled with its own rampart material at a date appropriate to the siege. The hoped-for story was complete.

Rik's last major dig was in every way a happy and satisfactory one. The students, whom he found 'a pleasant gang', benefited greatly from the field training and teaching; many of them were to win the command-ing heights of Pakistan archaeology. As for his lieutenants, in the first weeks he referred coolly to the 'two Cantabs'; they were 'settling down' and 'better than nothing'. But his regard and affection for David Stronach mounted, and by the last day (21 December) he told Molly, 'Stronach has been magnificent.' David, on his side, having never dug with Rik before, was astonished by the extent to which he delegated responsibility. He was put in charge of the mechanics of the cut down the mound and left to make his own mistakes, with only light supervision. One day, when he and his men had cut through a large wall without spotting it, Rik, on inspection, merely commented, 'A fine wall in its prime – that was!' On an occasion when the Director wanted him to take on another site on the mound and David dared to tell him he had not time for it Rik stumped off, barking over his shoulder, 'I'll do the damned thing myself.' They did the work together. Poor Hodson, meanwhile, who quite failed to please, was left to supervise the profoundly uninteresting cutting in the old river-bed.

Towards the end of the excavation the pressure, as usual, mounted and Rik declared that he was doing the work of three; it closed horribly in a 'cold torrential downpour and buckets of mud'. He spent Christmas in Lahore Fort, drawing and photographing the finds, a necessary chore since all had to be left behind. When, some eighteen months later, Rik was getting text and illustrations ready for publication he had a postal clash with F. A. Khan. He wrote him a very stiff letter, pointing out his failings and particularly his failures to publish. This was the real quarrel between them, for Rik, dreading low standards and endless delays in Pakistan, was determined to publish the Charsada Report in England, while Khan insisted that it must come from his department – as he said in his peppery but ludicrous reply. Rik, of course, had his way, the volume being published by the Oxford University Press 'for the Government of Pakistan and the British Academy'. This was not the last time they were to be on bad terms. Khan was certainly difficult and sometimes incompetent, but probably suffered from the nervousness of the small-minded and found Wheeler overbearing.

Through all the weeks of his absence Molly had been negotiating for the lease of Whitcomb Street and in almost every letter to her Rik enquired eagerly as to her progress, about yellow curtains from Liberty and coffee cups – he even bought some Afridi shawls for his bedroom curtains. In this rare access of domesticity he anticipated the fun it would be to get the house in order during his 'rare intervals in England'.

This was perhaps jokingly written, but not far from the truth. He escaped from Lahore Fort at the New Year, but within a month was cruising with Swans and by mid-February was in the heat of Ceylon for the start of his British Council lecture tour. Although his schedule seemed to leave him no time for eating or sleeping, and sweat oozed into the corners of his mouth as he lectured, he now knew he could count on the warmth of his reception by his old Indian associates, great and small, and his own feelings for them became less ambivalent. From Madras he wrote with satisfaction that there he was plain Dr Wheeler and no one had heard of television, 'but the doors are wide open to me and I'm smothered in flowers. . . . They're my people. . . .'

Near Hyderabad his old department was doing a rescue dig, and during a party given to him after dusk in a jungle clearing a senior made an oration: 'When you first came to us fifteen years ago, we thought for the first three days you were rough man, like soldier, but after three days we knew you had gold heart, and we belong to you and want you always with us.' It was all irresistible: Rik added, 'I had and still have a funny feeling inside. They're dears.'

He had to deliver special lectures at Baroda – and meanwhile to find time to prepare his last Anniversary Address to the Society of Antiquaries, due to be delivered soon after his return. Then in Delhi he had his spell among the elite, visiting the Vice-President, Radhakrishnan, whom he found very merry and 'more like Bertie Russell than ever', lunching with Malcolm MacDonald in the company of Julian and Juliette Huxley and lecturing with the Minister of Culture as his chairman. For the last week he sought rest in the wilds, disappearing on an archaeological mission.

By the time he was back in London Molly Myers had Whitcomb Street ready for him, the furnishing completed and his possessions moved from the flat. Even now, however, its enjoyment was to be a matter of 'intervals' since this was the year of his second journey to East Africa and his long pursuit of the 'Grandeur that was Rome'. Indeed, in his farewell address as President of the Antiquaries he apologized for his many absences from the Chair, but took the opportunity to speak mainly in praise of British archaeologists overseas, to announce the endowment of the East African Institute and to assure the assembled Fellows that his own persistence and Lord Nathan's legal acumen had defeated the sharks of the Inland Revenue, who had tried to rob the Society of its charitable status and so of its tax rebates. 'No President in his last moments could wish for the gift of a more congenial valediction.'

His very last moment, however, did not bring him inner satisfaction. He had to welcome as his successor Dr Joan Evans, the forty-year-younger half-sister of Sir Arthur, of Cretan fame. (Never were even half-brother and half-sister more unlike: the little, lizard-like gentleman, the large, stout, florid lady.) He had, in fact, opposed her presidency, wanting his friend Ian Richmond, the Romanist, to succeed him. Joan Evans was one of those against whom Rik cherished a prejudice, thinking that things had come too easily for her and that her work was careless. The rumour can be believed that he plotted a little to delay her damehood.

In spite of all his travelling at this period, Wheeler contrived to keep his many other commitments going – both private and public. He found less time for writing, it is true, but he had the Charsada Report on his hands and he was one of a galaxy of archaeologists invited to contribute to one of the grandest, most expensive projects ever undertaken by Thames and Hudson. This was a volume, edited by Stuart Piggott, to appear at last under the title of *The Dawn of Civilization*, lavishly illustrated with an apparatus of maps, tables and diagrams for the specialist and reconstruction scenes in colour for popular appeal. Rik was to describe it as very 'splendacious'. It was in this most hectic year of 1959 that he submitted his section, 'Ancient India', and was thanked by Stuart 'for making the editor's job so easy as to be virtually non-existent'.

The galleon was to sail into rougher water when an attempt was made further to popularize the book to please its American publishers. Rik commanded, 'Hands off my script' and he and Max Mallowan issued a declaration that they would work only with Stuart. In the end *The Dawn of Civilization* proved a great and deserved success.

Increasingly in these later years Wheeler gave more of his energies to public good works. Since its reconstruction, he had interested himself in the responsibilities of the Ancient Monuments Board, from the best way to conserve Hadrian's Wall to the provision of tea-rooms and car parks at Stonehenge. He must have been something of a trial to the Chief Inspector, to whom he addressed explosive criticisms. For instance, 'Your masons are making a perfectly ghastly mess of the south front of Colchester Castle. . . . I must ask you to stop *immediately*. . . . It's a perfectly bloody scandal, and you will shiver as I do when you see it.' Or again, 'Today I was at St. Albans and saw two of your workmen on the South corner. I was frankly horrified . . . the episode was completely shattering alike to the wall and myself.'

After ten years of constructive as well as critical service he was made Chairman of the Board and among other useful initiatives sought to improve its laboratory to meet the need for more technical services. Soon, however, he informed the Minister of his wish to retire, and, though urged to stay on, insisted, 'I have seen far too many old men overstay their welcome, and I should prefer not to risk being an addition to their number.'

Wheeler had been very much concerned with the theory and practice of museology ever since he was an outwardly humble Keeper at Cardiff, and his interest had not slackened. There is a certain melancholy repetitiveness in the museum affairs of the United Kingdom, cycles of high hopes, effort and disappointment. There has been progress, of course, but a halting one, bedevilled by a chronic lack of funds and, in the provinces, lack of bureaucratic standing and esteem. The efforts on behalf of what would now be called 'our heritage', in which Rik partici-pated in the fifties and sixties, had a dispiriting similarity with those of his London Museum days.

He had been made chairman of a committee for government assist-ance to museums which involved much liaison work with other cultural institutions, most obviously with the long-established but somewhat debilitated Museums Association. In 1956, when he addressed the Association at Bristol on 'The Plight of Our Museums', his name won publicity for his impassioned plea for more government expenditure on these Cinderellas of our cultural life. He also gave strong support to a scheme, then finding favour in the Association, for the setting-up of Regional Museums Boards to reduce over-centralization in London. A pilot project was to be started in the south-west and Rik did his best to arouse the sympathy of the county authorities concerned and to extract money for additional staff from his friends of the Pilgrim Trust.

In 1959, during one of those 'rare intervals' when he was at home, Wheeler brought that part of his work for museums that he most cared about to a head. He led a deputation to the Chancellor to discuss finances. It cannot be said that having reached the Chancellor's ear led to an immediate opening of his purse, but at least it made a shocking state of affairs more clearly known and perhaps helped Richard Griffiths to advance his new division at the Treasury.

This was all very decorous and correct, but the following year Rik let fly in a manner calculated to bring satisfaction to himself and many colleagues, and to elicit great huffing and indignation from the more complacent or cautious. His outburst concerned not all museums, but that national monument, the British Museum, Bloomsbury.

There had been widespread indignation that so long after the war the damage caused by the five bombs that hit the museum had still not been made good, and this affected particularly the department most con-cerned with prehistoric and Romano-British archaeology – though the whole place was shabby and overcrowded. The unimpressive plans for reconstruction announced the year before had been criticized, notably in a letter to *The Times* from Christopher Hawkes. Now (in October 1960) Sir Mortimer Wheeler, addressing an assembly celebrating the centenary of the Colchester Museum, described Bloomsbury as 'a mountainous corpse' and 'the worst of the world's great Museums'. The immediate furore was enough to make the BBC stage a confrontation between his attacker and Sir Frank Francis, Director of the British Museum, whom Rik considered to be a sensible chap who knew nothing whatever about museums. The Director, slightly shaken on being introduced as Sir Frank Fraser, made a reasonable but nerveless defence. He did venture to say that 'Sir Mortimer as a very practised public man probably recognized that striking phrases very often get further than more sober remarks.'

There followed an interview with the *Observer*; then, when, as he said, the 'mild disturbance' had died down Rik sent a letter to *The Times*, specifying his criticisms of dilatoriness in rebuilding, lack of gallery and storage space and, above all, a staff inadequate not only in numbers but in museum skills. He urged that recruits should be sent abroad to learn the business, then 'leave their ivory towers and take their coats off'. This was a point which he felt strongly about: we had agreed it was shocking that British Museum cases were left dusty and with curling, hand-scribbled labels, when a day's hard work could have set them right.

The letter in *The Times* led to a correspondence with Christopher Hawkes showing unusual friendliness and mutual regard, Rik seizing the opportunity to express himself very unkindly about some of those young denizens of ivory towers.

Whether sincere or not, Sir Frank's words about 'striking phrases' were true in relation to the British way of public life at that time, yet the explosive speech at Colchester seemed to signal the beginning of a slight change in Rik's deportment that came with advancing years. After his death Kathleen Kenyon wrote that as a result of his television celebrity 'an element of domineering developed'. I do not think this is true; he had always been inclined to domineer, and, if anything, became mellower in his human relationships in later life. But it could be observed that he grew more inclined to allow himself unrestrained outbursts in words and deeds. This tendency, and it was no more than that, may have been partly due to the inclination of the old, their careers behind them, not to give a damn about the Establishment proprieties, and still more to a fight with age itself, a determination that he would not 'go gentle into that good night'.

It was in the year of the British Museum ructions that Rik accepted another public good work which came to engage his interest and feelings. Sir David Eccles, as Minister of Education, was looking for someone to represent the United Kingdom in the international campaign being organized by UNESCO for the rescue of Nubian antiquities. The building of the High Dam at Aswan and the flooding of hundreds of miles of the Nile Valley in Egypt and the Sudan demanded advance surveying, excavation and the removal or protection of riverside temples. Wheeler, though no Egyptologist, was the obvious choice for a job that demanded mainly energy, reputation and an understanding of the problems. He agreed to be chairman of the British national committee and to represent it on the leading UNESCO body, the International Action Committee, while the Duke of Devonshire was to be its President and to sit on the International Committee of Honour under the King of Sweden. All was administratively *comme il faut*.

The British Committee (it included Sir Frank Francis) began its work with Professor Emery, the Egyptologist, as its 'principal archaeological executive' and working closely with the Egypt Exploration Society, which by now received a Treasury grant through the Academy and could be seen as a substitute for a British School in Egypt. Plans were drawn up and concessions obtained for an excavation at the Sudanese site of Buhen, for another at Qasr Ibrim in Egypt and for a ground survey, also within Egyptian Nubia, all to be under the general supervision of Professor Emery.

During the summer Wheeler met Dr Veronese, Director General of UNESCO, in London, attended a meeting of the Action Committee in Paris and was then ready for the inevitable battle to extract the necessary grants from the Treasury. It had from the first been government policy, in the political conditions of the time, not to fund the UNESCO campaign, but in drafting a letter for the Duke of Devonshire to send to Sir Edward Boyle, then Financial Secretary, Rik used arguments of national self-interest if the United Kingdom participated, national shame if it did not. The United States was voting very large sums; France, Germany and many other countries were contributing; 'We alone have so far refrained from direct contribution.' If this continued British Egyptology would suffer, especially since rewards in the shape of antiquities were being promised to generous participants. The Egypt Exploration Society would use its existing grant of £4500; all that was needed was to make this up to £15,000 for two years.

In the New Year the Duke, Professor Emery and Sir Mortimer Wheeler went to Sir Edward Boyle's room in the Treasury to plead their case in person. (This was the meeting at which Rik was able to make a quick pass at Sir Edward and get the money for his Persian Institute.) There was stiff argument, but the deputation left with the confirmation of a grant of £20,000, to be disbursed through the Academy.

Soon afterwards Rik joined his first Swans cruise on the Nile, for once going not as lecturer but to see something of UNESCO's own project in Egypt, dominated, to the great profit of France, by the formidable Madame Desroches Noblecourt, and to visit Emery's site at Buhen. There the British expedition was to uncover the Middle Kingdom fortress, conserve and move Queen Hapshetsut's temple and reveal a totally unexpected Old Kingdom town.

The British effort was, indeed, as Rik was to claim, among the most significant of all the purely archaeological research and rescue work in Nubia, but bitter disappointment came with the special appeal for the Abu Simbel temples. These uniquely sculptured monuments to Rameses II and his queen, cut deep into the sandstone cliffs beside the Nile, were by far the most famous of the threatened sites. As soon as the experts had determined that the best means of salvaging the temples was to excise them from the living rock and raise them to the cliff top Rik committed himself to a struggle to secure the twenty million pounds it was estimated this extraordinary project would cost. He had meanwhile been appointed to the new UNESCO Executive to spearhead the campaign.

His first step was an article in *The Times*. It was headed 'The Battle to Save Abu Simbel' – and he did want the temples to be saved, but for him it was far more a battle to win a sufficient British subscription to the fund. He declared that failure would be 'a defeat of the human spirit' and that Britain must have no part in such a failure. He ended that although the Treasury had already given some support, 'on the international plane today the crucial test is Abu Simbel.'

This was in June of 1961; soon he had prepared an eloquent memorandum for the Arts and Amenities Committee of the House of Commons, then staged a very successful Abu Simbel film show for Members. He attended meetings in London and Paris, he gave public lectures in London and the provinces. Government opposition, however, was firm, one of the political obstacles being the blocking of British assets in Egypt. He began to think of means by which the national gift could be made in kind: a British firm was one of the few capable of designing jacks to lift weights totalling 300,000 tons.

By the autumn Rik was beginning to despair, but then, after a meeting of the UNESCO Executive when the deadline for starting the work was postponed, he tried again, writing to Sir David Eccles, who had, after all, put the task on his shoulders. He told the Minister of the postponement and of the gifts being made by other and lesser countries, ending, 'Abu Simbel is *unique*, and on all grounds, including national prestige, I hope the U.K. will not stand down.'

Nearly a year later Wheeler had to report to Paris, 'In regard to the Abu Simbel business things are still not, I'm afraid, satisfactory,' but that the British committee was hammering away, while he himself was lecturing and making other propaganda to arouse public opinion. Then, in December of 1962, at the UNESCO Conference the 'assembled nations', including the United States, turned down a scheme for a loan to meet the initial cost of the salvage work, and it appeared that the temples really might be lost. Rik was moved to write one of his most indignant letters to *The Times*: '... the action of the British Delegation in helping to defeat the proposal is both deplorable now and will be increasingly deplored by future generations.' He could get some personal comfort from the fact that the Treasury agreed to find further funds for Emery's successful undertakings.

A few months later he went to UNESCO for a personal consultation with the admirable René Maheu, now Director General, and was able to report back to the Ministry that, urged on by John Kennedy himself, the United States might after all be generous, while a less expensive way of moving the temples was being sought. 'I and my colleagues remain bitterly ashamed of the British Government's negative action in the whole business....' By the summer, when the British committee met again, the Americans had indeed repented, while Swedish engineers had devised a scheme by which the Abu Simbel temples could be sawn into blocks, hoisted and reassembled on higher ground. A little more money was still needed, and the Chairman gave it as his opinion that 'A contribution of half a million pounds was necessary for the United Kingdom to maintain her position.'

Another appointment with the Minister was sought, but all to no purpose – the United Kingdom was niggardly to the end and could take no pride in the successful rescue which all the world was to applaud.

Rik's very last act in the long story was in 1966, when he wrote a sad letter to Maheu, pointing out that Britain had, after all, done excellent work in Nubia and asking to receive some small share in the distribution of rewards, in particular 'a good portrait head of Akhenaten' that was rumoured to be available. In this Rik showed himself to be sadly out of touch: the head was not available and, in fact, Britain was to receive an appropriately modest prize. I can witness how very strongly Rik felt over the Abu Simbel defeat: he had so far identified himself with the cause, and the cause with the national honour, that it hit him hard – and he was, of course, personally mortified.

Another undertaking at this time – undoubtedly welcome to Rik, since it took him to a part of Africa hitherto quite unknown to him – was a lecture tour for the British Council. For three weeks in January and February of 1962 he did a round of all three provinces of Nigeria, with a programme of lecturing in universities and Council centres, broadcasting, parties and visiting local dignitaries. (Among the last-mentioned he must have allowed himself at least a private grin when he learnt he was to go to Owe to be received by Sir Olateju Olagbegi II, Olowo of Owe.)

He was also able to make archaeological excursions, escorted, among others, by Frank Willett, who showed him not only much Ifé and Benin sculpture, but also the places from which it had come, and by Bernard Fagg, with whom he particularly enjoyed a visit to Jos, headquarters of the Antiquities Service and where the first of several good museums had been opened just ten years before. Nigeria was, indeed, something of an antidote to Rik's often-expressed sense of shame that British colonial rule in Africa had neglected cultural affairs in general and history and archaeology in particular.

On this tour Rik gave versions of two basic lectures, 'Archaeology in a Modern Society', discussing the place of scientific aids in archaeology, and 'The Importance of Nigeria in History'. Neither was of more than adequate distinction, but it is interesting to find that in the second lecture he discussed problems of diffusion versus independent invention. He was inclined to favour the view that, while novel forms of agriculture had undoubtedly been *developed* in West Africa, it was not, as had been claimed, an altogether independent centre, but had been sparked off by the *idea* of cultivation spreading from Asia. This was close to his controversial conviction that the Indus peoples absorbed the *idea* of urban civilization through contacts with Mesopotamia.

Apart from the many public affairs with which Rik busied himself by choice or necessity during the first half of the sixties, in his personal concerns he plunged into another spate of writing. The sharp decrease in his broadcasting left him with more time and some reduction of income. He did a little journalism, such as reviewing for the *Observer* under Terry Kilmartin, but mainly he undertook an amount of book-writing and editing that would have been a full-time job for most of us.

Neither his contributions to *The Dawn of Civilization* nor to Glyn's series had brought him into more than distant and sometimes irritable contact with the Neuraths, who had created Thames and Hudson, but now, with Juliet O'Hea as sympathetic go-between, he began to form a much more active association with Walter and Eva Neurath and Walter's son Thomas. Most of the books he was to produce for the general public were to be published by them – and nearly all to be at their suggestion. For, in contrast with his output on his return from India, these were not to be works that took shape in his own mind, although naturally the publishers' suggestions were tuned to his inclinations.

Closer collaboration began in a very small way in 1961 (the year in which the *Dawn* at last appeared), with Rik's agreement to write some fifteen thousand words on 'Roman Art and Architecture' for a volume, *The Birth of Western Civilization*, which Thames and Hudson were publishing under Michael Grant's editorship. His essay pleased everyone so much that Walter Neurath begged him to expand it into a book to go into his 'The World of Art' series and hailed it as 'splendid news' when he agreeed. It could not have been taken for granted, for he had not been altogether satisfied with his earlier encounter. He commented to Juliet, after she had made vain attempts to secure better terms, 'Between you and me they are an astonishing firm – recklessly extravagant in some directions and a little bit the other thing in others.' The truth was that Walter and Eva had suffered years of financial straits before Thames and Hudson's sudden success, and perhaps were still affected by the dismal contracts of their impoverished past.

This was the first coloured picture book Rik had done on his own account and he took as much trouble over the illustrations as he almost always did over every detail of a publication. He enjoyed the work because he liked the subject, but when he got his advance copies he found 'the coloured pictures shocking. Several have horrible green overtones.' He was pacified by excellent reviews. Meanwhile he had waded further into colour and into what could be classified as superior coffee-table volumes.

Thames and Hudson were in touch with a photographer, Roger Wood, and again Walter Neurath had little difficulty in persuading Rik to write a substantial introduction to a book that was to be published as *Roman Africa in Colour*. He had thought it would be a small task, but he had not reckoned with Wood's endless queries and problems: their correspondence went on, filling a bulging file, until towards the end Rik referred to Wood as 'that perpetual nuisance'. The publishers also gave him much extra trouble by changes in their briefing, and at the end of well over two years of toil and fuss he was to receive a meagre advance. He protested to Eva: 'I believe my reward in terms of horrid cash is £600, which quite frankly is no sort of compensation. (A rival firm had already offered me £1500 for a much simpler project.)' Eva, however, was quite unmoved, believing perhaps that penury is good for authors. She reminded him that, in theory at least, the £600 was only an advance on royalties, and these, she hoped, would increase the horrid cash. The royalties were at two per cent.

Before the tedious course of *Roman Africa* had reached its sticky ending Rik had agreed to take on a very different and much more extensive commitment with Thames and Hudson. This was to edit a series of books, 'New Aspects of Antiquity', in which he was to 'invite eminent archaeologists to record some of the discoveries which they themselves have recently made – discoveries which in many cases have revolutionized our knowledge of man's early history'. Unlike most claims on dust jackets, this one was to be fulfilled. Of the titles and authors originally contemplated (as early as 1963) a few, such as John Ward-Perkins on the Golden House of Nero, never materialized, while others, including Frank Willett on Ifé and Kathleen Kenyon on Jerusalem, made a valuable opening to a series that still continues. Lévi Strauss gave the stamp of his approval when he said of the first two volumes that while they made pleasant reading and were accessible to the layman, the texts left 'nothing to be desired in respect of scholarship at the highest level'. Indeed, of all Wheeler's output in general publishing during these latter years, 'New Aspects of Antiquity' has certainly proved the most valuable to his fellow-archaeologists.

Although Rik had so many dealings with Thames and Hudson – in addition to his own writing and editing he also served as an occasional reader and adviser – he kept an open ear for temptation from other publishers. In particular, George Weidenfeld, in partnership with Nigel Nicolson, had a dashing style, a readiness to flash his gold, in alluring contrast to the Neuraths' sometimes excessive carefulness. There is no doubt that when Rik mentioned to Eva the greater generosity of a 'rival firm' he was referring to Weidenfeld and Nicolson, who had given him a lump sum of £1500 to edit and write several portions of a grandiose tome to be called *Splendours of the East*, 'an ideal introduction to the art and architecture of Asia'. (I had the temerity to contribute a piece on Samarkhand, for which, it seems, I was paid more than the rest, 'to leaven the scholarly lump'.)

Although there had been some slight difficulties over the production, causing Rik to comment, 'I suggest there may be too many editors in the

pie', he was well pleased with *Splendours of the East* when it appeared
and the immediate sequel was that George Weidenfeld (whom Rik had
hardly met) invited him to follow their 'most happy and auspicious
collaboration' with another book that should lead to 'an exciting working relationship'. Nigel Nicolson was in charge of a series being
described as 'Cities in a Crucial Year', and Rik had suggested that he
would like to treat Persepolis in the year of its destruction by Alexander
the Great. He would call it *Flames Over Persepolis*. This was his own
conception and he really wanted to write about it. Not only would it be
centred on his own favourite hero, but it would allow him to introduce
the fascinating, little known 'Alexandria' on the Oxus, the Hellenistic
city recently explored by his friend Schlumberger, Gandharan art, and
his own contacts with Alexander at Charsada, all as part of a main theme
– the results of the destruction of the Persian Empire.

Nigel proved a spectral editor of a spectral series, seemingly out of
touch with the office and emerging infrequently from Sissinghurst with
little knowledge of what was going on. Rik had agreed with Weidenfeld
that he would write a short book, and when Nigel suddenly demanded
one more than twice as long he was told that the idea could not be so
expanded 'without becoming adipose', and when after a long interval he
materialized once more to ask Rik if he remembered the little book on
Persepolis the author good-humouredly replied that he was about to
send it in.

So far he had shown patience, for he had, as he said, 'written it for idle
pleasure'. Then the one deadly sin was committed: another editor had
altered his text without his consent. The blast he returned was certainly
the fiercest of all Rik's explosions over the ways of publishers:

My typescript, which had been carefully typed, was passed by somebody in
your office to some quite ignorant and, I should say, uneducated person for
what would, I suppose, be termed 'corrections'. The result is to land my
typescript in a complete mess in which idiocy after idiocy piles up. . . . In half a
century of close contact with publishers I have never seen anything like this.

The 'corrections' are of an unbelievably childish and quite often misguided
nature . . . even the re-writing of phrases in an infant-school style. Indeed the
very sight of the thing is so infuriating that I should welcome a change of
Publisher with a more civilized staff-method. . . .

Flames Over Persepolis came out at last in 1968, attractively produced
and in every way the freshest and most pleasing of Rik's picture books,
containing much that was new to all but the most specialized readers.
Rik, however, having been provoked, made further complaints about
the handling of the publication: that it was unobtainable when needed

for Christmas presents and other such frequent, and not infrequently justified, grievances of authors. In one of the pacifying letters from Weidenfeld and Nicolson he was assured, 'Your name is really synonymous with archaeology in the minds of the public.'

It could seem that Rik never brought himself to refuse an appealing suggestion for a book or an editorship. This is not altogether true: for instance, George Weidenfeld offered him £3000 for a history of the Moguls, which he turned down with the unvarnished explanation that he was incapable of the task – though he did leave himself a chink by adding that he might consider writing on Mogul art. Then John Hadfield, of George Rainbird, tempted him with the idea of following up their gorgeous and best selling *Tutankhamen*, to which he replied, 'It would indeed be an honour to compete with Madame Noblecourt. . . . It so happens, however, that at the moment I am either writing or editing a book with each hand and each foot, and really have nothing left to stand on.' There were, of course, plenty of less attractive offers that he had no difficulty in ignoring, and he certainly never undertook any work that did not have something to fire his mind or imagination. The trouble was that they were easily inflammable.

It was probably wrong of him to undertake the African book and *Splendours of the East*, for such was his scrupulousness that they took much time and labour. Why did a man long past the retiring age of ordinary mortals take on so huge a burden of publishing on top of all his other onerous concerns? It was quite simply true, as he said to Eva Neurath when she was being close-fisted, that he had to earn a living; he wanted, and to some extent needed, not to drop far behind the comfortable living that had come to him in the fifties. But far more, surely, he was driven by his demon, his need to be ceaselessly employed, a drive which, if possible, became greater rather than lesser as 'that good night' drew nearer.

It so happens that he was brutally reminded of mortality towards the height of these literary commitments. On 6 December 1963 he was taken in to the London Clinic for a prostate operation. Things went wrong and he was very ill indeed, being kept in the Clinic for just over a month before being moved to the King Edward VII Hospital, where he lay until 17 January. This was to be by far the longest sickness of his life, and it had been too serious a threat for even Rik to pretend to make light of. After Christmas he wrote to John Ward-Perkins about 'New Aspects of Antiquity' and by this time had recovered enough to be facetious: 'I am lying in bed between the surgeon and the physician – don't get me wrong! It has been a hell of a month.' To me he wrote on 11 January, inviting the contribution to *Splendours*, 'I'm dictating this from my bed in King Edward VII's Hospital where I suppose I shall be for a few more days.' He would, he said, have written sooner 'But for the intervention of providence in the shape of a surgeon and rather near-fatal complications.' Molly Myers attended him through this grim illness, combining the services of fond wife and perfect secretary – keeping in touch with his friends and enabling him, when the worst was past, to continue as an assiduous editor. During this last phase when survival was assured Rik grew anxious about his sexual future. The doctors reassured him – or so he said – with the information that he had been made 'infertile but not impotent'.

Rik left himself with only a little time to spare for any direct part in the pursuit of his old love: British archaeology. Not that he was ever out of touch with all that was going on, for through the Ancient Monuments Board, the Society of Antiquaries, the Academy, the British Museum, news-gathering friends such as Glyn Daniel and a still tenacious memory hardly a turf could be lifted in the name of archaeology without his knowledge. Often the younger generations who had now taken over excavation, with its costly technical apparatus, turned to him for grants or help with public fund-raising. He seldom failed them.

He was to be more directly associated with an excavation initiated in the west country, that of South Cadbury Castle in Somerset, a hill-fort which ever since the days of the Tudor antiquaries had been linked with King Arthur's Camelot. While the multiple ramparts were undoubtedly of Iron Age date, Ralegh Radford had recently identified some potsherds from the hilltop as a Mediterranean ware of round about AD 500, a rare discovery that at once gave some credence to the tradition.

It was a site that appealed to Rik and when, at the end of 1965, he was invited to be President of the Camelot Research Committee then being formed he 'accepted with alacrity'. Ralegh Radford was appointed Chairman and Leslie Alcock Field Director. The organizers had already determined to use the evocative name of Camelot, and so, after an interval of just forty years, he found himself once again using the powerful appeal of King Arthur to rouse the interest of the public and the press.

It proved on this occasion to be well justified. When, later, Rik invited Leslie Alcock to write a volume for his 'New Aspects of Antiquity' series he included in his Introduction a general defence of such appeals suggesting sore recollections of long past as well as recent criticisms.

... the site has offered rich rewards to Alcock and his colleagues, and has incidentally made kindly nonsense of those earnest scholars who, desperately anxious to preserve their scientific integrity from Arthurian pollution, hesitated to approve a serious venture amidst the half-memories which are happily an occasional and often decorative part of historic humanism. Let these young critics, bless them, in this sort of context recall the epic battles and victories of Troy long ago, and of a certain Heinrich Schliemann who was not afraid so to venture. . . .

Wheeler was very far from being a mere letter-head President. In the spring, when it had been determined that there should be a trial dig that year, he wrote the appeal for donations, announced he would be making a film at Cadbury (Paul Johnstone was to be concerned with this) and secured a grant from the Academy. After the successful trial he helped to secure the patronage of the *Observer*, beginning with a handsome fee for a conspicuous article on Camelot in the Magazine. He had so little repented his views about pleasing the press that he opined it was Leslie Alcock's 'duty within the confines of science, to produce something spectacular each year as far as may be feasible', a recognition of his debt to the *Observer*.

During the first full season Rik went down to Cadbury to inspect and give advice as of old. This must have been the last British excavation in which he had any down-to-earth share in the direction. He confided to Ralegh Radford his doubts as to whether Leslie was enough of a strategist for so expensive an undertaking, but they remained on good terms, and when all was done (by 1970) the excavator thanked Rik for having been his 'prop and goad'.

The dig was, in fact, more successful than the Camelot Research Committee had dared to hope. It was a bonus that it revealed remains going back to the Stone Age and on to Anglo-Saxon times, but the great triumph was the discovery of a large timber hall, where men had quaffed southern wine at a date to be identified with the lifetime of King Arthur. With such a lure, the public came in their thousands: it was happily reminiscent of Verulamium and Maiden Castle.

The exploration of Cadbury Castle undoubtedly brought Rik pleasure, but during these same years and beyond he accepted two other commitments, mainly of a money-raising kind that he could only have done from a persisting sense of obligation to British archaeology. He agreed to be Vice-Chairman of the Appeals Committee for a project to build a magnificent new museum and research centre at Salisbury. It all seemed propitious: it had the support of very important people, the promise of a fine site on the Avon, famous architects, even some money in the offing, but it never came to life. It was like a Rolls-Royce without the needful motor spirit. Wheeler himself launched the appeal, but the sum needed, not far short of a million, was too ambitious. A grandiose effort petered out.

The other undertaking lasted much longer and brought Rik much, mainly irritating, work. This was the organization of excavations at York Minster, to be made in advance of the extensive restoration of the fabric that had proved necessary. Wheeler was Chairman of the Archaeological Committee and devoted himself wholeheartedly to its responsibilities. A project with so many authorities involved was inevitably difficult: there were conflicts of interest between the archaeologists and both the Church and the builders and engineers; there had to be sackings and shifts of personnel; there were some fussy or even hysterical individuals concerned – and over all, year by year, a desperate shortage of money. When the scattered digging had been reasonably well completed Rik characteristically took pains over the Report, and was still troubling himself over it in 1974.

If Wheeler's renewed intimacy with India and Pakistan was already evident in the later fifties through the Swinford tour and Charsada it was to develop in many directions during the next decade. Indeed, it can be said that he was far more the accepted sage and elder there than he was at home. The warm relationship was not by any means limited to public services or archaeological science. Rik did an immense amount to help individuals, his former pupils and colleagues, in their everyday affairs. He helped them, or members of their families, to secure fellowships, grants and even doctorates or election to the Society of Antiquaries; equally he advised them on their professional problems at home, and did occasional examining and other such chores. Anyone believing that Rik never undertook modest and inconspicuous services should look through this vast correspondence.

In his contacts with those who were now running archaeological affairs in the subcontinent he was closer to the Indians but did just as much for the Pakistanis. For instance, soon after his passage of arms with F. A. Khan over the Charsada Report Rik shouldered the bulk of the work for the launch of his departmental journal, *Pakistan Archaeology*, assisted in placing his brother as a research student and his brother-in-law in an English textile firm, and rewrote an article of Khan's for the *Illustrated London News*. Unhappily, as will appear, all this did not prevent further friction between them.

In Delhi Rik maintained good working friendships, particularly with

Ghosh and B. B. Lal. Indeed, Ghosh and he not only entertained one another in London and Delhi, but Rik was on warm personal terms with Ghosh's family, exchanging bad verse and drawings with his daughter.

Wheeler's old associations with the Survey were most agreeably recalled when in December 1961 he made a brief stay in Delhi to celebrate the centenary of the department. There was an exhibition, Rik gave an address and Lal gave him a dinner party. It was this visit that evoked a letter from Bhag Singh, one-time store-keeper to the Survey:

Esteemed Sire,
My pleasure knew no bounds on hearing that your graciousness is visiting India in the recent future on the Centenary of your Department since I will once more meet my old master, companion Sir! . . . Respectable Lady Wheeler also towards whom I feel the possession of unforgettable sentiments?

In memoriam of our timetested strong relations if not in convenient, I, humbly, request for a wireless receiving set.

The trouble is too much yet I am sure your goodness will not mind it.
    Renew my old loyalty

                        I am Sir, Humbly, Your as ever
                        BHAG SINGH

A little over three years later, when Rik again went out, it so happened that he was engaged on commissions for both Pakistan and India. F. A. Khan had informed him some time before that Dr Harold Plenderleith, whom Rik had known well as head of the British Museum laboratory and who was now in Rome as Director of the international centre for cultural conservation studies, was concerned in a UNESCO scheme to save Mohenjodaro from the ill-effects of increasing salinization and waterlogging. Early in 1964 Plenderleith visited the ruins with specialist advisers and produced a preliminary report on *Preservation of Mohenjo Daro* which set the UNESCO project on course. Independently concerned with the enquiries was Dr George Dales of the Pennsylvania University Museum, whose digging on the coast had suggested that the flooding of the Indus capital had been due to a rise in land-level at the river mouth. He was now excavating at Mohenjodaro and making borings below the water-table and finding occupation at a depth far below that reached by Wheeler's unsuccessful venture of years gone by.

Also with a strong personal interest in the scheme was Robert Raikes, a professional hydrologist with a practice in Rome who had known Rik since the early sixties. They had argued the problems of the Indus

Valley waters from their two points of view, and it was to be the hydrologist who won over the archaeologist. Rik had believed that the impoverishment evident at Mohenjodaro before its fall was due in the main to climate change, tree-felling and soil exhaustion, but Raikes persuaded him that disastrous floods caused by the ponding back of water, as suggested also by Dales, had been the prime cause. He was to announce this changed interpretation in the last edition of his *Indus Civilization*.

Bobbie Raikes was much impressed by Rik's capacity to understand and accept new ideas, and, as he said, 'what started as an arm's length argument ended in friendship.' Rik took to staying with the Raikes whenever he was in Rome, and grew fond of them both.

Rik himself was not directly involved with the conservation project until 1965, when he spent a week in Pakistan en route for Delhi. He had business with the Department of Archaeology (Khan was friendly enough to lay on a lunch party), was concerned with new material for a book he was then contemplating – and was to visit Mohenjodaro. For this purpose he chartered a small aeroplane and flew three hundred miles up the Indus, taking with him Dr Dales, a worthy man who had a genius for provoking dislike (this was one subject on which Khan and Rik were agreed). Once arrived, they 'butted into a full-blown conference on the future of Mohenjodaro', as Rik put it in writing to Molly. This was a slight intervention indeed, but was to lead on to onerous work a few years later.

The next day he went up into the Baluch mountains, a day's journey by corkscrew gravel tracks, but through marvellous scenery. It moved him as much as ever, and so did the little family groups of Baluch tribesmen on their summer migration, 'with all their worldly goods piled high on camels, great sacks of dates and perhaps a baby or a puppy or a chicken or a tiny new-born camel, sweet and woolly and already wise, tied on the top of all'. In his seventy-fifth year and suffering from sleeplessness and a persistent cough after a bad bout of influenza, he still had the fresh response of youth.

In Delhi he was welcomed by Ghosh, who, as Director General of the Survey, had appointed Wheeler Chairman of a Review Committee set up under the Ministry of Education to assess its work and make recommendations for its future. The Ghoshs were to show him much hospitality and the Director General himself went to BOAC to book his return flight because 'the others don't understand', but unfortunately returned with the wrong timetable.

Rik spent a few days on preparatory work and picking up opinions, then he was received by the President, assembled the committee and plunged into an arduous programme. In Delhi they had meetings all day, while at night Rik drafted 'the Report-so-far'; then there were site tours to the new excavations at the Indus city of Kalibangan, to Agra, Hyderabad and elsewhere, involving those long, tedious train journeys which had once been so familiar.

However, he was well satisfied since he felt the committee was working well, which meant that it did not disagree too much with his own aims, which had not greatly changed with time. He attached most importance to raising the official status of the Survey, particularly by making the Director General Joint Secretary to government. For the rest, he still urged that the standing and prospects of the technical staff and museum curators should be much improved, believing that a little more expenditure in that direction would bring far better value.

After three hard weeks the report of the Review Committee was approved and on his very last day in Delhi, 4 April, the Chairman went for a little shopping expedition with the 'volatile' Mrs Ghosh and presented the report to the Minister of Education, Shri M. C. Chagla, before flying home. Ghosh himself was delighted with the recommendations, and although the government was to turn down Rik's strong advocacy for a Joint Secretaryship, he was reasonably satisfied with the compromise of giving the Director General direct access to ministers. In his thank-you letter Rik ended by telling Ghosh, 'Please do not forget that my luncheon and dinner table in London is always laid for you.'

Although the two men were to remain in touch over the Swans tours and over plans, never fulfilled, for them to write a guide book together and for Ghosh to be made Professor of Indian Archaeology in London, this was the last occasion on which Rik was able to do active work for his old department. The final assignment in his former domain was to be in Pakistan.

The next year, although Swans would bring him again to the subcontinent, Wheeler's most significant and entirely unexpected excursion overseas was to take him to a completely new quarter. There was something a little mysterious about his mid-March trip to Aden. Our former colony and protectorate was in turmoil and probably it was the scent of danger that lured him, a desire for his pulse to be quickened, that underlay the more prosaic reasons for his visit. That there was something of the sort seems to find support in a memory of Lord Robbins, then President of the British Academy. Rik had formed a relationship with him as close as with any of his predecessors, and probably more affectionate. Lord Robbins was struck by the fact that on only two occasions did Rik ever address him, except ironically, as 'Mr President', and the first of these was when he suddenly rang him up to request leave of absence from the Academy to go to South Arabia. Robbins felt there was something very odd about this call, not only in the form of address, but because there was no ruling for the Secretary to ask permission of this kind from the President and Rik had never thought to do so on similar occasions. The slight aura of excitement round this affair justifies its inclusion among those impulsive acts of Rik's old age.

It was not, in fact, altogether a sudden move (he had applied to the Academy in January for a grant to make an archaeological survey in South Arabia and the island of Socotra), although there may have been a change of plan, since Robbins remembers that he asked for several weeks of leave, while, in the event, he was to be there for just one week. The year before the constitutional talks had failed and the Speaker been assassinated; Britain had suspended the constitution and in Aden British lives were at risk.

Archaeologically, Rik's motive for his expedition was again his desire for imperial Britain's poor cultural record to be redeemed: in an article he was to write afterwards for *The Times* he said, 'How often have we as a colonial power handed over our trusts with wholly inadequate cultural provision and prevision? How rarely . . . have we realized the importance of equipping a new nation with an understanding of its past?' Yet in South Arabia there had already been some advance. At the end of the fifties public funds had been found for a superficial survey of ancient sites and subsequently a government architect in Aden had been turned into a most effective full-time Director of Antiquities. This was Brian Doe, who was to be Rik's conductor while he was in Arabia.

Although the aeroplane reached Aden at a very early hour, Rik (who was feeling sick) was met by the Governor-General and a contingent of the RAF and from then on was treated with all honour. There were the inevitable dinner party at Government House, reception for the British community ('astonishingly Kiplingesque') and session with the British Adviser. Brian Doe took him to as many inland sites as possible, and Rik performed his one ceremonial function, laying the foundation-stone of the much-needed new museum at Steamer Point in Aden. He was amused to find that while he, with his trowel, was at the centre of a ring of photographers and movie cameras, they in turn were encircled by police armed with machine-guns. Weapons were, indeed, very much in evidence wherever he went. In Aden itself a soldier with rifle or machine-gun was at every street-corner and bombs were to be heard at night.

All this was interesting but routine. That part of his visit which really delighted him, and which must have provided a sweet stab of excitement, was the two days that he spent on the remote and picturesque island of Socotra, which, although it lies well out into the Indian Ocean off the Horn of Africa, was administered from Arabia.

On the morning after his arrival at Aden he rose at 4 am, boarded a Dakota with an RAF crew and was flown to the island, to be greeted by the sight of another, crashed, Dakota and two Sultan Sahibs, with their armed police guard. These, as he told Molly, he inspected 'and was constantly presented arms to by'. After this, there being no roads, he tramped from site to site, returning to the aeroplane at dusk. There the airmen had prepared a good meal, and they sat together round the fire, drinking until they were ready to lie down where they were and sleep under the stars.

The next day the Sultan of Socotra, 'a big-eyed intelligent fellow as charming and evil as they make them', entertained him to a meal of many curries, eaten seated on the carpeted floor within the hierarchical ring of household and retainers. It was another adventure to be stored and enjoyed in memory.

During this year, before he went off for the Swans cruise in India, Rik took part in a little ceremony very different from the laying of foundation-stones. It deserves to be recorded since it was the summit of a personal relationship, quite unlike any other, that had threaded through his life for a very long time. The occasion was the eightieth birthday of Elsie Clifford – whom we used to regard as the uncrowned queen of Cotswold archaeology. In middle age she had bravely gone to Cambridge to take a course in the subject and had since established a high amateur reputation as a local excavator. She had tremendous will-power, a sharp perception and a way of uttering shrewd criticism of fellow-archaeologists in a most ladylike manner.

Elsie lived at Little Witcombe, at the foot of the Cotswolds, below Birdlip Hill, on her husband's death moving to a little, historic, timber-framed house in the same village that suited her perfectly. Rik developed a very real affection for her and she, of course, revered him, though far from blindly. He always visited her if in the neighbourhood, very often stayed with her to enjoy her talk and abundant food, lectured for her local society, wrote introductions for her work and put her up for Fellowship of the Antiquaries – although the first time she was (shamefully) blackballed.

Now she was eighty, and Glyn Daniel had suggested that she should be given a fine birthday party. Rik responded warmly to the idea and made an addition to it. He devised a brooch composed of copies of Celtic coins that Elsie herself had unearthed during her last important excavation, supervising its design and manufacture. On a pleasant early summer day about a score of us, more or less well-known archaeologists, with the addition of J. B. Priestley, enjoyed a good luncheon in Cheltenham, after which Rik presented the brooch. When all was over, as he recorded in the style he often assumed when some real feeling was aroused in him, 'The little lady was completely overwhelmed and tottered back into her cottage with a tearful, gratified little smile, which meant a lot.'

This gesture of friendship was in the sharpest contrast with a sad failure in another, closer, friendship occurring at much the same time. Cyril Fox had been failing and was partially paralyzed. He wanted to see Rik, and his wife urged him to come, but time went by and Rik did not go to see the man with whom he had so often worked and to whom he had poured out so many letters. In those written from India he had again and again expressed the greatest admiration for Cyril, for his energy and enthusiasm. More than this, he was the only man, other than Crawford and Alfred Clapham, with whom he could be quite at ease, dropping all masks and part-playing. Evidently Rik could not bear to see his friend with his precious vitality gone and in the helpless condition that he had long dreaded for himself.

In June of the following year, at the height of the Six Day War in Israel, Rik made a second excited telephone call to Lord Robbins. 'Mr President,' he said, 'I beg leave to go for a weekend to Jerusalem.' Startled by the timing of this request, Lord Robbins asked for an explanation and was told of Rik's concern on behalf of the British School (or Institute) in Jerusalem.

The story was that Dr Basil Hennessy, an Australian who had recently succeeded Kathleen Kenyon as Director, returned to Britain during the fighting, the position being complicated by the facts that the school was in the Jordanian sector of the city and most of the staff had pro-Arab sympathies. Rik, as Chairman of the Council for the British School, felt responsibility for its fortunes, while his own intense reaction to war and to civilians in time of war led him to suppose that

Hennessy should never have left and that he must certainly return at once. He would not send a man into danger without sharing in it and therefore resolved that he must go with him to Jerusalem. All this now seems excessive, an over-dramatization; the fact was that here, as at the time of the Aden visit, Rik was probably anxious to have the breath of war in his own nostrils. Writing to me much later, he gave as an example of his enjoyment of wars 'my visit to Jerusalem on the 7th day of the 6-day war when I travelled from London in an Israeli troop-plane full of noisy London taximen going out to drive tanks'. So it was that he flew with Hennessy back to Palestine – and was in truth exposed to considerable danger in the Holy City.

Kathleen Kenyon, involved that year with her last season of excavations in Jerusalem, was furious at such high-handed behaviour in what she regarded as very much her own domain. The row that ensued between the two did some lasting damage to their long relationship and was largely responsible for an unfortunate clash between them that autumn. To secure her realm, Kathleen wanted to take over the chairmanship of the Council, and when it met in London during October there was a confrontation between those who wanted to see Rik's chairmanship renewed and Kathleen's supporters. Rik himself, who had previously talked of retiring, now felt that there was much to be said for his continuing for one more year, 'to avoid any apparent association of my resignation with the present Arab–Israeli crisis'. He also considered Kathleen was unsuitable as Chairman because of her pro-Arab bias, recently exposed in a letter to *The Times*. Nevertheless, rather than continue the wrangle he withdrew, and an armistice was secured by the usual device of appointing a sub-committee – under Sir Eric (later Lord) Fletcher. The next day Rik wrote to Fletcher, confirming his refusal to stand against his 'oldest archaeological associate'. 'Kathleen and I have worked together for 37 years, and it would be a poor ending to that long association to meet in open combat.' He did, however, stick to his opinion as to her unsuitability for the chairmanship, suggesting that Eric Fletcher himself should take it on.

Kathleen, who had not been present at the Council, also wrote to Fletcher, confessing her anger that Rik should have spoken against her as Chairman because 'I am too much politically involved with the Arabs ... the real reason of course is that I opposed his treatment of Hennessy.' She then argued that she got on perfectly well with the Israeli archaeologists, and, indeed knew them better than Rik did and had their 'respect'. She ended with an accusation as unworthy as it was unwarranted: 'There is one real reason why I might not be considered suitable, and that is that there might be discrimination against the School in approaches to the Treasury through the British Academy. I am afraid things are as bad as that.'

It was true that Kathleen Kenyon had seen more of Israeli archaeologists and scholars than Rik could do, but it was also true that he was on more cordial terms with them, particularly with Yigael Yadin, whereas many of them felt her prejudice – which was to be apparent again at the time of the disgraceful UNESCO resolution against Israeli excavations in Jerusalem. Inevitably, however, Kathleen had her way – and Rik one chairmanship the less.

A month after this fracas Rik and Max Mallowan were making schemes for an excursion that would certainly serve as an antidote to any bitterness, if such were needed. Max applied to the British Academy on its Secretary's behalf, asking for the price of an air ticket to Teheran since the British Institute of Persian Studies were eager for a visit of inspection and also for Wheeler to see the progress of the digging at Siraf. The agreeable plan was for both Max and Agatha to go with him: Max to lecture and Agatha to give the pleasure of her company – which for Rik had always been very great. Rik would have the added pleasure of being looked after by David Stronach – with whose complicity, no doubt, the scheme had been devised – and going with him once more to join David Whitehouse at Siraf. Rik's enthusiasm and active participation in this excavation were so considerable that David Stronach would recognize it as his last active field work. This great mediaeval seaport had special appeal for him: more and more since Arikamedu he was stirred by evidence of the voyages of ancient seafarers, and here the ceramics proved contacts with Kilwa, where he himself had first dug before it was explored by the East African Institute.

The visit to Persia took place in January of 1968. It was a year in which the more routine demands of Wheeler's public commitments (there was a flurry for the York Excavation Committee over the discovery of the de Gray tomb) were interspersed by events pleasant and unpleasant. The first, brief, unpleasantness concerned the Queen's Lecture in West Berlin. Some time before, Lord Bridges, on behalf of the British Council, had invited Rik to deliver this annual address, a formal affair of some political significance, attended by the eminent and quite an event of the West Berlin year. It was laid down that 'the lectures should be academically distinguished and should relate to some present-day problem and make a contribution to the thinking of our time'; in accepting, Rik entitled his lecture, 'The Future of the Past: an Archaeologist looks forward.' It was to be delivered on 27 May as the climax of a full three-day programme, social and archaeological. The date proved to be a most unfortunate one, since it was at the height of the Berlin participation in the extraordinary outbreak of student unrest that was then shaking the West. Emergency regulations imposed by the West Berlin government had only increased the tension.

The Rector of the Technical University, where the lecture was to be held, had been warned by the police that trouble would be provoked by the attendance of the Governing Mayor and other bigwigs, but had turned down the offer of heavy police protection. When Rik, escorted by the British Ambassador and the GOC, arrived outside the university they found themselves on the pavement in semi-darkness amid a milling crowd of red-flag-waving students. Others had already rushed the entrances, occupied the hall and festooned it with more of their bunting. The three men, after hasty confabulation, decided the Queen's Lecture must be abandoned, since any other course might lead to violence. The Governing Mayor was meanwhile being whisked away in a police car.

In a lightly written report on the Berlin episode, submitted to Sir Paul Sinker of the British Council, Wheeler assured him that 'neither the Queen nor the lecturer nor the British Ambassador were in any way involved except as victims of a purely domestic conflict', and continued, 'I must add that all the other functions in connection with my visit went *perfectly*. The G.O.C., your nice people, and the Germans entertained me with the utmost kindliness, and at the civic reception after the episode the Governing Mayor and his charming wife were abjectly apologetic.' The lecture, though never delivered, was duly published.

The next, and most unpleasant, happening developed from the publication of the June number of *Antiquity*. It carried a critical review by Rik of the Report on Ian Richmond's excavations in the Iron Age and Roman fort on Hodhill, Dorset. This Report had been prepared in sad circumstances: Richmond had pressed ahead with it in the knowledge that he was dying and it had been completed by his principal assistant. The review, published within three years of his death and ten years after the end of the dig at Hodhill, caused such an extraordinary furore at the time and is so often quoted against its author still that it demands examination.

Rik had known Ian Richmond ever since he came to the Caernarvon dig as an undergraduate, respected his scholarship and style and had written a supplementary obituary for *The Times*, emphasizing his personal qualities as a friend, particularly 'that gift for genuine and quiet communication which to me – and others – was his most precious quality'. It cannot be said, then, that Rik did not appreciate the qualities of a man in many ways his opposite in personality and methods of work.

The review began with a very clear statement of Rik's position as he saw it: 'It is difficult to review the last book of one's oldest friend. The rival risks are to err on the alternative sides of the judicial median: adulation and apologia. As the time-range lengthens, the latter cannot be completely rejected in a fair appraisal.' Wheeler then plunged into what amounted to a severe critique not only of the Hodhill excavation and the Report, but of Richmond's career as an excavator. This he suggested was 'something of a tragedy' owing to his failure to publish his excavations, so that 'not more than a quarter of his fieldwork can now ever see the light of day'. This he attributed partly to Ian's slow, small-scale, 'lone hand' methods, partly to a kindliness which led him to 'spend an evening with the Much-Binding-in-the-Marsh Field Club' when he should have been writing a report. Rik's life-long belief in the duty of prompt publication, in the fact that without it excavation was the destruction of irreplaceable evidence, had tended to become obsessive as he saw around him too many colleagues falling into this deadly sin.

The review then went on to question the eight years Richmond had taken to dig Hodhill, work which Rik considered should have been done in four: again, he passed into generalization, declaring of his friend that 'In the field ... he was almost intolerably slow.' More particular criticisms were that even in so long a time he had failed to cut any section through the main Iron Age ramparts that discovered direct dating evidence for them, that he had somewhat neglected the Iron Age, and especially its pottery, because of his greater interest in things Roman. Even for the Roman period, where the historical writing showed Richmond 'at his brilliant best', Rik found fault with the field work.

It is interesting from the biographical point of view to find Rik returning to the old issue of the art of sectional drawings, on which he had expressed himself so forcefully in *Archaeology from the Earth*. Richmond's, he said, were 'of the obsolete Bersu type in which pictorial smudgery was substituted for hard-headed analysis' and had, moreover (another deadly sin), 'neglected the essential number of the layers'.

Hitherto Glyn Daniel had kept to Crawford's policy for *Antiquity*: reviews were not to be questioned. Now, without warning, he broke the rule, sending Rik copies of three letters of the 'indignant' variety that were to be published in the December number and inviting a final reply. He argued that to withhold them 'would give a sense of grievance to about three-quarters of the Roman Britons practising at the moment' – which would be 'bad editorial policy'. In his introductory words as editor Glyn mentioned one correspondent who had said of the review that 'these things badly needed saying' and congratulating author and editor on their courage – but published only the hostile letters. The principal one, very long and written 'with a sense of outrage', was signed, among others, by Sheppard Frere, himself not noted for prompt publication of reports, and Aileen Fox, now widowed. It called attention to some of Richmond's publications, and some cuts in the Hodhill ramparts, that the reviewer appeared to have overlooked, but in general defended him for virtues which Rik would never have denied. The accusation that Rik had stated that the 'central duty of a university professor' was to publish excavation reports was unjustified: he was speaking of the duty of an excavator. Taken together, the letters succeeded as a thinly veiled counter-attack against Wheeler on lines well established among his opponents. The implications were that if Ian Richmond dug too slowly and with too few helpers Rik dug too fast and delegated too much; that if Richmond published too slowly, too modestly or not at all Rik, with 'his enviable facility', published too fast and 'for reasons of ambition or prestige' preferred 'separate monographs or national journals'. There was even a return to the old issue of rampart chronology, with which Rik was said to be obsessed, versus the social and economic problems, which must now have priority.

Wheeler himself responded to all this behind the scenes with much of the petulance he had shown long ago when Nowell Myres criticized *Verulamium*. He was rightly vexed with Glyn for breaking the rule against the questioning of reviews and genuinely upset that his appreciation of the fine quality of his old friend could be doubted. He was, however, too inclined to dismiss his critics as 'little people' and, on sending his reply to Glyn, wrote of a 'farrago which in my opinion can only lower *Antiquity* to the level of a screaming kindergarten'. The printed reply itself was not unreasonable, though ending with an onslaught on Sheppard Frere for his own failures to publish.

Reading the notorious review again, I was astonished that it should have caused such great and lasting hostility. The tone is more one of sorrow than of anger, praise and censure are well balanced, and although it may have been a misjudgement to go beyond the book to the personality of the author, Richmond had been notorious for unconscionable delays. Perhaps, after all, Rik should have been pleased that no one thought of holding his fire because their opponent was in his seventy-eighth year.

There was pleasure in the warm reception of *Flames Over Persepolis*, but undoubtedly the supreme pleasant event of 1968 was the news that Sir Mortimer Wheeler had been made a Fellow of the Royal Society. This award, made under Statute 12 for outstanding contributions to science outside the regular subjects, gave Rik intense satisfaction. It seemed to prove that his original sense of mission to bring scientific method to archaeology had been fulfilled and recognized despite his later reactions as a humanist when he saw his subject being led away from its true historical aims. There was, of course, the added pleasure that no other archaeologist of recent times, not even Gordon Childe, had won this award.

The main working engagement of the year was a development from the UNESCO projects for Mohenjodaro. Since his hurried visit to the Indus capital four years before Rik had kept in touch with what was going on and it was natural for Dr F. A. Khan to appeal to him for help over a UNESCO mission, and in general to rally international support for the preservation of the ruins. Rik wrote a severe, indeed offensively severe, reply, blaming him, not for the first time, for having barred various foreign archaeologists from Pakistan and particularly for refusing both George Dales and his Pennsylvanian team and Robert Raikes the hydrologist permission to finish their work at Mohenjodaro and elsewhere, a policy which 'has created very bad feeling abroad'. He concluded, 'Briefly, the answer is, my dear Khan, that I will help you with all the power at my disposal, but only on the understanding that the wilful exclusiveness of your Department undergoes a drastic change.' This was in 1967, the year in which Khan's post as Director of Archaeology came to an end.

It was not until October of the following year that UNESCO sent a strong international mission to Pakistan, the party of half-a-dozen specialists including Wheeler and his old friend Claude Schaeffer. Rik failed to get Raikes made a member, but was armed with his clear statement of the technical problems of salinization and flooding to be faced at Mohenjodaro, a document prepared after the two had met in Rome that summer. It is noticeable that Raikes's recommendations dealt not only with conservation, but with the possibility of lowering the water-table, so that excavations could be carried down to the very first settlement on the site. This had been the aim of the Pennsylvanian project as well as Rik's own unsuccessful sounding so long before, and one in which he was still keenly interested for the light it could throw on the origins of the Indus civilization.

The mission spent only two October days at Mohenjodaro itself, but also visited Taxila and other sites with related problems. Everywhere the brickwork of the capital city was depressingly decayed, and Rik was particularly distressed by the deterioration of the granary walls, which had been in such good condition when he uncovered them in 1950. It was the combined effect of exposure to the weather, together with moisture and salt drawn up from saline ground water not far below the natural surface, that had wrought the havoc.

The mission deliberated: it seemed that the weathering could be averted by plastering in a manner known to the original builders, but the greater need, both for conservation and deep excavation, was for the lowering of the water-table. A recent report by experts from the Hague (NEDECO) had recommended that this should be achieved by encircling the entire city with a canal, but it was agreed by the missioners that this could not be dug deep enough for satisfactory 'de-watering', while for the archaeologists its probable destructiveness was unacceptable. It proved more difficult to agree on positive recommendations.

Rik wrote an interim report on their findings for the Director General of UNESCO, but it was determined that a meeting with the experts from the Hague and from the Rome Centre was essential. It was held in Paris during the following March, the scientists and engineers proved most co-operative, and decisions were reached for short- and long-term measures. These were to be supervised by an Advisory Committee for UNESCO, which should co-operate with an ambitious Mohenjodaro project, to be set up by the Pakistan government with international aid. Money was, of course, the limiting factor for all this hopeful plan.

It is a striking fact that there seems to have been no question but that the final report should be drawn up by the doyen of the mission. Molly Myers recalls how hard he worked at it on his return to London. As a result this document, his last considerable public undertaking of the kind, shows no diminution of powers. It is of just the right length, admirably laid out and written, and, in spite of the technical detail (and a gallant attempt at costing), never loses sight of the historic importance of this great city of the ancient world. Indeed, it can hardly be doubted that through his authorship Wheeler gave the report a stronger archaeological foundation than it would otherwise have had.

CHAPTER 12

The Last Phase

A NUMBER OF 'last things' in Rik's career have already been chronicled for these years leading up to his eightieth birthday. The end of 1968 can be seen as marking the close of the penultimate phase of his life. The remaining span, though he was still very active, able to travel and to enjoy the company of young girls, even to gain new friends and undertake a new kind of enterprise, seems to belong to its ending. Rik made a splendid resistance to old age and death, but they were with him on the stage.

Of course, their ascendancy came only gradually. The turning-point is chosen for one decisive event: it was at the end of 1968 that Rik resigned as Secretary of the British Academy. It has been said that there were Fellows who felt he had stayed too long and that he had to be eased out of office. This is entirely untrue, a fact confirmed by so close yet detached an observer as Lord Robbins, who assures me that he kept his drive and efficiency to the end and resigned entirely in his own time. At the close of his history of the Academy Wheeler himself gives some account of the event.

Having joked about himself as one who, having been the scourge of the old men, had remained in office until he was an old man, he continues, 'Happily that Secretary was the last of his kind. He was a throw back to the era when all officers of learned societies . . . were expected to be honorary'; he had never accepted more than modest expenses, even when past Presidents had urged him to do so, for he was convinced there could be no half-measures. If a Secretary was to be paid the Academy must wait until it could afford to pay him on a professorial scale. The government grant having by then increased to about £300,000, 'it was agreed that that happy situation was at last arising in 1968'.

By that time Rik's secretaryship had also been crowned by a triumph of a more domestic kind. When the Royal Society moved from its quarters on the east side of Burlington House (just across the courtyard from the Society of Antiquaries) Rik plotted to secure a part of them for the Academy, including the dignified lecture hall. One who particularly rejoiced in the move (which Molly Myers did not) was Lord Robbins, who had been shamed by the lack of decent accommodation whenever he took foreign visitors to the old premises.

It was not until the spring that the Academy staged a dinner to commemorate Rik's nineteen years of service, during which, as he wrote, 'the Academy's cares were rarely absent from my mind'. No doubt he appreciated it, but the greater pleasure was brought to him by a letter. It came from M. C. Knowles, 'in religion David', the greatly esteemed Benedictine and Cambridge historian. As Rik treasured this simple letter with a rarely admitted intensity of feeling it should be set down. It was written from Wimbledon on 9 April.

My dear Wheeler,

As I am not expecting to be present at the Academy dinner to salute you, I feel I must write just a word of appreciation of what you have done for the Academy. I always regard you – along with Webster – as the Second Founder of the Academy, and you have borne the burden and the heats of the day over the years when Webster could not do so. When I first became a Fellow I remember remarking that the Government Grant was about that given to a couple of dentists in the new Health Service. It still can scarcely compare with the salary of the chairman of I.C.S., but it is something, and the reputation of the Academy has undoubtedly risen. And the move to Burlington House is certainly due entirely to you. *Vivas felixque sis.*

Yours very sincerely,
David Knowles

Although any man might be pleased to be recognized as its second founder, Knowles's letter was far from overestimating what Rik had done for the British Academy. The fact that it meant so much to him surely affords a glimpse of inner humility, of uncertainty in himself, that lay concealed behind so many contrary attributes. The next year the Academy was to give him further recognition by establishing an annual Mortimer Wheeler lecture in honour of his eightieth birthday.

Rik had been very much more than an efficient driving force as Secretary of the Academy. His office, at least for those with whom he enjoyed mutual friendship and understanding, had been a stimulating and lively port of call. Directors of British Schools overseas, excavators, all those who were beneficiaries of the Academy and many more besides could drop in and be entertained by news of what was going on, by serious discussion, gossip and abrasive talk of personalities. Since his day, or so I have been told, all this has died away and there is little to attract visitors to a more formal, impersonal bureau.

Rik was succeeded as Secretary by Derek Allen, a numismatist and Fellow of the Academy who as a result of the war had become a civil servant. While excellently qualified for the job, he was perhaps a little dull and humourless. Rik Wheeler was culpable of aggravating the difficulties any successor would have had by retaining his own base at the Academy to the end of his days. Not only did he continue to do all his correspondence and other paper work there, but he retained the services of Molly Myers, although she was officially the assistant of the new Secretary. If anyone could handle the situation successfully it was Molly, but naturally she remained closer to Rik, all the more since she was now increasingly having to look after his physical needs as his health and memory, although still remarkable, began to decline. Rik sometimes made his little jokes at the expense of the new man, and there was occasional friction. Certainly, as Molly always recognized, it would have been wiser policy for Rik to have moved out, but it is unlikely that any other arrangement would have enabled him to remain productive or to enjoy the good things that still lay ahead.

The year 1969 was to prove a busy enough one to ease Rik into life without official employment. Even before the submission of the Mohenjodaro Report he was with the British School in Rome, where he was involved with a scheme for its overhaul and was to give an address; he went on no less than three Swans cruises, followed by the famous tour he led in southern India, with its feast of adulation. He had hardly digested that when, in December, he had the satisfaction of sharing in the success of an international symposium, 'The Impact of the Natural Sciences on Archaeology', staged jointly by the Royal Society and the British Academy to mark the twentieth anniversary of Willard Libby's public exposition of his revolutionary radiocarbon dating. This meeting was the product of 'the new spirit of co-operation' between the two bodies which Rik himself had done so much to foster. It was attended by, among many others, both Libby himself and Professor Suess, of 'the Suess effect', an adjustment based on the alternative tree-ring method of dating which had greatly affected the original Libby chronology.

Rik was proud of the joint meeting, but his attitude to the ingenious scientific aid to archaeology under discussion remained ambiguous. In the past, like many of us who were not young in 1949, he had been reluctant to put much trust in the 'absolute' dates it yielded. Already, on more than one occasion, he had vehemently opposed Glyn Daniel's intention of expounding the method to the public through print or broadcasting, and doubts had been reinforced by the shock of the 'Suess effect'. Some two years after the symposium he was again raising the issue with Glyn, though by now more judiciously. Having referred to the 'half-digested ideas' that were in circulation as a result of the 'Radiocarbon Revolution', he urged that 'when the varying veracity of radiocarbon has been more extensively established in principle and detail over a long enough period, a whole lot of our thinking ... will have to be rethought.' Although Rik was not fully in touch with research in the subject, and although his resistance was in part to new ideas, there was some wisdom in his plea. It can be added that although more advanced, the process of rethinking is still far from complete.

So Rik strode only a little less vigorously than before into his eightieth year, with much to occupy him. He was no longer on many official boards or councils, but he was still Professor of Ancient History with the Royal Academy, and was still a Trustee of the British Museum, a position he much enjoyed, despite his ferocious criticism of the Trustees at the time of his clash with Sir Frank Francis. (Not that he had ceased to be critical; during this year he so strongly disapproved of the plans for the extension to the museum that he wrote to Sir John Wolfenden, as Director, insisting that his disassociation from the scheme should be recorded and setting out his objection to the architect and all his works in most brutal terms.) Rik also remained on the Management Committee of the Archaeological Institute, and on the advisory panel of *Antiquity* – for which he continued regular reviewing. He was much concerned with the last season of excavations at Camelot.

In February he showed that he was still prepared for archaeological enterprise in extreme heat by spending a fortnight in Bahrein. He had taken a personal interest in Bibby's excavation of the tell of Qala'al al-Barein ever since it proved to be a port of call linked by trade with both the Indus civilization and Sumeria. He therefore took the chance to inspect the work and the local antiquities before joining the International Conference of Asian Archaeology meeting there at the invitation of the oil-rich Sheik Issa, ruler of Bahrein, whose hospitality added to the pleasures of archaeology.

When to all this was added his now customary cruises and his other undertakings as a Swan Director Rik was certainly busy enough, yet he might have begun to suffer from being no longer quite in the mainstream of archaeological affairs and from the loneliness that comes to the long-lived with the loss of their friends, even from some slight sense of neglect, had it not been for a most happy chain of events initiated by the imaginative enterprise of some university students. What followed, helping to lighten his last years, owed something to a stroke of luck, yet it was also good fortune fully deserved, just as the gift of Molly Myers had been. He deserved it for half a century of dedication to students – after pretty girls his most favoured section of humanity – and because the young man who lurks inside all old men who are not walking dead was quick in him and still eagerly responsive to a challenge.

The first move was made by undergraduates running the Archaeological Society of Southampton University. The society must have been well supported by Barry Cunliffe, then a brilliant young Professor of Archaeology at the university, but the initiative came from the students themselves. They were inspired to organize a national conference on 'The Iron Age and its Hillforts' as a tribute to Sir Mortimer Wheeler 'on the occasion of his Eightieth Year'.

Rik was, of course, wholly delighted to fall in with the idea and promised his attendance as patron of the conference. Knowledge of what was afoot first came to some of us through the editorial columns of *Antiquity* for September 1970. There, after noting that Rik's eccentric old friend Professor Creswell (victim in the Baedeker story) had been knighted just after his ninetieth birthday, Glyn Daniel hailed his Advisory Editor's eightieth, thanking him for all his services to the magazine since its foundation. He continued,

Wheeler has already set down some of his memories in *Still Digging*. . . . Is it not now time for a supplementary memoir dealing with the last fifteen years of archaeology since his autobiography was published? What should it be called? *No Longer Digging*? But with a sub-title which no publisher would print, namely, 'But still active in all aspects of Archaeology, and still a great power in the land'. And for that matter, in many other lands. Long may it be so.

Glyn followed this generous if rather oddly devised birthday salute by an announcement of the Southampton Conference, to be held at the university in the following March, giving some details of a distinguished programme. It was a unique event for a high-level conference to be planned and run from start to finish by an undergraduate society, and they did wonderfully well, in the face of a long postal strike, in securing an attendance of nearly five hundred. Rik joined them in the best of spirits, inwardly touched that the young were honouring him in this way and satisfied that they were doing it efficiently. So good was the general spirit that although a disgraceful sit-in by fellow students barred them from their conference hall, the three days went with a swing.

Sir Mortimer Wheeler was received by the Chairman, Professor A. L. F. Rivet, as 'one of the best-known figures of our time' and 'the modern representative of Renaissance Man'. The motto of the Royal Artillery, he suggested, might fittingly be Sir Mortimer's own: *Ubique, quo fas et gloria ducunt*. Rivet then ran through Wheeler's hill-fort digs from Lydney to Stanwick, reflecting, 'New techniques have been developed, new discoveries made and some of Sir Mortimer's own formulations have been superseded.' This did not distress him, since he knew his Plato and therefore that knowledge was advanced by the destruction of hypotheses, while 'the golden atoms of evidence on which Sir Mortimer based his remained as bright as ever and ready for future use'.

After these polished presidential words, to which Rik may have listened with slightly mixed feelings, he delivered his own address, most enthusiastically received, and the conference was on its way. One leading paper was read by Christopher Hawkes, now on far friendlier terms with Rik, and another by Barry Cunliffe, soon to succeed to Christopher's Oxford chair. Derek Allen, Rik's own successor at the Academy, was among more than a dozen others giving lectures – all to be promptly published as *The Iron Age and its Hill-forts*, papers presented to Sir Mortimer Wheeler in a useful volume that can be regarded as a novel variety of *Festschrift*.

That the hill-fort conference had been a great success was duly proclaimed in *Antiquity* and elsewhere, but it might have been no more than a single bright event to cheer Rik's first step into his eighties, had not the Goddess Fortuna sent a messenger to Southampton. Her emissary was an extraordinarily handsome and charming young producer at the BBC, David Collison, who at that time was working on the 'Chronicle' programmes.

He had gone down on the off-chance (as he supposed, knowing nothing of Fortuna) of securing something for 'Chronicle'. He was not very hopeful, for the word had spread at the BBC that since 'The Grandeur that was Rome' Mortimer Wheeler was a has-been, far past his peak of popularity with the viewers. There was also a notion that he had been cantankerous and difficult to work with: everyone, as David Collison discovered, 'was afraid to touch him'. The producer, however, was capable of forming and holding to his own opinions. Rik's opening address to the conference struck him as a *tour de force*, an impressive performance, showing no abatement of powers – and he was thankful for the instinct that had led him to have it filmed and recorded by a local man.

Rik had frankly admitted that he enjoyed his television fame while it lasted, but any suggestion that he owed his public recognition to the medium had always had a touchy response, and now, after a decade when he had rarely appeared on the box (as he liked to think on his own decision), his attitude was at best ambivalent. So it is not surprising that when David Collison waylaid him at the conference, when he was completely immersed in its doings and his role as hero, to ask him if he would consider some undertaking for 'Chronicle', Rik waved him off in 'a lordly way', showing little interest and referring him to a secretary.

Young Collison was not to be put off. He had been convinced that Rik could still be a good performer, and perhaps, too, he saw that there could be a deep appeal in an old man who still had so much fire in him. Rik's face, furrowed by the years, was still highly expressive, whether assuming noble or thoughtful expressions for the camera, breaking into remarkably youthful laughter in good company, varying with the moods of histrionic speech, or relapsing into the shared humour of his grin. On reflection, the idea came to David Collison that the best way to present the whole man through television would be in biographical form, rehearsing his archaeological career.

He took the idea to Paul Johnstone and won his support. Nor did it prove at all difficult to win over Rik when he was approached again in more normal surroundings. There is no question but that the idea in itself appealed to him, and when he learnt that Collison had been the producer of a programme on radio-carbon dating, which had impressed him very favourably, he felt able to agree to work with him. Having come so far, Collison had to consider how to avoid the instructive approach to the past that had marred 'The Grandeur that was Rome'. He determined to bring in Magnus Magnusson as 'a sounding board' and to do everything possible to make the life story 'more companionable and enthusiastic in spirit'.

The preliminaries took a long time. It was not until nearly a year after the Southampton conference that David Collison was able to send a definitive letter, setting out his ideas for the film. Three main themes were to run through what was above all to emerge as an autobiography of Sir Mortimer Wheeler: these were the development of scientific method in archaeology; purpose and strategy in excavation; good public relations. Collison suggested a number of locations at home and abroad where episodes could be shot, and concluded by recommending a start on 1 March.

Collison was happy to see that in his reply Sir Mortimer had struck out the typed surname and substituted David, while for the first time signing himself 'Rik'. David took this as a signal that they were now 'friends and colleagues', but he could have no idea how much this was to mean to both of them.

The decision was taken to begin filming very nearly at the beginning of the story: a trial run was to be made in Colchester, at that Balkerne Gate explored by Captain Wheeler and his men on their way to Passchendaele. The setting was good, for the King's Head pub, standing above dark tunnellings, was still there, though the name was now the more modish Hole in the Wall. It really was a trial run, Collison a little apprehensive that his hunch might be proved wrong. Although it was a decade since Rik had attempted anything so demanding for television, his now vast experience of addressing the assorted minds of Hellenic travellers may have relaxed his style, making him simpler and more direct in his appeal. Certainly David Collison could relax – Rik's performance was judged to be first-rate. So all secret doubts evaporated and a most imaginative enterprise was on its way. The filming was to last just a year, during which Rik, Magnus, and David with his little team were to travel near and far together, sharing all manner of labours and adventures. The young members of the team were soon drawn into the spirit of the thing, as David said, sometimes 'jollying Rik along', yet themselves inspired by his enthusiasm. Among them was David's assistant at the BBC, a girl called Alex, who became Rik's favourite.

David's original proposals for locations were to be modified, for once the wind was in their sails all were resolved that instead of tamely shooting the Director General's reminiscences of his Indian years in Whitcomb Street, they could not do less than pursue them to their source. Although this meant cutting out all the Welsh sequences, the decision was amply justified, for the Indian scenes splendidly dominate the latter part of the film and without them the immensity of Rik's esteem in the subcontinent could not have been conveyed. Perhaps it was only there that it was fully brought home to the film-makers themselves, when they saw the whole available staff of the Survey, from the Director downwards, gathered together outside the Delhi headquarters to welcome him. As the film commentary affirms, these were men of international standing, 'Yet when Wheeler returns to Delhi, they are once again his students, and he their teacher, coming home.' Complementary to the Delhi reception, but equally striking and far more exotic, was the scene at Arikamedu, where he was excitedly received by the clustering villagers, naked bar their loin cloths, against the unchanged background of thatched huts and the palm-fringed lagoon.

India made the effective climax of this curious pilgrimage to the high places, the shrines, as it were, of Rik's past life. For the rest, after Colchester, the party went to Verulamium, including Wheathampstead (where Rik, astonishingly, allowed himself to be shown failing to scale the ramparts), to Maiden Castle, very briefly to Normandy, with Swans to Athens to stage the Parthenon harangue, and to Dover. Then, at the last moment, in February 1973, there was an unexpected addition. Sir Mortimer Wheeler was invited as guest of honour to a symposium being held at Karachi to rally world support for the Mohenjodaro scheme – which had made little or no progress since Rik wrote his UNESCO report. David took the opportunity to send out one of the team with him, so that a record could be made of President Bhutto's address, of girls hanging Rik with flowers and of Rik, as chairman, making a brief, vehement declaration that the salvation of the famous ruins could and must be secured. These bonus shots were flown to London in time for them to be used for the end of the film – where the garlanding and the vehemence made a fitting final sequence, to be followed only by Rik's affirmation that he had done all that he wanted to do and 'had a very entertaining life. I've enjoyed living. I enjoy living still. Well, that's enough, those, I think, could be my last words, almost.'

The film, *Sir Mortimer Wheeler*, was divided into two 'Chronicle' programmes broadcast on 26 March and 2 April 1973 under the sub-headings 'Digging up People' and 'The Viceroy Sent for Me . . .'. It had an excellent reception, virtually without criticism and with praise also for David Collison's part in it – though probably few were aware how great it had been. This shared praise prompted Rik to confide to David, 'I feel warm and comfy inside about the whole thing.'

That autumn the BBC arranged a private showing of the entire film at a small studio behind the Courtauld Institute. Rik wrote to his friends, inviting our attendance – with characteristic deprecatory glosses, such as 'Of course this suggestion is perfectly preposterous!' A goodly company turned up and I believe we were all carried away by the sheer zest maintained through those hundred minutes that spanned a lifetime, as well as by the skill with which Rik, David and Magnus had woven it together. The three archaeological themes were there, but discreetly, and always Rik himself and his animated recollections and historical set-pieces prevailed over the monuments; biographical detail was slipped into the commentary while Magnus led his man on to talk of soldiering, war and death, of painting and poetry, chance and opportunity – even, briefly, of Tessa. The whole had grown, as David had hoped it would, into a vital autobiography, and one entirely without nostalgia.

It was also an autobiography without sex – save for an evocative description, delivered with much relish, of the tiny bronze figure of a dancing girl from Mohenjodaro.

There is her little Baluchi-style face with pouting lips and insolent look in the eye. She's about fifteen years old I should think, not more, but she stands there with bangles all the way up her arm and nothing else on. A girl perfectly, for the moment, perfectly confident of herself and the world. There's nothing like her, I think, in ancient art.

So Rik commented on his favourite statuette: he was to make use of the girl again at the end of his life.

There was nothing new in Rik's words – he had spoken or written on all subjects before – but being drawn into a whole gave them a new force. Again, read in cold blood, the praise and admiration expressed in the commentary and in one instance by a young archaeologist appear excessive: an heroic hagiography indeed. Yet on the screen Rik's mere presence, his enthusiasm and flashes of humour, overcame even this.

For me the most moving moment in *Sir Mortimer Wheeler* is at Maiden Castle, when, standing upright in the car, with hair streaming behind as they mount towards the entrance, he gazes up at the ramparts like some old Celtic chieftain returning in triumph from exile.

The making of this film provided Rik with the kind of purposeful activity that he craved. It remains a valuable document which one hopes will be seen by a future generation. Yet what I believe was of far greater moment to him during his last years was the friendship it created between himself and David Collison, an affection which extended to David's family, to Alex and other members of the team. The attachment was mutual. For David the six years granted to them were in many ways the most important in his life. Rik became one of his closest friends. He found their sessions together, and for him they were in part like seminars, wonderfully refreshing, a unique means 'of recharging his batteries'.

On Rik's side his letters show a fast-growing affection: after the turning-point marked by the striking-out of his producer's surname they are always handwritten and inscribed variously with love and blessings; there is a first invitation to the Athenaeum, dining at Stones, mention of how delightful and stimulating it has been to share a meal with David and Alex. Another advance was made with Rik's birthday, when the two of them celebrated it with him, bringing a gift of whisky glasses. He wrote, 'My dear David and Alex, that was for me one of the happiest evenings ever, and as for those delectable glasses . . . we must justify their elegant existence as often as we can.' A month later, when David wrote to tell him how successful their filming at Maiden Castle had been, Rik replied by return with his thanks: 'above all thank you for the brilliance, fantastic energy and infallible good humour with which you (to say nothing of dear Alex) conducted the whole operation. . . . The fact that I at least enjoyed every minute of it is a bonus beyond all acknowledgement. Let us all three meet again *soon* and bless the Bon Dieu.'

Although the relationship between Rik and David during the year was exceptional, it might have been expected to fade away when the work was done. Instead, it ripened into a purely personal attachment. David, with members of the old group, continued to meet Rik almost every week, often over picnic lunches at Whitcomb Street. At the same time the bond with David's wife, Sandy, and their two children grew closer. After the programmes had been broadcast the Collisons must have written warmly about them to Rik, for in response he told Sandy, 'those are just about the three nicest letters I've ever received. . . . You know the four of you seem to have become my little family, and I look forward more than I can say to gathering us all together again. . . .' The family did in fact continue to visit him frequently even after a third child was born and even after Rik moved to the country. When the children were expected Rik always went to Hatchards to choose them books and he got on with them very well – he who formerly had a reputation of ineptitude or worse with young children. Through the supreme good fortune of his and David's discovery of one another, quite new sentiments grew up within Rik during these late years. He himself wrote to David, 'How often I find myself blessing the fate that crossed our paths.'

Perhaps the growth of simpler and more gentle feelings made itself felt also with his own family. He was now more able to take pride in Michael's considerable success as a lawyer and probably saw rather more of him than before, dining with him in London from time to time. With his granddaughter Carol his relationship undoubtedly became more affectionate and towards the end he welcomed her visits to his eventual country retreat. There was, however, one alarming incident:

they had arranged for her to deliver some packet into his hands at the British Academy, Rik insisting that she should not park her car any-where near the entrance. She rashly broke this command, confident that she could quickly move away. Her grandfather saw what she was doing and came down the steps in genuine fury, belabouring her with his stick there in the public courtyard. Alarmed and much upset, she fled to park the car elsewhere. On her return his wrath had melted, but her tears of reconciliation roused it once more and the encounter ended in misery.

In the archaeological world it was agreed that Wheeler had 'mellowed' and some old hostilities were healed, notably, as we have seen, with his old opponents Nowell Myres and Christopher Hawkes. Nowell recalls that 'Rik never referred to our earlier differences but I think he came to regret them as much as I did.' Christopher last saw him in 1975 when he gave the Mortimer Wheeler Lecture at the Academy. Rik was in the front row and was well pleased by the appreciative references to his work. Afterwards he said to Christopher, 'It is a great pity that you and I haven't worked more together.'

Not that all was dissolved into sweetness and light. There were still opponents and revilers among this older generation, harbouring antagonisms such as had come to the surface over the affair of the Richmond review. As an outside observer, David Collison was much struck by the relative unfriendliness and neglect of this generation, in contrast with the younger archaeologists and students who had turned to the old master with enthusiasm. It is significant that two of the ablest of the younger men, Colin Renfrew and Barry Cunliffe, both used to see Rik and write to him for advice to the end. Barry, in particular, consulted him as to whether he should accept the Oxford chair. Rik was to speak and preside at Colin's inaugural when he in turn assumed the professorship at Southampton.

His advice, indeed, was a commodity widely sought throughout these years: his post was heavy with requests coming from all over the world and covering all his fields of experience, administrative, archaeological, personal. As his great dread was to be under-employed Rik welcomed such chores – as he did requests for more active partici-pation. There was, for instance, the Royal Asiatic Society. This distin-guished body, having, after inordinate delays, presented him with a *Festschrift*, the following year, 1973, invited him to take part in an International Symposium on 'The Undeciphered Languages' and he duly presided over the section dealing with the Indus script. The next night he was enjoying a dinner with Glyn and Ruth Daniel at the White Tower. Days such as these enlivened the intervals between his three Hellenic cruises of that year – all of them after the completion and televising of *Sir Mortimer Wheeler*.

With Molly Myers's constant help, Rik was able to live happily at 27 Whitcomb Street, still cherishing the rugs, the Persian plates and the Ivon Hitchens landscape which was his one considerable investment in contemporary art. So he remained, as he had long been, a familiar figure in and about Piccadilly as he walked between his little house, the Academy or Antiquaries and the Athenaeum. Or sometimes, if he just wanted an outing, he would go down to the embankment and walk up towards Westminster. His legs now had a slight sag in them and he carried his head forwards from his shoulders, but his old lope had not greatly changed; he still walked very freely, flinging out his feet as before. He could still squat, or sit clasping his knees: old age made him seem too loosely put together rather than stiffening him.

So long as Rik remained in London he was never without intimate girl-friends – as he liked us all to know. He still possessed, I feel sure, powers of sexual authority, and would have found his own means of pleasuring them. He left behind him passionate letters from a young girl who was evidently very much in love with him. Molly Myers read before destroying them, as she felt sure that (like Mavis of old) he wanted her to find them.

It was probably when he was in Rome in 1973 that Rik made a last attempt to see his wife. Kim was lodging in the British School while Rik was with the Raikes and, as usual, seeing something of Molly Cotton. It was arranged between them that he should go to the School and meet Kim at a small tea party. Kim, however, worked herself into such a state of emotion that she found it impossible to come downstairs into his company. Molly Cotton was made aware of how deeply hurt Rik was by what he regarded as Kim's refusal to see him. This incident, which became widely known, may well have contributed to his unshakeable resolve at the end of his life not to include his wife in his will.

In spite of the inevitable pangs of old age, and perhaps even occasional feelings of loneliness, Rik lived the first three years of his eighties with hardly diminished enjoyment. Throughout he was borne up by the work, interest and most of all by the young companionship that came from Southampton and David Collison's inspired enterprise. The sharper decline began with the bodily ills that struck in 1974.

It so happened that in the first week of that year he wrote me a letter so revealing of the high spirit that remained in him that it deserves to be quoted in part:

... you and I very much share our worship of *dynamism*: that's what my little life has been all about. Yes, we both understand it – both positive and negative dynamism. Incidentally that's why I've so much enjoyed my wars. ... Away back to 1943 and the battle of Medenine where I was suddenly put in command of ten thousand men in a day long battle – my first battle in major command. There I recall an example of *negative* dynamism. I remember how during the battle a young blonde German officer appeared nearby in a cleft in the hills. I froze and wondered whether to shoot. Somehow I couldn't, and eventually he turned back without seeing me. You know, that was for me a really dynamic moment – more so than if I had fired.

In March he went to Paris at the invitation of UNESCO. Towards the end of the six days he had, I believe, been unwell, and on board the aeroplane for his return flight he collapsed with a slight stroke. He came round to find himself on the floor at the centre of a ring of anxious faces and, hardly knowing what had happened, took command of the situation and turned the gathering into quite a merry party. That, at least, is how he was later to describe the event to his friends. When Molly Myers met him at Heathrow he was on his feet, but unsteady and over-excited, so that momentarily she thought he was drunk.

He spent the following week in the London Clinic, but, on coming out, made light of what had happened and few people realized its significance. He resumed his usual busy life and succeeded pretty well in concealing the fact that there was some loss of control on one side of his body, although it was enough to make his negotiation of the steep Whitcomb Street stairs more awkward than before. On one occasion he was to suffer the humiliation of becoming so helplessly stuck in his bath that Molly was obliged to send for help.

His memory for immediate things may also have worsened, making him more than ever dependent on Molly to get him to his engagements. It was at this time that I first became aware of it, for, because Molly herself was at a meeting, he failed to turn up for lunch at the Athenaeum Annexe, where he and I were to discuss with one Moss Eckhardt that young man's plans to write a book on General Pitt-Rivers. I had never thought it likely that we should be able to produce our own book on Rik's great predecessor: when he did at last turn up I realized it was impossible.

At the end of May he went as usual on his spring cruise, but it was noticeable, even to those who did not know him, that he was in poor form both as lecturer and social entertainer. Sometimes the evidence of his condition was obvious enough to be distressing.

In London that mid-summer he still had many engagements. So determined was he to keep going that in early August he set out on his second Swans cruise of that year. Within a week it ended in disaster. This was the moment when the Turks invaded Cyprus and since the *Ankara* was a Turkish ship the cruise itself was in difficulties. Then Rik fell ill and on 14 August had to be flown home from Athens and taken immediately into the King Edward VII Hospital.

Not only was his stay there very brief, but within three weeks he was off again, flying to Rome, principally on British School business. There he lodged with Bobbie and Janet Raikes, the last of many such visits. Once again Rik had to learn that will-power cannot triumph for ever. Falling on a slippery Roman floor, he suffered a hairline fracture of the pelvis. The Raikes had to struggle with all the difficulties of a chaotic medical system, made worse by the fact that most doctors were still on holiday, while hospitals were hardly functioning at all. Once the first crisis was past Rik was established in a wheelchair and Molly Myers flew out to help tend him. As Bobbie Raikes said, 'He must have been in considerable pain but did not complain and appeared to enjoy his regular before-lunch gin and vermouth and after-lunch cigar as much in a wheelchair as in any other.'

The fall had happened about a week before Rik's eighty-fifth birthday, but both he and his hosts were determined that this must be celebrated, however quietly. His old friend Molly Cotton, now living in Rome, was invited, and so, of course, was Molly Myers: these were the guests. Janet Raikes decided that she could and would meet Rik's exacting standards for roast beef and Yorkshire pudding, while Rik himself braved the pain of exchanging his dressing-gown for a suit – though not, as an heroic version of the story would have it, for full evening dress. His troubles were not to be mentioned: they talked together of old times, telling more or less familiar stories, all in great contentment together. Molly Cotton remembers how Rik unhesitatingly offered to help her with a book she had it in mind to write.

This little party, though shared by so few, had a quality that has made it widely known in archaeological tradition. It presents a scene that would find its place in any mosaic (in the map-maker's sense) of Rik's last years.

The events in Rome have some added significance as the prelude to a revolution in Rik's domestic affairs. With Molly Myers to look after him, he was able to fly home on 17 September. He went to Whitcomb Street, but was in no fit condition to be there and within a few days went down to Molly's house in Surrey for an intended stay of a week or so. He was to remain there for the rest of his life.

His new home was a most agreeable one. Molly lived in a long, low house on the outermost fringes of Leatherhead. The house had its own garden, set in the edge of the well-timbered property of a big house concealed in the background. Molly gave Rik a room with a fine view over miles of open countryside, a fact which proved of great solace to him. In the foreground, just across a lane, was a field where the horses and ponies of a riding stable were pastured. He did not feel either closed in or too much isolated.

The regime that gradually established itself as the visit extended into a kind of permanence suited Rik as well as anything that could have been devised. He kept on the lease of No. 27 and used it as his base for his at first not infrequent day trips to London, Molly driving him on her way to and from the Academy. He went up most usually for such occasions as meetings or dinners of the two Academies and the Royal Society, but also for social pleasures, including meals with the Collisons and members of their group – who, however, more often joined him in Leatherhead. It must be recorded that, when in London, Rik might refer to 'my cottage' or 'my little place' in the country.

On or within a day or two of his move to the country he had the diversion of once more meeting himself as a television performer. This was in the first of six weekly conversations with Magnus Magnusson which they had recorded earlier at No. 27 – David having devised the series as a worth-while but not too demanding sequel to the success of the *Sir Mortimer Wheeler* programmes. This opening talk was about his encounter with Winston Churchill and the little difficulty over Piltdown Man, to be followed by two on Stanwick and the Cartimandua story, others on Alexander the Great at Charsada and on Flinders Petrie. The final discussion was rather misleadingly entitled 'Schliemann and Gladstone – A Passage of Arms'. The main subject of the talk was, in fact, the balance between scientific technology and humanism in archaeology. Even now Rik admitted the advantages high science had brought, but spoke with feeling of the disadvantages. He made the point that the new technologies were on the whole more easily mastered than the 'old-fashioned disciplines', continuing, 'the result is that the old-fashioned humanities are getting thinner and thinner, the technology's getting thicker and thicker and is overlying a new generation of students of man, of mankind, in perspective which sometimes to my thinking forgets the man again'. It must have been the last time that he addressed the public on the issue which had vexed him for so long.

The talks were very informal, rather loosely organized and, as the brief extract shows, Rik's words were less well structured than of old. Occasionally Magnus had to supply some forgotten name. Yet Rik could still speak at length, still tell a story, and, above all, still had the vitality to attract and hold attention. The series made a not unworthy end to his career in television and the use he made of it to create a wider understanding of archaeology and the past. This was a theme to which he turned with pride during the last minutes of the final programme.

In spite of Rik's excursions to London and the visits to The Bothy of his family and friends, Rik had long days to fill in his country retreat. There was reading, of course, and he must sometimes have gone back to some of the favourites of his later years; for a time he had novels by Disraeli at his bedside for night reading and the autobiographies of Gibbon and Benvenuto Cellini were particular favourites. (Not long before he had been appalled to discover I had never read the great sculptor's book and sent me a copy, with a note to say that he would rather have been Cellini than anyone else except himself.)

He liked to do *The Times* crossword each day, and preparations for going to London were a labour and sometimes an ordeal for all concerned. But such chores and pastimes were not enough: Rik had always needed a challenge and now he set himself one commensurate with the powers that were, unbelievably, slipping from him. India remained the greatest of his memories. It was there that he had held a position appropriate to his stature, a position demanding everything that he could give; it was there that, in spite of some enmity, he had been most fully appreciated and most warmly revered. He would turn over in his mind a store of memories of the extraordinary enthusiasm with which he had been received on his return visits to the subcontinent. He resolved to write an account of all his doings there, drawing them together in what he hoped would be 'a succinct and essentially personal review'. The title chosen for it was *My Archaeological Mission to India and Pakistan*: a long echo from the idea of 'mission' he had so often expressed in the early days, when he first set himself to establish a scientific archaeology.

Molly Myers remembers how hard Rik drove himself to complete this task, and what a desperate struggle it sometimes became. It took months of labour to produce a brief text that he would formerly have tossed off in a night or two. Moreover, almost all of it had been culled from his past books or articles and assembled without any of his old mastery of form.

Yet, thankfully, it was finished: the challenge had been met. Early in 1976 Rik supervised the paste-up and Thames and Hudson made it an attractive-looking little book. It was ready in time for Rik to bring a copy to a meeting of the Antiquity Trust on 12 May, when several of us, friends and colleagues, saw him for the last time. He took care (I think) to hold it fully open in front of us in such a way that the splendid photograph of himself with a turbanned Arikamedu villager on the front cover appeared side by side with the Mohenjodaro dancer on the back, and we could rally him with the fact that he was clearly pointing across the spine of the book at that brazen young girl 'with the insolent look in her eye'.

The writing of this book was the backbone of Rik's refusal to surrender. He was the last man who would agree 'to go gently into that good night', and inevitably his resistance employed not only will but also temperament. He could be very difficult, could often lose his temper and make a show of ingratitude, yet Molly still recognized that essential 'sweetness and kindness' in him. He might give nurses a hard time, but they, like so many others who had served him, understood their bad patient well enough.

If it was most unlikely that Rik would go gently, it was surely unthinkable that he would make a late turn to religion. As far as we know, he suffered no qualms over his false passport into the Catholic Church. He had seldom spoken of his beliefs before and did not do so now, but, for a hint as to his possible thoughts, it is worth looking at the last essay in a small collection, *Alms for Oblivion*, which he had published ten years earlier.

It was about a curious work by Richard Burton, a character who attracted him by his courage and assumed vagabondage. In its final version this *Kasidah*, which the real author attributed to an imagined *Haji*, was much affected by FitzGerald's *Omar Khayyam*, but Rik recognized in Burton's original couplets the ideas of a man who, very unlike FitzGerald, had been 'truly in the saddle, amidst the wide and often pitiless horizons'. He printed a selection of the verses that meant most to him, knowing that, as poetry, they were indeed 'small beer'. To make a further selection:

> Do what thy manhood bids thee do, from
>   none but self expect applause;
> He noblest lives and noblest dies who makes
>   and keeps his self-made laws.

All other Life is living death, a world where
    none but Phantoms dwell,
A breath, a wind, a sound, a voice, a tinkling
    of the camel-bell.

To seek the True, to glad the heart, such
    is of life the HIGHER LAW,
Whose difference is the Man's degree, the
    Man of gold, the Man of straw.

Rik saw in his *Kasidah*, in spite of its Epicureanism and oriental trappings, Burton's brave affirmation of 'the pragmatic faith of the scientific revolution', of the fierce agnosticism of the later nineteenth century. Such thinking, Rik wrote, was not yet dead, and, in ending his own essays with Burton, 'let me confess that I do so, with high presumption, because I like to dream that my own faith, and in tiny measure, my own experience, have been the thin and lengthening shadow of his'. Here was a blend of the Romantic with the sternly rational that might be the lengthening shadow not only of Burton's ideas but of those Rik had absorbed from his own father.

As the summer advanced Rik's health was visibly cracking. Molly now drove home every evening through the worst of the rush hour to be sure of reaching him before the nurse left at six o'clock. Yet he still got up every day and enjoyed the society of David Collison, Carol and other favourite visitors.

There remained one worldly concern that troubled those close to him. It was the matter of the bestowal of Rik's modest possessions. Kim, whose relative riches had once embarrassed him, had, through lack of judgement and bad financial advice, lost almost all her money. Michael, supported by Molly, did his best to persuade him to make some provision for his legal wife, but he was absolute in his refusal. He had made Michael his literary legatee, but left all his treasures to Molly with the exception of his dress sword, which he assigned to Carol, together with one hundred pounds for its maintenance. Such an uneven assignment could not fail to cause some little hurt in the family, but all were agreed on the essential rightness of Rik's decision. Molly Myers had looked after him with a rare blend of high competence and fondness for over a quarter of a century, and over the last two years at great sacrifice to herself. He had not drawn her into much of his social life and yet she was and remained his 'Dear vif'. She was to contribute generously towards some endowment for Kim.

At the beginning of July Rik was still up, still able to go out of doors, and sufficiently inclined for company to ring up David Collison and invite him to lunch. David is very sad when he remembers that at the time it appeared quite impossible for him to accept. On 21 July Carol came to see her grandfather and they were able to go into the garden together. After she had left the last stroke came. The next morning he died, so escaping any long period of helplessness – which had been his greatest dread.

One would like to think that Rik's resolute shade might have lingered to watch his own obsequies. In London the newspaper placards read 'Sir Mortimer Wheeler dies' – he would have hated it if they had dismissed him as 'Famous Archaeologist'. He would have been satisfied, too, when flags were flown at half-mast on three of our greatest institutions, the British Academy, the Royal Academy and the Royal Society. Sorrow spread widely: I recall how a porter at Albany stopped me and said, 'I shall miss Sir Mortimer. I always liked to see him walking up Piccadilly. A funny walk he had. I shall miss him.'

All the grandeur was kept for that November memorial service in St James's Church, when Max Mallowan gave his address in honour of the hero who 'bestrode the world like a colossus', Lord Robbins and Nowell Myres read the lessons and afterwards a great congregation flowed across to Burlington House to drink and exchange memories. But it was the funeral at the crematorium, not many miles from The Bothy, attended only by about a score of friends, that Rik would have liked to see. It was, as he had wished, in all essentials a military funeral. He had particularly wanted the Last Post to be sounded, but he might well have been more amused than angered when the bugler lost his way and arrived almost, but not quite, too late to play his part. There is no doubt at all that he would have been delighted by the sergeants from his old regiment who attended, and who spontaneously formed a Guard of Honour as the coffin moved into the chapel. It was fitting, for, among all his loves, none was deeper or more lasting than his devotion to the 42nd Light Anti-Aircraft Regiment, Royal Artillery.

Bibliography

Segontium and the Roman Occupation of Wales (Y Cymmrodor *33*), London, 1923.

Prehistoric and Roman Wales, Oxford, 1925.

Roman Wales, Oxford, 1925.

The Roman Fort near Brecon (Y Cymmrodor *37*), London, 1926.

London and the Vikings (London Museum Catalogue), London, 1927.

London in Roman Times (London Museum Catalogue), London, 1930.

Report on the Excavation of the Prehistoric, Roman and Post-Roman Site in Lydney Park, Gloucestershire (Soc. Ant. Lond. Research Committee Report), London, 1932.

London and the Saxons (London Museum Catalogue), London, 1935.

Verulamium: A Belgic and Two Roman Cities (Soc. Ant. Lond. Research Committee Report), London, 1936.

Maiden Castle, Dorset (Soc. Ant. Lond. Research Committee Report), London, 1943.

Five Thousand Years of Pakistan, London, 1950.

The Indus Civilization (Cambridge History of India Supp. Vol.), Cambridge, 1953; 3rd edition, 1968.

The Stanwick Fortifications, North Riding of Yorkshire (Soc. Ant. Lond. Research Report), London, 1954.

Archaeology from the Earth, Oxford, 1954.

Rome beyond the Imperial Frontiers, London, 1954.

Still Digging, London, 1955.

Hill Forts of Northern France (Soc. Ant. Lond. Research Report), London, 1957.

Early India and Pakistan, London, 1959.

Charsada: A Metropolis of the North-West Frontier (Government of Pakistan and British Academy), London, 1962.

Roman Art and Architecture, London, 1964.

Alms for Oblivion: An Antiquary's Notebook, London, 1966.

Flames Over Persepolis, London, 1968.

The British Academy, 1949–1968, London, 1970.

My Archaeological Mission to India and Pakistan, London, 1976.

Index

Wheeler's writings are listed under the entry for Wheeler himself